T0332167

An Introduction to Description Logic

Description logic (DL) has a long tradition in computer science and knowledge representation, being designed so that domain knowledge can be described and so that computers can reason about this knowledge. DL has recently gained increased importance since it forms the logical basis of widely used ontology languages, in particular the web ontology language OWL.

Written by four renowned experts, this is the first textbook on Description Logic. It is suitable for self-study by graduates and as the basis for a university course. Starting from a basic DL, the book introduces the reader to its syntax, semantics, reasoning problems and model theory, and discusses the computational complexity of these reasoning problems and algorithms to solve them. It then explores a variety of different description logics, reasoning techniques, knowledge-based applications and tools, and describes the relationship between DLs and OWL.

An Introduction to Description Logic

FRANZ BAADER
Technische Universität, Dresden

IAN HORROCKS
University of Oxford

CARSTEN LUTZ
Universität Bremen

ULI SATTLER
University of Manchester

CAMBRIDGE
UNIVERSITY PRESS

CAMBRIDGE
UNIVERSITY PRESS

University Printing House, Cambridge CB2 8BS, United Kingdom

One Liberty Plaza, 20th Floor, New York, NY 10006, USA

477 Williamstown Road, Port Melbourne, VIC 3207, Australia

314-321, 3rd Floor, Plot 3, Splendor Forum, Jasola District Centre, New Delhi - 110025, India

79 Anson Road, #06-04/06, Singapore 079906

Cambridge University Press is part of the University of Cambridge.

It furthers the University's mission by disseminating knowledge in the pursuit of education, learning and research at the highest international levels of excellence.

www.cambridge.org
Information on this title: www.cambridge.org/9780521873611
DOI: 10.1017/9781139025355

First published 2017

A catalogue record for this publication is available from the British Library

ISBN   978-0-521-87361-1   Hardback
ISBN   978-0-521-69542-8   Paperback

Contents

1

Introduction

This is, to the best of our knowledge, the first textbook dedicated solely to Description Logic (DL), a very active research area in logic-based knowledge representation and reasoning that goes back to the late 1980s and that has a wide range of applications in knowledge-intensive information systems. In this introductory chapter we will sketch what DLs are, how they are used and where they come from historically. We will also explain how to use this book.

1.1 What are DLs and where do they come from?

Description logics (DLs) are a family of knowledge representation languages that can be used to represent knowledge of an application domain in a structured and well-understood way.[1] The name *description logics* is motivated by the fact that, on the one hand, the important notions of the domain are represented by concept *descriptions*, i.e., expressions that are built from atomic concepts (unary predicates) and atomic roles (binary predicates) using the concept and role constructors provided by the particular DL; on the other hand, DLs differ from their predecessors, such as semantic networks and frames, in that they are equipped with a *logic*-based semantics which, up to some differences in notation, is actually the same semantics as that of classical first-order logic.

Description logics typically separate domain knowledge into two components, a *terminological* part called the TBox and an *assertional* part called the ABox, with the combination of a TBox and an ABox being called a *knowledge base* (KB). The TBox represents knowledge about the structure of the domain (similar to a database schema), while the ABox represents knowledge about a concrete situation (similar to a database

---

[1] Note that we use *Description Logic* (singular) to refer to the research area, and *description logics* (plural) to refer to the relevant logical formalisms.

instance). TBox statements capturing knowledge about a university domain might include, e.g., *a teacher is a person who teaches a course*, *a student is a person who attends a course* and *students do not teach*, while ABox statements from the same domain might include *Mary is a person*, *CS600 is a course* and *Mary teaches CS600*. As already mentioned, a crucial feature of DLs is that such statements have a formal, logic-based semantics. In fact the above statements can be rendered as sentences in first-order logic as follows:

$$\forall x \, (\mathsf{Teacher}(x) \Leftrightarrow \mathsf{Person}(x) \wedge \exists y \, (\mathit{teaches}(x, y) \wedge \mathsf{Course}(y))),$$
$$\forall x \, (\mathsf{Student}(x) \Leftrightarrow \mathsf{Person}(x) \wedge \exists y \, (\mathit{attends}(x, y) \wedge \mathsf{Course}(y))),$$
$$\forall x \, ((\exists y \, \mathit{teaches}(x, y)) \Rightarrow \neg \mathsf{Student}(x)),$$
$$\mathsf{Person}(\mathsf{Mary}),$$
$$\mathsf{Course}(\mathsf{CS600}),$$
$$\mathit{teaches}(\mathsf{Mary}, \mathsf{CS600}).$$

Equivalently, these statements can be written in description logic syntax as follows:

$$\mathsf{Teacher} \equiv \mathsf{Person} \sqcap \exists \mathit{teaches}.\mathsf{Course},$$
$$\mathsf{Student} \equiv \mathsf{Person} \sqcap \exists \mathit{attends}.\mathsf{Course},$$
$$\exists \mathit{attends}.\top \sqsubseteq \neg \mathsf{Student},$$
$$\mathsf{Mary} : \mathsf{Person},$$
$$\mathsf{CS600} : \mathsf{Course},$$
$$(\mathsf{Mary}, \mathsf{CS600}) : \mathit{teaches}.$$

The first three statements of this knowledge base constitute its TBox, and the last three its ABox. Please note how the DL syntax does not use variables x or y. In Chapter 2 an extended version of the university KB example will be used to define and explain DL syntax and semantics in detail.

The logic-based semantics of DLs means that we have a well-defined, shared understanding of when a statement is *entailed* by a KB; for example, the above KB entails that Mary is a teacher. Moreover, we can use (automated) reasoning to determine those entailments, and thus reasoning can be used to support the development and application of DL KBs. Common reasoning tasks include checking the satisfiability of concepts and the consistency of KBs, determining when one concept is more specific than another (a reasoning task called *subsumption*) and answering different kinds of database-style queries over the KB.

The power of DLs derives from the fact that reasoning tasks are performed with respect to the whole KB, and in particular with respect to the conceptual domain knowledge captured in the TBox. Unfortunately, this power does not come without a computational cost, and one of the most important areas of DL research has been exploring the trade-off between the expressive power of the language available for making statements (particularly TBox statements) and the computational complexity of various reasoning tasks. The expressive power of DLs is invariably constrained so as to at least ensure that common reasoning tasks are decidable (i.e., they can always be correctly completed in a finite amount of time), and may even be sufficiently constrained so as to make them tractable (i.e., they can always be correctly completed in time that is polynomial with respect to the size of the KB). In another area of DL research, its *model theory*, we investigate which kinds of semantic structure, i.e., interpretations or models, we can describe in a KB. As well as theoretical investigations, e.g., determining the worst-case complexities for various DLs and reasoning problems, there has also been extensive practical work, e.g., developing systems and optimisation techniques, and empirically evaluating their behaviour when applied to benchmarks or KBs used in various applications. We will explore model theory in Chapter 3, theoretical complexity issues in Chapter 5 and DL reasoning techniques in Chapters 4, 6 and 7.

The emphasis on decidable and tractable formalisms is also the reason why a great variety of extensions of basic DLs have been considered – combining different extensions can easily lead to undecidability or intractability, even if each of the extensions is harmless when considered in isolation. While most DLs can be seen as decidable fragments of first-order logic, some extensions leave the realm of classical first-order logic, including, e.g., DLs with modal and temporal operators, fuzzy DLs and probabilistic DLs (for details, see [BCM+07, Chapter 6] and specialised survey articles such as [LWZ08, LS08]). If an application requires more expressive power than can be provided by a decidable DL, then one usually embeds the DL into an application program or another KR formalism rather than using an undecidable DL.

1.2 What are they good for and how are they used?

DL systems have been used in a range of application domains, including configuration (e.g., of telecommunications equipment) [MW98], software information and documentation systems [DBSB91] and databases [BCM+07], where they have been used to support schema design [CLN98, BCDG01], schema and data integration [CDGL+98b, CDGR99], and query answering [CDGL98a, CDGL99, HSTT00]. More recently, DLs

have played a central role in the semantic web [Hor08], where they
have been adopted as the basis for ontology languages such as OWL
[HPSvH03], and its predecessors OIL and DAML+OIL, and DL knowledge bases are now often referred to as ontologies. This has resulted
in a more widespread use of DL systems, with applications in fields as
diverse as agriculture [SLL⁺04], astronomy [DeRP06], biology
[RB11, OSRM⁺12], defence [LAF⁺05], education [CBV⁺14], energy
management [CGH⁺13], geography [Goo05], geoscience [RP05], medicine
[CSG05, GZB06, HDG12, TNNM13], oceanography [KHJ⁺15b] and oil
and gas [SLH13, KHJ⁺15a].

In a typical application, the first step will be to determine the relevant
vocabulary of the application domain and then formalise it in a suitable
TBox. This *ontology engineering* process may be manual or (semi-)
automatic. In either case a DL reasoner is invariably used to check
satisfiability of concepts and consistency of the ontology as a whole. This
reasoner is often integrated in an ontology editing tool such as Protégé
[KFNM04]. Some applications use only a terminological ontology (i.e.,
a TBox), but in others the ontology is subsequently used to structure
and access data in an ABox or even in a database. In the latter case a
DL reasoner will again be used to compute query answers.

The use of DLs in applications throws the above mentioned expressivity versus complexity trade-off into sharp relief. On the one hand,
using a very restricted DL might make it difficult to precisely describe
the concepts needed in the ontology and forces the modelling to remain
at a high level of abstraction; on the other hand, using a highly expressive DL might make it difficult to perform relevant reasoning tasks in a
reasonable amount of time. The OWL ontology language is highly expressive, and hence also highly intractable; however, the currently used
OWL 2 version of OWL also specifies several *profiles*, fragments of the
language that are based on less expressive but tractable DLs. We will
discuss OWL and OWL 2 in more detail in Chapter 8.

1.3 A brief history of description logic

The study of description logic grew out of research into knowledge representation systems, such as semantic networks and frames, and a desire to provide them with precise semantics and well-defined reasoning
procedures [WS92]. Early work was mainly concerned with the implementation of systems, such as KL-ONE, K-REP, BACK, and LOOM
[BS85, MDW91, Pel91, Mac91a]. These systems employed so-called
structural subsumption algorithms, which first normalise the concept de-

scriptions, and then recursively compare the syntactic structure of the normalised descriptions [Neb90a]. These algorithms are usually relatively efficient (polynomial), but they have the disadvantage that they are complete only for very inexpressive DLs, i.e., for more expressive DLs they cannot derive all relevant entailments. Early formal investigations into the complexity of reasoning in DLs showed that most DLs do not have polynomial-time inference problems [BL84, Neb90b]. Influenced by these results, the implementors of the CLASSIC system (the first industrial-strength DL system) chose to carefully restrict the expressive power of their DL so as to allow for tractable and complete reasoning [PSMB+91, Bra92].

The so-called *tableau* reasoning technique for DLs was first introduced by Schmidt-Schauß and Smolka in the early 1990s [SS91]. Tableau algorithms work on propositionally closed DLs (i.e., DLs with full Boolean operators), and are complete even for very expressive DLs. Moreover, an implementation of one such algorithm in the KRIS system showed that, with suitable optimisations, performance on realistic problems could be comparable with or even superior to existing structural approaches [BFH+92]. At the same time, there was a thorough analysis of the complexity of reasoning in various DLs [DLNN91a, DLNN91b, DHL+92], and it was observed that DLs are very closely related to modal logics [Sch91].

Initially, tableau algorithms and systems, including KRIS, considered only relatively restricted DLs (see Section 4.2.2). On the theoretical side, tableau algorithms were soon extended to deal with more expressive DLs [HB91, Baa91, BH91, BDS93]. It took several years, however, before the FaCT system demonstrated that suitably optimised implementations of such algorithms could be effective in practice [Hor97]. Subsequently, tableau algorithms were developed for increasingly expressive DLs [HST00], and implemented in FaCT and in other highly optimised DL systems including RACER [HM01], FaCT++ [TH06] and Pellet [SPC+07]. This line of research culminated in the development of $\mathcal{SROIQ}$ [HKS06], the DL that forms the basis for the OWL ontology language. In fact, a DL knowledge base can be seen as an OWL ontology. The standardisation of OWL gave DLs a stable, machine-processable and web-friendly syntax; this, and the central role of ontologies in the semantic web, sparked an increased development of DL knowledge bases (and OWL ontologies), and an increased development effort for tools such as reasoners to determine entailments, ontology editors to write knowledge bases and APIs to programmatically access ontologies and reasoners (see Section 8.2).

During the same period, the relationship to modal logics [DGL94a, Sch95] and to decidable fragments of first-order logic was also studied in more detail [Bor96, PST97, GKV97, Grä98, Grä99, LSW01], and first applications in databases (such as schema reasoning, query optimisation, and data integration) were investigated [LR96, BDNS98, CDGL98a, CDGL+98b].

Although highly optimised implementations of tableau algorithms were successful in many TBox reasoning applications, some larger-scale ontologies proved stubbornly resistant. Moreover, it remained unclear how tableau reasoning could deal effectively with very large ABoxes. This revived the interest in less expressive DLs, with the goal of developing tools that can deal with very large TBoxes and/or ABoxes, and led to the development of the $\mathcal{EL}$ and DL-Lite families of tractable DLs [BBL05, BBL08, CGL+05, CDL+07, ACKZ09], which are both included in OWL 2 as profiles. A main advantage of the $\mathcal{EL}$ family is that it is amenable to *consequence-based* reasoning techniques which scale also to large ontologies and are more robust than tableau reasoning [BBL05]. This was first demonstrated by the CEL system [BLS06]; other relevant implementations include ELK [KKS14] and SnoRocket [MJL13].

With the advent of the DL-Lite family of DLs, applications of description logics in databases started to receive increased interest. There are various benefits to enriching a database application with an ontology, such as adding domain knowledge, giving a formal definition to the symbols used in the database and providing an enriched and unified schema that can be used to formulate queries. These ideas have led to the study of *ontology-mediated querying* [BtCLW14] and to the *ontology-based data access (OBDA)* paradigm for data integration [CDL+09]; see also the recent surveys [KZ14, BO15]. DL-Lite is particularly suitable for such applications since its expressive power is sufficiently restricted so that database-style query answering with respect to ontologies can be reduced via query rewriting techniques to query answering in relational databases (see Chapter 7); this in turn allows standard database systems to be used for query answering in the presence of ontologies [CDL+07]. Implemented systems in this area include QuOnto and Mastro [ACG+05, CCD+13] as well as Ontop [KRR+14].

As DLs became increasingly used, researchers investigated a multitude of additional reasoning tasks that are intended to make DLs more usable in various applications. These included, among many others, computing *least common subsumers* and *concept difference, ontology difference,* and *explanation* [BK06, KWW08, HPS09]. The need to support the modularity of ontologies has been a strong driving force for studying new reasoning problems such as module extraction [GHKS08], conservative extensions [GLW06], and inseparability [BKL+16]. These tasks are now widely used to support ontology engineering, and so is explanation: module extraction and inseparability can be used to support ontology reuse, e.g., by highlighting interactions between statements in different ontologies, and explanation can be used to help debug errors in ontologies, e.g., by highlighting the causes of inconsistencies.

Description Logic continues to be a very active research area, with new theoretical results and new reasoning techniques and systems constantly being developed; see `http://dl.kr.org/`. These include the extension of tableau to hypertableau, as implemented in the HermiT system [GHM+14], the extension of rewriting techniques to the $\mathcal{EL}$ family of DLs and beyond [PUMH10, LTW09, BLW13, SMH13, BtCLW14], as implemented in the KARMA [SMH13] and Grind [HLSW15] systems, and the development of hybrid techniques, e.g., combining tableau with consequence-based approaches in the Konclude system [SLG14].

1.4 How to use this book

This book is intended as a textbook and not as a research monograph. Consequently, we have tried to cover all core aspects of DLs at a level of detail suitable for a novice reader with a little background in formal methods or logic. In particular, we expect the reader to understand the basic notions around sets, relations and functions, e.g., their union, intersection or composition. It will be useful, but not essential, for readers to have some knowledge of first-order logic and basic notions from theoretical computer science. Those lacking such background may wish to consult appropriate textbooks, e.g., `http://phil.gu.se/logic/books/ Gallier:Logic_For_Computer_Science.pdf` (which also contains a nice example of a guide for readers).

This book includes both basic and advanced level material suitable for undergraduate through to introductory graduate level courses on description logics. In the authors' experience, the material included here could be covered in a 36-hour lecture course for students with a good background in logic. For shorter courses, or those aimed at a different cohort, some of the more advanced material can easily be dropped.

Chapters 2 and 3 provide background material, including examples and definitions, that will prove useful in the remaining chapters. Some parts of these chapters are, however, quite long and detailed, and it may not be appropriate to read (or teach) them in full before continuing with the remainder of the book, but rather to dip into them as need arises. Also, the subsequent chapters are presented in an order that the authors find didactically convenient, but the order in which they are read and/or taught could easily be varied.

Chapter 4 deals with tableau-based reasoning techniques; these are typically used to reason about expressive DLs. It presents tableau algorithms for ABox and KB consistency in the basic DL $\mathcal{ALC}$, and shows how they can be extended to deal with other concept and role constructors. The chapter also includes a brief discussion of implementation issues. Chapter 5 discusses the computational complexity of satisfiability and subsumption in a variety of expressive DLs, and proves upper and lower complexity bounds for a suitable set of these problems. It also gives examples of extensions of DLs that are too expressive in the sense that they lead to undecidability. Chapter 6 looks at reasoning in the inexpressive DL $\mathcal{EL}$ and explains the consequence-based reasoning technique for this logic, and it also showcases an extension (with inverse roles) in which reasoning is more challenging. So far in this book, reasoning has been restricted to determining whether a DL knowledge base entails a DL axiom. Chapter 7 discusses more complex reasoning problems, namely query answering: the entailments to be checked are from a different language, in particular conjunctive queries and first-order queries. Finally, Chapter 8 explains the relationship between OWL and DLs, and describes the tools and applications of OWL.

In Chapters 2–7, citations have been kept to a minimum, but most chapters conclude with a short section providing historical context and a literature review.

The reader is cordially invited to *actively* read this book, especially the basic definitions. Throughout the book, we provide a lot of examples but strongly suggest that, whenever a new notion or term is introduced, the reader should consider their own examples of this notion or term – possibly by varying the ones presented – in order to make sure that the newly introduced notion is completely understood. We also show how to draw interpretations and models, and explain reasoning algorithms. Again, in addition to the examples given, the reader should draw their own models and run the algorithms on other inputs.

The running teaching example used throughout this book is made available on the book's website at `http://dltextbook.org/` in an OWL syntax. You will also find useful further examples and exercises there, as well as a list of errata, to which you can contribute by informing us about any errors that you find in the book.

2

A Basic Description Logic

In this chapter, we introduce and explain the basic notions of Description Logic, including syntax, semantics and reasoning services, and we explain how the latter are used in applications.

2.1 The concept language of the DL $\mathcal{ALC}$

In this section, we will describe the central notions of Description Logic first on an intuitive level and then on a more precise level. As a running example, we use the domain of university courses and teaching, and we will use a conceptualisation given informally, in graphical form, in Figure 2.1. Please note that this is *one* way of viewing university teaching – which might be very different from the reader's way of viewing it. Also, as it is an informal representation, different readers may interpret arrows in different ways; that is, our representation does not come with a well-defined semantics that would inform us in an unambiguous way how to interpret the different arrows.[1] In the next sections, we will describe our way of viewing university teaching in a DL knowledge base, thereby establishing some constraints on the meaning of terms like "Professor" and "teaches" used in Figure 2.1 and throughout this section.

In Description Logic, we assume that we want to describe some abstraction of some domain of interest, and that this abstraction is populated by *elements*.[2] We use three main building blocks to describe these elements:

- *Concepts* represent sets of elements and can be viewed as unary pred-

---

[1] Our graphical representation looks somewhat similar to an extended ER diagram, for which such a well-defined semantics has been specified [Che76, CLN94].

[2] We have chosen the term "elements" rather than "individuals" or "objects" to prevent the reader from making false assumptions.

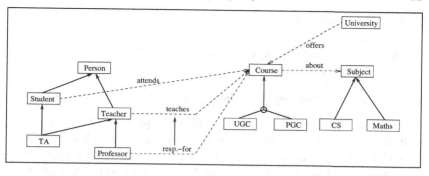

Fig. 2.1. An informal, graphical view of our running example.

icates. Concepts are built from *concept names* and *role names* (see below) using the constructors provided by the DL used. The set a concept represents is called its *extension*. For example, Person and Course are concept names, and m is an element in the extension of Person and c6 is in the extension of Course. To make our life a bit easier, we often use "is a" as an abbreviation for "is in the extension of" as, for example, in "m is a Person".

- *Role names* stand for binary relations on elements and can be viewed as binary predicates. If a role *r* relates one element with another element, then we call the latter one an *r-filler* of the former one. For example, if *m teaches* c6, then we call c6 a *teaches*-filler of *m*.

At the heart of a specific DL, we find a *concept language*; that is, a formal language that allows us to build *concept descriptions* (and *role descriptions*) from concept names, role names, and possibly other primitives. For example, Person ⊓ ∃*teaches*.Course is such a concept description built from the concept names Person and Course and the role name *teaches*. Next, we formalise the exact meaning of these notions.

Definition 2.1. Let **C** be a set of *concept names* and **R** be a set of *role names* disjoint from **C**. The set of *ALC concept descriptions* over **C** and **R** is inductively defined as follows:

- Every concept name is an *ALC* concept description.
- ⊤ and ⊥ are *ALC* concept descriptions.
- If C and D are *ALC* concept descriptions and r is a role name, then the following are also *ALC* concept descriptions:

$C \sqcap D$ (conjunction),

$C \sqcup D$ (disjunction),

$\neg C$ (negation),

$\exists r.C$, (existential restriction), and

$\forall r.C$ (value restriction).

As usual, we use parentheses to clarify the structure of concepts.

Definition 2.1 fixes the *syntax* of $\mathcal{ALC}$ concept descriptions; that is, it allows us to distinguish between expressions that are well formed and those that are not. For example, $\exists r.C$ and $A \sqcap \exists r.\forall s.(E \sqcap \neg F)$ are $\mathcal{ALC}$ concept descriptions, whereas $\exists C$ and $\forall s.s$ are not; in the former case since $\exists C$ is missing a role name, and in the latter case since s cannot be both a concept and a role name.

Next, we will introduce some DL parlance and abbreviations. First, we often use "$\mathcal{ALC}$ concept" as an abbreviation of "$\mathcal{ALC}$ concept description" and, if it is clear from the context that we talk about $\mathcal{ALC}$ concepts, we may even drop the $\mathcal{ALC}$ and use "concepts" for "$\mathcal{ALC}$ concepts". Moreover, when clear from the context, **C** and **R** are not mentioned explicitly.

Remark. Please note that in the DL setting a concept is, basically, a string, and is not to be confused with the notion of a "concept" in the sense of an abstract or general idea from philosophy. When we use a DL in an application, we may use a DL concept to describe a relevant application "concept", but the latter is far more subtle and intricate than the former.

Second, we sometimes distinguish between *atomic* and *compound* (also called complex) concepts. An atomic concept consists of a single lexical token, i.e., in $\mathcal{ALC}$, a concept name, $\top$, or $\bot$. A compound concept is constructed using at least one of the available operators, i.e., in $\mathcal{ALC}$, $\sqcap$, $\sqcup$, $\neg$, $\exists$ and $\forall$. In the following, we will use upper case letters A, B for concept names, upper case letters C, D for possibly compound concepts, and lower case letters r, s for role names.

Before we define the semantics, i.e., the meaning of concepts and roles, we will present an intuitive reading for compound concepts.

- A *negation* is written ¬Student and can be read as "not Student". It describes everything that is not in the extension of Student.
- A *conjunction* is written Student⊓Teacher and can be read as "Student and Teacher". It describes those elements that are in the extension of both Student and Teacher.

- A *disjunction* is written Student⊔Teacher and can be read as "Student or Teacher". It describes those elements that are in the extension of either Student or Teacher, or both.

- A *value restriction* is written ∀*teaches*.Course and can be read as "all *teaches*-fillers are Courses". It describes all those elements that have only elements in Course related to them via *teaches*. It is written with an upside-down A because of the "**all**" in its reading and its close relationship with universal quantification in first-order logic.

- An *existential restriction* is written ∃*teaches*.Course and can be read as "there exists a *teaches*-filler which is a Course". It describes all elements that have at least one *teaches*-filler that is in Course. It is written with a backwards E because of the "**there exists**" in its reading and its close relationship with existential quantification in first-order logic.

Now, to fix the meaning of concepts and roles, we make use of an *interpretation*, that is, a structure that:

- consists of a non-empty set called its *interpretation domain*. We call the elements of this interpretation domain simply "elements", but they are sometimes called individuals or objects elsewhere;

- fixes, for each concept name, its extension – that is, it tells us, for each concept name, which of the elements is (or isn't) in the extension of this concept;

- fixes, for each role name, its extension – that is, it tells us, for each role name, which pairs of elements are related to each other by this role.

Interpretations, as well as the extension of concept descriptions, are defined next.

Definition 2.2. An *interpretation* $\mathcal{I} = (\Delta^{\mathcal{I}}, \cdot^{\mathcal{I}})$ consists of a non-empty set $\Delta^{\mathcal{I}}$, called the *interpretation domain*, and a mapping $\cdot^{\mathcal{I}}$ that maps

- every concept name $A \in \mathbf{C}$ to a set $A^{\mathcal{I}} \subseteq \Delta^{\mathcal{I}}$, and
- every role name $r \in \mathbf{R}$ to a binary relation $r^{\mathcal{I}} \subseteq \Delta^{\mathcal{I}} \times \Delta^{\mathcal{I}}$.

The mapping $\cdot^{\mathcal{I}}$ is extended to $\top$, $\bot$ and compound concepts as follows:

$$\top^{\mathcal{I}} = \Delta^{\mathcal{I}},$$
$$\bot^{\mathcal{I}} = \emptyset,$$
$$(C \sqcap D)^{\mathcal{I}} = C^{\mathcal{I}} \cap D^{\mathcal{I}},$$
$$(C \sqcup D)^{\mathcal{I}} = C^{\mathcal{I}} \cup D^{\mathcal{I}},$$
$$(\neg C)^{\mathcal{I}} = \Delta^{\mathcal{I}} \setminus C^{\mathcal{I}},$$
$$(\exists r.C)^{\mathcal{I}} = \{d \in \Delta^{\mathcal{I}} \mid \text{there is an } e \in \Delta^{\mathcal{I}} \text{ with } (d, e) \in r^{\mathcal{I}} \text{ and } e \in C^{\mathcal{I}}\},$$
$$(\forall r.C)^{\mathcal{I}} = \{d \in \Delta^{\mathcal{I}} \mid \text{for all } e \in \Delta^{\mathcal{I}}, \text{ if } (d, e) \in r^{\mathcal{I}}, \text{ then } e \in C^{\mathcal{I}}\}.$$

We call

- $C^{\mathcal{I}}$ the *extension of* C in $\mathcal{I}$,
- $b \in \Delta^{\mathcal{I}}$ an *r-filler of a in $\mathcal{I}$* if $(a, b) \in r^{\mathcal{I}}$.

Please note that an interpretation is not restricted other than as explicitly specified above: its domain must be non-empty, but can be of any cardinality, and in particular it can be infinite; the extension of a concept can have any number of elements between "none" and "all"; and a role can relate any number of pairs of elements, from "none" to "all".

Also, please note that $A^{\mathcal{I}}$ stands for the result of applying the mapping $\cdot^{\mathcal{I}}$ to the concept name A; this is an unusual way of writing mappings, yet it is quite helpful and ink-saving. In the past, DL researchers have used different notations such as $\mathcal{I}(A)$ or $[[A]]_{\mathcal{I}}$, but the one used here is the one that stuck.

As an example, let us consider the following interpretation $\mathcal{I}$:

$$\Delta^{\mathcal{I}} = \{m, c6, c7, et\},$$
$$\mathsf{Teacher}^{\mathcal{I}} = \{m\},$$
$$\mathsf{Course}^{\mathcal{I}} = \{c6, c7, et\},$$
$$\mathsf{Person}^{\mathcal{I}} = \{m, et\},$$
$$\mathsf{PGC}^{\mathcal{I}} = \{c7\},$$
$$\textit{teaches}^{\mathcal{I}} = \{(m, c6), (m, c7), (et, et)\}.$$

We can easily modify $\mathcal{I}$ to obtain other interpretations $\mathcal{I}_1$, $\mathcal{I}_2$ etc., by adding or removing elements and changing the interpretation of concept and role names. An interpretation is often conveniently drawn as a directed, labelled graph with a node for each element of the interpretation domain and labelled as follows: a node is labelled with all concept names the corresponding element of the interpretation domain belongs to, and we find an edge from one node to another labelled with r if the element

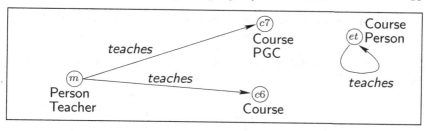

Fig. 2.2. A graphical representation of the example interpretation $\mathcal{I}$.

corresponding to the latter node is an r-filler of the element corresponding to the former node. As an example, Figure 2.2 shows a graphical representation of $\mathcal{I}$.

Let us take a closer look at $\mathcal{I}$. By definition, all elements are in the extension of $\top$, and no element is in the extension of $\bot$. The elements m and et are, for example, in the extension of Person, and et is a *teaches*-filler of itself. If we extend $\mathcal{I}$ to compound concepts as specified in Definition 2.2, then we can see that, for example, m is in the extension of Person⊓Teacher, and $c6$ is in the extension of Course⊓¬Person, because $c6$ is a Course and *not* a Person. Similarly, for existential restrictions, m and et are in the extension of ∃*teaches*.Course, but only m is in the extension of ∃*teaches*.¬Person. For value restrictions, all elements are in the extension of ∀*teaches*.Course: for m and et, this is clear, and for $c6$ and $c7$, this is because they do not have *any* *teaches*-fillers, and hence *all* their *teaches*-fillers vacuously satisfy any condition we may impose. In general, if an element has no r-filler, then it is in the extension of ∀$r.C$ for any concept C. In contrast, m is *not* in the extension of ∀*teaches*.(Course ⊓ PGC) because m has $c6$ as a *teaches*-filler that is *not* in the extension of Course ⊓ PGC since it is not a PGC. At this stage, we repeat our invitation to the reader to consider some more interpretations and concepts and determine which element is in the extension of which concept.

We can also investigate extensions of more compound concept descriptions such as Person⊓∃*teaches*.(Course⊓¬PGC): for example, m is in the extension of this concept since it is in the extension of both conjuncts: by definition of $\mathcal{I}$, it is in the extension of Person, and it also is in the extension of the second conjunct, because it has a *teaches*-successor, $c6$, that is in the extension of (Course ⊓ ¬PGC).

We have been rather generous in our syntax definition since we provide a non-minimal set of concept constructors, i.e., one with "syntactic sugar". The following lemma makes this observation precise.

Lemma 2.3. *Let $\mathcal{I}$ be an interpretation, C, D concepts, and r a role. Then*

$$
\begin{array}{rrcl}
\text{(i)} & \top^{\mathcal{I}} & = & (C \sqcup \neg C)^{\mathcal{I}}, \\
\text{(ii)} & \bot^{\mathcal{I}} & = & (C \sqcap \neg C)^{\mathcal{I}}, \\
\text{(iii)} & (\neg\neg C)^{\mathcal{I}} & = & C^{\mathcal{I}}, \\
\text{(iv)} & \neg(C \sqcap D)^{\mathcal{I}} & = & (\neg C \sqcup \neg D)^{\mathcal{I}}, \\
\text{(v)} & \neg(C \sqcup D)^{\mathcal{I}} & = & (\neg C \sqcap \neg D)^{\mathcal{I}}, \\
\text{(vi)} & (\neg(\exists r.C))^{\mathcal{I}} & = & (\forall r.\neg C)^{\mathcal{I}}, \\
\text{(vii)} & (\neg(\forall r.C))^{\mathcal{I}} & = & (\exists r.\neg C)^{\mathcal{I}}.
\end{array}
$$

Proof. These equations follow rather immediately from Definition 2.2:

By definition, $\top^{\mathcal{I}} = \Delta^{\mathcal{I}}$, and $(C \sqcup \neg C)^{\mathcal{I}} = C^{\mathcal{I}} \cup (\neg C)^{\mathcal{I}} = C^{\mathcal{I}} \cup (\Delta^{\mathcal{I}} \setminus C^{\mathcal{I}}) = \Delta^{\mathcal{I}}$. Hence Equation (i) holds.

Equation (ii) can be proven analogously and is left to the reader.

For Equation (iii), $(\neg\neg C)^{\mathcal{I}} = (\Delta^{\mathcal{I}} \setminus (\Delta^{\mathcal{I}} \setminus C^{\mathcal{I}}))$, which is of course the same as $C^{\mathcal{I}}$.

For Equation (iv), which is also known as one of de Morgan's laws, we have $\neg(C \sqcap D)^{\mathcal{I}} = \Delta^{\mathcal{I}} \setminus (C \sqcap D)^{\mathcal{I}}$. Now $d \in \Delta^{\mathcal{I}} \setminus (C \sqcap D)^{\mathcal{I}}$ if and only if $d \notin C^{\mathcal{I}}$ or $d \notin D^{\mathcal{I}}$ (or both), which is the case if and only if $d \in (\neg C)^{\mathcal{I}} \cup (\neg D^{\mathcal{I}}) = (\neg C \sqcup \neg D)^{\mathcal{I}}$.

Equation (v), another of de Morgan's laws, can be proven analogously.

For Equation (vi), by definition of the semantics,

$$
\begin{aligned}
&(\neg(\exists r.C))^{\mathcal{I}} \\
&= \Delta^{\mathcal{I}} \setminus \{d \in \Delta^{\mathcal{I}} \mid \text{there is an } e \in \Delta^{\mathcal{I}} \text{ with } (d,e) \in r^{\mathcal{I}} \text{ and } e \in C^{\mathcal{I}}\} \\
&= \{d \in \Delta^{\mathcal{I}} \mid \text{there is no } e \in \Delta^{\mathcal{I}} \text{ with } (d,e) \in r^{\mathcal{I}} \text{ and } e \in C^{\mathcal{I}}\} \\
&= \{d \in \Delta^{\mathcal{I}} \mid \text{for all } e \in \Delta^{\mathcal{I}} \text{ if } (d,e) \in r^{\mathcal{I}} \text{ then } e \notin C^{\mathcal{I}}\} \\
&= (\forall r.\neg C)^{\mathcal{I}}.
\end{aligned}
$$

Equation (vii) can be proven analogously and is left to the reader. $\square$

As a consequence of Lemma 2.3, and as we will see later, we can rewrite, e.g., $(C \sqcup D)$ to $\neg(\neg C \sqcap \neg D)$, and thus avoid explicit disjunctions.

2.2 $\mathcal{ALC}$ knowledge bases

If we were to use a DL-based system in an application, we would build concept descriptions that describe relevant notions from this application domain. For example, for a molecular biology application, we would build concepts describing proteins, genes and so on. We would then use these concepts in a *knowledge base*, and we can do this in (at least) four different ways:

(i) As in an encyclopedia, we define the meaning of some concept names in terms of concept descriptions. For example, we can define the meaning of UG-Student and CS-Teacher using the following equations:[3]

$$\text{UG-Student} \equiv \text{Student} \sqcap \forall attends.\text{UGC},$$
$$\text{CS-Teacher} \equiv \text{Teacher} \sqcap \exists teaches.(\text{Course} \sqcap \exists about.\text{CS}).$$

Intuitively, the first equation says that UG-Students are those students that attend only UGCs, and the second one says that CS-Teachers are those Teachers that teach some Course about CS.

(ii) We express background knowledge. For example, we can state that an undergraduate course (UGC) cannot be a postgraduate course (PGC), and that a University necessarily *offers* both UGCs and PGCs, using the following equations:

$$\text{UGC} \sqsubseteq \neg\text{PGC},$$
$$\text{University} \sqsubseteq \exists offers.\text{UGC} \sqcap \exists offers.\text{PGC}.$$

(iii) We assert that individual names stand for instances of (possibly compound) concept descriptions. For example, we can say that Mary stands for an instance of Teacher $\sqcap \exists teaches.$PGC and CS600 stands for an instance of Course.

(iv) We relate individual names by roles. For example, we can say that Mary *teaches* CS600.

Traditionally, we distinguish two parts of a DL knowledge base. The *terminological* part, called the *TBox*, contains statements of the form described in items (i) and (ii), and the *assertional* part, called the *ABox*, contains statements of form described in items (iii) and (iv). If we compare this to databases, then we can view a TBox as a schema because it expresses general constraints on what (our abstraction of) the world looks like. And we can view the ABox as the data since it talks about concrete elements, their properties and their relationships.

2.2.1 *ALC* **TBoxes**

We start by defining the syntax and semantics of TBoxes.

---

[3] The exact meaning of these equations will be defined later.

Definition 2.4. For C and D possibly compound $\mathcal{ALC}$ concepts, an expression of the form $C \sqsubseteq D$ is called an $\mathcal{ALC}$ *general concept inclusion* and abbreviated *GCI*. We use $C \equiv D$ as an abbreviation for $C \sqsubseteq D$, $D \sqsubseteq C$.

A finite set of GCIs is called an $\mathcal{ALC}$ *TBox*.

An interpretation $\mathcal{I}$ *satisfies* a GCI $C \sqsubseteq D$ if $C^{\mathcal{I}} \subseteq D^{\mathcal{I}}$. An interpretation that satisfies each GCI in a TBox $\mathcal{T}$ is called a *model* of $\mathcal{T}$.

As usual, if it is clear that we are talking about $\mathcal{ALC}$ concepts and TBoxes, we omit "$\mathcal{ALC}$" and use simply TBox or GCI. We will sometimes refer to abbreviations of the form $C \equiv D$ as an *equivalence axiom*, and use *axiom* to refer to either an equivalence axiom or a GCI.

The interpretation $\mathcal{I}$ given in Figure 2.2 satisfies each of the GCIs in

$$\mathcal{T}_1 = \{\text{Teacher} \quad \sqsubseteq \quad \text{Person},$$
$$\text{PGC} \quad \sqsubseteq \quad \neg\text{Person},$$
$$\text{Teacher} \quad \sqsubseteq \quad \exists\textit{teaches}.\text{Course},$$
$$\exists\textit{teaches}.\text{Course} \quad \sqsubseteq \quad \text{Person}\}$$

and thus $\mathcal{I}$ is a model of $\mathcal{T}_1$. To verify this, for each GCI $C \sqsubseteq D$, we determine $C^{\mathcal{I}}$ and $D^{\mathcal{I}}$ and then check whether $C^{\mathcal{I}}$ is indeed a subset of $D^{\mathcal{I}}$. For the first GCI, we observe that $\text{Teacher}^{\mathcal{I}} = \{m\} \subseteq \{m, et\} = \text{Person}^{\mathcal{I}}$. Similarly, for the second one, we have $\text{PGC}^{\mathcal{I}} = \{c7\} \subseteq \{c6, c7\} = (\neg\text{Person})^{\mathcal{I}}$. For the third one, m is the only element in the extension of Teacher and also in the extension of $\exists\textit{teaches}.\text{Course}$, hence it is also satisfied by $\mathcal{I}$. Finally $(\exists\textit{teaches}.\text{Course})^{\mathcal{I}} = \{m, et\}$ and both m and et are in the extension of Person.

In contrast, $\mathcal{I}$ does not satisfy the GCIs

$$\text{Course} \quad \sqsubseteq \quad \neg\text{Person}, \tag{2.1}$$

$$\exists\textit{teaches}.\text{Course} \quad \sqsubseteq \quad \text{Teacher}, \tag{2.2}$$

because et is both a Person and a Course, and because et *teaches* some Course, but is not a Teacher.

In general, a TBox $\mathcal{T}$ allows us to distinguish between those interpretations that are and those that are not models of $\mathcal{T}$. In practice, this means that we can use a TBox to restrict our attention to those interpretations that fit our intuitions about the domain. For example, Formula (2.1) should be in our TBox if we think that a Course cannot be a Person, and Formula (2.2) should be in our TBox if we think that only Teachers can teach Courses. In general, the more GCIs our TBox contains, the fewer models it has. This is expressed in the following lemma.

$$
\begin{array}{rcll}
\mathcal{T}_{ex} = \{\text{Course} & \sqsubseteq & \neg\text{Person}, & (\mathcal{T}_{ex}.1)\\
\text{UGC} & \sqsubseteq & \text{Course}, & (\mathcal{T}_{ex}.2)\\
\text{PGC} & \sqsubseteq & \text{Course}, & (\mathcal{T}_{ex}.3)\\
\text{Teacher} & \equiv & \text{Person} \sqcap \exists \textit{teaches}.\text{Course}, & (\mathcal{T}_{ex}.4)\\
\exists \textit{teaches}.\top & \sqsubseteq & \text{Person}, & (\mathcal{T}_{ex}.5)\\
\text{Student} & \equiv & \text{Person} \sqcap \exists \textit{attends}.\text{Course}, & (\mathcal{T}_{ex}.6)\\
\exists \textit{attends}.\top & \sqsubseteq & \text{Person} \} & (\mathcal{T}_{ex}.7)
\end{array}
$$

Fig. 2.3. The example TBox $\mathcal{T}_{ex}$.

Lemma 2.5. *If $\mathcal{T} \subseteq \mathcal{T}'$ for two TBoxes $\mathcal{T}$, $\mathcal{T}'$, then each model of $\mathcal{T}'$ is also a model of $\mathcal{T}$.*

Proof. The proof is rather straightforward: let $\mathcal{T} \subseteq \mathcal{T}'$ be two TBoxes and $\mathcal{I}$ a model of $\mathcal{T}'$. By definition, $\mathcal{I}$ satisfies all GCIs in $\mathcal{T}'$ and thus, since $\mathcal{T} \subseteq \mathcal{T}'$, also all GCIs in $\mathcal{T}$. Hence $\mathcal{I}$ is, as required, also a model of $\mathcal{T}$. □

Next, in Figure 2.3, we define a TBox $\mathcal{T}_{ex}$ that partially captures our intuition of teaching as presented in Figure 2.1. Axiom $\mathcal{T}_{ex}.4$ is an equivalence that defines a Teacher as a Person who *teaches* a Course. That is, every Teacher is a Person who *teaches* a Course and, vice versa, if a Person *teaches* a Course, then they are a Teacher. Axiom $\mathcal{T}_{ex}.5$ ensures that only Persons can teach a course. As mentioned above, the interpretation depicted in Figure 2.2 is not a model of $\mathcal{T}_{ex}$ since it violates axiom $\mathcal{T}_{ex}.1$.

2.2.2 ALC ABoxes

Next, we define ABoxes and knowledge bases.

Definition 2.6. Let **I** be a set of *individual names* disjoint from **R** and **C**. For $a, b \in \mathbf{I}$ individual names, C a possibly compound ALC concept, and $r \in \mathbf{R}$ a role name, an expression of the form

- $a : C$ is called an ALC *concept assertion*, and
- $(a, b) : r$ is called an ALC *role assertion*.

A finite set of ALC concept and role assertions is called an ALC *ABox*.

An interpretation function $\cdot^{\mathcal{I}}$ is additionally required to map every individual name $a \in \mathbf{I}$ to an element $a^{\mathcal{I}} \in \Delta^{\mathcal{I}}$. An interpretation $\mathcal{I}$ *satisfies*

- a concept assertion $a : C$ if $a^{\mathcal{I}} \in C^{\mathcal{I}}$, and

- a role assertion $(a, b) : r$ if $(a^{\mathcal{I}}, b^{\mathcal{I}}) \in r^{\mathcal{I}}$.

An interpretation that satisfies each concept assertion and each role assertion in an ABox $\mathcal{A}$ is called a *model* of $\mathcal{A}$.

Again, if it is clear that we are talking about $\mathcal{ALC}$ concepts and ABoxes, we omit "$\mathcal{ALC}$" and use simply ABox, concept assertion etc. Moreover, for the sake of brevity, we will occasionally use "individual" as an abbreviation for "individual name".

In Figure 2.4, we present an example ABox $\mathcal{A}_{ex}$ with concept and role assertions. The following interpretation $\mathcal{I}$ is a model of this ABox:

$$
\begin{aligned}
\Delta^{\mathcal{I}} &= \{h, m, c6, p4\}, \\
\mathsf{Mary}^{\mathcal{I}} &= m, \\
\mathsf{Betty}^{\mathcal{I}} &= \mathsf{Hugo}^{\mathcal{I}} = h, \\
\mathsf{CS600}^{\mathcal{I}} &= c6, \\
\mathsf{Ph456}^{\mathcal{I}} &= p4, \\
\mathsf{Person}^{\mathcal{I}} &= \{h, m, c6, p4\}, \\
\mathsf{Teacher}^{\mathcal{I}} &= \{h, m\}, \\
\mathsf{Course}^{\mathcal{I}} &= \{c6, p4\}, \\
\mathsf{PGC}^{\mathcal{I}} &= \{p4\}, \\
\mathsf{UGC}^{\mathcal{I}} &= \{c6\}, \\
\mathsf{Student}^{\mathcal{I}} &= \emptyset, \\
\mathit{teaches}^{\mathcal{I}} &= \{(m, c6), (h, p4)\}, \\
\mathit{attends}^{\mathcal{I}} &= \{(h, p4), (m, p4)\}.
\end{aligned}
$$

Please observe that the individual names Hugo and Betty are interpreted as the same element: h. This is allowed by our definition of the semantics. Some logics, including many early description logics, make the so-called *Unique Name Assumption* (UNA) which requires that $a^{\mathcal{I}} \neq b^{\mathcal{I}}$ in the case $a \neq b$, and would thus rule out such an interpretation. Throughout this book, we do not make the UNA unless it is stated to the contrary.

We can further observe that, in $\mathcal{I}$, the extension of $\mathsf{Teacher}$ has more elements than strictly required by $\mathcal{A}_{ex}$: nothing in $\mathcal{A}_{ex}$ requires m, $c6$ or $p4$ to be in the extension of $\mathsf{Teacher}$. Moreover, $\mathcal{I}$ interprets the concept UGC, although this concept isn't mentioned in $\mathcal{A}_{ex}$. Again, all this is allowed by our definition of the semantics. Also, please note that $\mathcal{I}$ is not a model of the TBox $\mathcal{T}_{ex}$ given in Figure 2.3; for example, $h \in (\mathsf{Person} \sqcap \exists \mathit{attends}.\mathsf{Course})^{\mathcal{I}}$, but $h \notin \mathsf{Student}$, and thus $\mathcal{I}$ does not satisfy the axiom $\mathcal{T}_{ex}.6$.

Next, we combine TBoxes and ABoxes in knowledge bases: this allows us to specify terms and their meaning in a TBox, and then make use of these in our ABox.

Definition 2.7. An $\mathcal{ALC}$ *knowledge base* $\mathcal{K} = (\mathcal{T}, \mathcal{A})$ consists of an $\mathcal{ALC}$ TBox $\mathcal{T}$ and an $\mathcal{ALC}$ ABox $\mathcal{A}$. An interpretation that is both a model of $\mathcal{A}$ and of $\mathcal{T}$ is called a *model* of $\mathcal{K}$.

Hence for an interpretation to be a model of $\mathcal{K}$, it has to satisfy all assertions in $\mathcal{K}$'s ABox and all GCIs in $\mathcal{K}$'s TBox. As an example, consider $\mathcal{K}_{ex} = (\mathcal{T}_{ex}, \mathcal{A}_{ex})$, with $\mathcal{T}_{ex}$ and $\mathcal{A}_{ex}$ as presented in Figures 2.3 and 2.4. As mentioned earlier, the interpretation $\mathcal{I}$ given above is *not* a model of $\mathcal{K}_{ex}$, because $\mathcal{I}$ does not satisfy two of the axioms in $\mathcal{T}_{ex}$ and hence is not a model of $\mathcal{T}_{ex}$:

  (i) m and h are Persons attending a Course, $p4$, but they are not in the extension of Student in $\mathcal{I}$, thereby violating axiom $\mathcal{T}_{ex}.6$.
 (ii) We have two elements, $c6$ and $p4$, that are both in the extension of Person and of Course, thereby violating axiom $\mathcal{T}_{ex}.1$.

We can, however, easily construct a model $\mathcal{I}'$ of $\mathcal{K}_{ex}$ as follows:

$$
\begin{aligned}
\Delta^{\mathcal{I}'} &= \{h, m, b, c6, p4, c5\}, \\
\mathsf{Mary}^{\mathcal{I}'} &= m, \\
\mathsf{Betty}^{\mathcal{I}'} &= b, \\
\mathsf{Hugo}^{\mathcal{I}'} &= h, \\
\mathsf{CS600}^{\mathcal{I}'} &= c6, \\
\mathsf{Ph456}^{\mathcal{I}'} &= p4, \\
\mathsf{Person}^{\mathcal{I}'} &= \{h, m, b\}, \\
\mathsf{Teacher}^{\mathcal{I}'} &= \{h, m, b\}, \\
\mathsf{Course}^{\mathcal{I}'} &= \{c6, p4, c5\}, \\
\mathsf{PGC}^{\mathcal{I}'} &= \{p4\}, \\
\mathsf{UGC}^{\mathcal{I}'} &= \{c6\}, \\
\mathsf{Student}^{\mathcal{I}'} &= \{h, m, b\}, \\
\mathit{teaches}^{\mathcal{I}'} &= \{(m, c6), (h, p4), (b, c5)\}, \\
\mathit{attends}^{\mathcal{I}'} &= \{(h, p4), (m, p4), (b, p4)\}.
\end{aligned}
$$

An important difference relative to databases and other similar formalisms can be illustrated using this example. In $\mathcal{A}_{ex}$, we have stated that Betty is a Teacher, and we know from axiom $\mathcal{T}_{ex}.4$ in Figure 2.3 that Betty must therefore teach at least one course, but we have not said which course she teaches; i.e., there is no role assertion of the form (Betty, ?) : *teaches* in $\mathcal{A}_{ex}$. In a database setting, an *integrity constraint*

$$
\begin{array}{rl}
\mathcal{A}_{ex} = \{ \text{Mary} : \text{Person}, & (\mathcal{A}_{ex}.1) \\
\text{CS600} : \text{Course}, & (\mathcal{A}_{ex}.2) \\
\text{Ph456} : \text{Course} \sqcap \text{PGC}, & (\mathcal{A}_{ex}.3) \\
\text{Hugo} : \text{Person}, & (\mathcal{A}_{ex}.4) \\
\text{Betty} : \text{Person} \sqcap \text{Teacher}, & (\mathcal{A}_{ex}.5) \\
(\text{Mary}, \text{CS600}) : \textit{teaches}, & (\mathcal{A}_{ex}.6) \\
(\text{Hugo}, \text{Ph456}) : \textit{teaches}, & (\mathcal{A}_{ex}.7) \\
(\text{Betty}, \text{Ph456}) : \textit{attends}, & (\mathcal{A}_{ex}.8) \\
(\text{Mary}, \text{Ph456}) : \textit{attends} \} & (\mathcal{A}_{ex}.9)
\end{array}
$$

Fig. 2.4. The example ABox $\mathcal{A}_{ex}$.

can be used to make an apparently similar statement (i.e., that teachers must teach at least one course), but such a constraint would make it mandatory to explicitly specify at least one course that Betty teaches, and failure to do so would be treated as a violation of the integrity constraint (an error). In contrast, in our DL setting it is perfectly fine for a knowledge base to contain such *incomplete information* – we know that Betty stands for an element that is *teaches*-related to some Course, but we do not know to which element; i.e., $\mathcal{K}_{ex}$ has other models in which Betty teaches different courses.

Similarly, in $\mathcal{I}'$, we have that Hugo *attends* Ph456 thanks to $(h, p4) \in$ *attends*$^{\mathcal{I}'}$, yet this is not enforced by $\mathcal{K}_{ex}$. Due to this interpretation of *attends*, however, it is crucial that $h \in \text{Student}^{\mathcal{I}'}$ (which it is) since, otherwise, $\mathcal{I}'$ would not satisfy axiom $\mathcal{T}_{ex}.6$ in Figure 2.3. So, in $\mathcal{I}'$, Hugo is in the extension of Student, although this is not enforced by $\mathcal{K}_{ex}$; i.e., $\mathcal{K}_{ex}$ has other models in which Hugo is not in the extension of Student. In contrast, in a database setting interpretations can only model those facts that explicitly occur in the database.

Furthermore, assume that we add the following axiom to $\mathcal{T}_{ex}$:

$$\text{PG-Student} \equiv \text{Student} \sqcap \forall \textit{attends}.\text{PGC}.$$

Since $\mathcal{A}_{ex}$ explicitly asserts that Betty *attends* Ph456, which is a PGC, and this is the only course that she attends, we might assume that, in each model of our extended $\mathcal{K}_{ex}$, Betty is interpreted as an element in the extension of PG-Student. However, this is not the case: nothing in $\mathcal{K}_{ex}$ rules out the possibility that Betty might attend other courses, and we could construct a model $\mathcal{I}''$ of $\mathcal{K}_{ex}$ that extends $\mathcal{I}'$ by setting *teaches*$^{\mathcal{I}''}$ = *teaches*$^{\mathcal{I}'} \cup \{(b, c6)\}$. In $\mathcal{I}''$ $c6$ is not in the extension of PGC, and so Betty is not in the extension of PG-Student. Thus Betty is not interpreted as a PG-Student in every model of $\mathcal{K}_{ex}$; i.e., $\mathcal{K}_{ex}$ does *not* entail Betty : PG-student. In the general AI literature, this important principle is referred to as the *open world assumption*, and we will come back to it later.

2.2.3 Restricted TBoxes and concept definitions

In Section 2.1, we introduced $C \equiv D$ as an abbreviation for $C \sqsubseteq D$, $D \sqsubseteq C$, and used it in our TBox $\mathcal{T}$ to define the meaning of Teacher and Student:

$$\text{Teacher} \equiv \text{Person} \sqcap \exists teaches.\text{Course},$$
$$\text{Student} \equiv \text{Person} \sqcap \exists attends.\text{Course}.$$

For A a concept name, we call an axiom of the form $A \equiv C$ a *concept definition* of A, and an axiom of the form $A \sqsubseteq C$ a *primitive* concept definition of A. Before we discuss these in detail, let us first convince ourselves that we can restrict our attention to (non-primitive) concept definitions, as formalised in the following lemma.

Lemma 2.8. *Let $A \sqsubseteq C$ be a primitive concept definition in which A_C does not occur. Every model of $A \sqsubseteq C$ can be extended to a model of $A \equiv A_C \sqcap C$ and, vice versa, any model of $A \equiv A_C \sqcap C$ is a model of $A \sqsubseteq C$.*

As a consequence of Lemma 2.8, we can faithfully transform primitive concept definitions into non-primitive ones, and therefore restrict our attention to the latter.

Proof of Lemma 2.8. Let $\mathcal{I}$ be a model of $A \sqsubseteq C$, i.e., $A^{\mathcal{I}} \subseteq C^{\mathcal{I}}$. Since A_C does not occur in C, we are free to extend $\mathcal{I}$ by setting $A_C^{\mathcal{I}} = A^{\mathcal{I}}$, thereby obtaining an extended interpretation $\mathcal{I}$ with $A^{\mathcal{I}} = A_C^{\mathcal{I}} \cap C^{\mathcal{I}}$, i.e., a model of $A \equiv A_C \sqcap C$.

Vice versa, consider a model $\mathcal{I}$ of $A \equiv A_C \sqcap C$. Since $(A_C \sqcap C)^{\mathcal{I}} \subseteq C^{\mathcal{I}}$, we have that $A^{\mathcal{I}} \subseteq C^{\mathcal{I}}$, and thus $\mathcal{I}$ is also a model of $A \sqsubseteq C$. $\qquad\square$

Now consider the concept definition

$$\text{Happy} \equiv \text{Person} \sqcap \forall likes.\text{Happy}. \qquad (2.3)$$

First, observe that this concept definition is *cyclic*: the definition of Happy involves the concept Happy on its right-hand side. Next, we consider an interpretation $\mathcal{I}$ with $\{(p, m), (m, p)\} = \text{likes}^{\mathcal{I}}$ and $\{p, m\} = \text{Person}^{\mathcal{I}}$, and ask ourselves whether p is Happy in $\mathcal{I}$. Since Happy is a defined concept, we might expect that we can determine this by simply considering the interpretation of other concepts and roles. This is, however, not the case: we can choose either $\mathsf{Happy}^{\mathcal{I}} = \{p, m\}$ or $\mathsf{Happy}^{\mathcal{I}} = \emptyset$, and both choices would make $\mathcal{I}$ a model of the concept definition (2.3).

To give TBoxes more *definitorial power*, we can restrict them so as to avoid cyclic references as in the example above.

Definition 2.9. An $\mathcal{ALC}$ *concept definition* is an expression of the form $A \equiv C$ for A a concept name and C a possibly compound $\mathcal{ALC}$ concept.

Let $\mathcal{T}$ be a finite set of concept definitions. We say that A *directly uses* B if there is a concept definition $A \equiv C \in \mathcal{T}$ such that B occurs in C. We say that A *uses* B if A directly uses B, or if there is a concept name B' such that A *uses* B' and B' directly uses B; i.e., *uses* is the transitive closure of *directly uses*.

We call a finite set $\mathcal{T}$ of concept definitions an *acyclic TBox* if

- there is no concept name in $\mathcal{T}$ that uses itself, and
- no concept name occurs more than once on the left-hand side of a concept definition in $\mathcal{T}$.

If $\mathcal{T}$ is an acyclic TBox with $A \equiv C \in \mathcal{T}$, we say that A is *exactly defined in* $\mathcal{T}$, and call C the *definition of* A in $\mathcal{T}$.

In an acyclic TBox we cannot, by definition, have a situation such as follows:

$$
\begin{aligned}
A_1 &\equiv \ldots A_2 \ldots \\
A_2 &\equiv \ldots A_3 \ldots \\
&\vdots \qquad \vdots \\
A_n &\equiv \ldots A_1 \ldots
\end{aligned}
$$

Since acyclic TBoxes are a syntactic restriction of TBoxes, we do not need to define their semantics since it follows directly from the semantics for (general) TBoxes.

To see how an acyclic TBox $\mathcal{T}$ does *not* restrict the interpretation of the concepts that are not defined in $\mathcal{T}$, we make the following observation.

Lemma 2.10. *Let $\mathcal{T}$ be an acyclic TBox, and $\mathcal{I}$ be an interpretation. Then there exists a model $\mathcal{J}$ of $\mathcal{T}$ that coincides with $\mathcal{I}$ on the interpretation of all role and concept names that are not defined in $\mathcal{T}$.*

In other words, any interpretation of terms that are not defined in $\mathcal{T}$ can be extended to a model of $\mathcal{T}$ by interpreting defined concept names in a suitable way.

Proof of Lemma 2.10. Let $\mathcal{T}$ be an acyclic TBox, $\mathcal{I}$ an interpretation and $\{A_1, \ldots, A_k\}$ the set of concept names that are not defined in $\mathcal{T}$. By definition, $\mathcal{T}$ is of the form $A_1 \equiv C_1, \ldots, A_k \equiv C_k$. Without loss of generality and because $\mathcal{T}$ is acyclic, we can assume that the indices $\cdot_i$ are such that, if A_i directly uses A_j, then $j < i$. We define the following series of interpretations $\mathcal{I}_i$ as modifications of $\mathcal{I}$:

- for each i, we set

$$\Delta^{\mathcal{I}_i} = \Delta^{\mathcal{I}},$$
$$r^{\mathcal{I}_i} = r^{\mathcal{I}} \text{ for all role names in } \mathcal{T}, \text{ and}$$
$$A^{\mathcal{I}_i} = A^{\mathcal{I}} \text{ for all concept names not defined in } \mathcal{T}, \text{ and}$$

- we fix the interpretation of defined concepts as follows:

$$A_1^{\mathcal{I}_1} = C_1^{\mathcal{I}}, A_j^{\mathcal{I}_1} = \emptyset \text{ for all } j > 1,$$
$$A_1^{\mathcal{I}_2} = A_1^{\mathcal{I}_1}, A_2^{\mathcal{I}_2} = C_2^{\mathcal{I}_1}, A_j^{\mathcal{I}_2} = \emptyset \text{ for all } j > 2,$$
$$\ldots$$
$$A_1^{\mathcal{I}_k} = A_1^{\mathcal{I}_{k-1}}, A_2^{\mathcal{I}_k} = A_2^{\mathcal{I}_{k-1}}, \ldots, A_k^{\mathcal{I}_k} = C_k^{\mathcal{I}_{k-1}}.$$

By our assumption on the naming of concept names, A_1 uses no defined concept name, and each concept name A_i uses only concept names A_j with $j < i$. Hence the interpretation $\mathcal{I}_k$ is well defined. By definition, $\mathcal{I}_k$ coincides with $\mathcal{I}$ on the interpretation of all role names and concept names that are not defined in $\mathcal{T}$. Moreover, $\mathcal{I}_k$ is a model of $\mathcal{T}$ since it satisfies each axiom in $\mathcal{T}$. $\qquad\square$

Next, we will discuss how to *expand* or *unfold* acyclic TBoxes by treating concept definitions like macros. In a nutshell, assume we are given a knowledge base $\mathcal{K} = (\mathcal{T}, \mathcal{A})$ where $\mathcal{T}$ is acyclic, and that we obtain $\mathcal{A}'$ from $\mathcal{A}$ by recursively replacing all occurrences of concept names in $\mathcal{A}$ with their definitions from $\mathcal{T}$, then we can show that $(\mathcal{T}, \mathcal{A})$ and $\mathcal{A}'$ carry the same meaning in the sense that they have (essentially) the same models.

Definition 2.11. Let $\mathcal{K} = (\mathcal{T}, \mathcal{A})$ be an $\mathcal{ALC}$ knowledge base, where $\mathcal{T}$ is acyclic and of the form $\mathcal{T} = \{A_i \equiv C_i \mid 1 \leq i \leq m\}$. Let $\mathcal{A}_0 = \mathcal{A}$ and let $\mathcal{A}_{j+1}$ be the result of carrying out the following replacement:

(i) find some $a : D \in \mathcal{A}_j$ in which some A_i occurs in D, for some $1 \leq i \leq m$;
(ii) replace all occurrence of A_i in D with C_i.

If no more replacements can be applied to $\mathcal{A}_k$, we call $\mathcal{A}_k$ the *result of unfolding $\mathcal{T}$ into $\mathcal{A}$*.

Please note that, if $\mathcal{A}_k$ is the result of unfolding $\mathcal{T}$ into $\mathcal{A}$ and $A \equiv C \in \mathcal{T}$, then A does not occur in the right-hand side of any assertions in $\mathcal{A}_k$ (otherwise we could apply the replacement from Definition 2.11 to produce $\mathcal{A}_{k+1}$). Next, we show that the meaning of $(\mathcal{T}, \mathcal{A})$ is the same as the meaning of $\mathcal{A}_k$.

Lemma 2.12. *Let $\mathcal{K} = (\mathcal{T}, \mathcal{A})$ be an $\mathcal{ALC}$ knowledge base with $\mathcal{T}$ being acyclic. Then the result of unfolding $\mathcal{T}$ into $\mathcal{A}$ exists and, for $\mathcal{A}'$ the result of unfolding $\mathcal{T}$ into $\mathcal{A}$, we have that*

(i) *each model of $\mathcal{K}$ is a model of $\mathcal{A}'$, and*
(ii) *each model $\mathcal{I}$ of $\mathcal{A}'$ can be modified to one of $\mathcal{K}$ that coincides with $\mathcal{I}$ on the interpretation of roles and concepts that are not defined in $\mathcal{T}$.*

Proof. Let $\mathcal{K} = (\mathcal{T}, \mathcal{A})$, $\mathcal{A}_0 = \mathcal{A}$, and $\mathcal{A}_j$ be as described in Definition 2.11. To prove that unfolding indeed terminates, consider the graph $G(\mathcal{A}_j)$ where

- for each concept name in $\mathcal{T}$ and each individual name in $\mathcal{A}_j$, there is a node in $G(\mathcal{A}_j)$,
- there is an edge from A to B if A directly uses B in $\mathcal{T}$, and
- there is an edge from a to A if there is a concept assertion $a : C \in \mathcal{A}_j$ such that A occurs in C.

Since $\mathcal{T}$ is acyclic, the graph $G(\mathcal{A}_0)$ is acyclic, and the replacement rule does not introduce cycles into $G(\mathcal{A}_j)$. Moreover, by Definition 2.11, the edges between concept names do not change from $\mathcal{A}_j$ to $\mathcal{A}_{j+1}$, and the set of nodes remains stable as well. Most importantly, the replacement rule in Definition 2.11 strictly shortens the length of at least one path from an individual name in $\mathcal{A}$ to a leaf node B, and does not lengthen any path. As a consequence, the replacement rule will eventually no longer be applicable, unfolding will therefore terminate, and the result of unfolding $\mathcal{T}$ into $\mathcal{A}$ exists.

For (i), we show by induction on j that $\mathcal{I}$ being a model of $(\mathcal{T}, \mathcal{A}_j)$ implies that $\mathcal{I}$ is a model of $(\mathcal{T}, \mathcal{A}_{j+1})$. Let $\mathcal{I}$ be a model of $(\mathcal{T}, \mathcal{A}_j)$, and let $\mathcal{A}_{j+1}$ be the result of replacing all occurrences of A_i with C_i in an assertion $a : D$ in $\mathcal{A}_j$. Then $\mathcal{I}$ being a model of $\mathcal{T}$ and $A_i \equiv C_i \in \mathcal{T}$ implies that $A_i^{\mathcal{I}} = C_i^{\mathcal{I}}$, and thus $(D')^{\mathcal{I}} = D^{\mathcal{I}}$ for D' the result of this replacement. Hence $\mathcal{I}$ satisfies $a : D'$ and thus is a model of $(\mathcal{T}, \mathcal{A}_{j+1})$.

For (ii), let $\mathcal{I}$ be a model of $\mathcal{A}'$. As in the proof of Lemma 2.10, we assume that the concept name indices are such that, if A_i directly uses

A_j, then $j < i$. If $\mathcal{I}$ is not a model of $\mathcal{T}$, then modify $\mathcal{I}$ in the following way, starting from $i = 0$ and considering A_i in ascending order:

if $\mathcal{I}$ does not satisfy $A_i \equiv C_i \in \mathcal{T}$, then set $A_i^{\mathcal{I}}$ to $C_i^{\mathcal{I}}$.

Call the result of this modification $\mathcal{J}$. First, $\mathcal{J}$ is well defined: the order in which we modify $\mathcal{I}$ ensures that the interpretation of a defined concept name A_i only depends on concept names already considered, and the fact that each concept name occurs at most once on the left-hand side of an axiom in $\mathcal{T}$ ensures that $\mathcal{J}$ is well defined. Secondly, $\mathcal{J}$ coincides with $\mathcal{I}$ on the interpretation of roles and concepts not defined in $\mathcal{T}$. Third, by construction, $\mathcal{J}$ is a model of $\mathcal{T}$. Finally, $\mathcal{J}$ is a model of $\mathcal{A}$: $\mathcal{J}$ satisfies

- each role assertion in $\mathcal{A}$ because $\mathcal{I}$ and $\mathcal{J}$ coincide on the interpretation of individual and role names, and $\mathcal{I}$ is a model of $\mathcal{A}$;
- each concept assertion in $\mathcal{A}$: let $a : C \in \mathcal{A}$. Then there is some $a : C' \in \mathcal{A}'$ where C' is the result of replacing concept names defined in $\mathcal{T}$ with their definition. Since there are no defined concept names occurring in C', the construction of $\mathcal{J}$ and $\mathcal{J}$ being a model of $\mathcal{T}$ implies that $(C')^{\mathcal{J}} = C^{\mathcal{I}}$, and thus $\mathcal{J}$ satisfies $a : C$. □

Hence we have shown that acyclic TBox definitions are like macros that can be expanded directly into an ABox. It should be noted, however, that unfolding of acyclic definitions may cause an exponential blow-up of the size of the ABox, as demonstrated by the following example.

Example 2.13. Consider the ABox $\mathcal{A} = \{A : a\}$ together with the acyclic TBox $\mathcal{T}$ consisting of the following definitions:

$$
\begin{aligned}
A_0 &\equiv \forall r.A_1 \sqcap \forall s.A_1, \\
A_1 &\equiv \forall r.A_2 \sqcap \forall s.A_2, \\
&\vdots \\
A_{n-1} &\equiv \forall r.A_n \sqcap \forall s.A_n.
\end{aligned}
$$

The knowledge base $\mathcal{K} = (\mathcal{T}, \mathcal{A})$ has a size that is linear in n, but the ABox obtained by unfolding $\mathcal{T}$ into $\mathcal{A}$ contains the concept name A_n 2^n times.

We will see in Section 4.2.2 an improved *lazy* way to unfold an acyclic TBox, and discuss how this avoids the exponential blow-up that the *eager* unfolding introduced above and used in the example may cause.

2.3 Basic reasoning problems and services

So far, we have defined the components of a DL knowledge base and what it means for an interpretation to be a model of such a knowledge base. Next, we define the reasoning problems commonly considered in DLs, and discuss their relationships. We start by defining the basic reasoning problems in DLs upon which the basic system services of a DL *reasoner* are built, and then provide a number of examples.

Definition 2.14. Let $\mathcal{K} = (\mathcal{T}, \mathcal{A})$ be an $\mathcal{ALC}$ knowledge base, C, D possibly compound $\mathcal{ALC}$ concepts, and b an individual name. We say that

(i) C is *satisfiable* with respect to $\mathcal{T}$ if there exists a model $\mathcal{I}$ of $\mathcal{T}$ and some $d \in \Delta^{\mathcal{I}}$ with $d \in C^{\mathcal{I}}$;

(ii) C is *subsumed by* D with respect to $\mathcal{T}$, written $\mathcal{T} \models C \sqsubseteq D$, if $C^{\mathcal{I}} \subseteq D^{\mathcal{I}}$ for every model $\mathcal{I}$ of $\mathcal{T}$;

(iii) C and D are *equivalent* with respect to $\mathcal{T}$, written $\mathcal{T} \models C \equiv D$, if $C^{\mathcal{I}} = D^{\mathcal{I}}$ for every model $\mathcal{I}$ of $\mathcal{T}$;

(iv) $\mathcal{K}$ is *consistent* if there exists a model of $\mathcal{K}$;

(v) b is an *instance of* C with respect to $\mathcal{K}$, written $\mathcal{K} \models b : C$, if $b^{\mathcal{I}} \in C^{\mathcal{I}}$ for every model $\mathcal{I}$ of $\mathcal{K}$.

We use the standard entailment symbol $\models$ because the semantics of DL entailment coincides with the semantics of entailment in first-order logic (see Section 2.6.1). To underline the fact that, once $\mathcal{T}$ is fixed, subsumption and equivalence with respect to $\mathcal{T}$ is a binary relation between (possibly compound) concepts, we often use $C \sqsubseteq_{\mathcal{T}} D$ for $\mathcal{T} \models C \sqsubseteq D$ and $C \equiv_{\mathcal{T}} D$ for $\mathcal{T} \models C \equiv D$.

Please note that satisfiability and subsumption are defined with respect to a TBox, whereas consistency and instance are defined with respect to a TBox and an ABox. We can always assume that the TBox (or the TBox and ABox) are empty: in this case, "all models of $\mathcal{T}$ (or $\mathcal{K}$)" becomes simply "all interpretations". We will sometimes talk about the consistency of a TBox $\mathcal{T}$ or an ABox $\mathcal{A}$, which is equivalent to the consistency of $\mathcal{K} = (\mathcal{T}, \emptyset)$ and $\mathcal{K} = (\emptyset, \mathcal{A})$ respectively.

Please make sure you understand the difference between an element being *in the extension of* a concept C in an interpretation $\mathcal{I}$, and an individual name being *an instance of* a concept C: an individual name b can be interpreted in many different ways, and $b^{\mathcal{I}_1}$ can have quite different properties from $b^{\mathcal{I}_2}$. A knowledge base $\mathcal{K}$ can, however, enforce that $b^{\mathcal{I}}$ is in the extension of C in *every* model $\mathcal{I}$ of $\mathcal{K}$, which is why we define the notion of an instance for individual names. For example, consider our TBox $\mathcal{T}_{ex}$ and ABox $\mathcal{A}_{ex}$ from Figures 2.3 and 2.4, and our example model $\mathcal{I}'$ of $\mathcal{K}_{ex} = (\mathcal{T}_{ex}, \mathcal{A}_{ex})$. In $\mathcal{I}'$, h is in the extension of Teacher, but there can be other interpretations $\mathcal{I}'$ where $h \notin \text{Teacher}^{\mathcal{I}'}$ and even where $h \notin \Delta^{\mathcal{I}}$. However, in every model $\mathcal{I}$ of $\mathcal{K}$, the element of $\Delta^{\mathcal{I}}$ that interprets Hugo (i.e., $\text{Hugo}^{\mathcal{I}}$) *must* be in the extension of Teacher; i.e., $\mathcal{K} \models \text{Hugo} : \text{Teacher}$.

So far, most of the concepts we have seen were satisfiable, but we have also seen concepts such as $A \sqcap \neg A$ that are unsatisfiable even with respect to the empty TBox, i.e., we cannot find any interpretation $\mathcal{I}$ in which $(A \sqcap \neg A)^{\mathcal{I}} \neq \emptyset$, because this would mean that we have some element in both the extension of A and of $\neg A$. Thus $\bot$ and $A \sqcap \neg A$ are equivalent (with respect to the empty TBox). In fact there are (infinitely) many such concepts; for example, $\exists r.A \sqcap \forall r.\neg A$ is also unsatisfiable, because any element in the extension of this concept would need to have an r-filler that is in the extension of both A and $\neg A$. More interesting are concepts that are satisfiable with respect to some but not all TBoxes. For example, consider again the TBox $\mathcal{T}_{ex}$; Course $\sqcap \exists teaches.\text{Course}$ is *not* satisfiable with respect to $\mathcal{T}_{ex}$ because axioms $\mathcal{T}_{ex}.1$ and $\mathcal{T}_{ex}.5$ prevent an element in the extension of Course from having a *teaches*-filler.

Similarly, (infinitely) many subsumption relations are entailed even by the empty TBox; for example, it is easy to see that $\emptyset \models A \sqcap B \sqsubseteq A$, $\emptyset \models A \sqsubseteq A \sqcup B$, and $\emptyset \models \exists r.A \sqcap B \sqsubseteq \exists r.A$. Slightly more tricky is $\emptyset \models \exists r.A \sqcap \forall r.B \sqsubseteq \exists r.B$: every element x in the extension of $\exists r.A \sqcap \forall r.B$ has an r-filler in A, and the second conjunct implies that this r-filler also needs to be in the extension of B; hence x is also in the extension of $\exists r.B$. If we again consider $\mathcal{T}_{ex}$, we have that $\mathcal{T}_{ex} \models \text{PGC} \sqsubseteq \neg \text{Person}$, and that $\mathcal{T}_{ex} \models \exists teaches.\text{Course} \sqsubseteq \neg \text{Course}$. To see the latter, try to find a model $\mathcal{I}$ of $\mathcal{T}_{ex}$ with $x \in (\exists teaches.\text{Course})^{\mathcal{I}}$: since x has a *teaches*-filler, x must be in $\text{Person}^{\mathcal{I}}$ and, if x were in $\text{Course}^{\mathcal{I}}$, then x would need to be in $(\neg \text{Person})^{\mathcal{I}}$ – thereby contradicting $x \in \text{Person}^{\mathcal{I}}$. We will formalise this in Theorem 2.17 (ii).

As we have already seen, the knowledge base $\mathcal{K}_{ex} = (\mathcal{T}_{ex}, \mathcal{A}_{ex})$ is consistent since we have built a model $\mathcal{I}'$ of it. In contrast, the knowledge base $(\mathcal{T}_{ex}, \mathcal{A}_2)$, with $\mathcal{A}_2$ defined as follows, is not consistent:

$$\mathcal{A}_2 = \{\text{ET} : \text{Course}, (\text{ET}, \text{Foo}) : teaches\}.$$

If we try to build a model $\mathcal{I}$ of $(\mathcal{T}_{ex}, \mathcal{A}_2)$, we will fail because $\text{ET}^{\mathcal{I}}$ would need to be in $\text{Course}^{\mathcal{I}}$, therefore *not* in $\text{Person}^{\mathcal{I}}$ due to the axiom $\mathcal{T}_{ex}.1$, yet *in* Person$^\mathcal{I}$ because ET$^\mathcal{I}$ has a *teaches*-filler. Removing either of the two assertions from $\mathcal{A}_2$ results in an ABox that is consistent with $\mathcal{T}_{ex}$.

Next, we would like to point out that it is possible for a knowledge base $(\mathcal{T}, \mathcal{A})$ to be consistent and for a concept C to be unsatisfiable with respect to $\mathcal{T}$: clearly, $\bot$ is unsatisfiable with respect to every TBox since, by Definition 2.2, $\bot^\mathcal{I} = \emptyset$ for every interpretation $\mathcal{I}$. Even if C is defined in $\mathcal{T}$ (see Definition 2.9), it is possible that C is unsatisfiable with respect to $\mathcal{T}$ while $\mathcal{T}$ is consistent; consider, for example, the TBox $\mathcal{T} = \{A \equiv B \sqcap \neg B\}$ which has infinitely many models, but in all of them the extension of A is empty.

Finally, Mary and Hugo are instances of Teacher with respect to $\mathcal{K}_{ex} = (\mathcal{T}_{ex}, \mathcal{A}_{ex})$, because $\mathcal{A}_{ex}$ contains assertions that they are both Persons and teach some Courses, and because axiom $\mathcal{T}_{ex}.4$ implies that a Person who *teaches* a Course is a Teacher. Hence, in every model $\mathcal{I}$ of $\mathcal{K}_{ex}$, Mary$^\mathcal{I} \in$ Teacher$^\mathcal{I}$ and Hugo$^\mathcal{I} \in$ Teacher$^\mathcal{I}$.

To deepen the readers' understanding of the reasoning problems, we discuss some important properties of the subsumption relationship.

Lemma 2.15. *Let C, D and E be concepts, b an individual name, and $(\mathcal{T}, \mathcal{A})$, $(\mathcal{T}', \mathcal{A}')$ knowledge bases with $\mathcal{T} \subseteq \mathcal{T}'$ and $\mathcal{A} \subseteq \mathcal{A}'$.*

- (i) *$C \sqsubseteq_\mathcal{T} C$.*
- (ii) *If $C \sqsubseteq_\mathcal{T} D$ and $D \sqsubseteq_\mathcal{T} E$, then $C \sqsubseteq_\mathcal{T} E$.*
- (iii) *If b is an instance of C with respect to $(\mathcal{T}, \mathcal{A})$ and $C \sqsubseteq_\mathcal{T} D$, then b is an instance of D with respect to $(\mathcal{T}, \mathcal{A})$.*
- (iv) *If $\mathcal{T} \models C \sqsubseteq D$ then $\mathcal{T}' \models C \sqsubseteq D$.*
- (v) *If $\mathcal{T} \models C \equiv D$ then $\mathcal{T}' \models C \equiv D$.*
- (vi) *If $(\mathcal{T}, \mathcal{A}) \models b : E$ then $(\mathcal{T}', \mathcal{A}') \models b : E$.*

Part (ii) of Lemma 2.15 says that the subsumption relationship is transitive, and parts (iv)–(vi) say that $\mathcal{ALC}$ is *monotonic*: the more statements a knowledge base contains, the more entailments it has.

Proof. Let C, D, E, b and $(\mathcal{T}, \mathcal{A})$ be as described in Lemma 2.15.

- (i) For any interpretation $\mathcal{I}$ and any concept C, we obviously have $C^\mathcal{I} = C^\mathcal{I}$, and thus $C^\mathcal{I} \subseteq C^\mathcal{I}$. Hence we have $C \sqsubseteq_\mathcal{T} C$.
- (ii) Let $C \sqsubseteq_\mathcal{T} D$ and $D \sqsubseteq_\mathcal{T} E$ and consider a model $\mathcal{I}$ of $\mathcal{T}$: we have that $C^\mathcal{I} \subseteq D^\mathcal{I}$ and $D^\mathcal{I} \subseteq E^\mathcal{I}$. Hence we have, by transitivity of $\subseteq$, $C^\mathcal{I} \subseteq E^\mathcal{I}$. Since $\mathcal{I}$ was an arbitrary model of $\mathcal{T}$, this implies $C \sqsubseteq_\mathcal{T} E$.

(iii) Let b be an instance of C with respect to $(\mathcal{T}, \mathcal{A})$ and $C \sqsubseteq_\mathcal{T} D$. Hence, for each model $\mathcal{I}$ of $(\mathcal{T}, \mathcal{A})$, we have that $b^\mathcal{I} \in C^\mathcal{I}$ and $C^\mathcal{I} \subseteq D^\mathcal{I}$. Thus, for each model $\mathcal{I}$ of $(\mathcal{T}, \mathcal{A})$, we have that $b^\mathcal{I} \in D^\mathcal{I}$, and thus b is an instance of D with respect to $(\mathcal{T}, \mathcal{A})$.

(iv) This is an immediate consequence of the fact that $\mathcal{T} \subseteq \mathcal{T}'$ and Lemma 2.5.

(v) and (vi) can be proven analogously to Lemma 2.5 and are left to the reader. $\qquad\square$

Now we reconsider our observation about the generosity of the set of operators to build $\mathcal{ALC}$ concept descriptions and take Lemma 2.3 a bit further.

Lemma 2.16. *Let C and D be concepts, r a role, $\mathcal{T}_0 = \emptyset$ the empty TBox, and $\mathcal{T}$ an arbitrary TBox.*

(i) $\mathcal{T}_0 \models \top \equiv (\neg C \sqcup C)$.

(ii) $\mathcal{T}_0 \models \bot \equiv (\neg C \sqcap C)$.

(iii) $\mathcal{T}_0 \models C \sqcup D \equiv \neg(\neg C \sqcap \neg D)$.

(iv) $\mathcal{T}_0 \models \forall r.C \equiv \neg(\exists r.\neg C)$.

(v) $\mathcal{T} \models C \sqsubseteq D$ *if and only if* $\mathcal{T} \models \top \sqsubseteq (\neg C \sqcup D)$.

As a consequence of Lemma 2.16, we can indeed rewrite every concept description into an equivalent one that does not use $\top$, $\bot$, disjunction or universal restrictions. Also, we could formulate an alternative form of this lemma that would allow us to drop conjunction rather than disjunction, and existential rather than universal restrictions. As a further consequence of Lemma 2.15, these equivalences are entailed by all TBoxes – and thus we call them *tautologies*.

Proof of Lemma 2.16. Equivalences (i) and (ii) are an immediate consequence of Lemma 2.3 (i) and (ii) which state that $\top^\mathcal{I} = (C \sqcup \neg C)^\mathcal{I}$ and $\bot^\mathcal{I} = (C \sqcap \neg C)^\mathcal{I}$ hold in any interpretation. Hence $\emptyset \models \top \equiv (\neg C \sqcup C)$ and $\emptyset \models \bot \equiv (\neg C \sqcap C)$.

For (iii), Lemma 2.3 (iii) and (v) imply that, for any interpretation $\mathcal{I}$, $(C \sqcup D)^\mathcal{I} = (\neg\neg(C \sqcup D))^\mathcal{I} = (\neg(\neg C \sqcap \neg D))^\mathcal{I}$, and thus $\emptyset \models C \sqcup D \equiv \neg(\neg C \sqcap \neg D)$.

For (iv), Lemma 2.3 (iii) and (vii) imply that, for any interpretation $\mathcal{I}$, $(\forall r.C)^\mathcal{I} = (\neg\neg(\forall r.C))^\mathcal{I} = (\neg(\exists r.\neg C))^\mathcal{I}$, and thus $\emptyset \models \forall r.C \equiv \neg(\exists r.\neg C)$.

For (v), assume that $\mathcal{T} \models C \sqsubseteq D$, and consider a model $\mathcal{I}$ of $\mathcal{T}$ and some $a \in \Delta^\mathcal{I}$. Since $\mathcal{I}$ is a model of $\mathcal{T}$, $C^\mathcal{I} \subseteq D^\mathcal{I}$. If $a \in C^\mathcal{I}$, then

$\mathcal{T} \models C \sqsubseteq D$ implies that $a \in D^{\mathcal{I}}$, and thus $a \in (\neg C \sqcup D)^{\mathcal{I}}$. Otherwise, $a \in (\neg C)^{\mathcal{I}}$ and thus also in $(\neg C \sqcup D)^{\mathcal{I}}$. Hence $\mathcal{T} \models \top \sqsubseteq (\neg C \sqcup D)$. The other direction is analogous.　　　　　　　　　　　　　　　　　□

Next, we formalise some of the implicit relationships between DL reasoning problems that we have used intuitively in our considerations above.

Theorem 2.17. *Let* $\mathcal{K} = (\mathcal{T}, \mathcal{A})$ *be an* $\mathcal{ALC}$ *knowledge base,* C, D *possibly compound* $\mathcal{ALC}$ *concepts and* b *an individual name.*

  (i) $C \equiv_{\mathcal{T}} D$ *if and only if* $C \sqsubseteq_{\mathcal{T}} D$ *and* $D \sqsubseteq_{\mathcal{T}} C$.
  (ii) $C \sqsubseteq_{\mathcal{T}} D$ *if and only if* $C \sqcap \neg D$ *is not satisfiable with respect to* $\mathcal{T}$.
  (iii) C *is satisfiable with respect to* $\mathcal{T}$ *if and only if* $C \not\sqsubseteq_{\mathcal{T}} \bot$.
  (iv) C *is satisfiable with respect to* $\mathcal{T}$ *if and only if* $(\mathcal{T}, \{b : C\})$ *is consistent.*
  (v) $(\mathcal{T}, \mathcal{A}) \models b : C$ *if and only if* $(\mathcal{T}, \mathcal{A} \cup \{b : \neg C\})$ *is* not *consistent.*
  (vi) *if* $\mathcal{T}$ *is acyclic, and* $\mathcal{A}'$ *is the result of unfolding* $\mathcal{T}$ *into* $\mathcal{A}$, *then* $\mathcal{K}$ *is consistent if and only if* $(\emptyset, \mathcal{A}')$ *is consistent.*

As a consequence of this theorem, we can focus our attention on knowledge base consistency, since all the reasoning problems introduced in Definition 2.14 can be *reduced* to knowledge base consistency; i.e., we can use an algorithm for knowledge base consistency to decide all of these other reasoning problems. Note, however, that there are other reasoning problems not mentioned yet for which such a reduction is not possible, and even if it is possible it may in some cases incur an exponential blow-up in the size of the problem. In particular, conjunctive query answering (see Chapter 7) is 2ExpTime-complete for $\mathcal{ALCI}$, whereas $\mathcal{ALCI}$ knowledge base consistency is "only" ExpTime-complete [Lut08], and for $\mathcal{SROIQ}$, the decidability of conjunctive query answering is still open, whereas knowledge base consistency is known to be decidable and N2ExpTime-complete [GLHS08, Kaz08].

Next, we will prove Theorem 2.17.

Proof. Let $\mathcal{K} = (\mathcal{T}, \mathcal{A})$ be an $\mathcal{ALC}$ knowledge base, C, D possibly compound $\mathcal{ALC}$ concepts and b an individual name.

  (i) Let $C \equiv_{\mathcal{T}} D$. By definition, this means that $C^{\mathcal{I}} = D^{\mathcal{I}}$, for each model $\mathcal{I}$ of $\mathcal{T}$. This implies that, for each model $\mathcal{I}$ of $\mathcal{T}$, we have $C^{\mathcal{I}} \subseteq D^{\mathcal{I}}$ and $D^{\mathcal{I}} \subseteq C^{\mathcal{I}}$. Hence we have, by definition, that $C \sqsubseteq_{\mathcal{T}} D$ and $D \sqsubseteq_{\mathcal{T}} C$.

Now let $C \sqsubseteq_{\mathcal{T}} D$ and $D \sqsubseteq_{\mathcal{T}} C$. We can use an analogous way of reasoning to conclude that $C \equiv_{\mathcal{T}} D$.[4]

(ii) Let $C \sqsubseteq_{\mathcal{T}} D$. By definition, this means that, in every model $\mathcal{I}$ of $\mathcal{T}$, we have $C^{\mathcal{I}} \subseteq D^{\mathcal{I}}$. Hence there cannot be a model $\mathcal{I}$ of $\mathcal{T}$ in which there is some $x \in C^{\mathcal{I}}$ with $x \notin D^{\mathcal{I}}$. This means that there cannot be a model $\mathcal{I}$ of $\mathcal{T}$ in which there is some $x \in C^{\mathcal{I}}$ with $x \in (\neg D)^{\mathcal{I}}$, and thus $C \sqcap \neg D$ is not satisfiable with respect to $\mathcal{T}$.

For the other direction, let $C \sqcap \neg D$ be unsatisfiable with respect to $\mathcal{T}$. Hence in every model $\mathcal{I}$ of $\mathcal{T}$, we have that $(C \sqcap \neg D)^{\mathcal{I}} = \emptyset$, and thus $C^{\mathcal{I}} \subseteq D^{\mathcal{I}}$ holds in every model $\mathcal{I}$ of $\mathcal{T}$.

(iii) First, remember that, by Definition 2.2, $\bot^{\mathcal{I}} = \emptyset$ in every interpretation $\mathcal{I}$. Now let C be satisfiable with respect to $\mathcal{T}$. Hence there is some model $\mathcal{I}$ of $\mathcal{T}$ with $C^{\mathcal{I}} \neq \emptyset$, and thus $C^{\mathcal{I}} \not\subseteq \bot^{\mathcal{I}}$.

Similarly, if $C \sqsubseteq_{\mathcal{T}} \bot$, then $C^{\mathcal{I}} = \emptyset$ in every model $\mathcal{I}$ of $\mathcal{T}$, and thus C is not satisfiable with respect to $\mathcal{T}$.

(iv) Let C be satisfiable with respect to $\mathcal{T}$. Hence there exists some $\mathcal{I}$ with $C^{\mathcal{I}} \neq \emptyset$. Take some $x \in C^{\mathcal{I}}$ and extend $\mathcal{I}$ by setting $b^{\mathcal{I}} = x$. This clearly preserves $\mathcal{I}$ being a model of $\mathcal{T}$, and also makes $\mathcal{I}$ a model of the ABox $\{b : C\}$. Hence $(\mathcal{T}, \{b : C\})$ is consistent.

If $(\mathcal{T}, \{b : C\})$ is consistent, then it has some model, say $\mathcal{I}$. By definition, $b^{\mathcal{I}} \in C^{\mathcal{I}}$, and thus $C^{\mathcal{I}} \neq \emptyset$.

(v) Let b be an instance of C with respect to $\mathcal{K}$. By definition, we have $b^{\mathcal{I}} \in C^{\mathcal{I}}$, for every model $\mathcal{I}$ of $\mathcal{K}$. Together with the fact that $C^{\mathcal{I}}$ and $(\neg C)^{\mathcal{I}}$ are disjoint, this implies that there is no model $\mathcal{I}$ of $\mathcal{T}$ and $\mathcal{A}$ in which $b^{\mathcal{I}} \in (\neg C)^{\mathcal{I}}$, and thus $(\mathcal{T}, \mathcal{A} \cup \{b : \neg C\})$ is not consistent. Please note that the above line of reasoning is independent of $\mathcal{K}$'s consistency.

Let $(\mathcal{T}, \mathcal{A} \cup \{b : \neg C\})$ be inconsistent. If $(\mathcal{T}, \mathcal{A})$ is also inconsistent, we are done since any model of $(\mathcal{T}, \mathcal{A})$ satisfies everything because there are no such models. Otherwise, there are models of $(\mathcal{T}, \mathcal{A})$, but there cannot be a model $\mathcal{I}$ of $(\mathcal{T}, \mathcal{A})$ with $b^{\mathcal{I}} \in (\neg C)^{\mathcal{I}}$ because this would contradict our assumption. Hence in every model $\mathcal{I}$ of $(\mathcal{T}, \mathcal{A})$, we have $b^{\mathcal{I}} \notin (\neg C)^{\mathcal{I}}$, which is, by Definition 2.2, the same as $b^{\mathcal{I}} \in C^{\mathcal{I}}$. Hence b is an instance of C with respect to $\mathcal{K}$.

(vi) This is an immediate consequence of Lemma 2.12. □

In general, when designing or changing a knowledge base, it is helpful to see the *effects* of the current TBox and ABox statements. We will use

---

[4] And we cordially invite the reader to verify this.

the reasoning problems from Definition 2.14 to formalise some of these effects and formulate them in terms of *reasoning services*. The following is a list of the most basic DL reasoning services.

(i) Given a TBox $\mathcal{T}$ and a concept C, check whether C is *satisfiable* with respect to $\mathcal{T}$.

(ii) Given a TBox $\mathcal{T}$ and two concepts C and D, check whether C is *subsumed by* D with respect to $\mathcal{T}$.

(iii) Given a TBox $\mathcal{T}$ and two concepts C and D, check whether C and D are *equivalent* with respect to $\mathcal{T}$.

(iv) Given a knowledge base $(\mathcal{T}, \mathcal{A})$, check whether $(\mathcal{T}, \mathcal{A})$ is *consistent*.

(v) Given a knowledge base $(\mathcal{T}, \mathcal{A})$, an individual name a, and a concept C, check whether a is an *instance of* C with respect to $(\mathcal{T}, \mathcal{A})$.

Please note that these basic reasoning services correspond one-to-one to the basic reasoning problems from Definition 2.14. As a consequence, we know exactly *what* each of these reasoning services should do, even though we might not know *how* such a service could be implemented – this will be discussed in Chapter 4. To put it differently, the behaviour of a service has been described independently of a specific algorithm or its implementation, and thus we can expect that, for example, every satisfiability checker for $\mathcal{ALC}$ gives the same answer when asked whether a certain concept is satisfiable with respect to a certain TBox – regardless of how this satisfiability checker works.

Clearly, we might be able to compute these services by hand, yet this is unfeasible for larger knowledge bases, and it has turned out to be quite useful to have implementations of these services. In the past, numerous DLs have been investigated with respect to their *decidability* and *complexity*, i.e., whether or which of the reasoning problems are decidable and, if they are, how complex they are in terms of computation time and space. As we saw in Theorem 2.17, we can reduce all these basic reasoning problems to knowledge base consistency, and thus use an algorithm that decides consistency, for example, as a sub-routine in an algorithm that checks subsumption.

Using these most basic reasoning services, we can specify slightly more sophisticated reasoning services as follows.

- *Classification* of a TBox: given a TBox $\mathcal{T}$, compute the *subsumption hierarchy* of all concept names occurring in $\mathcal{T}$ with respect to $\mathcal{T}$. That is, for each pair A, B of concept names occurring in $\mathcal{T}$, check whether A is subsumed by B with respect to $\mathcal{T}$ and whether B is subsumed by A with respect to $\mathcal{T}$.

- Checking the *satisfiability* of concepts in $\mathcal{T}$: given a TBox $\mathcal{T}$, for each concept name A in $\mathcal{T}$, test whether A is satisfiable with respect to $\mathcal{T}$. If it is not, then this is usually an indication of a modelling error.

- *Instance retrieval*: given a concept C and a knowledge base $\mathcal{K}$, return all those individual names b such that b is an instance of C with respect to $\mathcal{K}$. That is, for each individual name b occurring in $\mathcal{K}$, check whether it is an instance of C with respect to $\mathcal{K}$, and return the set of those individual names for which this test is positive.

- *Realisation* of an individual name: given an individual name b and a knowledge base $\mathcal{K}$, test, for each concept name A occurring in $\mathcal{T}$, whether b is an instance of A with respect to $\mathcal{K}$, and return the set of those concept names for which this test is positive.

The result of classification is usually presented in form of a *subsumption hierarchy*, that is, a graph whose nodes are labelled with concept names from $\mathcal{T}$ and where we find an edge from a node labelled A to a node labelled B if A is subsumed by B with respect to $\mathcal{T}$. We may want to choose a slightly more succinct representation: from Lemma 2.15, we know that the subsumption relationship $\sqsubseteq_\mathcal{T}$ is a *pre-order*, i.e., a reflexive and transitive relation. It is common practice to consider the induced *strict partial order* $\sqsubset_\mathcal{T}$, i.e., an irreflexive and transitive (and therefore anti-symmetric) relation, by identifying all concepts participating in a cycle $C \sqsubseteq_\mathcal{T} \ldots \sqsubseteq_\mathcal{T} C$ – or collapsing them all into a single node in our graphical representation. In addition, we might want to show only direct edges; that is, we might not want to draw an edge from a node labelled C to a node labelled E in case there is a node labelled D such that $C \sqsubseteq_\mathcal{T} D \sqsubseteq_\mathcal{T} E$: this is commonly known as the *Hasse diagram* of a partial order.

In Figure 2.5, we present the subsumption hierarchy for the TBox $\mathcal{T}_{ex}$ from Figure 2.3. Please make sure you understand the difference between this graphical representation of a subsumption hierarchy and the graphical representation of an interpretation such as the one presented in Figure 2.2: both are graphs, but with very different meanings.

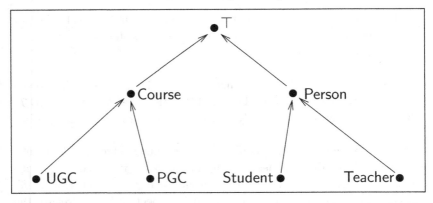

Fig. 2.5. A graphical representation of the subsumption hierarchy for the TBox $\mathcal{T}_{ex}$ from Figure 2.3.

2.4 Using reasoning services

Here, we sketch how DL reasoning services can be used during the construction of a DL knowledge base. Assume we want to design a DL knowledge base about universities, courses, students etc. First, we would need to fix some set of interesting *terms* and decide which of them are concept names and which are role names. Then we could explicate some background knowledge, for example that Courses and Persons are disjoint and that only a Person ever *teaches* somebody or *attends* something; see axioms $\mathcal{T}_{ex}.1$, $\mathcal{T}_{ex}.5$ and $\mathcal{T}_{ex}.7$ in Figure 2.3. Next, we could define some relevant concepts, for example UGC and PGC as kinds of Course, Teacher as a Person who *teaches* a Course, and Student as a Person who *attends* a Course; see axioms $\mathcal{T}_{ex}.2$, $\mathcal{T}_{ex}.3$, $\mathcal{T}_{ex}.4$ and $\mathcal{T}_{ex}.6$ in Figure 2.3. Then it might be useful to see the subsumption hierarchy of our TBox $\mathcal{T}_{ex}$. In our example, we can easily compute this hierarchy by hand; see Figure 2.5.

Now assume that we extend $\mathcal{T}_{ex}$ by adding the following concept definition:

$$\text{Professor} \equiv \exists \textit{teaches}.\text{PGC}.$$

For $\mathcal{T}'_{ex}$ this extended TBox, it is a bit more tricky to see that, in addition to the subsumptions above, we also have $\mathcal{T}'_{ex} \models \text{Professor} \sqsubseteq \text{Person}$. However, this still fits our intuition, and we can continue extending our knowledge base. Assume we extend $\mathcal{T}'_{ex}$ with the following GCI that expresses that a LazyStudent does not *attend* any Courses:

$$\text{LazyStudent} \sqsubseteq \forall \textit{attends}.\neg\text{Course}.$$

Let $\mathcal{T}''_{ex}$ be the result of this extension. It is not too hard to see that a LazyStudent is *not* a Student (because every Student *attends* at least one Course), i.e., $\mathcal{T}''_{ex} \not\models$ LazyStudent $\sqsubseteq$ Student. This is no longer consistent with our intuition or concept naming scheme. We might try to fix this perceived problem by modifying the newly added GCI, for example, by turning it into the following concept definition:

$$\text{LazyStudent} \equiv \text{Student} \sqcap \forall attends.\neg\text{Course}.$$

This modification now makes make LazyStudent unsatisfiable with respect to the resulting TBox since axiom $\mathcal{T}_{ex}.6$ states that a Student necessarily *attends* some Course. We might consider introducing a new role, *activelyAttends*, and defining lazy students as those who do not actively attend a course; however, the DL $\mathcal{ALC}$ is too weak to capture the interaction between active attendance and attendance, so we will abandon our efforts to model lazy students, and go back to $\mathcal{T}'_{ex}$.

Now assume we add some knowledge about concrete individuals; for example, we add our ABox $\mathcal{A}_{ex}$ from Figure 2.4 to give $\mathcal{K} = (\mathcal{T}'_{ex}, \mathcal{A}_{ex})$. Then it would be quite helpful to learn that Mary and Hugo are instances of Teacher and that Hugo is an instance of Professor with respect to $\mathcal{K}$– even though this knowledge is not explicitly stated in our knowledge base, it follows from it, and thus should be made available to the user. For example, if one asks to retrieve all Teachers in $\mathcal{K}$, then Betty, Mary and Hugo should be returned.

The design of ontology editors that help users to build, maintain and use a DL knowledge base is a very active research area, partly due to the fact that the web ontology language OWL is based on DLs, and DL reasoning services can thus be used to support *ontology engineering* in OWL; we will discuss this in more detail in Chapter 8.

2.5 Extensions of the basic DL $\mathcal{ALC}$

We next motivate and introduce the syntax and semantics for a number of important extensions of the basic DL $\mathcal{ALC}$, namely inverse roles, number restrictions, nominals, role inclusions and transitive roles.

2.5.1 Inverse roles

Consider our running example and assume that we want to add to our TBox $\mathcal{T}_{ex}$ from Figure 2.3 the following GCIs to express that Professors are Teachers, and that Courses are not taught by Professors:

$$\text{Professor} \sqsubseteq \text{Teacher},$$
$$\text{Course} \sqsubseteq \forall \textit{taught-by}.\neg\text{Professor}.$$

Let us call the resulting TBox $\mathcal{T}'_{ex}$. Intuitively, Professor should be un-satisfiable with respect to $\mathcal{T}'_{ex}$: due to the first GCI above, an element p in the extension of Professor would also need to be in the extension of Teacher, and hence axiom $\mathcal{T}_{ex}.4$ implies that p has a *teaches*-filler, say c, that is a Course. Now, if p *teaches* c, then c should be taught-by p, and thus the second statement above implies that p is a $\neg$Professor, con-tradicting our assumption. Now this argumentation contains a serious flaw: *teaches* and *taught-by* are interpreted as some arbitrary binary re-lations, and thus it is *not* the case that, if p *teaches* c, then c is taught-by p. Indeed, Professor is satisfiable with respect to $\mathcal{T}'_{ex}$: any model $\mathcal{I}$ of $\mathcal{T}_{ex}$ in which Professor$^{\mathcal{I}} \subseteq$ Teacher$^{\mathcal{I}}$ holds and *taught-by*$^{\mathcal{I}} = \emptyset$ is a model of $\mathcal{T}'_{ex}$.

In order to relate roles such as *teaches* and *taught-by* in the desired way, DLs can be extended with *inverse roles*. The fact that a DL pro-vides inverse roles is normally indicated by the letter $\mathcal{I}$ in its name. Since we will discuss and name many different DLs (e.g., $\mathcal{ALC}$, $\mathcal{ALCO}$, $\mathcal{ALCOI}$, $\mathcal{SHIQ}$), we will use $\mathcal{L}$ as a placeholder for the name of a DL.

Definition 2.18. For R a role name, R^- is an *inverse role*. The set of $\mathcal{I}$ *roles* is $\mathbf{R} \cup \{R^- \mid R \in \mathbf{R}\}$.

Let $\mathcal{L}$ be a description logic. The set of $\mathcal{LI}$ *concepts* is the smallest set of concepts that contains all $\mathcal{L}$ concepts and where $\mathcal{I}$ roles can occur in all places of role names.

In addition to what is said in Definition 2.1, an interpretation $\mathcal{I}$ maps inverse roles to binary relations as follows:

$$(r^-)^{\mathcal{I}} = \{(y, x) \mid (x, y) \in r^{\mathcal{I}}\}.$$

Following this definition, in the DL $\mathcal{ALCI}$, inverse roles can occur in existential and universal restrictions, for example, in the following concept:

$$\exists r^-.(\forall s.(\exists r.A \sqcap \forall s^-.B)).$$

In $\mathcal{ALCI}$, we now have indeed that $(x, y) \in r^{\mathcal{I}}$ if and only if $(y, x) \in (r^-)^{\mathcal{I}}$, and we can thus rephrase our new constraints using *teaches*$^-$

instead of *taught-by*:

$$\begin{aligned}
\mathsf{Professor} &\sqsubseteq \mathsf{Teacher}, \\
\mathsf{Course} &\sqsubseteq \forall \textit{teaches}^-.\neg\mathsf{Professor}.
\end{aligned}$$

We use $\mathcal{T}''_{ex}$ for the extension of the TBox $\mathcal{T}_{ex}$ from Figure 2.3 with the above two GCIs. Please note that Professor is indeed unsatisfiable with respect to $\mathcal{T}''_{ex}$: assume we had an interpretation $\mathcal{I}$ with $p \in \mathsf{Professor}^{\mathcal{I}}$. Again, this implies that $p \in \mathsf{Teacher}^{\mathcal{I}}$, and hence $\mathcal{T}_{ex}.4$ implies that there exists some c with $(p, c) \in \textit{teaches}^{\mathcal{I}}$ and $c \in \mathsf{Course}^{\mathcal{I}}$. Now $(c, p) \in (\textit{teaches}^-)^{\mathcal{I}}$, and thus the second GCI above implies that $p \in (\neg\mathsf{Professor})^{\mathcal{I}}$, contradicting our assumption.

In any system based on a DL with inverse roles, it would clearly be beneficial to allow the user to introduce names for inverse roles, such as *taught-by* for *teaches*$^-$, *child-of* for *has-child*$^-$, or *part-of* for *has-part*$^-$. Indeed, as we will see in Chapter 8, state-of-the-art ontology languages do this.

The above line of reasoning has been repeated numerous times in DL related research:

- we want to express something, e.g., that courses are not taught by professors;
- this seems to be not possible in a satisfactory way: in contrast to our intuition, Professor was satisfiable with respect to $\mathcal{T}'_{ex}$;
- we extend our DL with a new constructor, e.g., inverse roles, which involves extending the syntax (i.e., allowing roles r^- in the place of role names r) *and* the semantics (i.e., fixing $(r^-)^{\mathcal{I}}$).

2.5.2 Number restrictions

Next, assume we want to restrict the number of courses attended by students to, say, at least three and at most seven: so far, we have only said that each student attends at least one course – see $\mathcal{T}_{ex}.8$ in Figure 2.3. Again, we can try hard, e.g., using the following GCI:

$$\begin{aligned}
\mathsf{Student} \sqsubseteq\ &\exists \textit{attends}.(\mathsf{Course} \sqcap A) \sqcap \\
&\exists \textit{attends}.(\mathsf{Course} \sqcap \neg A \sqcap B) \sqcap \\
&\exists \textit{attends}.(\mathsf{Course} \sqcap \neg A \sqcap \neg B).
\end{aligned}$$

This will ensure that any element in the extension of Student attends at least three courses due to the usage of the mutually contradictory concepts A, $\neg A \sqcap B$, and $\neg A \sqcap \neg B$. We will see in Section 3.2 that we cannot use a similar trick to ensure that a Student attends at most seven courses. As a consequence, (*qualified*) *number restrictions* were introduced in DLs. The fact that a DL provides number restrictions (respectively qualified number restrictions) is normally indicated by the letter $\mathcal{N}$ (respectively $\mathcal{Q}$) in its name.

Definition 2.19. For n a non-negative number, r an $\mathcal{L}$ role and C a (possibly compound) $\mathcal{L}$ concept description, a *number restriction* is a concept description of the form $(\leqslant n\,r)$ or $(\geqslant n\,r)$, and a *qualified number restriction* is a concept description of the form $(\leqslant n\,r.C)$ or $(\geqslant n\,r.C)$, where C is the qualifying concept.

Let $\mathcal{L}$ be a description logic. The description logic $\mathcal{LN}$ (respectively $\mathcal{LQ}$) is obtained from $\mathcal{L}$ by, additionally, allowing number restrictions (respectively qualified number restrictions) as concept constructors.

For an interpretation $\mathcal{I}$, its mapping $\cdot^{\mathcal{I}}$ is extended as follows, where $\#M$ is used to denote the cardinality of a set M:

$$
\begin{aligned}
(\leqslant n\,r)^{\mathcal{I}} &= \{d \in \Delta^{\mathcal{I}} \mid \#\{e \mid (d,e) \in r^{\mathcal{I}}\} \leq n\}, \\
(\geqslant n\,r)^{\mathcal{I}} &= \{d \in \Delta^{\mathcal{I}} \mid \#\{e \mid (d,e) \in r^{\mathcal{I}}\} \geq n\}, \\
(\leqslant n\,r.C)^{\mathcal{I}} &= \{d \in \Delta^{\mathcal{I}} \mid \#\{e \mid (d,e) \in r^{\mathcal{I}} \text{ and } e \in C^{\mathcal{I}}\} \leq n\}, \\
(\geqslant n\,r.C)^{\mathcal{I}} &= \{d \in \Delta^{\mathcal{I}} \mid \#\{e \mid (d,e) \in r^{\mathcal{I}} \text{ and } e \in C^{\mathcal{I}}\} \geq n\}.
\end{aligned}
$$

Concept descriptions $(=nr)$ and $(=n\,r.C)$ may be used as abbreviations for $(\leqslant n\,r) \sqcap (\geqslant n\,r)$ and $(\leqslant n\,r.C) \sqcap (\geqslant n\,r.C)$ respectively.

A qualified number restriction allows us to restrict the number of r-fillers that are *in the extension of* a concept C. In contrast, an unqualified number restriction only allows us to restrict the number of r-fillers, regardless of which concepts' extensions they belong to; this is equivalent to a qualified number restriction where the qualifying concept is $\top$, i.e., $(\leqslant n\,r) \equiv (\leqslant n\,r.\top)$ and $(\geqslant n\,r) \equiv (\geqslant n\,r.\top)$. Naming conventions are such that, in $\mathcal{ALCIQ}$, both role names and inverse roles can occur in number restrictions whereas, of course, in $\mathcal{ALCQ}$, only role names can.

In the example interpretation $\mathcal{I}$ in Figure 2.2, $m \in (\leqslant 2\ \textit{teaches}.\mathsf{Course})^{\mathcal{I}}$ and $m \in (\geqslant 2\ \textit{teaches}.\mathsf{Course})^{\mathcal{I}}$ because m has exactly two *teaches*-fillers in $\mathsf{Course}^{\mathcal{I}}$. The element et is in $(\geqslant 1\ \textit{teaches}.\mathsf{Course})^{\mathcal{I}}$, but not in $(\geqslant 2\ \textit{teaches}.\mathsf{Course})^{\mathcal{I}}$. Finally, every element in every interpretation $\mathcal{I}$ is in $(\geqslant 0\,r.C)^{\mathcal{I}}$; the concept $\exists r.C$ is equivalent to $(\geqslant 1\,r.C)$; and $\forall r.C$ is equivalent to $(\leqslant 0\,r.\neg C)$.

2.5.3 Nominals

So far, we have used individual names in ABoxes, where we have used concepts and roles to constrain their interpretation. Now, assume we want to use individual names inside concepts, e.g., we want to define the class CourseOfMary as those Courses that are taught by Mary. Clearly, we could try the following $\mathcal{ALCI}$ concept definition

$$\text{CourseOfMary} \equiv \text{Course} \sqcap \exists \textit{teaches}^-.\text{Mary}, \qquad (2.4)$$

but this would not work for the following two reasons. First, when combined with the ABox from Figure 2.4, the Concept Definition 2.4 would lead to a syntax error since, in Definition 2.6, we have said that individual names are disjoint from concept names, hence Mary cannot occur both as an individual and as a concept name. Second, if we were to allow Mary to occur in place of a concept, we would need to say what this means for Mary's interpretation: in every interpretation $\mathcal{I}$, Mary$^{\mathcal{I}}$ is an element of the interpretation domain, but concepts are interpretated as *sets* of elements. To enable the use of individual names in concepts and avoid these problems, *nominals* have been introduced. The fact that a DL provides nominals is normally indicated by the letter $\mathcal{O}$ in its name, for the "o" in nominal and because $\mathcal{N}$ is already used for unqualified number restrictions.

Definition 2.20. For b an individual name in **I**, $\{b\}$ is called a *nominal*.

Let $\mathcal{L}$ be a description logic. The description logic $\mathcal{LO}$ is obtained from $\mathcal{L}$ by allowing nominals as additional concepts.

For an interpretation $\mathcal{I}$, its mapping $\cdot^{\mathcal{I}}$ is extended as follows:

$$(\{a\})^{\mathcal{I}} = \{a^{\mathcal{I}}\}.$$

Hence in $\mathcal{ALCOI}$, we can define the above mentioned concept using the following $\mathcal{ALCOI}$ concept definition:

$$\text{CourseOfMary} \equiv \text{Course} \sqcap \exists \textit{teaches}^-.\{\text{Mary}\}. \qquad (2.5)$$

So, by putting curly brackets around the individual name Mary, we have turned it into a concept and can therefore use it inside a concept. To see the additional expressive power provided by $\mathcal{ALCOI}$ over $\mathcal{ALCI}$, please note that, for example, CS600 is an instance of CourseOfMary with respect to Concept Definition 2.5 and $\mathcal{A}_{ex}$ from Figure 2.4.

2.5.4 Role hierarchies

Coming back to our example on lazy students, assume that we want to define lazy students as those who do not actively attend anything (and thus also no course):

$$\text{LazyStudent} \equiv \text{Student} \sqcap \forall \textit{attendsActively}.\bot. \tag{2.6}$$

Let $\mathcal{T}'_{ex}$ be the TBox from Figure 2.3 extended with the above definition, and consider the ABox $\mathcal{A} = \{(\text{Bob}, \text{CS600}) : \textit{attendsActively}\}$; then the KB $\mathcal{K} = (\mathcal{T}'_{ex}, \mathcal{A})$ should entail that Bob is a student, but not a lazy one. However, we find that $\mathcal{K} \not\models \text{Bob} : \text{Student}$ since we did not capture the intended relationship between *attendsActively* and *attends*, namely that the former implies the latter. *Role inclusion axioms* are the DL constructors that can capture this implication. Their availability is indicated by the letter $\mathcal{H}$ in the logic's name.

Definition 2.21. Let $\mathcal{L}$ be a description logic.

A *role inclusion axiom* (RIA) is an axiom of the form $r \sqsubseteq s$ for r, s $\mathcal{L}$ roles.[5]

The DL $\mathcal{LH}$ is obtained from $\mathcal{L}$ by allowing, additionally, role inclusion axioms in TBoxes.

For an interpretation $\mathcal{I}$ to be a *model of* a role inclusion axiom $r \sqsubseteq s$, it has to satisfy

$$r^{\mathcal{I}} \subseteq s^{\mathcal{I}}.$$

An interpretation is a *model of* a TBox if it satisfies all concept and role inclusion axioms in it.

Continuing our lazy student example, we can now add the following role inclusion axiom to $\mathcal{T}'_{ex}$ and call the result $\mathcal{T}''_{ex}$:

$$\textit{attendsActively} \sqsubseteq \textit{attends}. \tag{2.7}$$

We will then find that $(\mathcal{T}''_{ex}, \mathcal{A}) \models \text{Bob} : \text{Student}$, while LazyStudent is satisfiable with respect to $\mathcal{T}''_{ex}$.

2.5.5 Transitive roles

As a last extension, we consider transitive roles. Consider our running example $\mathcal{T}_{ex}$ in Figure 2.3 extended with the following axioms that in-

---

[5] That is, $r, s \in \mathbf{R}$ if $\mathcal{L}$ does not support inverse roles, and r, s possibly inverse roles if $\mathcal{L}$ supports inverse roles.

troduce the notion of a section:

$$
\begin{aligned}
\text{Course} &\sqsubseteq \exists hasPart.\text{Section} \sqcap \forall hasPart.\text{Section}, \\
\text{Section} &\sqsubseteq \forall hasPart.\text{Section}, \\
\text{TeachableCourse} &\equiv \text{Course} \sqcap \forall hasPart.\text{Ready}.
\end{aligned}
$$

Given that sections of a course can contain other sections which, in turn, can contain sections, the question arises what we mean by a teachable course. Consider the following example interpretation $\mathcal{I}$:

$$
\begin{aligned}
\Delta^{\mathcal{I}} &= \{c, s_1, s_2, s_3, \ldots\}, \\
\text{Section}^{\mathcal{I}} &= \{s_1, s_2, s_3\}, \\
\text{Ready}^{\mathcal{I}} &= \{s_1, s_2\}, \\
\text{Course}^{\mathcal{I}} &= \{c\}, \\
hasPart^{\mathcal{I}} &= \{(c, s_1), (c, s_2), (s_1, s_3)\}.
\end{aligned}
$$

Now $c \in (\text{TeachableCourse})^{\mathcal{I}}$ because it is a Course and all of its (immediate) sections are *Ready*. Intuitively, however, we might not expect this, because c *hasPart* s_1, s_1 *hasPart* s_3, and s_3 is not Ready. We might try to address this issue by using the following stricter definition of TeachableCourse:

$$\text{TeachableCourse} \equiv \text{Course} \sqcap \forall hasPart.(\text{Ready} \sqcap \forall hasPart.\text{Ready}).$$

This would work for the above interpretation $\mathcal{I}$, but not for others where we have longer *hasPart*-paths. In particular, if we wanted to define TeachableCourse as those courses all of whose *direct and indirect* sections are ready, regardless of the lengths of paths that relate a course to its (direct or indirect) sections, then we need to consider *transitive roles*.

Definition 2.22. Let $\mathcal{L}$ be a description logic. A *role transitivity axiom* is an axiom of the form $\text{Trans}(r)$ for r an $\mathcal{L}$ role.[6]

The name of the DL that is the extension of $\mathcal{L}$ by allowing, additionally, transitivity axioms in TBoxes, is usually given by replacing $\mathcal{ALC}$ in $\mathcal{L}$'s name with $\mathcal{S}$.

For an interpretation $\mathcal{I}$ to be a *model of* a role transitivity axiom $\text{Trans}(r)$, $r^{\mathcal{I}}$ must be transitive.

An interpretation $\mathcal{I}$ is a *model of* a TBox $\mathcal{T}$ if $\mathcal{I}$ satisfies each of the axioms in $\mathcal{T}$.

Naming conventions are slightly more complicated for transitive roles.

---

[6] That is, $r \in \mathbf{R}$ if $\mathcal{L}$ does not support inverse roles, and r is a possibly inverse role if $\mathcal{L}$ supports inverse roles.

In order to avoid having longer and longer names for DLs, the extension of $\mathcal{ALC}$ with role transitivity axioms is usually called $\mathcal{S}$ (due to similarities with the modal logic **S4**); e.g., the extension of $\mathcal{ALCIQ}$ with transitive roles is called $\mathcal{SIQ}$, and the extension of $\mathcal{ALCHIQ}$ with transitive roles is called $\mathcal{SHIQ}$. However, in some cases $_{R^+}$ is used to indicate transitive roles; using this naming scheme, $\mathcal{SHIQ}$ would be written $\mathcal{ALCHIQ}_{R^+}$.

It is important to understand the difference between transitive roles and the transitive closure of roles. Transitive closure is a role *constructor*: given a role r, transitive closure can be used to construct a role r^+, with the semantics being that $(r^+)^{\mathcal{I}} = (r^{\mathcal{I}})^+$. In a logic that includes both transitive roles and role inclusion axioms, e.g., $\mathcal{SH}$, adding axioms $\mathsf{Trans}(s)$ and $r \sqsubseteq s$ to a TBox $\mathcal{T}$ ensures that in every model $\mathcal{I}$ of $\mathcal{T}$, $s^{\mathcal{I}}$ is transitive, and $r^{\mathcal{I}} \subseteq s^{\mathcal{I}}$. However, we cannot enforce that s is the smallest such transitive role: s is just *some* transitive role that includes r. In contrast, the transitive closure r^+ of r is, by definition, the *smallest* transitive role that includes r; thus we have:

$$\{\mathsf{Trans}(s), r \sqsubseteq s\} \models r \sqsubseteq r^+ \sqsubseteq s.$$

This finishes our overview of various extensions of $\mathcal{ALC}$. Although we have covered several of the most prominent extensions, the overview is far from exhaustive, and many other extensions have been studied in the literature, including concrete domains (see Section 5.3.2), role value maps (see Section 5.3.1) and role boxes (see Section 8.1.2); the Appendix summarises the syntax and semantics of the DL constructors and axioms used in this book.

2.6 DLs and other logics

This section explains the close relationship between DLs and other logics, namely first-order logic (also known as first-order predicate logic or first-order predicate calculus) and modal logic. It is aimed at those readers who know one or both of these logics, and should provide these readers with a deeper understanding of the material and of the field. We suggest that readers not familiar with these logics skip this section.

2.6.1 DLs as decidable fragments of first-order logic

Most DLs can be seen as decidable fragments of first-order logic, although some provide operators such as transitive closure of roles or fixpoints that make them decidable fragments of second-order logic [Bor96]. Viewing role names as binary relations and concept names as unary relations, we can translate TBox axioms and ABox assertions into first-order logic formula, e.g.,

$$\exists attends.\top \ \sqsubseteq \ \textsf{Person},$$
$$\textsf{Teacher} \ \equiv \ \textsf{Person} \sqcap \exists teaches.\textsf{Course},$$
$$\textsf{Mary} : \textsf{Teacher}$$

can be translated into

$$\forall x.(\exists y.attends(x,y) \Rightarrow \textsf{Person}(x)),$$
$$\forall x.(\textsf{Teacher}(x) \Leftrightarrow \textsf{Person}(x) \wedge \exists y.(teaches(x,y) \wedge \textsf{Course}(y))),$$
$$\textsf{Teacher}(\textsf{Mary}).$$

Please note how TBox axioms correspond to universally quantified (bi-) implications without free variables, and how ABox assertions correspond to ground facts.

To formalise this translation, we define two translation functions, π_x and π_y, that inductively map $\mathcal{ALC}$ concepts into first-order formulae with one free variable, x or y:[7]

$$\pi_x(A) = A(x), \qquad\qquad\qquad \pi_y(A) = A(y),$$
$$\pi_x(C \sqcap D) = \pi_x(C) \wedge \pi_x(D), \qquad \pi_y(C \sqcap D) = \pi_y(C) \wedge \pi_y(D),$$
$$\pi_x(C \sqcup D) = \pi_x(C) \vee \pi_x(D), \qquad \pi_y(C \sqcup D) = \pi_y(C) \vee \pi_y(D),$$
$$\pi_x(\exists r.C) = \exists y.r(x,y) \wedge \pi_y(C), \qquad \pi_y(\exists r.C) = \exists x.r(y,x) \wedge \pi_x(C),$$
$$\pi_x(\forall r.C) = \forall y.r(x,y) \Rightarrow \pi_y(C), \qquad \pi_y(\forall r.C) = \forall x.r(y,x) \Rightarrow \pi_x(C).$$

Next, we translate a TBox $\mathcal{T}$ and an ABox $\mathcal{A}$ as follows, where $\psi[x \mapsto a]$ is the formula obtained from ψ by replacing all free occurrences of x with a:

$$\pi(\mathcal{T}) \ = \ \forall x. \bigwedge_{C \sqsubseteq D \in \mathcal{T}} (\pi_x(C) \Rightarrow \pi_x(D)),$$
$$\pi(\mathcal{A}) \ = \ \bigwedge_{a:C \in \mathcal{A}} \pi_x(C)[x \mapsto a] \wedge \bigwedge_{(a,b):r \in \mathcal{A}} r(a,b).$$

This translation clearly preserves the semantics: we can easily view DL interpretations as first-order interpretations and vice versa.

Theorem 2.23. *Let $(\mathcal{T}, \mathcal{A})$ be an $\mathcal{ALC}$-knowledge base, C, D possibly compound $\mathcal{ALC}$ concepts and b an individual name. Then*

(i) *$(\mathcal{T}, \mathcal{A})$ is satisfiable if and only if $\pi(\mathcal{T}) \wedge \pi(\mathcal{A})$ is satisfiable,*

---

[7] This definition is inductive (or recursive), with π_x calling π_y and vice versa, from compound concepts to their constituent parts.

(ii) $C \sqsubseteq_{\mathcal{T}} D$ *if and only if* $\pi(\mathcal{T}) \Rightarrow \forall x.(\pi_x(C) \Rightarrow \pi_x(D))$ *is valid, and*

(iii) b *is an instance of* C *with respect to* $(\mathcal{T}, \mathcal{A})$ *if and only if* $(\pi(\mathcal{T}) \wedge \pi(\mathcal{A})) \Rightarrow \pi_x(C)[x \mapsto b]$ *is valid.*

This translation not only provides an alternative way of defining the semantics of $\mathcal{ALC}$, but also tells us that all reasoning problems for $\mathcal{ALC}$ knowledge bases are decidable: the translation of a knowledge base uses only variables x and y, and thus yields a formula in the *two-variable fragment of first-order logic*, for which satisfiability is known to be decidable in nondeterministic exponential time [GKV97]. Similarly, the translation of a knowledge base uses quantification only in a rather restricted way, and therefore yields a formula in the *guarded fragment* [ANvB98], for which satisfiability is known to be decidable in deterministic exponential time [Grä99]. As we can see, the exploration of the relationship between DLs and first-order logics even gives us upper complexity bounds for free.

The translation of more expressive DLs may be straightforward, or more difficult, depending on the additional constructs: inverse roles can be captured easily in both the guarded and the two-variable fragments by simply swapping the variable places; e.g., $\pi_x(\exists r^-.C) = \exists y.r(y, x) \wedge \pi_y(C)$. Number restrictions can be captured using (in)equality or so-called *counting quantifiers*. It is known that the two-variable fragment with counting quantifiers is still decidable in nondeterministic exponential time [PST00]. The guarded fragment, when restricted carefully to the so-called *action guarded fragment* [GG00], can still capture a variety of features such as number restrictions, inverse roles and fixpoints, while remaining decidable in deterministic exponential time.

2.6.2 DLs as cousins of modal logic

Description logics are closely related to modal logic, yet they have been developed independently. This close relationship was discovered only rather late [Sch91], and has been exploited quite successfully to transfer complexity and decidability results as well as reasoning techniques [Sch94, DGL94a, HPS98, Are00]. It is not hard to see that $\mathcal{ALC}$ concepts can be viewed as syntactic variants of formulae of multi-modal $\mathbf{K}_{(m)}$: Kripke structures can easily be viewed as DL interpretations, and vice versa; we can then view concept names as propositional variables, and role names as modal parameters, and realise this correspondence through the mapping π as follows:

$$
\begin{aligned}
\pi(A) &= A, \text{ for concept names } A, \\
\pi(C \sqcap D) &= \pi(C) \wedge \pi(D), \\
\pi(C \sqcup D) &= \pi(C) \vee \pi(D), \\
\pi(\neg C) &= \neg\pi(C), \\
\pi(\forall r.C) &= [r]\pi(C), \\
\pi(\exists r.C) &= \langle r \rangle \pi(C).
\end{aligned}
$$

The translation of DL knowledge bases is slightly more tricky: a TBox $\mathcal{T}$ is satisfied only in those structures where, for each $C \sqsubseteq D$, $\neg\pi(C) \vee \pi(D)$ holds *globally*, i.e., in each world of our Kripke structure (or equivalently, in each element of our interpretation domain). We can express this using the *universal modality*, that is, a special modal parameter U that is interpreted as the total relation in all interpretations. Before we discuss ABoxes, let us first state the properties of our correspondence so far.

Theorem 2.24. *Let $\mathcal{T}$ be an $\mathcal{ALC}$ TBox and E, F possibly compound $\mathcal{ALC}$ concepts. Then:*

(i) *F is satisfiable if and only if $\pi(F)$ is satisfiable;*

(ii) *F is satisfiable with respect to $\mathcal{T}$ if and only if $\bigwedge_{C \sqsubseteq D \in \mathcal{T}} [U](\pi(C) \Rightarrow \pi(D)) \wedge \pi(F)$ is satisfiable;*

(iii) *$E \sqsubseteq_{\mathcal{T}} F$ if and only if $\bigwedge_{C \sqsubseteq D \in \mathcal{T}} [U](\pi(C) \Rightarrow \pi(D)) \Rightarrow [U](\pi(E) \Rightarrow \pi(F))$ is valid.*

Like TBoxes, ABoxes do not have a direct correspondence in modal logic, but they can be seen as a special case of a modal logic constructor, namely *nominals*.[8] These are special propositional variables that hold in exactly one world; they are the basic ingredient of *hybrid logics* [ABM99].[9] Usually, modal nominals come with a special modality, the @-operator, that allows one to refer to the (only) world in which a nominal a holds. For example, $@_a\psi$ holds if, in the world where a holds, ψ holds as well. Hence an ABox assertion of the form $a : C$ corresponds to the modal formula $@_a\pi(C)$, and an ABox assertion $(a, b) : r$ corresponds to $@_a\langle r \rangle b$. In this latter formula, we see how nominals can act both as a parameter to the @ operator, like a, and as a propositional variable, like

---

[8] Description logic nominals as introduced in Section 2.5.3 have received their name from modal logic.

[9] Please note that modal nominals are special propositional variables, whereas DL nominals are concepts constructed from individual names by enclosing them in curly brackets.

b. In DLs that provide nominals, such as $\mathcal{ALCO}$, there is traditionally no counterpart to the @ operator: for example, the concept $A \sqcap \exists r.\{b\}$ corresponds to the modal formula $A \wedge \langle r \rangle b$, where b is a nominal, but the formula $A \wedge \langle r \rangle (B \vee @_b B)$ does not have an $\mathcal{ALCO}$ counterpart since it uses the @ operator to say "B holds at the place where b holds".

2.7 Historical context and literature review

This chapter tries to introduce the basic, standard notions relevant in Description Logic: concepts, GCIs and assertions, TBoxes and ABoxes, interpretations and models, entailments and reasoning services. We left out the history of the area, and will only sketch it very briefly here. Description logics have had various other names in the past, e.g., terminological knowledge representation systems, concept languages, frame languages etc. They were developed to give a well-defined semantics to knowledge representation systems, in particular KL-ONE [BS85]. When it turned out that the DL underlying KL-ONE was undecidable [Sch89], a lot of work was carried out in trying to understand the sources of undecidability (see, e.g., [PS89]) and to identify useful, decidable DLs: the DL underlying the CLASSIC system [PSMB+91] was designed to be tractable, and the CLASSIC system was the first one to be used by non-experts (in an application that supported engineers in configuring communication systems). With $\mathcal{ALC}$ [SS91], the first propositionally closed DL was introduced and proven to be decidable, but of a computational complexity that was believed to preclude practically useful implementations (see Chapter 5). Research in the 1990s and 2000s saw a plethora of results regarding decidability and computational complexity for a wide range of DLs that differed in

- the constructors they allowed for forming concepts and roles, e.g., inverse role, number restrictions, concrete domains,
- the kind of axioms they allowed, in particular regarding roles, e.g., role hierarchies, but also axioms that expressed default or probabilistic statements and
- the semantics they employed, e.g., least or greatest fixpoint semantics for cyclic TBoxes, fuzzy or probabilistic semantics,

with the interest in a specific DL usually driven by some specific knowledge representation application. This period also saw the design of various algorithms to decide subsumption, satisfiability, consistency etc., together with proofs of their correctness, i.e., together with proofs that they always terminate and never give the wrong answer. It also saw implementations and optimisations of these algorithms, and further algorithms for TBox classification.

In this way, DLs developed into a rich family of logics for which sources of complexity and undecidability are well understood. In parallel, researchers in this area noticed the close relationship between DLs and other logics: the relationship between modal and description logics is first discussed in [Sch91] and explored further in [Sch94, DGL94a, DGL94b]. The relationship between a wide range of DLs and first-order logic was first described in [Bor96].

There is a huge and still growing body of work describing these results, far too big to list here in a suitable way. We suggest consulting *The Description Logic Handbook* [BCM$^+$07] for a general overview, the informal proceedings of the annual International Workshop of Description Logics, which are almost all available electronically at `dl.kr.org`, as well as the proceedings of meetings on artificial intelligence, knowledge representation and reasoning such as AAAI (the conference of the Association for the Advancement of Artificial Intelligence), CADE (the International Conference on Automated Deduction), ECAI (the European Conference on Artificial Intelligence), IJCAI (the International Joint Conference on Artificial Intelligence), IJCAR (the International Joint Conference on Automated Reasoning), and KR (the International Conference on Principles of Knowledge Representation and Reasoning). Furthermore, journals that are often used by researchers in Description Logic to publish their work include AIJ (*Artificial Intelligence – an International Journal*), JAIR (*Journal of Artificial Intelligence Research*), and JLC (*Journal of Logic and Computation*).

3

A Little Bit of Model Theory

The main purpose of this chapter is to show that sets of models of $\mathcal{ALC}$ concepts or knowledge bases satisfy several interesting properties, which can be used to prove expressivity and decidability results. To be more precise, we will introduce the notion of *bisimulation* between elements of $\mathcal{ALC}$ interpretations, and prove that $\mathcal{ALC}$ concepts cannot distinguish between bisimilar elements. On the one hand, we will use this to show restrictions of the *expressive power* of $\mathcal{ALC}$: number restrictions, inverse roles and nominals cannot be expressed within $\mathcal{ALC}$. On the other hand, we will employ bisimulation invariance of $\mathcal{ALC}$ to show that $\mathcal{ALC}$ has the *tree model property* and satisfies *closure under disjoint union* of models. We will also show that $\mathcal{ALC}$ has the *finite model property*, though not as a direct consequence of bisimulation invariance. These properties will turn out to be useful in subsequent chapters and of interest to people writing knowledge bases: for example, $\mathcal{ALC}$'s tree model property implies that it is too weak to describe the ring structure of many chemical molecules since any $\mathcal{ALC}$ knowledge base trying to describe such a structure will also have acyclic models. In the present chapter, we will only use the finite model property (or rather the stronger *bounded model property*) to show a basic, not complexity-optimal decidability result for reasoning in $\mathcal{ALC}$. For the sake of simplicity, we concentrate here on the terminological part of $\mathcal{ALC}$, i.e., we consider only concepts and TBoxes, but not ABoxes.

To obtain a better intuitive view of the definitions and results introduced below, one should recall that interpretations of $\mathcal{ALC}$ can be viewed as *graphs*, with edges labelled by roles and nodes labelled by sets of concept names. More precisely, in such a graph

- the nodes are the elements of the interpretation and they are labelled with all the concept names to which this element belongs in the interpretation;

- an edge with label r between two nodes says that the corresponding two elements of the interpretation are related by the role r.

Examples for this representation of interpretations by graphs can be found in the previous chapter (see Figure 2.2) and in Figure 3.1.

3.1 Bisimulation

We define the notion of a bisimulation directly for interpretations, rather than for the graphs representing them.

Definition 3.1 (Bisimulation). Let $\mathcal{I}_1$ and $\mathcal{I}_2$ be interpretations. The relation $\rho \subseteq \Delta^{\mathcal{I}_1} \times \Delta^{\mathcal{I}_2}$ is a *bisimulation* between $\mathcal{I}_1$ and $\mathcal{I}_2$ if

(i) $d_1 \, \rho \, d_2$ implies

$$d_1 \in A^{\mathcal{I}_1} \text{ if and only if } d_2 \in A^{\mathcal{I}_2}$$

for all $d_1 \in \Delta^{\mathcal{I}_1}$, $d_2 \in \Delta^{\mathcal{I}_2}$, and $A \in \mathbf{C}$;

(ii) $d_1 \, \rho \, d_2$ and $(d_1, d_1') \in r^{\mathcal{I}_1}$ implies the existence of $d_2' \in \Delta^{\mathcal{I}_2}$ such that

$$d_1' \, \rho \, d_2' \text{ and } (d_2, d_2') \in r^{\mathcal{I}_2}$$

for all $d_1, d_1' \in \Delta^{\mathcal{I}_1}$, $d_2 \in \Delta^{\mathcal{I}_2}$, and $r \in \mathbf{R}$;

(iii) $d_1 \, \rho \, d_2$ and $(d_2, d_2') \in r^{\mathcal{I}_2}$ implies the existence of $d_1' \in \Delta^{\mathcal{I}_1}$ such that

$$d_1' \, \rho \, d_2' \text{ and } (d_1, d_1') \in r^{\mathcal{I}_1}$$

for all $d_1 \in \Delta^{\mathcal{I}_1}$, $d_2, d_2' \in \Delta^{\mathcal{I}_2}$, and $r \in \mathbf{R}$.

Given $d_1 \in \Delta^{\mathcal{I}_1}$ and $d_2 \in \Delta^{\mathcal{I}_2}$, we define

$$(\mathcal{I}_1, d_1) \sim (\mathcal{I}_2, d_2) \quad \text{if there is a bisimulation } \rho \text{ between } \mathcal{I}_1 \text{ and } \mathcal{I}_2$$
$$\text{such that } d_1 \, \rho \, d_2,$$

and say that $d_1 \in \mathcal{I}_1$ is *bisimilar* to $d_2 \in \mathcal{I}_2$.

Intuitively, d_1 and d_2 are bisimilar if they belong to the same concept names and, for each role r, have bisimilar r-successors. The reason for calling the relation ρ a *bi*simulation is that we require both property (ii) and (iii) in the definition. These two properties together are sometimes also called the back-and-forth property. Strictly speaking, the notion of

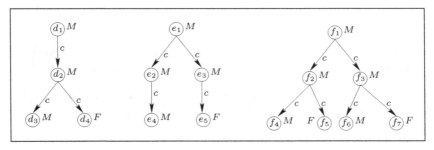

Fig. 3.1. Three interpretations $\mathcal{I}_1, \mathcal{I}_2, \mathcal{I}_3$ represented as graphs.

a bisimulation needs to be parametrised with respect to the employed set of concept names **C** and role names **R**. In the following, we assume that these two sets are fixed, and thus do not mention them explicitly. It should also be noted that the interpretations $\mathcal{I}_1$ and $\mathcal{I}_2$ in Definition 3.1 are not required to be distinct. In addition, the empty relation is always a bisimulation, though not a very interesting one.

Given the three interpretations depicted in Figure 3.1 (where c is supposed to represent the role *child*, M the concept Male and F the concept Female), it is easy to see that $(d_1, \mathcal{I}_1)$ and $(f_1, \mathcal{I}_3)$ are bisimilar, whereas $(d_1, \mathcal{I}_1)$ and $(e_1, \mathcal{I}_2)$ are not.

The following theorem states that $\mathcal{ALC}$ cannot distinguish between bisimilar elements.

Theorem 3.2. *If* $(\mathcal{I}_1, d_1) \sim (\mathcal{I}_2, d_2)$, *then the following holds for all* $\mathcal{ALC}$ *concepts* C:

$$d_1 \in C^{\mathcal{I}_1} \quad \text{if and only if} \quad d_2 \in C^{\mathcal{I}_2}.$$

Proof. Since $(\mathcal{I}_1, d_1) \sim (\mathcal{I}_2, d_2)$, there is a bisimulation ρ between $\mathcal{I}_1$ and $\mathcal{I}_2$ such that $d_1 \, \rho \, d_2$. We prove the theorem by induction on the structure of C. Since, up to equivalence, any $\mathcal{ALC}$ concept can be constructed using only the constructors conjunction, negation and existential restriction (see Lemma 2.16), we consider only these constructors in the induction step. The base case is the one where C is a concept name.

• Assume that $C = A \in \mathbf{C}$. Then

$$d_1 \in A^{\mathcal{I}_1} \quad \text{if and only if} \quad d_2 \in A^{\mathcal{I}_2}$$

is an immediate consequence of $d_1 \, \rho \, d_2$ (see part (i) of Definition 3.1).

- Assume that $C = D \sqcap E$. Then

$$
\begin{aligned}
d_1 \in (D \sqcap E)^{\mathcal{I}_1} \quad &\text{if and only if} \quad d_1 \in D^{\mathcal{I}_1} \text{ and } d_1 \in E^{\mathcal{I}_1}, \\
&\text{if and only if} \quad d_2 \in D^{\mathcal{I}_2} \text{ and } d_2 \in E^{\mathcal{I}_2}, \\
&\text{if and only if} \quad d_2 \in (D \sqcap E)^{\mathcal{I}_2},
\end{aligned}
$$

where the first and third equivalences are due to the semantics of conjunction, and the second is due to the induction hypothesis applied to D and E.
- Negation ($\neg$) can be treated similarly.
- Assume that $C = \exists r.D$. Then

$$
\begin{aligned}
d_1 \in (\exists r.D)^{\mathcal{I}_1} \quad &\text{if and only if} \quad \text{there is } d_1' \in \Delta^{\mathcal{I}_1} \text{ such that} \\
&\qquad\qquad\qquad (d_1, d_1') \in r^{\mathcal{I}_1} \text{ and } d_1' \in D^{\mathcal{I}_1}, \\
&\text{if and only if} \quad \text{there is } d_2' \in \Delta^{\mathcal{I}_2} \text{ such that} \\
&\qquad\qquad\qquad (d_2, d_2') \in r^{\mathcal{I}_2} \text{ and } d_2' \in D^{\mathcal{I}_2}, \\
&\text{if and only if} \quad d_2 \in (\exists r.D)^{\mathcal{I}_2}.
\end{aligned}
$$

Here the first and third equivalences are due to the semantics of existential restrictions. The second equivalence is due to parts (ii) and (iii) of Definition 3.1 and the induction hypothesis.

This completes the proof of the theorem. $\qquad\qquad\qquad\qquad\square$

Applied to our example, the theorem says that d_1 in $\mathcal{I}_1$ belongs to the same $\mathcal{ALC}$ concepts as f_1 in $\mathcal{I}_3$. For instance, both belong to the concept

$$
\exists c.(M \sqcap \exists c.M \sqcap \exists c.F),
$$

which contains those male individuals that have a son that has both a son and a daughter. In contrast, e_1 in $\mathcal{I}_2$ does not belong to this concept because e_1 does not have a son that has both a son and a daughter. It only has a son that has a son and another son that has a daughter.

3.2 Expressive power

In Section 2.5, we introduced extensions of $\mathcal{ALC}$ with the concept constructors *number restrictions* and *nominals*, and the role constructor *inverse roles*. How can we prove that these constructors really extend $\mathcal{ALC}$, i.e., that they *cannot be expressed* using just the constructors of $\mathcal{ALC}$? For this purpose, we need to show that, using any of these constructors (in addition to the constructors of $\mathcal{ALC}$), we can construct

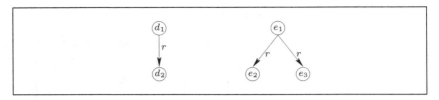

Fig. 3.2. Two interpretations $\mathcal{I}_1$ and $\mathcal{I}_2$ represented as graphs.

concepts that cannot be expressed by $\mathcal{ALC}$ concepts, i.e, there is no equivalent $\mathcal{ALC}$ concept. At first sight, this may sound like a formidable task. In fact, given such a concept C, we need to show that $C \not\equiv D$ holds for *all* $\mathcal{ALC}$ concepts D, and there are *infinitely many* such concepts D. This is where bisimulation comes into play: if we can show that C can distinguish between two bisimilar elements, then obviously it cannot be equivalent to an $\mathcal{ALC}$ concept by Theorem 3.2.

First, we consider the case of number restrictions. Remember that $\mathcal{ALCN}$ is the extension of $\mathcal{ALC}$ with unqualified number restrictions, i.e., concepts of the form $(\leqslant n\, r.\top)$ and $(\geqslant n\, r.\top)$, for $r \in \mathbf{R}$ and $n \geq 0$.

Proposition 3.3. $\mathcal{ALCN}$ *is more expressive than $\mathcal{ALC}$; that is, there is an $\mathcal{ALCN}$ concept C such that $C \not\equiv D$ holds for all $\mathcal{ALC}$ concepts D.*

Proof. We show that no $\mathcal{ALC}$ concept is equivalent to the $\mathcal{ALCN}$ concept $(\leqslant 1\, r.\top)$. Assume to the contrary that D is an $\mathcal{ALC}$ concept with $(\leqslant 1\, r.\top) \equiv D$. In order to lead this assumption to a contradiction, we consider the interpretations $\mathcal{I}_1$ and $\mathcal{I}_2$ depicted in Figure 3.2. Since

$$\rho = \{(d_1, e_1), (d_2, e_2), (d_2, e_3)\}$$

is a bisimulation, we have $(\mathcal{I}_1, d_1) \sim (\mathcal{I}_2, e_1)$, and thus $d_1 \in D^{\mathcal{I}_1}$ if and only if $e_1 \in D^{\mathcal{I}_2}$. This contradicts our assumption $(\leqslant 1\, r.\top) \equiv D$ since $d_1 \in (\leqslant 1\, r.\top)^{\mathcal{I}_1}$, but $e_1 \notin (\leqslant 1\, r.\top)^{\mathcal{I}_2}$. $\qquad\square$

Recall that $\mathcal{ALCI}$ denotes the extension of $\mathcal{ALC}$ by inverse roles.

Proposition 3.4. $\mathcal{ALCI}$ *is more expressive than $\mathcal{ALC}$; that is, there is an $\mathcal{ALCI}$ concept C such that $C \not\equiv D$ holds for all $\mathcal{ALC}$ concepts D.*

Proof. We show that no $\mathcal{ALC}$ concept is equivalent to the $\mathcal{ALCI}$ concept $\exists r^-.\top$. Assume to the contrary that D is an $\mathcal{ALC}$ concept with $\exists r^-.\top \equiv D$. In order to lead this assumption to a contradiction, we consider the interpretations $\mathcal{I}_1$ and $\mathcal{I}_2$ depicted in Figure 3.3.

Since $\rho = \{(d_2, e_2)\}$ is a bisimulation, we have $(\mathcal{I}_1, d_2) \sim (\mathcal{I}_2, e_2)$, and

Fig. 3.3. Two more interpretations $\mathcal{I}_1$ and $\mathcal{I}_2$ represented as graphs.

thus $d_2 \in D^{\mathcal{I}_1}$ if and only if $e_2 \in D^{\mathcal{I}_2}$. This contradicts our assumption $\exists r^-.\top \equiv D$ since $d_2 \in (\exists r^-.\top)^{\mathcal{I}_1}$, but $e_2 \notin (\exists r^-.\top)^{\mathcal{I}_2}$. $\qquad\square$

Recall that $\mathcal{ALCO}$ denotes the extension of $\mathcal{ALC}$ by nominals.

Proposition 3.5. *$\mathcal{ALCO}$ is more expressive than $\mathcal{ALC}$; that is, there is an $\mathcal{ALCO}$ concept C such that $C \not\equiv D$ holds for all $\mathcal{ALC}$ concepts D.*

Proof. We show that no $\mathcal{ALC}$ concept is equivalent to the $\mathcal{ALCO}$ concept $\{a\}$. Using the same pattern as in the previous two proofs, it is enough to show that there are bisimilar elements that can be distinguished by this concept. For this, we consider the interpretation $\mathcal{I}_1$ with $\Delta^{\mathcal{I}_1} = \{d\}$, $a^{\mathcal{I}_1} = d$ and $A^{\mathcal{I}_1} = \emptyset = r^{\mathcal{I}_1}$ for all $A \in \mathbf{C}$ and $r \in \mathbf{R}$; and the interpretation $\mathcal{I}_2$ with $\Delta^{\mathcal{I}_2} = \{e_1, e_2\}$, $a^{\mathcal{I}_2} = e_1$ and $A^{\mathcal{I}_2} = \emptyset = r^{\mathcal{I}_2}$ for all $A \in \mathbf{C}$ and $r \in \mathbf{R}$.

Since $\rho = \{(d, e_2)\}$ is a bisimulation, we have $(\mathcal{I}_1, d) \sim (\mathcal{I}_2, e_2)$, but $d \in \{a\}^{\mathcal{I}_1}$ and $e_2 \notin \{a\}^{\mathcal{I}_2}$. $\qquad\square$

In summary, we have now convinced ourselves that extending $\mathcal{ALC}$ with one of inverse roles, nominals or number restrictions indeed increases its ability to describe certain models. In the following sections, we will look more closely into statements that we cannot make in $\mathcal{ALC}$. For example, the results of the next section imply that $\mathcal{ALC}$ cannot enforce finiteness of a model, whereas the subsequent section shows that it cannot enforce infiniteness either. Finally, the tree model property proved in the last section of this chapter implies that $\mathcal{ALC}$ cannot enforce cyclic role relationships.

3.3 Closure under disjoint union

Given two interpretations $\mathcal{I}_1$ and $\mathcal{I}_2$ with disjoint domains, one can put them together into one interpretation $\mathcal{I}$ by taking as its domain the union of the two domains, and defining the extensions of concept and role names in $\mathcal{I}$ as the union of the respective extensions in $\mathcal{I}_1$ and $\mathcal{I}_2$. It can then be shown that the extension of a (possibly complex) concept C in $\mathcal{I}$ is also the union of the extensions of C in $\mathcal{I}_1$ and $\mathcal{I}_2$. Below, we define and prove this in the more general setting where the interpretation domains are not necessarily disjoint and where we may have more than two interpretation. Before we can then build the *disjoint* union of these interpretations, we must make them disjoint by an appropriate renaming of the domain elements.

Definition 3.6 (Disjoint union). Let $\mathfrak{N}$ be an index set and $(\mathcal{I}_\nu)_{\nu \in \mathfrak{N}}$ a family of interpretations $\mathcal{I}_\nu = (\Delta^{\mathcal{I}_\nu}, \cdot^{\mathcal{I}_\nu})$. Their *disjoint union* $\mathcal{J}$ is defined as follows:

$$
\begin{aligned}
\Delta^{\mathcal{J}} &= \{(d, \nu) \mid \nu \in \mathfrak{N} \text{ and } d \in \Delta^{\mathcal{I}_\nu}\}; \\
A^{\mathcal{J}} &= \{(d, \nu) \mid \nu \in \mathfrak{N} \text{ and } d \in A^{\mathcal{I}_\nu}\} \text{ for all } A \in \mathbf{C}; \\
r^{\mathcal{J}} &= \{((d, \nu), (e, \nu)) \mid \nu \in \mathfrak{N} \text{ and } (d, e) \in r^{\mathcal{I}_\nu}\} \text{ for all } r \in \mathbf{R}.
\end{aligned}
$$

In the following, we will sometimes denote such a disjoint union as $\biguplus_{\nu \in \mathfrak{N}} \mathcal{I}_\nu$. Note that the interpretations $\mathcal{I}_\nu$ are not required to be distinct from each other. In particular, if all members $\mathcal{I}_\nu$ of the family are the same interpretation $\mathcal{I}$ and $\mathfrak{N} = \{1, \ldots, n\}$, then we call $\biguplus_{\nu \in \mathfrak{N}} \mathcal{I}_\nu$ the n-fold disjoint union of $\mathcal{I}$ with itself. Similarly, if $\mathfrak{N} = \mathbb{N}$ and all elements of the family are equal to $\mathcal{I}$, then we call $\biguplus_{\nu \in \mathfrak{N}} \mathcal{I}_\nu$ the countably infinite disjoint union of $\mathcal{I}$ with itself.

As an example, consider the three interpretations $\mathcal{I}_1$, $\mathcal{I}_2$ and $\mathcal{I}_3$ depicted in Figure 3.1. We can view the three graphs in this figure as a single graph, which then is the graph representation of the disjoint union of these three interpretations (modulo appropriate renaming of nodes).

Lemma 3.7. *Let $\mathcal{J} = \biguplus_{\nu \in \mathfrak{N}} \mathcal{I}_\nu$ be the disjoint union of the family $(\mathcal{I}_\nu)_{\nu \in \mathfrak{N}}$ of interpretations. Then we have*

$$
d \in C^{\mathcal{I}_\nu} \quad \text{if and only if} \quad (d, \nu) \in C^{\mathcal{J}}
$$

for all $\nu \in \mathfrak{N}$, $d \in \Delta^{\mathcal{I}_\nu}$ and $\mathcal{ALC}$ concept descriptions C.

Proof. It is easy to see that, for all $\nu \in \mathfrak{N}$, the relation

$$
\rho = \{(d, (d, \nu)) \mid d \in \Delta^{\mathcal{I}_\nu}\}
$$

is a bisimulation between $\mathcal{I}_\nu$ and $\mathcal{J}$. Thus, the bi-implication in the statement of the lemma follows immediately from Theorem 3.2. □

As an easy consequence of this lemma, we obtain that the class of all models of a TBox is closed under disjoint union.

Theorem 3.8. *Let $\mathcal{T}$ be an $\mathcal{ALC}$ TBox and $(\mathcal{I}_\nu)_{\nu \in \mathfrak{N}}$ a family of models of $\mathcal{T}$. Then its disjoint union $\mathcal{J} = \biguplus_{\nu \in \mathfrak{N}} \mathcal{I}_\nu$ is also a model of $\mathcal{T}$.*

Proof. Assume that $\mathcal{J}$ is not a model of $\mathcal{T}$. Then there is a GCI $C \sqsubseteq D$ in $\mathcal{T}$ and an element $(d, \nu) \in \Delta^{\mathcal{J}}$ such that $(d, \nu) \in C^{\mathcal{J}}$, but $(d, \nu) \notin D^{\mathcal{J}}$. By Lemma 3.7, this implies $d \in C^{\mathcal{I}_\nu}$ and $d \notin D^{\mathcal{I}_\nu}$, which contradicts our assumption that $\mathcal{I}_\nu$ is a model of $\mathcal{T}$. $\square$

As an example of an application of this theorem we show that extensions of satisfiable concepts can always be made infinite.

Corollary 3.9. *Let $\mathcal{T}$ be an $\mathcal{ALC}$ TBox and C an $\mathcal{ALC}$ concept that is satisfiable with respect to $\mathcal{T}$. Then there is a model $\mathcal{J}$ of $\mathcal{T}$ in which the extension $C^{\mathcal{J}}$ of C is infinite.*

Proof. Since C is satisfiable with respect to $\mathcal{T}$, there is a model $\mathcal{I}$ of $\mathcal{T}$ and an element $d \in \Delta^{\mathcal{I}}$ such that $d \in C^{\mathcal{I}}$. Let $\mathcal{J} = \biguplus_{n \in \mathbb{N}} \mathcal{I}_n$ be the countably infinite disjoint union of $\mathcal{I}$ with itself. By Theorem 3.8, $\mathcal{J}$ is a model of $\mathcal{T}$, and by Lemma 3.7, $(d, n) \in C^{\mathcal{J}}$ for all $n \in \mathbb{N}$. $\square$

In this section, we have restricted our attention to TBoxes. We can extend our observations to knowledge bases, but we need to be a little bit careful: in particular, since individual names can have only one extension in an interpretation, we would need to pick a single index $\nu \in \mathfrak{N}$ and set $a^{\mathcal{J}} = (a^{\mathcal{I}_\nu}, \nu)$ for all individual names occurring in this knowledge base. Then, being a model of a knowledge base is preserved when taking the disjoint union of such models.

3.4 Finite model property

As we saw in the previous chapter, in $\mathcal{ALC}$ we cannot force models to be finite. As we will see next, we cannot enforce them to be infinite either.

Definition 3.10. *The interpretation $\mathcal{I}$ is a model of a concept C with respect to a TBox $\mathcal{T}$ if $\mathcal{I}$ is a model of $\mathcal{T}$ such that $C^{\mathcal{I}} \neq \emptyset$. We call this model finite if $\Delta^{\mathcal{I}}$ is finite.*

In the following, we show that $\mathcal{ALC}$ has the *finite model property* (fmp), i.e., every $\mathcal{ALC}$ concept that is satisfiable with respect to an $\mathcal{ALC}$ TBox has a finite model. Interestingly, this can be used to show that satisfiability of $\mathcal{ALC}$ concepts with respect to $\mathcal{ALC}$ TBoxes is decidable since we can actually determine a concrete bound on the size of such a finite model.

Before we can prove that $\mathcal{ALC}$ has the fmp, we need to introduce some technical notions. Given an $\mathcal{ALC}$ concept C, we define its *size* $\mathsf{size}(C)$ and the set of its *subconcepts* $\mathsf{sub}(C)$ by induction on the structure of C:

- If $C = A \in N_C \cup \{\top, \bot\}$, then $\mathsf{size}(C) = 1$ and $\mathsf{sub}(C) = \{A\}$.
- If $C = C_1 \sqcap C_2$ or $C = C_1 \sqcup C_2$, then $\mathsf{size}(C) = 1 + \mathsf{size}(C_1) + \mathsf{size}(C_2)$ and $\mathsf{sub}(C) = \{C\} \cup \mathsf{sub}(C_1) \cup \mathsf{sub}(C_2)$.
- If $C = \neg D$ or $C = \exists r.D$ or $C = \forall r.D$, then $\mathsf{size}(C) = 1 + \mathsf{size}(D)$ and $\mathsf{sub}(C) = \{C\} \cup \mathsf{sub}(D)$.

The size just counts the number of occurrences of concept names (including $\top$ and $\bot$), role names and Boolean operators. For example,

$$\mathsf{size}(A \sqcap \exists r.(A \sqcup B)) = 1 + 1 + (1 + (1 + 1 + 1)) = 6.$$

For the same concept, the set of its subconcepts is

$$\mathsf{sub}(A \sqcap \exists r.(A \sqcup B)) = \{A \sqcap \exists r.(A \sqcup B), A, \exists r.(A \sqcup B), A \sqcup B, B\}.$$

We can extend these notions to $\mathcal{ALC}$ TBoxes as follows:

$$\mathsf{size}(\mathcal{T}) = \sum_{C \sqsubseteq D \in \mathcal{T}} \mathsf{size}(C) + \mathsf{size}(D) \text{ and } \mathsf{sub}(\mathcal{T}) = \bigcup_{C \sqsubseteq D \in \mathcal{T}} \mathsf{sub}(C) \cup \mathsf{sub}(D).$$

It is easy to see[1] that the number of subconcepts of a concept or TBox is bounded by the size of the concept or TBox:

Lemma 3.11. *Let C be an $\mathcal{ALC}$ concept and $\mathcal{T}$ be an $\mathcal{ALC}$ TBox. Then*

$$|\mathsf{sub}(C)| \leq \mathsf{size}(C) \ \text{and} \ |\mathsf{sub}(\mathcal{T})| \leq \mathsf{size}(\mathcal{T}).$$

We call a set S of $\mathcal{ALC}$ concepts *closed* if $\bigcup\{\mathsf{sub}(C) \mid C \in S\} \subseteq S$. Obviously, if S is the set of subdescriptions of an $\mathcal{ALC}$ concept or TBox, then S is closed.

Definition 3.12 (*S*-type). Let S be a set of $\mathcal{ALC}$ concepts and $\mathcal{I}$ an interpretation. The *S-type* of $d \in \Delta^{\mathcal{I}}$ is defined as

$$t_S(d) = \{C \in S \mid d \in C^{\mathcal{I}}\}.$$

Since an *S*-type is a subset of S, there are at most as many *S*-types as there are subsets:

Lemma 3.13. *Let S be a finite set of $\mathcal{ALC}$ concepts and $\mathcal{I}$ an interpretation. Then $|\{t_S(d) \mid d \in \Delta^{\mathcal{I}}\}| \leq 2^{|S|}$.*

---

[1] A formal proof can be done by induction on the structure of concepts.

The main idea underlying our proof that $\mathcal{ALC}$ has the fmp is that, in order to find a model of an $\mathcal{ALC}$ concept C with respect to an $\mathcal{ALC}$ TBox $\mathcal{T}$, it is sufficient to consider only interpretations in which every S-type is realised by at most one element, i.e., $d = d'$ if and only if $t_S(d) = t_S(d')$, where S is the set of subconcepts of C and $\mathcal{T}$. Starting with an arbitrary model of C with respect to $\mathcal{T}$, we can obtain a model satisfying this property by merging elements that have the same S-type into a single element using the filtration technique introduced below.

Definition 3.14 (S-filtration). Let S be a finite set of $\mathcal{ALC}$ concepts and $\mathcal{I}$ an interpretation. We define the equivalence relation $\simeq_S$ on $\Delta^{\mathcal{I}}$ as follows:

$$d \simeq_S e \quad \text{if} \quad t_S(d) = t_S(e).$$

The $\simeq_S$-*equivalence class* of $d \in \Delta^{\mathcal{I}}$ is denoted by $[d]_S$, i.e.,

$$[d]_S = \{e \in \Delta^{\mathcal{I}} \mid d \simeq_S e\}.$$

The S-*filtration of* $\mathcal{I}$ is the following interpretation $\mathcal{J}$:

$$
\begin{aligned}
\Delta^{\mathcal{J}} &= \{[d]_S \mid d \in \Delta^{\mathcal{I}}\}; \\
A^{\mathcal{J}} &= \{[d]_S \mid \text{there is } d' \in [d]_S \text{ with } d' \in A^{\mathcal{I}}\} \text{ for all } A \in \mathbf{C}; \\
r^{\mathcal{J}} &= \{([d]_S, [e]_S) \mid \text{there are } d' \in [d]_S, e' \in [e]_S \text{ with } (d', e') \in r^{\mathcal{I}}\} \\
&\quad \text{for all } r \in \mathbf{R}.
\end{aligned}
$$

Lemma 3.15. *Let S be a finite, closed set of $\mathcal{ALC}$ concepts, $\mathcal{I}$ an interpretation and $\mathcal{J}$ the S-filtration of $\mathcal{I}$. Then we have*

$$d \in C^{\mathcal{I}} \quad \text{if and only if} \quad [d]_S \in C^{\mathcal{J}}$$

for all $d \in \Delta^{\mathcal{I}}$ and $C \in S$.

Proof. By induction on the structure of C, where we again restrict our attention to concept names, negation, conjunction and existential restriction (see Lemma 2.16):

• Assume that $C = A \in \mathbf{C}$.

  – If $d \in A^{\mathcal{I}}$, then $[d]_S \in A^{\mathcal{J}}$ by the definition of $\mathcal{J}$ since $d \in [d]_S$.
  – If $[d]_S \in A^{\mathcal{J}}$, then there is $d' \in [d]_S$ with $d' \in A^{\mathcal{I}}$. Since $d \simeq_S d'$ and $A \in S$, $d' \in A^{\mathcal{I}}$ implies $d \in A^{\mathcal{I}}$.

- Assume that $C = D \sqcap E$. Then the following holds:

$$d \in (D \sqcap E)^{\mathcal{I}} \quad \text{if and only if} \quad d \in D^{\mathcal{I}} \text{ and } d \in E^{\mathcal{I}}$$
$$\text{if and only if} \quad [d]_S \in D^{\mathcal{J}} \text{ and } [d]_S \in E^{\mathcal{J}}$$
$$\text{if and only if} \quad [d]_S \in (D \sqcap E)^{\mathcal{J}}.$$

The first and last bi-implications hold because of the semantics of conjunction. The second holds by induction: since S is closed, we have $D, E \in S$, and thus the induction hypothesis applies to D and E.

- Negation $C = \neg D$ can be treated similarly to conjunction.
- Assume that $C = \exists r.D$. Since S is closed, we have $D \in S$, and thus the induction hypothesis applies to D.
  - If $d \in (\exists r.D)^{\mathcal{I}}$, then there is $e \in \Delta^{\mathcal{I}}$ such that $(d, e) \in r^{\mathcal{I}}$ and $e \in D^{\mathcal{I}}$. We have $([d]_S, [e]_S) \in r^{\mathcal{J}}$ since $d \in [d]_S$ and $e \in [e]_S$. In addition, induction (applied to $D \in S$) yields $[e]_S \in D^{\mathcal{J}}$. This shows $[d]_S \in (\exists r.D)^{\mathcal{J}}$.
  - If $[d]_S \in (\exists r.D)^{\mathcal{J}}$, then there is $[e]_S \in \Delta^{\mathcal{J}}$ such that $([d]_S, [e]_S) \in r^{\mathcal{J}}$ and $[e]_S \in D^{\mathcal{J}}$. Induction (applied to $D \in S$) yields $e \in D^{\mathcal{I}}$. In addition, there are $d' \in [d]_S$ and $e' \in [e]_S$ such that $(d', e') \in r^{\mathcal{I}}$. Since $e \simeq_S e'$ and $D \in S$, we know that $e \in D^{\mathcal{I}}$ implies $e' \in D^{\mathcal{I}}$. Consequently, we have $d' \in (\exists r.D)^{\mathcal{I}}$. But then $d \simeq_S d'$ and $\exists r.D \in S$ yield $d \in (\exists r.D)^{\mathcal{I}}$. $\square$

One may be tempted to show the lemma in a simpler way using bisimulation invariance of $\mathcal{ALC}$ and the relation

$$\rho = \{(d, [d]_S) \mid d \in \Delta^{\mathcal{I}}\}$$

between elements of the domain of $\mathcal{I}$ and elements of the domain of $\mathcal{J}$. Unfortunately, this relation is in general not a bisimulation. First of all, (i) of Definition 3.1 is obviously only guaranteed to hold if S contains all concept names in $\mathbf{C}$. But even if this is assumed, (iii) of Definition 3.1 need not hold. In fact, assume that $S = \{\top, A, \exists r.\top\}$ where $\mathbf{C} = \{A\}$ and $\mathbf{R} = \{r\}$, and consider the interpretation $\mathcal{I}$ consisting of the elements d_1, d_2, d'_1, d'_2 depicted on the left-hand side of Figure 3.4. Then $\simeq_S$ has three equivalence classes, $[d_1]_S = [d_2]_S$, $[d'_1]_S$ and $[d'_2]_S$, and the S-filtration $\mathcal{J}$ of $\mathcal{I}$ is the interpretation depicted on the right-hand side of Figure 3.4. It is easy to see that the relation ρ defined above is not a bisimulation in this example. In fact, we have $(d_1, [d_1]_S) \in \rho$, but $[d_1]_S$ has an r-successor in $\mathcal{J}$ that does not belong to the extension of A, whereas d_1 does not have such an r-successor in $\mathcal{I}$.

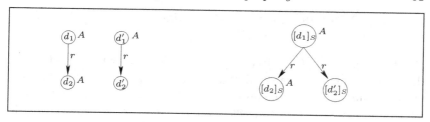

Fig. 3.4. An interpretation $\mathcal{I}$ and its S-filtration $\mathcal{J}$ for $S = \{\top, A, \exists r.\top\}$.

As a consequence of Lemma 3.15, we can show that $\mathcal{ALC}$ satisfies a property that is even stronger than the finite model property: the *bounded model property*. For the bounded model property, it is not sufficient to know that there is a finite model. One also needs to have an explicit bound on the cardinality of this model in terms of the size of the TBox and concept.

Theorem 3.16 (Bounded model property). *Let $\mathcal{T}$ be an $\mathcal{ALC}$ TBox, C an $\mathcal{ALC}$ concept and $n = \mathsf{size}(\mathcal{T}) + \mathsf{size}(C)$. If C has a model with respect to $\mathcal{T}$, then it has one of cardinality at most 2^n.*

Proof. Let $\mathcal{I}$ be a model of $\mathcal{T}$ with $C^{\mathcal{I}} \neq \emptyset$, and $S = \mathsf{sub}(\mathcal{T}) \cup \mathsf{sub}(C)$. Then we have $|S| \leq n$, and thus the domain of the S-filtration $\mathcal{J}$ of $\mathcal{I}$ satisfies $|\Delta^{\mathcal{J}}| \leq 2^n$ by Lemma 3.13. Thus, it remains to show that $\mathcal{J}$ is a model of C with respect to $\mathcal{T}$.

Let $d \in \Delta^{\mathcal{I}}$ be such that $d \in C^{\mathcal{I}}$. Since $C \in S$, we know that $d \in C^{\mathcal{I}}$ implies $[d]_S \in C^{\mathcal{J}}$ by Lemma 3.15, and thus $C^{\mathcal{J}} \neq \emptyset$. In addition, it is easy to see that $\mathcal{J}$ is a model of $\mathcal{T}$. In fact, let $D \sqsubseteq E$ be a GCI in $\mathcal{T}$, and $[e]_S \in D^{\mathcal{J}}$. We must show $[e]_S \in E^{\mathcal{J}}$. Since $D \in S$, Lemma 3.15 yields $e \in D^{\mathcal{I}}$, and thus $e \in E^{\mathcal{I}}$ since $\mathcal{I}$ is a model of $\mathcal{T}$. But then $E \in S$ implies $[e]_S \in E^{\mathcal{J}}$, again by Lemma 3.15.   □

Obviously, the finite model property of $\mathcal{ALC}$ is an immediate consequence of the bounded model property.

Corollary 3.17 (Finite model property). *Let $\mathcal{T}$ be an $\mathcal{ALC}$ TBox and C an $\mathcal{ALC}$ concept. If C has a model with respect to $\mathcal{T}$, then it has one of finite cardinality.*

Another interesting consequence of the bounded model property of $\mathcal{ALC}$ is that the *satisfiability problem* for $\mathcal{ALC}$ concepts with respect to $\mathcal{ALC}$ TBoxes is decidable.

Corollary 3.18 (Decidability). *Satisfiability of $\mathcal{ALC}$ concepts with respect to $\mathcal{ALC}$ TBoxes is decidable.*

Proof. Let $n = \mathsf{size}(\mathcal{T}) + \mathsf{size}(C)$. If C is satisfiable with respect to $\mathcal{T}$, then it has a model of cardinality at most 2^n. Up to isomorphism (i.e., up to renaming of the domain elements), there are only finitely many interpretations satisfying this size bound. Thus, we can enumerate all of these interpretations, and then check (using the inductive definition of the semantics of concepts) whether one of them is a model of C with respect to $\mathcal{T}$. □

Not all description logics have the fmp. For example, if we add number restrictions and inverse roles to $\mathcal{ALC}$, then the fmp is lost.

Theorem 3.19 (No finite model property). *$\mathcal{ALCIN}$ does not have the finite model property.*

Proof. Let $C = \neg A \sqcap \exists r.A$ and $\mathcal{T} = \{A \sqsubseteq \exists r.A, \top \sqsubseteq (\leqslant 1\, r^-)\}$. We claim that C does not have a finite model with respect to $\mathcal{T}$.

Assume to the contrary that $\mathcal{I}$ is such a finite model, and let $d_0 \in \Delta^{\mathcal{I}}$ be such that $d_0 \in C^{\mathcal{I}}$. Then $d_0 \in (\exists r.A)^{\mathcal{I}}$, and thus there is $d_1 \in \Delta^{\mathcal{I}}$ such that $(d_0, d_1) \in r^{\mathcal{I}}$ and $d_1 \in A^{\mathcal{I}}$. Because of the first GCI in $\mathcal{T}$, there is $d_2 \in \Delta^{\mathcal{I}}$ such that $(d_1, d_2) \in r^{\mathcal{I}}$ and $d_2 \in A^{\mathcal{I}}$. We can continue this argument to obtain a sequence $d_0, d_1, d_2, d_3, \ldots$ of individuals in $\Delta^{\mathcal{I}}$ such that

- $d_0 \notin A^{\mathcal{I}}$,
- $(d_{i-1}, d_i) \in r^{\mathcal{I}}$ and $d_i \in A^{\mathcal{I}}$ for all $i \geq 1$.

Since $\Delta^{\mathcal{I}}$ is finite, there are two indices $0 \leq i < j$ such that $d_i = d_j$. We may assume without loss of generality that i is chosen minimally, i.e., for all $k < i$ there is no $\ell > k$ such that $d_k = d_\ell$.

Since $j > 0$, we have $d_i = d_j \in A^{\mathcal{I}}$, and thus $i = 0$ is not possible. However, $i > 0$ and $j > 0$ imply that d_{i-1} and d_{j-1} are r-predecessors of $d_i = d_j$, i.e., $(d_i, d_{i-1}) \in (r^-)^{\mathcal{I}}$ and $(d_i, d_{j-1}) \in (r^-)^{\mathcal{I}}$. Consequently, the second GCI in $\mathcal{T}$ enforces $d_{i-1} = d_{j-1}$, which contradicts our minimal choice of i. □

So, we have seen that $\mathcal{ALC}$ cannot enforce infinity of models, but $\mathcal{ALCIN}$ can. In fact, it is known that both $\mathcal{ALCI}$ and $\mathcal{ALCN}$ still enjoy the fmp (and so does $\mathcal{ALCQ}$). Thus, it is indeed the *combination* of number restrictions and inverse roles that destroys the fmp.

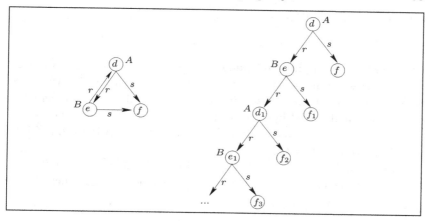

Fig. 3.5. Unravelling of a model $\mathcal{I}$ into a tree model $\mathcal{J}$.

3.5 Tree model property

Another interesting model-theoretic property of $\mathcal{ALC}$ is that every satisfiable concept has a tree model. For the purpose of this section, a *tree* is a directed graph $\mathcal{G} = (V, E)$ such that

- V contains a unique *root*, i.e., a node $v_r \in V$ such that there is no $v \in V$ with $(v, v_r) \in E$;
- every node $v \in V \setminus \{v_r\}$ has a unique predecessor, i.e., there is a unique node $v' \in V$ such that $(v', v) \in E$.

Basically, a tree model is a model whose graph representation is a tree.

Definition 3.20 (Tree model). Let $\mathcal{T}$ be an $\mathcal{ALC}$ TBox and C an $\mathcal{ALC}$ concept description. The interpretation $\mathcal{I}$ is a *tree model* of C with respect to $\mathcal{T}$ if $\mathcal{I}$ is a model of C with respect to $\mathcal{T}$, and the graph

$$\mathcal{G}_\mathcal{I} = \left(\Delta^\mathcal{I}, \bigcup_{r \in \mathbf{R}} r^\mathcal{I} \right)$$

is a tree whose root belongs to $C^\mathcal{I}$.

In order to show that every concept that is satisfiable with respect to $\mathcal{T}$ has a tree model with respect to $\mathcal{T}$, we use the well-known *unravelling* technique. Before introducing unravelling formally, we illustrate it by an example. The graph on the left-hand side of Figure 3.5 describes an interpretation $\mathcal{I}$. It is easy to check that $\mathcal{I}$ is a model of the concept A

with respect to the TBox

$$\mathcal{T} = \{A \sqsubseteq \exists r.B, \quad B \sqsubseteq \exists r.A, \quad A \sqcup B \sqsubseteq \exists s.\top\}.$$

The graph on the right-hand side of Figure 3.5 describes (a finite part of) the corresponding unravelled model $\mathcal{J}$, where d was used as the start node for the unravelling. Basically, one considers all paths starting with d in the original model but, rather than re-entering a node, one makes a copy of it. Like $\mathcal{I}$, the corresponding unravelled interpretation $\mathcal{J}$ is a model of $\mathcal{T}$ and it satisfies $d \in A^{\mathcal{J}}$.

More formally, let $\mathcal{I}$ be an interpretation and $d \in \Delta^{\mathcal{I}}$. A d-*path in* $\mathcal{I}$ is a finite sequence $d_0, d_1, \ldots, d_{n-1}$ of $n \geq 1$ elements of $\Delta^{\mathcal{I}}$ such that

- $d_0 = d$,
- for all $i, 1 \leq i < n$, there is a role $r_i \in \mathbf{R}$ such that $(d_{i-1}, d_i) \in r_i^{\mathcal{I}}$.

Given a d-path $p = d_0, d_1, \ldots, d_{n-1}$, we define its *length* to be n and its *end node* to be $\mathsf{end}(p) = d_{n-1}$.

In the unravelled model, such paths constitute the elements of the domain. In our example, the node with label d_1 corresponds to the path d, e, d, the one with label f_1 to d, e, f, the one with label e_1 to d, e, d, e etc.

Definition 3.21 (Unravelling). Let $\mathcal{I}$ be an interpretation and $d \in \Delta^{\mathcal{I}}$. The *unravelling of* $\mathcal{I}$ *at* d is the following interpretation $\mathcal{J}$:

$$\Delta^{\mathcal{J}} = \{p \mid p \text{ is a } d\text{-path in } \mathcal{I}\},$$
$$A^{\mathcal{J}} = \{p \in \Delta^{\mathcal{J}} \mid \mathsf{end}(p) \in A^{\mathcal{I}}\} \text{ for all } A \in \mathbf{C},$$
$$r^{\mathcal{J}} = \{(p, p') \in \Delta^{\mathcal{J}} \times \Delta^{\mathcal{J}} \mid p' = (p, \mathsf{end}(p')) \text{ and } (\mathsf{end}(p), \mathsf{end}(p')) \in r^{\mathcal{I}}\}$$
$$\text{for all } r \in \mathbf{R}.$$

In our example, $d_1 = d, e, d \in A^{\mathcal{J}}$ because $\mathsf{end}(d_1) = d \in A^{\mathcal{I}}$, and $((d, e, d), (d, e, d, e)) \in r^{\mathcal{J}}$ because $(d, e) \in r^{\mathcal{I}}$.

Next, we will see that the relation that connects a d-path with its end node is a bisimulation.

Lemma 3.22. *The relation*

$$\rho = \{(p, \mathsf{end}(p)) \mid p \in \Delta^{\mathcal{J}}\}$$

is a bisimulation between $\mathcal{J}$ *and* $\mathcal{I}$.

Proof. By definition of the extensions of concept names in the interpretation $\mathcal{J}$, we have $p \in A^{\mathcal{J}}$ if and only if $\mathsf{end}(p) \in A^{\mathcal{I}}$, and thus Condition (i) of Definition 3.1 is satisfied.

To show that Condition (ii) of Definition 3.1 is also satisfied, we assume that $(p, p') \in r^{\mathcal{J}}$ and $(p, e) \in \rho$. Since $\text{end}(p)$ is the only element of $\Delta^{\mathcal{I}}$ that is ρ-related to p, we have $e = \text{end}(p)$. Thus, we must show that there is an $f \in \Delta^{\mathcal{I}}$ such that $(p', f) \in \rho$ and $(\text{end}(p), f) \in r^{\mathcal{I}}$. We define $f = \text{end}(p')$. Because $(p', \text{end}(p')) \in \rho$, it is thus enough to show $(\text{end}(p), \text{end}(p')) \in r^{\mathcal{I}}$. This is, however, an immediate consequence of the definition of the extensions of roles in $\mathcal{J}$.

To show that Condition (iii) of Definition 3.1 is satisfied, we assume that $(e, f) \in r^{\mathcal{I}}$ and $(p, e) \in \rho$ (i.e., $\text{end}(p) = e$). We must find a path p' such that $(p', f) \in \rho$ and $(p, p') \in r^{\mathcal{J}}$. We define $p' = p, f$. This is indeed a d-path since p is a d-path with $\text{end}(p) = e$ and $(e, f) \in r^{\mathcal{I}}$. In addition, $\text{end}(p') = f$, which shows $(p', f) \in \rho$. Finally, we clearly have $p' = p, \text{end}(p')$ and $(\text{end}(p), \text{end}(p')) \in r^{\mathcal{I}}$ since $\text{end}(p) = e$ and $\text{end}(p') = f$. This yields $(p, p') \in r^{\mathcal{J}}$. $\qquad\square$

The following proposition is an immediate consequence of this lemma and Theorem 3.2.

Proposition 3.23. *For all $\mathcal{ALC}$ concepts C and all $p \in \Delta^{\mathcal{J}}$, we have*

$$p \in C^{\mathcal{J}} \quad \text{if and only if} \quad \text{end}(p) \in C^{\mathcal{I}}.$$

We are now ready to show the tree model property of $\mathcal{ALC}$.

Theorem 3.24 (Tree model property). *$\mathcal{ALC}$ has the tree model property, i.e., if $\mathcal{T}$ is an $\mathcal{ALC}$ TBox and C an $\mathcal{ALC}$ concept such that C is satisfiable with respect to $\mathcal{T}$, then C has a tree model with respect to $\mathcal{T}$.*

Proof. Let $\mathcal{I}$ be a model of $\mathcal{T}$ and $d \in \Delta^{\mathcal{I}}$ be such that $d \in C^{\mathcal{I}}$. We show that the unravelling $\mathcal{J}$ of $\mathcal{I}$ at d is a tree model of C with respect to $\mathcal{T}$.

(i) To prove that $\mathcal{J}$ is a model of $\mathcal{T}$, consider a GCI $D \sqsubseteq E$ in $\mathcal{T}$, and assume that $p \in \Delta^{\mathcal{J}}$ satisfies $p \in D^{\mathcal{J}}$. We must show $p \in E^{\mathcal{J}}$. By Proposition 3.23, we have $\text{end}(p) \in D^{\mathcal{I}}$, which yields $\text{end}(p) \in E^{\mathcal{I}}$ since $\mathcal{I}$ is model of $\mathcal{T}$. But then Proposition 3.23 applied in the other direction yields $p \in E^{\mathcal{J}}$.

(ii) We show that the graph

$$\mathcal{G}_{\mathcal{J}} = \left(\Delta^{\mathcal{J}}, \bigcup_{r \in N_R} r^{\mathcal{J}}\right)$$

is a tree with root d, where d is viewed as a d-path of length 1. First, note that d is the only d-path of length 1. By definition of the extensions of roles in $\mathcal{J}$ and the definition of d-paths, all and only d-paths of length > 1 have a predecessor with respect to some role. Consequently, d is the unique node without predecessor, i.e., the root. Assume that p is a d-path of length > 1. Then there is a unique d-path p' such that $p = p', \mathsf{end}(p)$. Thus, p' is the unique d-path with $(p', p) \in E$, which completes our proof that $\mathcal{G}_{\mathcal{J}}$ is a tree with root d.

(iii) It remains to show that the root d of this tree belongs to the extension of C in $\mathcal{J}$. However, this follows immediately by Proposition 3.23 since $d = \mathsf{end}(d)$ and $d \in C^{\mathcal{I}}$.

This completes the proof of the theorem.   □

Note that, in case the model we start with has a cycle, the tree constructed in the proof is an infinite tree, i.e., it has infinitely many nodes. Although $\mathcal{ALC}$ has the finite model property and the tree model property, it does not have the finite tree model property. In fact, it is easy to see that the concept A does not have a finite tree model with respect to the TBox $\{A \sqsubseteq \exists r.A\}$.

It should also be noted that, in our definition of a tree model, we do not consider edge labels. Thus, $(u, v) \in r^{\mathcal{I}}$ yields the same edge (u, v) in E as $(u, v) \in s^{\mathcal{I}}$. Consequently, in a tree model as introduced in Definition 3.20, there can be several roles connecting two nodes u and v with $(u, v) \in E$. Alternatively, we could have required that, for every element d of $\Delta^{\mathcal{I}}$ excepting the root, there is exactly one role r and element $d' \in \Delta^{\mathcal{I}}$ such that $(d', d) \in r^{\mathcal{I}}$. One can show that $\mathcal{ALC}$ also satisfies the tree model property for this stronger notion of tree model, but the definition of unravelling gets a bit more complicated since role names need to be remembered in the paths.

We remark that many extensions of $\mathcal{ALC}$, such as $\mathcal{ALCIQ}$, also enjoy the tree model property. However, in the presence of inverse roles, a more liberal definition of trees is needed that also allows edges to be oriented towards the root. An example of a description logic that does not enjoy the tree model property is $\mathcal{ALCO}$: the concept $\{o\} \sqcap \exists r.\{o\}$ can clearly only have a non-empty extension in an interpretation that has a reflexive r-edge.

Finally, let us point out that the tree model property can also be used to show decidability of satisfiability of concepts with respect to TBoxes in $\mathcal{ALC}$, using the so-called *automata-based approach*. The automata used in this approach are automata working on infinite trees. In general, there are various types of such automata such as *Büchi, Rabin* and *parity automata*, but for $\mathcal{ALC}$ the simpler *looping automata* (which have a trivial acceptance condition) are sufficient. An important property of all these automata is that their emptiness problem (i.e., the question whether a given automaton accepts at least one tree) is decidable, for looping automata even in linear time. In principle, the automata approach for $\mathcal{ALC}$ works as follows:

- Devise a translation from each pair $C, \mathcal{T}$, where C is an $\mathcal{ALC}$ concept description and $\mathcal{T}$ is an $\mathcal{ALC}$ TBox, into a looping tree automaton $\mathcal{A}_{C,\mathcal{T}}$ such that $\mathcal{A}_{C,\mathcal{T}}$ accepts exactly the tree models of C with respect to $\mathcal{T}$.
- Apply the emptiness test for looping tree automata to $\mathcal{A}_{C,\mathcal{T}}$ to test whether C has a (tree) model with respect to $\mathcal{T}$: if $\mathcal{A}_{C,\mathcal{T}}$ accepts some trees, then these are (tree) models of C with respect to $\mathcal{T}$; if $\mathcal{A}_{C,\mathcal{T}}$ accepts no trees, then C has no tree models with respect to $\mathcal{T}$, and thus no models.

We do not go into more detail here, but just want to point out that the states of these automata are types (as introduced in Section 3.4) and that the emptiness test for them boils down to the type elimination procedure described in Section 5.1.2.

3.6 Historical context and literature review

In Section 2.6.2, the close relationship between description and modal logics was described. The model-theoretic notions and properties considered in this chapter in the context of description logics have originally been introduced and proved for modal logics (see, e.g., [BdRV01, Bv07, GO07]). For the modal logic $\mathbf{K}_{(m)}$, it was also shown that bisimulations satisfy additional interesting properties that are stronger than Theorem 3.2. Expressed for the syntactic variant $\mathcal{ALC}$ of $\mathbf{K}_{(m)}$, two famous ones are the following:

(a) A formula of first-order logic with one free variable is equivalent to the translation of an $\mathcal{ALC}$ concept if and only if it is invariant under bisimulation.

(b) If $\mathcal{I}_1$ and $\mathcal{I}_2$ are interpretations of finite outdegree (that is, in which every element has only finitely many role successors) and $d_1 \in \Delta^{\mathcal{I}_1}$ and $d_2 \in \Delta^{\mathcal{I}_2}$, then d_1 and d_2 belong to the same $\mathcal{ALC}$ concepts if and only if $(d_1, \mathcal{I}_1) \sim (d_2, \mathcal{I}_2)$. Note that every finite interpretation satisfies this property. For interpretations in which elements can have an unrestricted number of successors, this bi-implication need not hold.

Basically, Property (a) says that the notion of bisimulation that we have introduced in Definition 3.1 is exactly the right one for $\mathcal{ALC}$. An analogue of Property (a) also exists for TBoxes instead of for concepts, saying that a sentence of first-order logic is equivalent to the translation of an $\mathcal{ALC}$ TBox if and only if it is invariant under bisimulation and disjoint unions [LPW11].

It is important to note that many notions and constructions in this section are tailored specifically to the description logic $\mathcal{ALC}$. For example, proving non-expressibility results for logics other than $\mathcal{ALC}$ requires other versions of bisimulations. For $\mathcal{ALCI}$, one needs to admit also inverse roles in Conditions (ii) and (iii) of bisimulations. For $\mathcal{ALCQ}$, these conditions need to consider more than one successor at the time and involve some counting. An overview is given in [LPW11]; other relevant references are [KdR97, Kd99] in the description logic literature and [dR00, GO07] in that of modal logic. An interesting case is provided by description logics that are weaker than $\mathcal{ALC}$, such as $\mathcal{EL}$, which admits only the constructors $\top$, $\sqcap$ and $\exists r.C$, and which we study in Chapters 6 and 8. For this DL, bisimulations need to be replaced by simulations, which intuitively are "half a bisimulation" as they only go "forth" from $\mathcal{I}_1$ to $\mathcal{I}_2$, but not "back" from $\mathcal{I}_2$ to $\mathcal{I}_1$. Concepts formulated in a logic without disjunction such as $\mathcal{EL}$ also have another important model-theoretic property, namely that they are preserved under forming direct products, an operation well known from classical model theory [Hod93]. In fact, in analogy to Property (a), a formula of first-order logic with one free variable is equivalent to the translation of an $\mathcal{EL}$ concept if and only if it is preserved under simulations and direct products [LPW11].

Properties like the tree model property and the finite model property can also be shown as a consequence of the completeness of tableau algorithms (see Chapter 4). For example, the original tableau algorithm for satisfiability of $\mathcal{ALC}$ concepts (without TBoxes) [SS91] in principle constructs a finite tree model whenever the input concept is satisfiable.

4

Reasoning in DLs with Tableau Algorithms

A variety of reasoning techniques can be used to solve (some of) the reasoning problems introduced in Chapter 2. These include resolution and consequence-based approaches (see Chapter 6), automata-based approaches (see Section 3.5) and query rewriting approaches (see Chapter 7). For reasoning with expressive DLs,[1] however, the most widely used technique is the tableau-based approach.

We will concentrate on knowledge base consistency because, as we saw in Theorem 2.17, this is a very general problem to which many others can be reduced. For example, given a knowledge base $\mathcal{K} = (\mathcal{T}, \mathcal{A})$, a concept C is subsumed by a concept D with respect to $\mathcal{K}$ ($\mathcal{K} \models C \sqsubseteq D$) if and only if $(\mathcal{T}, \mathcal{A} \cup \{x : C \sqcap \neg D\})$ is not consistent, where x is a new individual name (i.e., one that does not occur in $\mathcal{K}$). Similarly, an individual name a is an instance of a concept C with respect to $\mathcal{K}$ ($\mathcal{K} \models a : C$) if and only if $(\mathcal{T}, \mathcal{A} \cup \{a : \neg C\})$ is not consistent. In practice, highly optimised tableau algorithms for deciding knowledge base consistency form the core of several implemented systems, including FaCT, FaCT++, Pellet, RACER and Konclude.

In the following we will:

- describe the general principles of the tableau approach;
- present an algorithm for the case of the basic DL $\mathcal{ALC}$ and prove that it is a decision procedure (i.e., that it is sound, complete and terminating);
- show how the algorithm can be extended to deal with some of the extensions described in Section 2.5, and how the proofs of soundness, completeness and termination can be adapted accordingly; and

---

[1] By "expressive" we mean here DLs that require some form of reasoning by case, for example to handle disjunction.

$\mathcal{T}_1 =$	{ Course $\equiv$ UGC $\sqcup$ PGC,
	PGC $\sqsubseteq \neg$UGC,
	Professor $\sqsubseteq$ Teacher $\sqcap$ $\exists$*teaches*.PGC }
$\mathcal{A}_1 =$	{ Betty : Professor,
	Hugo : Student,
	CS600 : Course,
	(Betty, CS600) : *teaches*,
	(Hugo, CS600) : *attends* }

Fig. 4.1. Example TBox and ABox.

- briefly review some of the techniques that are used in order to improve the performance of tableau-based reasoners in practice.

4.1 Tableau basics

We recall from Definition 2.14 that a knowledge base $\mathcal{K}$ is consistent if there exists some model $\mathcal{I}$ of $\mathcal{K}$. For example, given the knowledge base $\mathcal{K}_1 = (\mathcal{T}_1, \mathcal{A}_1)$ with $\mathcal{T}_1$ and $\mathcal{A}_1$ defined as in Figure 4.1, it is easy to see that the following interpretation $\mathcal{I}_1$ is a model of $\mathcal{K}_1$ (to really *see* this, we cordially invite the reader to draw the model below following the example given in Figure 2.2):

$$
\begin{aligned}
\Delta^{\mathcal{I}_1} &= \{b, h, c\}, & \text{Betty}^{\mathcal{I}_1} &= b, \\
\text{Hugo}^{\mathcal{I}_1} &= h, & \text{CS600}^{\mathcal{I}_1} &= c, \\
\text{PGC}^{\mathcal{I}_1} &= \{c\}, & \text{UGC}^{\mathcal{I}_1} &= \emptyset, \\
\text{Teacher}^{\mathcal{I}_1} &= \{b\}, & \text{Professor}^{\mathcal{I}_1} &= \{b\}, \\
\text{Student}^{\mathcal{I}_1} &= \{h\}, & \text{Course}^{\mathcal{I}_1} &= \{c\}, \\
\textit{teaches}^{\mathcal{I}_1} &= \{(b, c)\}, & \textit{attends}^{\mathcal{I}_1} &= \{(h, c)\}.
\end{aligned}
$$

The existence of $\mathcal{I}_1$ proves that $\mathcal{K}_1$ is consistent; we say that such a model is a *witness* of the consistency of $\mathcal{K}_1$.

The idea behind tableau-based techniques is to try to prove the consistency of a knowledge base $\mathcal{K} = (\mathcal{A}, \mathcal{T})$ by demonstrating the existence of a suitable witness, i.e., an interpretation $\mathcal{I}$ such that $\mathcal{I} \models \mathcal{K}$. They do this constructively, starting from $\mathcal{A}$ and extending it as needed to explicate constraints implied by the semantics of concepts and axioms in $\mathcal{A}$ and $\mathcal{T}$. This results either in the construction of (an ABox representation of) a witness,[2] or in the discovery of obvious contradictions that

---

[2] For convenience and brevity, we will sometimes conflate the notions of a witness and the ABox representation of a witness – when our intended meaning is obvious from the context.

prove that no such witness can exist, and thus that $\mathcal{K}$ is not consistent. Note that, in contrast, the consequence-based techniques to be described in Chapter 6 prove that a subsumption follows from a knowledge base by deriving new GCIs (consequences) from the given ones.

The tree model property (see Section 3.5), or some generalisation of it, is critical to the effectiveness and correctness of tableau-based techniques. On the one hand, an algorithm can restrict itself to constructing tree-like witnesses; this is critical for effectiveness, as it greatly reduces the number of possible witnesses that need to be considered, and for completeness, as the non-existence of a tree-like witness is sufficient to prove the non-existence of *any* witness. On the other hand, the structure of tree-like witnesses makes it relatively easy to identify when the construction of some branch of the tree has become repetitive; this is critical for termination, as we can halt the construction of such branches, and for soundness, as we can show that such partially constructed witnesses imply the existence of a complete (but possibly infinite) witness.

4.2 A tableau algorithm for $\mathcal{ALC}$

In this section we will present an algorithm that takes as input an $\mathcal{ALC}$ knowledge base $\mathcal{K} = (\mathcal{T}, \mathcal{A})$ and returns either "consistent" or "inconsistent". We will show that the algorithm terminates, and that it returns "consistent" if and only if $\mathcal{K}$ is consistent; i.e., that it is a decision procedure for $\mathcal{ALC}$ knowledge base consistency.

We will do this in three stages: first, we will present an algorithm for deciding $\mathcal{ALC}$ *ABox consistency*; second, we will show how this algorithm can be extended to one deciding $\mathcal{ALC}$ *knowledge base consistency* in the case where $\mathcal{T}$ is acyclic; and third, we will show how this algorithm can further be extended to deal with the case where $\mathcal{T}$ is an arbitrary TBox.

In the following, unless stated to the contrary, we will assume that A, B, C and D are concepts, that r and s are roles, and that a, b, c and d are individual names. To simplify the presentation, and without loss of generality, we will assume that all concepts occurring in $\mathcal{T}$ or $\mathcal{A}$ are in *negation normal form* (NNF), i.e., that negation is applied only to concept names, that $\mathcal{A}$ is non-empty and that every individual name occurring in $\mathcal{A}$ occurs in at least one assertion of the form $a : C$; we will call such an ABox *normalised*. An arbitrary $\mathcal{ALC}$ concept can be transformed into an equivalent one in NNF by pushing negations inwards using a combination of de Morgan's laws and the duality between existential and universal restrictions, as well as eliminating double negation (see Lemma 2.3):

$$\begin{array}{rclcrcl}
\neg(C \sqcap D) & \equiv & \neg C \sqcup \neg D, & & \neg(C \sqcup D) & \equiv & \neg C \sqcap \neg D, \\
\neg \exists r.C & \equiv & \forall r.\neg C, & & \neg \forall r.C & \equiv & \exists r.\neg C, \\
\neg\neg C & \equiv & C.
\end{array}$$

For a concept C, we will use $\dot{\neg} C$ to denote the NNF of $\neg C$. Finally, for any individual name a occurring in $\mathcal{A}$ we can add to $\mathcal{A}$ a vacuous assertion $a : \top$, and if $\mathcal{A}$ is empty we can add the assertion $a : \top$ for some new individual name a.

It will be useful to extend the definition of subconcept (see Section 3.4) to ABoxes and to knowledge bases in the obvious way:

$$\mathsf{sub}(\mathcal{A}) = \bigcup_{a : C \in \mathcal{A}} \mathsf{sub}(C),$$

and, for $\mathcal{K} = (\mathcal{T}, \mathcal{A})$, $\mathsf{sub}(\mathcal{K}) = \mathsf{sub}(\mathcal{T}) \cup \mathsf{sub}(\mathcal{A})$.

4.2.1 ABox consistency

We will first describe an algorithm for deciding ABox consistency, i.e., for the case where $\mathcal{K} = (\emptyset, \mathcal{A})$. This algorithm is very simple because, when the TBox is empty, the expansion rules only need to explicate the semantics of the concepts occurring in concept assertions in $\mathcal{A}$. Moreover, because these rules syntactically decompose concepts, the algorithm naturally terminates when all concepts have been fully decomposed.

As we saw in Section 3.5, $\mathcal{ALC}$ has the tree model property; i.e., every satisfiable concept has a tree model. However, since $\mathcal{A}$ might include individual names connected via arbitrary role assertions, this must be generalised to a *forest model property* for $\mathcal{ALC}$ knowledge bases: if $\mathcal{K}$ is consistent, then it has a model that consists of one or more disjoint trees, where the root of each tree interprets some individual name in $\mathcal{A}$, and where the roots are arbitrarily connected by edges. The algorithm will try to construct a forest-shaped ABox. It will do this by applying *expansion rules* so as to extend $\mathcal{A}$ until it is *complete*. In a complete ABox, consistency can be checked by looking for obvious contradictions (clashes).

Definition 4.1 (Complete and clash-free ABox). An ABox $\mathcal{A}$ contains a *clash* if, for some individual name a, and for some concept C, $\{a : C, a : \neg C\} \subseteq \mathcal{A}$; it is *clash-free* if it does not contain a clash. A

⊓-rule: if 1. $a : C \sqcap D \in \mathcal{A}$, and
2. $\{a : C, a : D\} \not\subseteq \mathcal{A}$
then $\mathcal{A} \longrightarrow \mathcal{A} \cup \{a : C, a : D\}$

⊔-rule: if 1. $a : C \sqcup D \in \mathcal{A}$, and
2. $\{a : C, a : D\} \cap \mathcal{A} = \emptyset$
then $\mathcal{A} \longrightarrow \mathcal{A} \cup \{a : X\}$ for some $X \in \{C, D\}$

∃-rule: if 1. $a : \exists r.C \in \mathcal{A}$, and
2. there is no b such that $\{(a, b) : r, b : C\} \subseteq \mathcal{A}$,
then $\mathcal{A} \longrightarrow \mathcal{A} \cup \{(a, d) : r, d : C\}$, where d is new in $\mathcal{A}$

∀-rule: if 1. $\{a : \forall r.C, (a, b) : r\} \subseteq \mathcal{A}$, and
2. $b : C \notin \mathcal{A}$
then $\mathcal{A} \longrightarrow \mathcal{A} \cup \{b : C\}$

Fig. 4.2. The syntax expansion rules for $\mathcal{ALC}$ ABox consistency.

is *complete* if it contains a clash, or if none of the expansion rules is applicable.

The definition of a complete ABox refers to the applicability of expansion rules. In the context of this section, these are the expansion rules of Figure 4.2. In later sections we will modify and/or extend the set of rules to deal with TBoxes and additional concept and role constructors. The notion of a complete ABox will remain the same, relative to the modified/extended set of rules, but the notion of a clash may need to be extended to deal with additional constructors.

We are now ready to define an algorithm consistent for deciding the consistency of a normalised $\mathcal{ALC}$ ABox $\mathcal{A}$. Nondeterministic algorithms are often used for this purpose, and have the advantage of being very simple and elegant: a typical definition simply says that $\mathcal{A}$ is consistent if and only if the rules can be applied to it in such a way as to construct a complete and clash-free ABox. However, such an algorithm cannot be directly implemented, and it conflates *relevant* (sometimes called *don't know*) nondeterminism, where different choices may affect the outcome of the algorithm, with *irrelevant* (sometimes called *don't care*) nondeterminism, where the choices made do not affect the outcome. We will instead define a deterministic algorithm that uses search to explore only relevant nondeterministic choices.

In the case of $\mathcal{ALC}$, there is only one such choice: the choice associated with the ⊔-rule. Unlike the other rules, where application of the rule leads deterministically to a unique expanded ABox, the ⊔-rule can be applied in different ways, and applying the rule in the "wrong" way can change $\mathcal{A}$ from being consistent to being inconsistent. For example, $\{a : \neg D, a : C \sqcup D\}$ is clearly consistent, and can be expanded using the $\sqcup$-rule into the complete and clash-free ABox $\{a : \neg D, a : C \sqcup D, a : C\}$; however, applying the $\sqcup$-rule in the other way would give $\{a : \neg D, a : C \sqcup D, a : D\}$, which is clearly inconsistent – in fact it already contains a clash. In a nondeterministic algorithm we simply say that $\mathcal{A}$ is consistent if we can choose *some* way of applying the $\sqcup$-rule that results in a consistent ABox; in our deterministic algorithm we will (recursively) check the consistency of the ABoxes resulting from *each* possible way of applying the $\sqcup$-rule, and we will say that $\mathcal{A}$ is consistent if *any* of these ABoxes is consistent.

Note that our algorithm does not search different possible orders of rule applications. This is because the order of rule applications does not affect consistency, although it can (dramatically) affect the efficiency of the algorithm. For this reason, an implementation typically chooses the order of rule applications using heuristics that aim to reduce the size of the search space; e.g., they may choose to apply the $\sqcup$-rule only if no other rule is applicable (see Section 4.4). Moreover, we can freely choose the order in which to explore the different expansion choices offered by the $\sqcup$-rule – if any choice leads to a consistent ABox, then our algorithm will (eventually) find it – and in practice this order may also be heuristically determined.

To facilitate the description of our deterministic algorithm we introduce a function exp that takes as input a normalised and clash-free $\mathcal{ALC}$ ABox $\mathcal{A}$, a rule R and an assertion or pair of assertions α such that R is applicable to α in $\mathcal{A}$; it returns a set $\exp(\mathcal{A}, R, \alpha)$ containing each of the ABoxes that can result from applying R to α in $\mathcal{A}$. For example,

- $\exp(\{a : \neg D, a : C \sqcup D\}, \sqcup\text{-rule}, a : C \sqcup D)$ returns a set containing two ABoxes: $\{a : \neg D, a : C \sqcup D, a : C\}$ and $\{a : \neg D, a : C \sqcup D, a : D\}$;
- $\exp(\{b : \neg D, a : \forall r.D, (a, b) : r\}, \forall\text{-rule}, (a : \forall r.D, (a, b) : r))$ returns a singleton set consisting of the ABox $\{b : \neg D, a : \forall r.D, (a, b) : r, b : D\}$.

For deterministic rules exp returns singleton sets, whereas for non-deterministic rules it returns sets of cardinality greater than one. In the case of $\mathcal{ALC}$, the $\sqcup$-rule is the only such nondeterministic rule, always returning sets of cardinality two, but, as we will see in Section 4.3, extending the algorithm to deal with additional constructors may necessitate the introduction of additional nondeterministic rules, which may also return sets of larger cardinality.

Algorithm consistent()

Input: a normalised $\mathcal{ALC}$ ABox $\mathcal{A}$

if expand($\mathcal{A}$) $\neq \emptyset$ **then**
 return "consistent"
else
 return "inconsistent"

Algorithm expand()

Input: a normalised $\mathcal{ALC}$ ABox $\mathcal{A}$

if $\mathcal{A}$ is not complete **then**
 select a rule R that is applicable to $\mathcal{A}$ and an assertion
 or pair of assertions α in $\mathcal{A}$ to which R is applicable
 if there is $\mathcal{A}' \in \exp(\mathcal{A}, R, \alpha)$ with expand($\mathcal{A}'$) $\neq \emptyset$ **then**
  return expand($\mathcal{A}'$)
 else
  return $\emptyset$
else
 if $\mathcal{A}$ contains a clash **then**
  return $\emptyset$
 else
  return $\mathcal{A}$

Fig. 4.3. The tableau algorithm consistent for $\mathcal{ALC}$ ABox consistency and the ABox expansion algorithm expand.

Definition 4.2 (Algorithm for $\mathcal{ALC}$ ABox consistency). The algorithm consistent for $\mathcal{ALC}$ ABox consistency takes as input a normalised $\mathcal{ALC}$ ABox $\mathcal{A}$ and uses the algorithm expand to apply the rules from Figure 4.2 to $\mathcal{A}$; both algorithms are given in Figure 4.3.

Before discussing the properties of the algorithm consistent in detail, and proving that it is in fact a decision procedure for $\mathcal{ALC}$ ABox consistency, we will use the following example ABox to illustrate some important features of consistent:

$$\mathcal{A}_{ex} = \{a : A \sqcap \exists s.F, \qquad (a,b) : s,$$
$$a : \forall s.(\neg F \sqcup \neg B), (a,c) : r,$$
$$b : B, \qquad c : C \sqcap \exists s.D\}.$$

Note that $\mathcal{A}_{ex}$ is already normalised, and so the algorithm can be applied to it.

First, we note that a precondition for the application of each rule to an ABox $\mathcal{A}$ is the presence in $\mathcal{A}$ of a concept assertion $e : E$, where E is of the relevant type ($\sqcap$, $\sqcup$, $\exists$ or $\forall$), and in each case the rule only adds concept assertions of the form $e : E'$ or $f : E'$, where E' is a subconcept of E and f an individual name such that $(e, f) : t \in \mathcal{A}$ for a role t.

For example, applying the $\sqcap$-rule to the first assertion in $\mathcal{A}_{ex}$ yields $\mathcal{A} = \mathcal{A}_{ex} \cup \{a : A,\ a : \exists s.F\}$. Note that we could instead have chosen to apply the $\sqcap$-rule to $c : C \sqcap \exists s.D$; however, as mentioned above, such choices do not affect the eventual outcome (i.e., whether the algorithm returns "consistent" or "inconsistent"), as rules remain applicable until their consequents have been satisfied (in this case, until both $c : C$ and $c : \exists s.D$ have been added).

Second, new individual names are introduced by the $\exists$-rule (and by no other rule), and such individual names are connected to an existing individual name by a single role assertion. Hence such individual names form trees whose roots are the individual names that occur in the input ABox; the resulting ABox can thus be said to form a forest.

In our example, applying the $\exists$-rule to $a : \exists s.F$ adds the assertions $(a, x) : s$, $x : F$, where x is a new individual name (i.e., different from the individual names a, b, c already occurring in the ABox). In subsequent steps, we can apply the $\forall$-rule to $a : \forall s.(\neg F \sqcup \neg B)$ together with $(a, b) : s$ and $(a, x) : s$. For the first role assertion, the rule adds $b : \neg F \sqcup \neg B$; for the second, it adds $x : \neg F \sqcup \neg B$.

Third, as discussed above, the $\sqcup$-rule is nondeterministic, and we have to explore all possible ways of applying it until we find one that leads to the construction of a complete and clash-free ABox, or determine that none of them does. In our example, we can apply the $\sqcup$-rule to $x : \neg F \sqcup \neg B$ in the current ABox $\mathcal{A}$, and in this case $\exp(\mathcal{A}, \sqcup\text{-rule}, x : \neg F \sqcup \neg B) = \{\mathcal{A} \cup \{x : \neg F\}, \mathcal{A} \cup \{x : \neg B\}\}$. If we first try $\mathcal{A}' = \mathcal{A} \cup \{x : \neg F\}$, then we will find that $\expand(\mathcal{A}') = \emptyset$ ($\mathcal{A}'$ already contains a clash); we will then try $\mathcal{A}' = \mathcal{A} \cup \{x : \neg B\}$. Similarly, we can apply the $\sqcup$-rule to $b : \neg F \sqcup \neg B \in \mathcal{A}$; in this case, if we first try $\mathcal{A}' = \mathcal{A} \cup \{b : \neg F\}$, then we will find that it is consistent and we won't try $\mathcal{A}' = \mathcal{A} \cup \{b : \neg B\}$.

We can now finish the example, assuming that we have so far extended

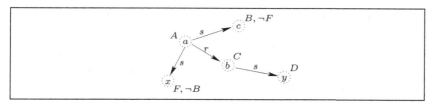

Fig. 4.4. A graphical representation of the complete and clash-free ABox generated for $\mathcal{A}_{ex}$ by the tableau algorithm in Figure 4.3.

the ABox $\mathcal{A}_{ex}$ to

$$\mathcal{A} = \{a : A \sqcap \exists s.F, \quad (a, b) : s,$$
$$a : \forall s.(\neg F \sqcup \neg B), (a, c) : r,$$
$$b : B, \quad c : C \sqcap \exists s.D,$$
$$a : A, \quad a : \exists s.F,$$
$$x : F, \quad (a, x) : s,$$
$$b : \neg F \sqcup \neg B, \quad x : \neg F \sqcup \neg B,$$
$$b : \neg F, \quad x : \neg B\}.$$

Only the $\sqcap$-rule is applicable to $c : C \sqcap \exists s.D \in \mathcal{A}$, and its application adds $c : C$ and $c : \exists s.D$ to $\mathcal{A}$. Now the $\exists$-rule is applicable to $c : \exists s.D \in \mathcal{A}$, and its application adds $(c, y) : s$ and $y : D$ to $\mathcal{A}$. We have now constructed a complete and clash-free ABox $\mathcal{A}$, and thus the tableau algorithm returns "consistent". A graphical representation of $\mathcal{A}$ can be found in Figure 4.4, where we leave out all complex concept expressions.

Before we analyse the algorithm in detail, we introduce some useful notation: as individual names introduced by the $\exists$-rule form part of a tree, we will call them *tree individuals*, and we will call the individual names that occur in the input ABox *root individuals*. It will sometimes be convenient to refer to the *predecessor* and *successor* of an individual name, defining them in the obvious way: if the $\exists$-rule adds a tree individual b and a role assertion of the form $(a, b) : r$, then b is a $(r$-) successor of a and a is a predecessor of b. We will use *ancestor* and *descendant* for the transitive closure of predecessor and successor, respectively; i.e., if a is the predecessor (successor) of b, then a is also an ancestor (descendant) of b, and if a is an ancestor (descendant) of b' and b' is an ancestor (descendant) of b, then a is an ancestor (descendant) of b. Note that root individuals may have successors (and hence descendants), but they have no predecessor (and hence no ancestors).

We will denote by $\text{con}_{\mathcal{A}}(a)$ the set of concepts C in concept assertions of the form $a : C$, i.e.,

$$\mathsf{con}_{\mathcal{A}}(a) = \{C \mid a : C \in \mathcal{A}\}.$$

The following lemma is an immediate consequence of the fact that $|\mathsf{sub}(C)| \leq \mathsf{size}(C)$, which was shown in Lemma 3.11.

Lemma 4.3. *For each $\mathcal{ALC}$ ABox $\mathcal{A}$, we have that $|\mathsf{sub}(\mathcal{A})| \leq \sum_{a : C \in \mathcal{A}} \mathsf{size}(C)$.*

As a consequence of Lemma 4.3, we can say that the cardinality of $\mathsf{sub}(\mathcal{A})$ is linear in the size of $\mathcal{A}$.

Please note that, in our example, the tree individuals form rather trivial trees; we invite the reader to run the algorithm again on the given ABox extended with $b : \exists r.A \sqcap \exists r.B \sqcap \forall r.(\exists s.A \sqcap \exists s.B)$ to see a less trivial tree of six freshly introduced tree individuals.

We will now prove that, for any $\mathcal{ALC}$ ABox $\mathcal{A}$, the algorithm terminates, returns "consistent" only if $\mathcal{A}$ is consistent (i.e., it is sound), and returns "consistent" whenever $\mathcal{A}$ is consistent (i.e., it is complete).

Lemma 4.4 (Termination). *For each $\mathcal{ALC}$ ABox $\mathcal{A}$, consistent($\mathcal{A}$) terminates.*

Proof. Let $m = |\mathsf{sub}(\mathcal{A})|$. Termination is a consequence of the following properties of the expansion rules:

(i) The expansion rules never remove an assertion from $\mathcal{A}$, and each rule application adds a new assertion of the form $a : C$, for some individual name a and some concept $C \in \mathsf{sub}(\mathcal{A})$. Moreover, we saw in Lemmas 3.11 and 4.3 that the size of $\mathsf{sub}(\mathcal{A})$ is bounded by the size of $\mathcal{A}$, and thus there can be at most m rule applications adding a concept assertion of the form $a : C$ for any individual name a, and $|\mathsf{con}_{\mathcal{A}}(a)| \leq m$.

(ii) A new individual name is added to $\mathcal{A}$ only when the $\exists$-rule is applied to an assertion of the form $a : C$ with C an existential restriction (a concept of the form $\exists r.D$), and for any individual name each such assertion can trigger the addition of at most one new individual name. As there can be no more than m different existential restrictions in $\mathcal{A}$, a given individual name can cause the addition of at most m new individual names, and the out-degree of each tree in the forest-shaped ABox is thus bounded by m.

(iii) The ∃- and ∀-rules are triggered by assertions of the form $a : \exists r.C$ and $a : \forall r.C$, respectively, and they only add concept assertions of the form $b : C$, where b is a successor of a; in either case, C is a strict subdescription of the concept $\exists r.C$ or $\forall r.C$ in the assertion to which the rule was applied, and it is clearly strictly smaller than these concepts. Further rule applications may be triggered by the presence of $b : C$ in $\mathcal{A}$, adding additional concept assertions $b : D$, but then D is a subdescription of C that is smaller than C, etc. Consequently, $\mathsf{sub}(\mathsf{con}_{\mathcal{A}}(b)) \subseteq \mathsf{sub}(\mathsf{con}_{\mathcal{A}}(a))$ and the size of the largest concept in $\mathsf{con}_{\mathcal{A}}(b)$ is smaller than the size of the largest concept in $\mathsf{con}_{\mathcal{A}}(a)$. The second fact shows that the inclusion stated by the first fact is actually strict; i.e., for any tree individual b whose predecessor is a, $\mathsf{sub}(\mathsf{con}_{\mathcal{A}}(b)) \subsetneq \mathsf{sub}(\mathsf{con}_{\mathcal{A}}(a))$. Consequently, the depth of each tree in the forest-shaped ABox is bounded by m.

These properties ensure that there is a bound on the size of the ABox that can be constructed via rule applications, and thus a bound on the number of recursive applications of expand. □

Lemma 4.5 (Soundness). *If* consistent($\mathcal{A}$) *returns "consistent", then $\mathcal{A}$ is consistent.*

Proof. Let $\mathcal{A}'$ be the set returned by expand($\mathcal{A}$). Since the algorithm returns "consistent", $\mathcal{A}'$ is a complete and clash-free ABox.

The proof then follows rather easily from the very close correspondence between $\mathcal{A}'$ and an interpretation $\mathcal{I} = (\Delta^{\mathcal{I}}, \cdot^{\mathcal{I}})$ that is a model of $\mathcal{A}'$, i.e., that satisfies each assertion in $\mathcal{A}'$. Given that the expansion rules never delete assertions, we have that $\mathcal{A} \subseteq \mathcal{A}'$, so $\mathcal{I}$ is also a model of $\mathcal{A}$, and is a witness to the consistency of $\mathcal{A}$. We use $\mathcal{A}'$ to construct a suitable interpretation $\mathcal{I}$ as follows:

$$\Delta^{\mathcal{I}} = \{a \mid a : C \in \mathcal{A}'\},$$
$$a^{\mathcal{I}} = a \text{ for each individual name } a \text{ occurring in } \mathcal{A}',$$
$$A^{\mathcal{I}} = \{a \mid A \in \mathsf{con}_{\mathcal{A}'}(a)\} \text{ for each concept name } A \text{ in } \mathsf{sub}(\mathcal{A}'),$$
$$r^{\mathcal{I}} = \{(a, b) \mid (a, b) : r \in \mathcal{A}'\} \text{ for each role } r \text{ occurring in } \mathcal{A}'.$$

Note that each individual name a that occurs in $\mathcal{A}'$ occurs in at least one concept assertion: for root individuals this follows from our assumptions on the structure of $\mathcal{A}$, and for tree individuals this follows from the definition of the ∃-rule. It is easy to see that $\mathcal{I}$ is an interpretation: by assumption, $\mathcal{A}$ contains at least one assertion of the form $a : C$, so $\Delta^{\mathcal{I}}$

is non-empty, and by construction $\cdot^{\mathcal{I}}$ maps every individual name in $\mathcal{A}'$ to an element of $\Delta^{\mathcal{I}}$, every concept name $A \in \mathsf{sub}(\mathcal{A}')$ to a subset of $\Delta^{\mathcal{I}}$, and every role r occurring in $\mathcal{A}'$ to a subset of $\Delta^{\mathcal{I}} \times \Delta^{\mathcal{I}}$. From Definition 2.6, $\mathcal{I}$ is a model of $\mathcal{A}'$ if it satisfies each concept and role assertion in $\mathcal{A}'$. The construction of $\mathcal{I}$ means that it trivially satisfies all role assertions in $\mathcal{A}'$. By induction on the structure of concepts, we show the following property (P1):

$$\text{if } a : C \in \mathcal{A}', \text{ then } a^{\mathcal{I}} \in C^{\mathcal{I}}. \tag{P1}$$

Induction Basis C is a concept name: by definition of $\mathcal{I}$, if $a : C \in \mathcal{A}'$, then $a^{\mathcal{I}} \in C^{\mathcal{I}}$ as required.

Induction Steps

- $C = \neg D$: since $\mathcal{A}'$ is clash-free, $a : \neg D \in \mathcal{A}'$ implies that $a : D \notin \mathcal{A}'$. Since all concepts in $\mathcal{A}$ are in NNF, D is a concept name. By definition of $\mathcal{I}$, $a^{\mathcal{I}} \notin D^{\mathcal{I}}$, which implies $a^{\mathcal{I}} \in \Delta^{\mathcal{I}} \setminus D^{\mathcal{I}} = C^{\mathcal{I}}$ as required.

- $C = D \sqcup E$: if $a : D \sqcup E \in \mathcal{A}'$, then completeness of $\mathcal{A}'$ implies that $\{a : D, a : E\} \cap \mathcal{A}' \neq \emptyset$ (otherwise the $\sqcup$-rule would be applicable). Thus $a^{\mathcal{I}} \in D^{\mathcal{I}}$ or $a^{\mathcal{I}} \in E^{\mathcal{I}}$ by induction, and hence $a^{\mathcal{I}} \in D^{\mathcal{I}} \cup E^{\mathcal{I}} = (D \sqcup E)^{\mathcal{I}}$ by the semantics of $\sqcup$.

- $C = D \sqcap E$: this case is analogous to but easier than the previous one and is left to the reader as a useful exercise.

- $C = \forall r.D$: let $a : \forall r.D \in \mathcal{A}'$ and consider b with $(a^{\mathcal{I}}, b^{\mathcal{I}}) \in r^{\mathcal{I}}$. For $a^{\mathcal{I}}$ to be in $(\forall r.D)^{\mathcal{I}}$, we need to ensure that $b^{\mathcal{I}} \in D^{\mathcal{I}}$. By definition of $\mathcal{I}$, $(a, b) : r \in \mathcal{A}'$. Since $\mathcal{A}'$ is complete and $a : \forall r.D \in \mathcal{A}'$, we have that $b : D \in \mathcal{A}'$ (otherwise the $\forall$-rule would be applicable). By induction, $b^{\mathcal{I}} \in D^{\mathcal{I}}$, and since the above holds for all b with $(a^{\mathcal{I}}, b^{\mathcal{I}}) \in r^{\mathcal{I}}$, we have that $a^{\mathcal{I}} \in (\forall r.D)^{\mathcal{I}}$ by the semantics of $\forall$.

- $C = \exists r.D$: again, this case is analogous to and easier than the previous one and is left to the reader as a useful exercise.

As a consequence, $\mathcal{I}$ satisfies all concept assertions in $\mathcal{A}'$ and thus in $\mathcal{A}$, and it satisfies all role assertions in $\mathcal{A}'$ and thus in $\mathcal{A}$ by definition. Hence $\mathcal{A}$ has a model and thus is consistent. $\qquad \square$

Lemma 4.6 (Completeness). *If $\mathcal{A}$ is consistent, then* $\mathsf{consistent}(\mathcal{A})$ *returns "consistent".*

Proof. Let $\mathcal{A}$ be consistent, and consider a model $\mathcal{I} = (\Delta^{\mathcal{I}}, \cdot^{\mathcal{I}})$ of $\mathcal{A}$. Since $\mathcal{A}$ is consistent, it cannot contain a clash.

If $\mathcal{A}$ is complete – since it does not contain a clash – expand simply returns $\mathcal{A}$ and consistent returns "consistent". If $\mathcal{A}$ is not complete, then expand calls itself recursively until $\mathcal{A}$ is complete; each call selects a rule and applies it. We will show that rule application preserves consistency by a case analysis according to the type of rule:

- The $\sqcup$-rule: If $a : C \sqcup D \in \mathcal{A}$, then $a^{\mathcal{I}} \in (C \sqcup D)^{\mathcal{I}}$ and Definition 2.2 implies that either $a^{\mathcal{I}} \in C^{\mathcal{I}}$ or $a^{\mathcal{I}} \in D^{\mathcal{I}}$. Therefore, at least one of the ABoxes $\mathcal{A}' \in \exp(\mathcal{A}, \sqcup\text{-rule}, a : C \sqcup D)$ is consistent. Thus, one of the calls of expand is applied to a consistent ABox.
- The $\sqcap$-rule: If $a : C \sqcap D \in \mathcal{A}$, then $a^{\mathcal{I}} \in (C \sqcap D)^{\mathcal{I}}$ and Definition 2.2 implies that both $a^{\mathcal{I}} \in C^{\mathcal{I}}$ and $a^{\mathcal{I}} \in D^{\mathcal{I}}$. Therefore, $\mathcal{I}$ is still a model of $\mathcal{A} \cup \{a : C, a : D\}$, so $\mathcal{A}$ is still consistent after the rule is applied.
- The $\exists$-rule: If $a : \exists r.C \in \mathcal{A}$, then $a^{\mathcal{I}} \in (\exists r.C)^{\mathcal{I}}$ and Definition 2.2 implies that there is some $x \in \Delta^{\mathcal{I}}$ such that $(a^{\mathcal{I}}, x) \in r^{\mathcal{I}}$ and $x \in C^{\mathcal{I}}$. Therefore, there is a model $\mathcal{I}'$ of $\mathcal{A}$ such that, for some new individual name d, $d^{\mathcal{I}'} = x$, and that is otherwise identical to $\mathcal{I}$. This model $\mathcal{I}'$ is still a model of $\mathcal{A} \cup \{(a, d) : r, d : C\}$, so $\mathcal{A}$ is still consistent after the rule is applied.
- The $\forall$-rule: If $\{a : \forall r.C, (a, b) : r\} \subseteq \mathcal{A}$, then $a^{\mathcal{I}} \in (\forall r.C)^{\mathcal{I}}$, $(a^{\mathcal{I}}, b^{\mathcal{I}}) \in r^{\mathcal{I}}$, and Definition 2.2 implies that $b^{\mathcal{I}} \in C^{\mathcal{I}}$. Therefore, $\mathcal{I}$ is still a model of $\mathcal{A} \cup \{b : C\}$, so $\mathcal{A}$ is still consistent after the rule is applied.

$\square$

Theorem 4.7. *The tableau algorithm presented in Definition 4.2 is a decision procedure for the consistency of $\mathcal{ALC}$ ABoxes.*

Proof. That the algorithm is a decision procedure for normalised $\mathcal{ALC}$ ABoxes follows from Lemmas 4.4, 4.5 and 4.6; and as we showed at the beginning of this subsection, an arbitrary $\mathcal{ALC}$ ABox can be transformed into an equivalent normalised ABox. $\square$

A few comments on the complexity of the algorithm are appropriate at this point. As we will see in Section 5.1, the complexity of the $\mathcal{ALC}$ ABox consistency problem is PSPACE-complete; however, the fully expanded ABox may be exponentially larger than the input ABox, and applications of nondeterministic rules may lead to the exploration of exponentially many different ABoxes, so the algorithm as presented above requires exponential time and space. The algorithm can, however, easily be adapted to use only polynomial space via a so-called trace technique [SS91]. This relies firstly on the fact that individual names introduced

$\sqsubseteq$-rule: if 1. $a:A \in \mathcal{A}$, $A \sqsubseteq C \in \mathcal{T}$, and
2. $a:C \notin \mathcal{A}$
then $\mathcal{A} \longrightarrow \mathcal{A} \cup \{a:C\}$
$\equiv_1$-rule: if 1. $a:A \in \mathcal{A}$, $A \equiv C \in \mathcal{T}$, and
2. $a:C \notin \mathcal{A}$
then $\mathcal{A} \longrightarrow \mathcal{A} \cup \{a:C\}$
$\equiv_2$-rule: if 1. $a:\neg A \in \mathcal{A}$, $A \equiv C \in \mathcal{T}$, and
2. $a:\dot{\neg}C \notin \mathcal{A}$
then $\mathcal{A} \longrightarrow \mathcal{A} \cup \{a:\dot{\neg}C\}$

Fig. 4.5. The axiom unfolding rules for $\mathcal{ALC}$.

by the $\exists$-rule form part of a tree, and secondly on the fact that the order of rule applications can be chosen arbitrarily. Exploiting the second property, we can exhaustively apply the $\sqcap$, $\sqcup$ and $\forall$-rules to existing individual names before considering the $\exists$-rule. We can then construct the tree parts of the forest model one branch at a time, reusing space once we have completed the construction of a given branch. For example, if $\mathcal{A} = \{a:\exists r.C, a:\exists r.D, a:\forall r.A\}$, then we can apply the $\exists$- and $\forall$-rules to introduce new individual names b and c with $\{b:C, b:A\} \subseteq \mathcal{A}$ and $\{c:D, c:A\} \subseteq \mathcal{A}$. The consistency of $\{b:C, b:A\}$ and $\{c:D, c:A\}$ can then be treated as independent sub-problems, with the space used to solve each of them being subsequently reused.

4.2.2 Acyclic knowledge base consistency

We can use the algorithm from Definition 4.2 to decide the consistency of a knowledge base $\mathcal{K} = (\mathcal{T}, \mathcal{A})$ where $\mathcal{T}$ is acyclic as per Definition 2.9, i.e., where all axioms in $\mathcal{T}$ are of the form $A \equiv C$ or $A \sqsubseteq C$ for A a concept name and C a possibly compound $\mathcal{ALC}$ concept that does not use A either directly or indirectly. In such cases, we can unfold $\mathcal{T}$ into $\mathcal{A}$ to give $\mathcal{A}'$ as per Definition 2.11, and from Lemma 2.12 it follows that $\mathcal{K} = (\mathcal{T}, \mathcal{A})$ is consistent if and only if $\mathcal{K}' = (\emptyset, \mathcal{A}')$ is consistent.

As shown in Example 2.13, this *eager* unfolding procedure could lead to an exponential increase in the size of the ABox. This can be avoided by unfolding definitions only as required by the progress of the algorithm, so-called *lazy* unfolding. Suitable lazy unfolding rules are presented in Figure 4.5; when used in conjunction with the syntax expansion rules from Figure 4.2 the resulting algorithm is a decision procedure for acyclic $\mathcal{ALC}$ knowledge bases. Rather than adapting the proofs from the previous section to this case, we are going to generalise both the approach and the proofs to general TBoxes, i.e., those possibly involving cyclic dependencies between concept names such as $A \sqsubseteq \exists r.A$ and axioms with complex concepts on the left-hand side such as $\exists r.B \sqsubseteq \forall s.E$. For the interested reader who wants to adapt the proofs to the acyclic TBox case, termination is rather straightforward, as is completeness, with the main changes to be done in the soundness proof. To construct a model from a complete and clash-free ABox $\mathcal{A}'$, one can use the same definitions as in the proof of Lemma 4.5 to obtain an interpretation $\mathcal{J}$ of all role names and of the concept names that do not have definitions in $\mathcal{T}$. This can then be extended to a model $\mathcal{I}$ of $\mathcal{T}$ by interpreting defined concepts A with definition $A \equiv C \in \mathcal{T}$ in the same way as $\mathcal{J}$ interprets C (see the proof of Lemma 2.10). It remains to show that $\mathcal{I}$ is also a model of $\mathcal{A}'$, where the main problem is showing Property (P1) by induction. For this, one needs to define a well-founded order in which any concept is larger than its strict subconcepts *and* A is larger than C if $A \equiv C \in \mathcal{T}$.

4.2.3 General knowledge base consistency

Next, we present a tableau algorithm that deals with "full" $\mathcal{ALC}$ knowledge bases, i.e., an ABox and a general TBox.

As a consequence of Lemma 2.16, we have the following two equivalences, and we can thus assume without loss of generality that all our TBox axioms are of the form $\top \sqsubseteq E$:

$\mathcal{I}$ satisfies $C \sqsubseteq D$ if and only if $\mathcal{I}$ satisfies $\top \sqsubseteq D \sqcup \neg C$,
$\mathcal{I}$ satisfies $C \equiv D$ if and only if $\mathcal{I}$ satisfies $\top \sqsubseteq (D \sqcup \neg C) \sqcap (C \sqcup \neg D)$.

We will extend our notion of *normalised* to TBoxes and knowledge bases accordingly: we will say that a TBox is normalised if its constituent axioms are all of the form $\top \sqsubseteq E$, where E is in NNF; and that a knowledge base $\mathcal{K} = (\mathcal{T}, \mathcal{A})$ is normalised if both $\mathcal{T}$ and $\mathcal{A}$ are normalised.

In order to deal with these GCIs, we extend the tableau algorithm from Section 4.2.1 to use the expansion rules shown in Figure 4.6: they are identical to the ones shown for ABoxes in Figure 4.2 apart from the addition of the $\sqsubseteq$-rule and the third clause in the $\exists$-rule. The former deals with GCIs, the latter ensures termination, and both will be explained later – after we have explained why termination needs to be dealt with explicitly. Regarding the latter, please note that, without the third clause in the $\exists$-rule, the resulting algorithm can still be proven to be sound and complete, but it would no longer be guaranteed to terminate.

> ⊓-rule: if 1. $a : C \sqcap D \in \mathcal{A}$, and
>   2. $\{a : C, a : D\} \not\subseteq \mathcal{A}$
>   then $\mathcal{A} \longrightarrow \mathcal{A} \cup \{a : C, a : D\}$
>
> ⊔-rule: if 1. $a : C \sqcup D \in \mathcal{A}$, and
>   2. $\{a : C, a : D\} \cap \mathcal{A} = \emptyset$
>   then $\mathcal{A} \longrightarrow \mathcal{A} \cup \{a : X\}$ for some $X \in \{C, D\}$
>
> ∃-rule: if 1. $a : \exists r.C \in \mathcal{A}$,
>   2. there is no b such that $\{(a, b) : r, b : C\} \subseteq \mathcal{A}$, and
>   3. a is not blocked,
>   then $\mathcal{A} \longrightarrow \mathcal{A} \cup \{(a, d) : r, d : C\}$, where d is new in $\mathcal{A}$
>
> ∀-rule: if 1. $\{a : \forall r.C, (a, b) : r\} \subseteq \mathcal{A}$, and
>   2. $b : C \notin \mathcal{A}$
>   then $\mathcal{A} \longrightarrow \mathcal{A} \cup \{b : C\}$
>
> ⊑-rule: if 1. $a : C \in \mathcal{A}$, $\top \sqsubseteq D \in \mathcal{T}$, and
>   2. $a : D \notin \mathcal{A}$
>   then $\mathcal{A} \longrightarrow \mathcal{A} \cup \{a : D\}$

Fig. 4.6. The syntax expansion rules for $\mathcal{ALC}$ KB consistency.

The termination problem stems from the fact that a naive combination of the ∃- and ⊑-rules could introduce a successor b of a such that $\mathsf{sub}(\mathsf{con}_{\mathcal{A}}(b))$ is no longer a strict subset of $\mathsf{sub}(\mathsf{con}_{\mathcal{A}}(a))$, and so the depth of trees in the forest-shaped ABox is no longer naturally bounded; as an example, consider the knowledge base $(\{A \sqsubseteq \exists r.A\}, \{a : A\})$ or its normalised equivalent $(\{\top \sqsubseteq \neg A \sqcup \exists r.A\}, \{a : A\})$.

For $\mathcal{K} = (\mathcal{T}, \mathcal{A})$ and any individual name a in the ABox during the run of the tableau algorithm, the set $\mathsf{con}_{\mathcal{A}}(a)$ is contained in $\mathsf{sub}(\mathcal{K}) = \mathsf{sub}(\mathcal{T}) \cup \mathsf{sub}(\mathcal{A})$, and thus any branch in a tree can contain at most $2^{|\mathsf{sub}(\mathcal{K})|}$ individual names before it contains two different individual names a and b such that $\mathsf{con}_{\mathcal{A}}(a) = \mathsf{con}_{\mathcal{A}}(b)$. If this situation arises, then the rules could clearly be applied to b so as to (eventually) introduce another individual name b' with $\mathsf{con}_{\mathcal{A}}(b) = \mathsf{con}_{\mathcal{A}}(b')$, and the construction could continue like this indefinitely. However, as we will see later, if the ABox is clash-free, then we can stop our ABox construction and use the regularity of such branches to define a suitable ABox (and hence model) without explicitly introducing b' or further "clones" of a.

To formalise this idea and thus ensure termination,[3] we halt construction of a given branch once it contains two individual names that can be considered "clones" of each other, a technique known as *blocking*.

---

[3] We could do this simply by imposing the relevant depth limit on the construction, but the approach presented is more efficient.

Definition 4.8 ($\mathcal{ALC}$ blocking). An individual name b in an $\mathcal{ALC}$ ABox $\mathcal{A}$ is *blocked by an individual name* a if

- a is an ancestor of b, and
- $\mathrm{con}_{\mathcal{A}}(a) \supseteq \mathrm{con}_{\mathcal{A}}(b)$.

An individual name b is *blocked in* $\mathcal{A}$ if it is blocked by some individual name a, or if one or more of its ancestors is blocked in $\mathcal{A}$. When it is clear from the context, we may not mention the ABox explicitly; e.g., we may simply say that b is *blocked*.

Please note the following two consequences of this definition: (a) when an individual name is blocked, all of its descendants are also blocked; and (b) since a root individual has no ancestors it can never be blocked.

As mentioned above, blocking guarantees termination without compromising soundness. To prove soundness of our algorithm, we construct, from a complete and clash-free ABox $\mathcal{A}$, a model of the input knowledge base. For this construction, if b is blocked by a in $\mathcal{A}$, then we have two equally valid choices:

(i) we repeat the structure of the section between a and b infinitely often, leading to an infinite tree model, or

(ii) instead of introducing b, the branch loops back to a, leading to a finite model with cycles.

As we saw in Sections 3.4 and 3.5, $\mathcal{ALC}$ TBoxes have both the finite model property and the tree model property. Given a consistent knowledge base $\mathcal{K}$, the first choice above leads to an (infinite) tree model[4] witness (of the consistency of $\mathcal{K}$), whereas the second choice leads to a finite (non-tree) model witness. As mentioned in Section 3.5, there are $\mathcal{ALC}$ concepts that, with respect to a general TBox, do not have a model that is both finite *and* tree-shaped. This implies that there are $\mathcal{ALC}$ knowledge bases that do not have a model that is both finite *and* forest-shaped, and explains why we must choose which of these two properties is guaranteed by our construction.

We can modify the algorithm from Definition 4.2 to additionally deal with a normalised $\mathcal{ALC}$ TBox $\mathcal{T}$ simply by substituting the rules from Figure 4.6 for those from Figure 4.2. For the sake of completeness, we will recapitulate the (modified) definition here.

---

[4] Recall that, with the addition of ABoxes, we introduced *forest* models as a generalisation of *tree* models (see Section 4.2.1).

Algorithm consistent()
Input: a normalised $\mathcal{ALC}$ KB $(\mathcal{T},\mathcal{A})$
if expand$(\mathcal{T},\mathcal{A}) \neq \emptyset$ **then**
    return "consistent"
else
    return "inconsistent"

Algorithm expand()
Input: a normalised $\mathcal{ALC}$ KB $(\mathcal{T},\mathcal{A})$
if $\mathcal{A}$ is not complete **then**
    select a rule R that is applicable to $\mathcal{A}$ and an assertion
    or pair of assertions α in $\mathcal{A}$ to which R is applicable
    if there is $\mathcal{A}' \in \exp(\mathcal{A}, R, \alpha)$ with expand$(\mathcal{T},\mathcal{A}') \neq \emptyset$ **then**
        return expand$(\mathcal{T},\mathcal{A}')$
    else
        return $\emptyset$
else
    if $\mathcal{A}$ contains a clash **then**
        return $\emptyset$
    else
        return $\mathcal{A}$

Fig. 4.7. The tableau algorithm, consistent, for $\mathcal{ALC}$ knowledge base consistency, and the ABox expansion algorithm expand.

Definition 4.9 (Algorithm for $\mathcal{ALC}$ KB consistency). The algorithm consistent for $\mathcal{ALC}$ KB consistency takes as input a normalised $\mathcal{ALC}$ knowledge base $\mathcal{K} = (\mathcal{T}, \mathcal{A})$ and uses the algorithm expand to apply the rules from Figure 4.6 to $\mathcal{A}$ with respect to the axioms in the TBox $\mathcal{T}$; both algorithms are given in Figure 4.7.

We will now prove that, for any $\mathcal{ALC}$ knowledge base $\mathcal{K} = (\mathcal{T}, \mathcal{A})$, the algorithm is terminating, sound and complete.

Lemma 4.10 (Termination). *For each $\mathcal{ALC}$ knowledge base $\mathcal{K}$,* consistent$(\mathcal{K})$ *terminates.*

Proof. The proof is very similar to the proof of Lemma 4.4, the only difference being with respect to the third part of the proof that concerns the depth bound on trees in the forest-shaped ABox. Let $m = |\operatorname{sub}(\mathcal{K})|$. By definition of the rules in Figure 4.6, we have $\operatorname{con}_{\mathcal{A}}(a) \subseteq \operatorname{sub}(\mathcal{K})$, and thus there are at most 2^m different such sets.

(i) There can be at most m rule applications in respect of any given individual name (see Lemma 4.4).

(ii) The outdegree of each tree in the forest-shaped ABox is thus bounded by m (see Lemma 4.4).

(iii) Since $\text{con}_{\mathcal{A}}(a) \subseteq \text{sub}(\mathcal{K})$ and $|\text{sub}(\mathcal{K})| = m$, any path along tree individuals in the ABox generated can contain at most 2^m individual names before it contains two different individual names a and b such that b is a descendant of a, $\text{con}_{\mathcal{A}}(a) \supseteq \text{con}_{\mathcal{A}}(b)$, and application of the $\exists$-rule to b and all of its descendants is thus blocked. The depth of each tree in the forest-shaped ABox is thus bounded by 2^m.

The second and third properties imply that only finitely many new individual names can be generated, and thus the first property yields termination. $\qquad \square$

Lemma 4.11 (Soundness). *If* consistent($\mathcal{K}$) *returns "consistent", then* $\mathcal{K}$ *is consistent.*

Proof. As in the proof of Lemma 4.5, we use the complete and clash-free ABox $\mathcal{A}'$ returned by expand($\mathcal{K}$) to construct a suitable model $\mathcal{I} = (\Delta^{\mathcal{I}}, \cdot^{\mathcal{I}})$ of $\mathcal{K}$, with the only additional difficulty being how to deal with blocked individual names. This can most easily be achieved in two steps: first by constructing a new ABox $\mathcal{A}''$ that contains those axioms in $\mathcal{A}'$ that do not involve blocked individual names, plus a new "loop-back" role assertion $(a, b') : r$ to replace each $(a, b) : r \in \mathcal{A}'$ in which a is not blocked and b is blocked by b'; and second by using $\mathcal{A}''$ to construct a model of $\mathcal{K}$.

We construct $\mathcal{A}''$ as follows:

$$\mathcal{A}'' = \{a : C \mid a : C \in \mathcal{A}' \text{ and } a \text{ is not blocked}\} \cup$$
$$\{(a, b) : r \mid (a, b) : r \in \mathcal{A}' \text{ and } b \text{ is not blocked}\} \cup$$
$$\{(a, b') : r \mid (a, b) : r \in \mathcal{A}', a \text{ is not blocked and } b \text{ is blocked by } b'\}.$$

It is not hard to see that $\mathcal{A} \subseteq \mathcal{A}''$ because $\mathcal{A} \subseteq \mathcal{A}'$ and, for all assertions $a : C$ and $(a, b) : r$ in $\mathcal{A}$, both a and b are root individuals and so can never be blocked. Note that indeed none of the individual names occurring in $\mathcal{A}''$ is blocked. For concept assertions $a : C$ this is the case by definition. For role assertions, we need to consider two cases. In the first case, if $(a, b) : r \in \mathcal{A}'$ and b is not blocked, then obviously a also cannot be blocked since successors of blocked individual names are also blocked. In the second case, it is sufficient to show that b' is not blocked. In fact, if b is blocked, the fact that its predecessor a is not blocked implies that b is blocked by some predecessor b' of b in $\mathcal{A}'$. Since either $b' = a$ or b' is a predecessor of a, the fact that a is not blocked implies that b' cannot be blocked.

The following Property (P2) is an immediate consequence of the definition of $\mathcal{A}''$ and will be used repeatedly:

$$\mathsf{con}_{\mathcal{A}''}(a) = \mathsf{con}_{\mathcal{A}'}(a). \tag{P2}$$

Since $\mathcal{A}'$ is clash-free, $\mathcal{A}''$ is also clash-free: Property (P2) implies that if $\mathcal{A}''$ contains a clash, then so does $\mathcal{A}'$. Moreover, $\mathcal{A}'$ being complete implies that $\mathcal{A}''$ is also complete:

- For the ⊓-rule, if $a : C \sqcap D \in \mathcal{A}''$, then Property (P2) implies $a : C \sqcap D \in \mathcal{A}'$. Completeness of $\mathcal{A}'$ implies that $\{a : C, a : D\} \subseteq \mathcal{A}'$ and then Property (P2) implies $\{a : C, a : D\} \subseteq \mathcal{A}''$.

- Analogous arguments hold for the ⊔- and ⊑-rules and are left to the reader as a useful exercise.

- For the ∃-rule, if $a : \exists r.C \in \mathcal{A}''$, then $a : \exists r.C \in \mathcal{A}'$ and a is not blocked in $\mathcal{A}'$; hence there is a b such that $\{(a, b) : r, b : C\} \subseteq \mathcal{A}'$ (otherwise $\mathcal{A}'$ would not be complete). We distinguish two cases:

  – If b is not blocked, then $\{(a, b) : r, b : C\} \subseteq \mathcal{A}''$.
  – If b is blocked, the fact that its predecessor a is not blocked implies that b is blocked by some b' in $\mathcal{A}'$, and that b' is not blocked (see the argument given for this fact above). Hence $(a, b') : r \in \mathcal{A}''$, and $\mathsf{con}_{\mathcal{A}'}(b) \subseteq \mathsf{con}_{\mathcal{A}'}(b')$ which, together with Property (P2), yields $b' : C \in \mathcal{A}''$. We therefore have $\{(a, b') : r, b' : C\} \subseteq \mathcal{A}''$.

  In both cases, the ∃-rule is not applicable in $\mathcal{A}''$.

- For the ∀-rule, if $\{a : \forall r.C, (a, b') : r\} \subseteq \mathcal{A}''$, then $a : \forall r.C \in \mathcal{A}'$ and neither a nor b' is blocked in $\mathcal{A}'$. We distinguish two cases:

  – If $(a, b') : r \in \mathcal{A}'$, then $b' : C \in \mathcal{A}'$ (since $\mathcal{A}'$ is complete), and Property (P2) implies $b' : C \in \mathcal{A}''$.
  – If $(a, b') : r \notin \mathcal{A}'$, then there is a b such that $(a, b) : r \in \mathcal{A}'$, with b blocked by b' in $\mathcal{A}'$, and $b : C \in \mathcal{A}'$ (since $\mathcal{A}'$ is complete). Then the definition of blocking implies $b' : C \in \mathcal{A}'$, and Property (P2) yields $b' : C \in \mathcal{A}''$.

  In both cases, the ∀-rule is not applicable in $\mathcal{A}''$.

We can construct an interpretation $\mathcal{I}$ from $\mathcal{A}''$ exactly as in the proof of

Lemma 4.5:

$$\Delta^{\mathcal{I}} \;=\; \{a \mid a \text{ is an individual name occurring in } \mathcal{A}''\},$$
$$a^{\mathcal{I}} \;=\; a \;\text{ for each individual name } a \text{ occurring in } \mathcal{A}'',$$
$$A^{\mathcal{I}} \;=\; \{a \mid A \in \mathsf{con}_{\mathcal{A}''}(a)\} \;\text{ for each concept name } A \text{ occurring in } \mathcal{A}'',$$
$$r^{\mathcal{I}} \;=\; \{(a,b) \mid (a,b):r \in \mathcal{A}''\} \;\text{ for each role } r \text{ occurring in } \mathcal{A}''.$$

From Definition 2.7, $\mathcal{I}$ is a model of $\mathcal{K}$ if it is a model of both $\mathcal{T}$ and $\mathcal{A}$. The proof that $\mathcal{I}$ is a model of $\mathcal{A}''$ and hence of $\mathcal{A}$ is exactly as for Lemma 4.5. In particular, we can show that $a : C \in \mathcal{A}''$ implies $a^{\mathcal{I}} \in C^{\mathcal{I}}$ via an induction on the structure of concepts, as a consequence of $\mathcal{A}''$ being complete and clash-free. From Definition 2.4, it is a model of $\mathcal{T}$ if it satisfies each GCI in $\mathcal{T}$. For each GCI $\top \sqsubseteq D \in \mathcal{T}$,[5] and each individual name a occurring in $\mathcal{A}''$, we have $a : D \in \mathcal{A}''$ (otherwise the $\sqsubseteq$-rule would be applicable) and, as $\mathcal{I}$ is a model of $\mathcal{A}''$, we have $a = a^{\mathcal{I}} \in D^{\mathcal{I}}$. Since a was an arbitrary element of $\Delta^{\mathcal{I}}$, this shows that $\Delta^{\mathcal{I}} \subseteq D^{\mathcal{I}}$ as required.   □

Lemma 4.12 (Completeness). *If $\mathcal{K}$ is consistent, then* consistent($\mathcal{K}$) *returns "consistent".*

Proof. As in the proof of Lemma 4.6, recursive applications of expand preserve consistency. Blocking makes no difference – it only means that the construction will eventually terminate (as per Lemma 4.10) – so the only difference is with respect to the addition of the $\sqsubseteq$-rule, and this is rather trivial: if $a : C \in \mathcal{A}$ and $\top \sqsubseteq D \in \mathcal{T}$, then Definition 2.4 implies that $a^{\mathcal{I}} \in D^{\mathcal{I}}$ in any model $\mathcal{I}$ of $(\mathcal{T}, \mathcal{A})$, so $\mathcal{I}$ is still a model of $(\mathcal{T}, \mathcal{A} \cup \{a : D\})$.   □

Theorem 4.13. *The algorithm presented in Definition 4.9 is a decision procedure for the consistency of $\mathcal{ALC}$ knowledge bases.*

Proof. This follows directly from Lemmas 4.10, 4.11 and 4.12.   □

Next, let us discuss the complexity of this algorithm. First, note that the transformation of GCIs into the form $\top \sqsubseteq D$ at most doubles the size of the input knowledge base. Next, we have explained in the proof of Lemma 4.10 that the algorithm generates new individual names that form trees in the forest-shaped ABox whose outdegree is bounded by m, and whose depth is bounded by 2^m, for m the number of sub-concepts in the input $\mathcal{K}$. As a consequence, the algorithm presented

---

[5] Remember that, at the beginning of this section, we assume that all our GCIs are of this form, which is without loss of generality thanks to Lemma 2.16.

requires space that is double exponential in the size of the input knowledge base. This is clearly suboptimal since deciding $\mathcal{ALC}$ consistency with respect to general TBoxes is known to be an ExpTime-complete problem (see Section 5.4 for pointers to the literature), and indeed optimal decision procedures exist, even tableau-based ones, the first one presented in [DGM00]. In [GN13], a more economical form of blocking is used to ensure termination, and so-called global cashing is used to deal with nondeterminism, resulting in a conceptually relatively simple ExpTime tableau algorithm for $\mathcal{ALC}$ with general knowledge bases.

4.3 A tableau algorithm for $\mathcal{ALCIN}$

The algorithm described in Section 4.2.3 can be extended to deal with a wide range of additional constructors; this typically involves modifying existing or adding new expansion rules, and may also require the modification of other parts of the algorithm, such as the definitions of clash-free and blocking. In this section we will consider the changes necessary to deal with $\mathcal{ALCIN}$, which extends $\mathcal{ALC}$ with inverse roles and number restrictions. This is an interesting case for several reasons: inverse roles mean that tree individuals can influence their predecessors as well as their successors; number restrictions mean that we need to deal with equality (of individual names); and the combination of the two means that the logic no longer has the finite model property (see Theorem 3.19), which means that blocks must be assumed to represent infinitely repeating rather than cyclical models.

In the following sections we will discuss these issues in more detail, but still not on a completely formal level. Instead, we will only sketch the ideas behind correctness proofs. The interested reader is referred to [HS04] for details and full proofs.

4.3.1 Inverse roles

In $\mathcal{ALCI}$, roles are no longer restricted to being role names, but can also be inverse roles as per Definition 2.19. Consequently, tree individuals can influence not only their successors (as in the case of $\mathcal{ALC}$), but also their predecessors. For example, if $\{a : \forall r.C, b : \forall r^-.D, (a, b) : r\} \subseteq \mathcal{A}$, then we can infer not only that $\mathcal{A} \models b : C$, due to the interaction between $a : \forall r.C$ and $(a, b) : r$, but also that $\mathcal{A} \models a : D$, due to the interaction between $b : \forall r^-.D$ and the (only implicitly present) role assertion $(b, a) : r^-$.

To make it easier to deal with inverse roles, we define a function Inv

∃-rule: if 1. $a : \exists r.C \in \mathcal{A}$,
         2. there is no b such that b is an r-neighbour of a
           with $b : C \in \mathcal{A}$, and
         3. a is not blocked,
        then $\mathcal{A} \longrightarrow \mathcal{A} \cup \{(a, d) : r, d : C\}$, where d is new in $\mathcal{A}$
∀-rule: if 1. $a : \forall r.C \in \mathcal{A}$, b is an r-neighbour of a, and
         2. $b : C \notin \mathcal{A}$
        then $\mathcal{A} \longrightarrow \mathcal{A} \cup \{b : C\}$

Fig. 4.8. ∃- and ∀-rules for $\mathcal{ALCI}$.

that allows us to "flip" backwards and forwards between a role and its inverse, so we can avoid the need to consider semantically equivalent roles such as r and $(r^-)^-$, and we introduce the notion of an r-neighbour, so we can avoid the need to consider semantically equivalent role assertions such as $(a, b) : r$ and $(b, a) : r^-$. We define Inv as follows:

$$\mathsf{Inv}(r) = \left\{ \begin{array}{ll} r^- & \text{if } r \in \mathbf{R}, \\ s & \text{if } r = s^- \text{ and } s \in \mathbf{R}; \end{array} \right.$$

and we say that an individual name b is an r-*neighbour* of an individual name a in an ABox $\mathcal{A}$ if either $(a, b) : r \in \mathcal{A}$ or $(b, a) : \mathsf{Inv}(r) \in \mathcal{A}$. In our example ABox $\mathcal{A}$ above, b is an r-neighbour of a and a is an r^--neighbour of b.

We can then modify the definitions of the ∃- and ∀-rules so as to allow for inverse roles simply by referring to "an r-neighbour b of a" (see Fig. 4.8). Note that, as in $\mathcal{ALC}$, successor and predecessor relationships depend on the structure of the tree-shaped parts of the ABox, whereas a neighbour can be a successor, a predecessor or neither (i.e., when two root individuals are neighbours).

In addition, to ensure soundness, we need to modify the definition of blocking (see Definition 4.8).

Definition 4.14 (Equality blocking). An individual name b in an $\mathcal{ALCI}$ ABox $\mathcal{A}$ is *blocked by an individual name* a if

- a is an ancestor of b, and
- $\mathsf{con}_\mathcal{A}(a) = \mathsf{con}_\mathcal{A}(b)$.

An individual name b is *blocked in* $\mathcal{A}$ if it is blocked by some individual name a, or if one or more of its ancestors is blocked in $\mathcal{A}$. When it is clear from the context, we may not mention the ABox explicitly; e.g., we may simply say that b is *blocked*.

For $\mathcal{ALC}$, it sufficed that $\mathsf{con}_{\mathcal{A}}(b) \subseteq \mathsf{con}_{\mathcal{A}}(a)$ for b to be blocked by a; in the presence of inverse roles, we require that $\mathsf{con}_{\mathcal{A}}(b) = \mathsf{con}_{\mathcal{A}}(a)$; i.e., with inverse roles we use *equality blocking* rather than *subset blocking*. This is because, if b is blocked by a, b is an r-successor of c and c is not blocked, then we replace $(c, b):r$ with $(c, a):r$ when constructing the ABox $\mathcal{A}''$ in the proof of Lemma 4.11. This is harmless in $\mathcal{ALC}$, but in $\mathcal{ALCI}$ it makes c an $\mathsf{Inv}(r)$-neighbour of a, and the $\forall$-rule might be applicable to an assertion of the form $a : \forall\,\mathsf{Inv}(r).C$ if $\forall\,\mathsf{Inv}(r).C \in \mathsf{con}_{\mathcal{A}'}(a) \setminus \mathsf{con}_{\mathcal{A}'}(b)$; $\mathcal{A}''$ might thus be incomplete, and the algorithm could return "consistent" when $\mathcal{A}$ is inconsistent (i.e., the algorithm would be unsound).

For example, consider the KB $\mathcal{K} = (\mathcal{T}, \mathcal{A})$, where

$$
\begin{aligned}
\mathcal{T} &= \{\top \sqsubseteq \exists r.C, \top \sqsubseteq \forall r^{-}.(\forall r^{-}.\neg C)\}, \\
\mathcal{A} &= \{a : C\}.
\end{aligned}
$$

With subset blocking, the modified expansion rules would construct a complete and clash-free ABox $\mathcal{A}'$ with $(a, x):r \in \mathcal{A}'$, $\mathsf{con}_{\mathcal{A}'}(x) = \{C, \exists r.C, \forall r^{-}.(\forall r^{-}.\neg C)\}$, $\mathsf{con}_{\mathcal{A}'}(a) = \mathsf{con}_{\mathcal{A}'}(x) \cup \{\forall r^{-}.\neg C\}$ and x blocked by a. However, the construction of $\mathcal{A}''$ would replace $(a, x):r$ with $(a, a):r$, and the resulting ABox would no longer be complete as the $\forall$-rule would be applicable to $a : \forall r^{-}.C$ and $(a, a):r$. Moreover, applying this rule would add $a : \neg C$, resulting in a clash – in fact it is easy to see that $\mathcal{K}$ is inconsistent.

The use of equality blocking ensures that, in the $\mathcal{ALCI}$ version of the proof of Lemma 4.11, $\mathcal{A}''$ is still complete. This is because, if b is an r-successor of a, and b is blocked by b', then $\forall\,\mathsf{Inv}(r).C \in \mathsf{con}_{\mathcal{A}'}(b')$ implies that $\forall\,\mathsf{Inv}(r).C \in \mathsf{con}_{\mathcal{A}'}(b)$, and the completeness of $\mathcal{A}'$ implies that $a : C \in \mathcal{A}'$. Moreover, we can adapt the model construction part of the proof simply by using the notion of an r-neighbour when constructing role interpretations.

In the above example, $\mathsf{con}_{\mathcal{A}'}(x) \neq \mathsf{con}_{\mathcal{A}'}(a)$, so x is not equality-blocked by a, and the construction continues with the addition of $(x, y):r$ and, eventually, $y : \forall r^{-}.(\forall r^{-}.\neg C)$ to $\mathcal{A}'$. This will in turn lead to the addition of $x : \forall r^{-}.\neg C$, at which point $\mathsf{con}_{\mathcal{A}'}(x) = \mathsf{con}_{\mathcal{A}'}(a)$, and x is equality-blocked by a. However, the $\forall$-rule is now applicable to $x : \forall r^{-}.C$ and $(a, x):r$, and applying this rule adds $a : \neg C$, resulting in a clash.

4.3.2 Number restrictions

With the introduction of number restrictions (see Section 2.5.2) it becomes necessary to deal with (implicit) equalities and inequalities between individual names. For example, if

$$\{(a, x) : r, (a, y) : r, a : (\leqslant 1\, r)\} \subseteq \mathcal{A},$$

then we can infer that x and y are equal, i.e., that in every model $\mathcal{I}$ of $\mathcal{A}$, $x^{\mathcal{I}} = y^{\mathcal{I}}$. Note that in $\mathcal{ALC}$ there is no way to enforce such an equality: for every $\mathcal{ALC}$ knowledge base $\mathcal{K} = (\mathcal{T}, \mathcal{A})$, and individual names a and b, there exists a model $\mathcal{I}$ of $\mathcal{K}$ in which $a^{\mathcal{I}} \neq b^{\mathcal{I}}$.[6] Similarly, given an assertion of the form $a : (\geqslant n\, r) \in \mathcal{A}$, we can infer that a has at least n r-successors $x_1, \ldots, x_n$ that are pairwise unequal (necessarily interpreted as different elements of the domain).

We can explicate such equalities and inequalities by extending the definition of an ABox to include equality and inequality assertions of the form $a = b$ and $a \neq b$, where a and b are individual names. The semantics of these assertions is straightforward: an interpretation $\mathcal{I}$ satisfies an equality assertion $a = b$ if $a^{\mathcal{I}} = b^{\mathcal{I}}$, and it satisfies an inequality assertion $a \neq b$ if $a^{\mathcal{I}} \neq b^{\mathcal{I}}$. We will use such assertions in our algorithm, but we can assume without loss of generality that they are not present in the ABox of the input knowledge base $\mathcal{K} = (\mathcal{T}, \mathcal{A})$: an inequality $a \neq b \in \mathcal{A}$ can be replaced with assertions $a : C$ and $b : \neg C$, where C is new in $\mathcal{K}$, and an equality $a = b \in \mathcal{A}$ can be eliminated by rewriting $\mathcal{A}$ so as to replace all occurrences of b with a (or vice versa) – for example, if b is replaced with a, then $b : C$ would be rewritten as $a : C$ and $(b, d) : r$ would be rewritten as $(a, d) : r$. We will use $\mathcal{A}[b \mapsto a]$ to denote the ABox obtained by replacing each occurrence of b in $\mathcal{A}$ with a.

As usual, the $\mathcal{ALCN}$ expansion rules will only deal with non-negated concepts, and we therefore need to extend our transformation into NNF to deal with negated number restrictions as follows:

$$\neg(\geqslant n\, r) \equiv \begin{cases} \bot & \text{if } n = 0, \\ (\leqslant (n-1)\, r) & \text{otherwise,} \end{cases}$$
$$\neg(\leqslant n\, r) \equiv (\geqslant (n+1)\, r),$$

where n is a non-negative number and r is a role.

The idea for a $\geqslant$-rule is quite intuitive: it is applicable to $a : (\geqslant n\, r) \in \mathcal{A}$ if a has *fewer* than n r-successors, and, when applied, the rule adds n new r-successors of a. Similarly, it is not hard to see that we need

---

[6] See also Proposition 3.3 in Chapter 3, where it is shown that $\mathcal{ALCN}$ is strictly more expressive than $\mathcal{ALC}$.

a $\leqslant$-rule that is applicable to $a : (\leqslant n\, r) \in \mathcal{A}$ if a has *more* than n r-successors, and when applied, it *merges* two of a's r-successors using the rewriting procedure described above, i.e., when merging b_1, b_2, being two of a's r-successors, a $\leqslant$-rule would return $\mathcal{A}[b_2 \mapsto b_1]$. Of course, this $\leqslant$-rule is nondeterministic: it nondeterministically selects two of a's r-successors and merges them. Moreover, in contrast to the other rules we have discussed, the $\leqslant$-rule does not strictly expand the ABox: it merges one individual name into another, which changes and/or removes ABox assertions. For example, if $\mathcal{A} = \{(a, x) : r, (a, y) : r, x : C, y : D, a : (\leqslant 1\, r)\}$, then applying the $\leqslant$-rule to $a : (\leqslant 1\, r)$ and merging y into x will result in the ABox $\mathcal{A}' = \{(a, x) : r, x : C, x : D, a : (\leqslant 1\, r)\}$.

Ensuring termination becomes much more problematical when we no longer have a monotonically growing ABox (see proof of Lemma 4.10): even if we can establish an upper bound on the size of the ABox, non-termination could result from repeated expansion and contraction of the ABox. Indeed, it is easy to see that conflicting number restrictions could lead to such non-termination; e.g., if $\mathcal{A} = \{a : (\geqslant 2\, r), a : (\leqslant 1\, r)\}$, then the $\geqslant$- and $\leqslant$-rules could be used to repeatedly add and merge r-successors of a. Moreover, a more insidious form of the problem can arise when tree individuals are merged with root individuals; consider, for example, the KB $\mathcal{K} = (\mathcal{T}, \mathcal{A})$, where

$$\begin{aligned}
\mathcal{T} &= \{\top \sqsubseteq \exists r.A\}, \\
\mathcal{A} &= \{(a, a) : r, a : (\leqslant 1\, r)\}.
\end{aligned}$$

We can use $\sqsubseteq$- and $\exists$-rule applications to construct an ABox:

$$\mathcal{A}_1 = \mathcal{T}(\{(a, a) : r, a : (\leqslant 1\, r), (a, x) : r, x : A, (x, y) : r, y : A\}),$$

where $\mathcal{T}(\mathcal{A})$ is shorthand for the ABox resulting from exhaustive application of the $\sqsubseteq$-rule to $(\mathcal{T}, \mathcal{A})$.[7] The $\leqslant$-rule can now be used to merge x into a to give

$$\mathcal{A}_2 = \mathcal{T}(\{(a, a) : r, a : (\leqslant 1\, r), a : A, (a, y) : r, y : A\}),$$

after which applications of the $\exists$- and $\sqsubseteq$-rules lead to the ABox

$$\mathcal{A}_3 = \mathcal{T}(\{(a, a) : r, a : (\leqslant 1\, r), a : A, (a, y) : r, y : A, (y, z) : r, z : A\}).$$

We can now merge y into a, producing an ABox that is isomorphic to $\mathcal{A}_2$ (i.e., they are identical but for individual names), and the process can be repeated indefinitely.[8] Please note that the expansion rules,

---

[7] We will sometimes use this notation to make examples more readable.
[8] This kind of example has, for obvious reasons, sometimes been called a "yo-yo".

⩾-rule: if 1. $a : (\geqslant n\, r) \in \mathcal{A}$, a is not blocked, and
2. there do not exist distinct $b_1, \ldots, b_n$ such that
$(a, b_i) : r \in \mathcal{A}$ for $1 \leq i \leq n$
then $\mathcal{A} \longrightarrow \mathcal{A} \cup \bigcup_{1 \leq i \leq n} \{(a, d_i) : r\} \cup \bigcup_{1 \leq i < j \leq n} \{d_i \neq d_j\}$
where $d_1, \ldots, d_n$ are new in $\mathcal{A}$.

⩽-rule: if 1. $a : (\leqslant n\, r) \in \mathcal{A}$, and
2. there exist distinct $b_0 \ldots b_n$ such that
$(a, b_i) : r \in \mathcal{A}$ for $0 \leq i \leq n$
then $\mathcal{A} \longrightarrow (\mathsf{prune}(\mathcal{A}, b_j))[b_j \mapsto b_i] \cup \{b_i = b_j\}$
for some $0 \leq i < j \leq n$,
such that, if b_j is a root individual, then so is b_i.

Fig. 4.9. The ⩾- and ⩽-rules for $\mathcal{ALCN}$.

when applied in a different order to this example, can result in a clash-free and complete ABox but, so far, we have striven to design tableau algorithms that are sound, complete and terminating *regardless* of the order in which rules are applied, i.e., without imposing any priorities on rule application.

In order to regain termination, both the ⩾- and ⩽-rules are augmented as shown in Figure 4.9. The ⩾-rule is augmented so that, as well as adding new r-successors, it adds pairwise inequality assertions between the newly added individual names, the purpose of which is to prevent the merging of individual names added by the same ⩾-rule application. The introduction of inequality assertions also necessitates the definition of a new kind of clash: in addition to the condition from Definition 4.1, an ABox $\mathcal{A}$ contains a clash if, for some individual name a, $a \neq a \in \mathcal{A}$; this would require that $a^{\mathcal{I}} \neq a^{\mathcal{I}}$, which clearly precludes any satisfying interpretation. This new clash condition means that, although it is still possible to apply the ⩽-rule in an "obviously silly" way, i.e., by merging two individual names b_1 and b_2 with $b_1 \neq b_2 \in \mathcal{A}$, such a rule application will immediately result in a clash of the form $b_1 \neq b_1$ in $\mathcal{A}[b_2 \mapsto b_1]$. This ensures that the ⩾-rule can be applied at most once in respect of any given ABox assertion.

The extended ⩾-rule and clash conditions allow us to bound the number of successors that can be added to any given individual name by applications of the ∃- and ⩾-rules. However, unlike in the case of $\mathcal{ALC}$, successors can also be added by the ⩽-rule: in the above yo-yo example, y is originally added as a successor of x, but subsequently becomes a successor of a when x is merged into a. To address this issue, the ⩽-rule is augmented so as to use a procedure called *pruning* to remove all descendants of an individual name before it is merged into another individual name, and to add an equality assertion that allows us to "remember" which individual names have been merged.[9] More precisely, $\mathsf{prune}(\mathcal{A}, a)$ is defined to be the ABox that results from removing all assertions of the form $x : C$ or $(y, x) : r$ from $\mathcal{A}$, where x is a descendant of a. The $\leqslant$-rule also ensures that a root individual is never merged into a tree individual: this could cause the ABox to lose its forest shape, which is a fundamental assumption underlying the algorithm, and could even result in the entire ABox being removed by pruning.

We can now adapt the termination argument from Lemma 4.10 to establish a bound on the number of individual names that can be added to $\mathcal{A}$ – which clearly also bounds the size of $\mathcal{A}$. There can still be at most $m = |\mathsf{sub}(\mathcal{K})|$ applications of the $\exists$- and $\geqslant$-rules in respect of any given individual name. For the $\exists$-rule, if assertions $(a, x) : r$ and $x : C$ are added to $\mathcal{A}$ as a result of the $\exists$-rule being applied to an assertion $a : \exists r.C \in \mathcal{A}$, and x is subsequently merged into y, then it must be the case that $(a, y) : r \in \mathcal{A}$; otherwise the $\leqslant$-rule would not have been applicable; thus, after the merge, $\{(a, y) : r, y : C\} \subseteq \mathcal{A}$, and the $\exists$-rule cannot be applied again to $a : \exists r.C$. For the $\geqslant$-rule, the inequality assertions mean that merging two individual names added by any given rule application will immediately result in a clash, and hence the rule cannot be applied twice in respect of the same assertion. Thus $\exists$- and $\geqslant$-rules can add at most $m \times n$ successors to an individual name a, where n is the largest number occurring in a $\geqslant$-restriction in $\mathcal{A}$. Moreover, because of pruning, these are the *only* individual names that can ever be successors of a. Thus the number of individual names that can be added at depth d of each tree in the forest-shaped ABox is bounded by mn^d (assuming $d = 0$ for root individuals), and when combined with the 2^m depth bound due to blocking this gives a bound of mn^{2^m} on the number of individual names that can be added to any such tree.

For soundness, the proof is similar to the one for Lemma 4.11, but the construction of $\mathcal{A}''$ must be modified so that it leads to a complete and clash-free ABox. For example, if $\{a : (\geqslant 2\, r), (a, x) : r, (a, y) : r, x \neq y\} \subseteq \mathcal{A}'$, and both x and y are blocked by z, then replacing $(a, x) : r$ and $(a, y) : r$ with $(a, z) : r$ in $\mathcal{A}''$ would effectively merge x and y into z, resulting in a clash (or, equivalently, in the applicability of the $\geqslant$-rule to $a : (\geqslant 2\, r)$). However, we can extend $\mathcal{A}'$ by adding copies of blocking

---

[9] The equality assertion is not used during expansion, but it will be useful in the completeness proof to construct a model of the input knowledge base from a complete and clash-free ABox.

individual names for each of the individual names that they block; for example, if x is blocked by z, then we can introduce a new individual name xz and add concept assertions $xz : C$ for each concept C with $z : C \in \mathcal{A}'$ and role assertions $(xz, y) : r$ for each role r and individual name y with $(z, y) : r \in \mathcal{A}'$. It is easy to see that $\mathcal{A}''$ is still complete and clash-free (any clash or rule applicable to one of the copy individual names would have applied to the individual name from which it was copied), and we can proceed with the construction of $\mathcal{A}''$ as per Lemma 4.11, except that when x is blocked by z we treat it as being blocked by xz. Finally, we can copy the equality assertions from $\mathcal{A}'$ to $\mathcal{A}''$ and use these in the model construction to ensure that each individual name occurring in $\mathcal{A}$ is appropriately interpreted.

The completeness proof only requires a straightforward extension of the case analysis from Lemma 4.6 to include the $\geqslant$- and $\leqslant$-rules. Remember that, like the $\sqcup$-rule, the $\leqslant$-rule is nondeterministic, and a knowledge base is consistent if and only if at least one such selection yields a consistent knowledge base. As with the $\sqcup$-rule, the algorithm expand from Figure 4.3 will recursively explore all possible ways of applying the $\leqslant$-rule, the number of which can escalate rapidly with larger number restrictions; e.g., if $a : (\leqslant 5\, r) \in \mathcal{A}$ and a has ten r-successors in $\mathcal{A}$, then there are

$$\frac{10!}{(5-1)!(10-(5-1))!} = 210$$

different ways of merging these successors so as to satisfy the number restriction, and this increases to 167,960 for $a : (\leqslant 10\, r)$ with twenty r-successors.

4.3.3 Combining inverse roles and number restrictions

It might seem that we can combine inverse roles with number restrictions simply by modifying the $\geqslant$- and $\leqslant$-rules from Figure 4.9 such that the b_i are r-neighbours of a. However, interactions between inverse roles and number restrictions introduce some additional difficulties that require careful handling.

First, the merging performed by the $\leqslant$-rule could destroy the forest shape of the ABox. Consider, for example, an ABox

$$\mathcal{A} \supseteq \{(w, x) : r, (x, y) : r^-, (y, z) : r, y : (\leqslant 1\, r)\},$$

where w, x, y and z are tree individuals, and x, y and z are successors of, respectively, w, x and y. Both x and z are r-neighbours of y, so the $\leqslant$-rule is applicable to $y : (\leqslant 1\, r)$; however, merging x into z would result in the ABox

$$\mathcal{A}' \supseteq \{(w, z) : r, (z, y) : r^-, (y, z) : r, y : (\leqslant 1\, r)\},$$

in which the tree individuals are no longer arranged in a tree shape: even if we ignore the semantically redundant assertion $(z, y) : r^-$, the individual name y has no predecessor. In order to deal with this problem, we can modify the $\leqslant$-rule so that it never merges an individual name into one of its descendants and, although not strictly necessary, the rule can also remove semantically redundant role assertions that result from merging an individual name into one of its ancestors, as these would complicate the model construction in the soundness proof. In the above example, this would result in z being merged into x, and the removal of the rewritten role assertion $(y, x) : r$ (which is semantically equivalent to $(x, y) : r^-$), to give

$$\mathcal{A} \supseteq \{(w, x) : r, (x, y) : r^-, y : (\leqslant 1\, r)\}.$$

Second, the construction of a finite model used in the proof of Lemma 4.11 clearly cannot work, as $\mathcal{ALCIN}$ does not have the finite model property (see Theorem 3.19). In particular, if $(y, z) : r \in \mathcal{A}'$ and z is blocked by x, then the construction of $\mathcal{A}''$ replaces $(y, z) : r$ with $(y, x) : r$ (in the proof of Lemma 4.11) or $(y, zx) : r$ (in the adapted construction for $\mathcal{ALCN}$); but in either case, if $x : (\leqslant 1\, r^-) \in \mathcal{A}'$ and x (and hence also zx) already has an unblocked r^--neighbour in $\mathcal{A}'$, then it would get a second one. As a consequence, $\mathcal{A}''$ would no longer be complete. Consider, for example, the KB $\mathcal{K} = (\mathcal{T}, \mathcal{A})$, where

$$\mathcal{T} = \{\top \sqsubseteq \exists r.A, \top \sqsubseteq (\leqslant 1\, r^-)\},$$
$$\mathcal{A} = \{a : \neg A\}.$$

We can use expansion rule applications to generate an ABox

$$\mathcal{A}' = \mathcal{T}(\{a : \neg A, (a, x) : r, x : A, (x, y) : r, y : A\}).$$

The ABox $\mathcal{A}'$ is complete, with y being blocked by x, but if we replace $(x, y) : r$ with $(x, x) : r$ in the construction of $\mathcal{A}''$, then $\mathcal{A}''$ is no longer complete as both x and a are r^--neighbours of x, and the $\leqslant$-rule would be applicable to $x : (\leqslant 1\, r^-) \in \mathcal{A}''$. Moreover, applying the rule would merge x into a, resulting in a clash ($\{a : A, a : \neg A\} \subseteq \mathcal{A}''$). The same problem arises if we use a copy yx of the blocking node; we leave it as an exercise for the reader to work through the example.

This problem can be overcome by using a stronger *pairwise* blocking condition[10] which ensures that $\mathcal{A}'$ can be used to construct a (possibly infinite) forest-shaped $\mathcal{A}''$ that is complete and clash-free and from which we can construct a (possibly infinite) model in the usual way.

Definition 4.15 (Pairwise blocking). An individual name b is *blocked by an individual name a* in an $\mathcal{ALCIN}$ ABox $\mathcal{A}$ if, for some role r, b has ancestors a', a and b' such that:

(i) a is an r-successor of a' and b is an r-successor of b';
(ii) $\mathsf{con}_{\mathcal{A}}(a) = \mathsf{con}_{\mathcal{A}}(b)$ and $\mathsf{con}_{\mathcal{A}}(a') = \mathsf{con}_{\mathcal{A}}(b')$.

An individual name b is *blocked in $\mathcal{A}$* if it is blocked by some individual name a, or if one or more of its ancestors is blocked in $\mathcal{A}$. When it is clear from the context, we may not mention the ABox explicitly; e.g., we may simply say that b is *blocked*.

When $\mathcal{A}'$ contains blocked individual names, we can construct a forest-shaped ABox by replacing them with a copies of the subtrees rooted in the corresponding blocking individual names. A subtree rooted in a blocking individual name necessarily includes the individual names that it blocks, and so the copying process is infinitely recursive, a procedure that is sometimes referred to as "unravelling" (see Definition 3.21). More precisely, the construction of $\mathcal{A}''$ follows the same pattern as in the proof of Lemma 4.11, but in the situation where $(a, b) : r \in \mathcal{A}'$, with a not blocked and b blocked by b', we add $\{(a, b'') : r\} \cup \mathsf{copy}(b'', b')$ to $\mathcal{A}''$, where b'' is new in $\mathcal{A}''$, and $\mathsf{copy}(x, y)$ is defined as the smallest set that includes:

- $\{x : C\}$ for each concept assertion $y : C \in \mathcal{A}'$;
- $\{(x, z') : r\} \cup \mathsf{copy}(z', z)$ for each role assertion $(y, z) : r \in \mathcal{A}'$, where z is not blocked in $\mathcal{A}'$ and z' is new in $\mathcal{A}''$;
- $\{(x, z') : r\} \cup \mathsf{copy}(z', w)$ for each role assertion $(y, z) : r \in \mathcal{A}'$, where z is blocked by w in $\mathcal{A}'$ and z' is new in $\mathcal{A}''$.

In the above example, where

$$\mathcal{A}' \quad = \quad \mathcal{T}(\{a : \neg A, (a, x) : r, x : A, (x, y) : r, y : A\}),$$

and y is blocked by x, unravelling $(x, y) : r$ would add $\{(x, x') : r\} \cup \mathsf{copy}(x', x)$ to $\mathcal{A}''$, which adds concept assertions such that $\mathsf{con}_{\mathcal{A}''}(x') = \mathsf{con}_{\mathcal{A}'}(x)$ and a role assertion $(x', x'') : r$ such that x'' is new in $\mathcal{A}''$, and

---

[10] Sometimes called double blocking.

x'' is (recursively) a copy of x. The recursion will result in a complete and clash-free set of assertions[11] that includes an infinite sequence of r-successors, each of which is a copy of x. In general, however, simple equality blocking (see Definition 4.14) is not sufficient to guarantee that we can use unravelling to construct such an ABox (and hence to construct a model). Consider, for example, the KB $\mathcal{K} = (\mathcal{T}, \mathcal{A})$, where

$$\mathcal{T} = \{\top \sqsubseteq \exists r.A, \top \sqsubseteq \exists r^-.\neg A, \top \sqsubseteq (\leqslant 1\, r^-)\},$$
$$\mathcal{A} = \{a : \neg A, (a, a) : r\}.$$

We can use expansion rule applications to generate an ABox

$$\mathcal{A}' = \mathcal{T}(\{a : \neg A, (a, a) : r, (a, x) : r, x : A, (x, y) : r, y : A\}),$$

in which y is equality blocked by x. Note that the $\exists$-rule is not applicable to $x : \exists r^-.\neg A$, because a is an r-neighbour of x with $a : \neg A \in \mathcal{A}'$. However, when we start unravelling, we replace y with a copy x' of x, and the $\exists$-rule *is* applicable to $x' : \exists r^-.\neg A$, because x is the only r-neighbour of x', and $x : \neg A \notin \mathcal{A}'$. Moreover, applying the $\exists$-rule to $x' : \exists r^-.\neg A$ will add $(x', z) : r^-$ and $z : \neg A$, and the $\leqslant$-rule will merge z into x, revealing a clash – indeed it is easy to see that $\mathcal{K}$ is inconsistent, and that pairwise blocking (rather than equality blocking) is indeed required to detect this.

Pairwise blocking ensures that, when a blocked individual name y is replaced with a copy x' of the individual name x that blocks y, the neighbours of x' are indistinguishable from those of x. This is clearly the case for the successors of x', as these are copies of the successors of x, and pairwise blocking ensures that this is also the case for the predecessors of x' and of x (note that pairwise blocking ensures that both blocked and blocking individual names are tree individuals, and so each has exactly one predecessor, and no neighbours other than its predecessor and successors). Thus if any expansion rule were to be applicable to x', then it would have been applicable to x. Moreover, the construction of $\mathcal{A}''$ cannot introduce a clash, as for each newly introduced individual name x', $\mathsf{con}_{\mathcal{A}''}(x') = \mathsf{con}_{\mathcal{A}'}(x)$ for some individual name x in $\mathcal{A}'$. Thus, if $\mathcal{A}'$ is complete and clash-free, then so is $\mathcal{A}''$.

---

[11] This set is not strictly speaking an ABox since ABoxes are *finite* sets of assertions, but the semantics is the same.

4.4 Some implementation issues

As we have seen, tableau algorithms prove that a knowledge base $\mathcal{K} = (\mathcal{T}, \mathcal{A})$ is consistent by constructing a sequence of ABoxes $\mathcal{A}_0, \mathcal{A}_1, \ldots, \mathcal{A}_n$ where $\mathcal{A}_0 = \mathcal{A}$ and each $\mathcal{A}_i$ is obtained from $\mathcal{A}_{i-1}$ by an application of one of the expansion rules. Some of these rules may be nondeterministic, e.g., the ⊔-rule: if $a : C \sqcup D \in \mathcal{A}$, then either $a : C$ or $a : D$ (or both) must be satisfied, and the algorithm may have to make a nondeterministic guess as to which one to add to $\mathcal{A}$. If the first such guess leads to a clash, then the algorithm must backtrack and try each of the other possible choices in turn, with $\mathcal{K}$ being inconsistent only if all such choices lead to a clash. This process is sometimes referred to as *or-branching*. Other rules can cause new individual names to be added to the ABox, e.g., the ∃-rule: if $a : \exists r.C \in \mathcal{A}$, then the algorithm may have to add an assertion $b : C$ to $\mathcal{A}$, where b is an individual name that did not previously occur in $\mathcal{A}$. This process is sometimes referred to as *and-branching*.

Both kinds of branching can be a cause of scalability problems in practice: or-branching may lead to the exploration of an infeasibly large number of expansion choices, while and-branching may lead to the construction of an infeasibly large ABox. Modern tableau reasoners include numerous optimisations aimed at curbing both kinds of branching.

In practice, DL reasoners are typically used not to perform single KB consistency tests, but to perform large numbers of reasoning tasks with respect to the same KB. A prominent example is classification: the computation of all subsumption relationships between concept names in the input KB (see Section 2.3). Tableau-based reasoners invariably include optimisations whose goal is to minimise the number of KB consistency tests performed during classification.

A comprehensive survey of these and other optimisation techniques is beyond the scope of this chapter (the interested reader is referred to [THPS07] for such a survey, and to [GHM+14] for some more recent work), but we will briefly discuss some of the most important and widely used techniques.

4.4.1 Or-branching

The technique for dealing with arbitrary GCIs described in Section 4.2.3 is simple, but extremely inefficient in practice. In fact, a GCI of the form $C \sqsubseteq D$ is transformed into the GCI $\top \sqsubseteq D \sqcup \neg C$, and thus for each GCI $C \sqsubseteq D$ in $\mathcal{T}$ and each individual name occurring in the ABox, the ⊑-rule causes an assertion of the form $a : D \sqcup \neg C$ to be added. Given a KB with a TBox containing only 10 GCIs and an ABox containing only 10 individual names, the $\sqsubseteq$-rule would thus add at least 100 such assertions to the ABox, and as many as 2^{100} different sequences of nondeterministic expansion choices may thus need to be explored. Moreover, this will happen even if the KB falls within a fragment of the logic for which deterministic reasoning is possible (see, e.g., Chapter 6).

Lazy unfolding and *absorption* are optimisation techniques that address this problem; they are among the most important and widely used optimisation techniques for tableau algorithms, and without them tableau algorithms for general knowledge base consistency would be hopelessly impractical. As we saw in Section 4.2.2, acyclic TBox axioms can be dealt with deterministically. This technique does not work for general TBox axioms, but a general TBox $\mathcal{T}$ can be divided into two disjoint subsets $\mathcal{T}_a$ and $\mathcal{T}_g$ such that $\mathcal{T} = \mathcal{T}_a \cup \mathcal{T}_g$ and $\mathcal{T}_a$ is acyclic. The lazy expansion rules from Fig. 4.5 can then be used to deal with axioms in $\mathcal{T}_a$, with the $\sqsubseteq$-rule being used only for axioms in $\mathcal{T}_g$.

Although much more efficient, even this approach may be impractical unless $\mathcal{T}_g$ is small. Absorption is a technique that tries to rewrite axioms so as to increase the size of $\mathcal{T}_a$ and reduce the size of $\mathcal{T}_g$. In its most basic form, absorption rewrites axioms of the form $A \sqcap B \sqsubseteq C$ as $A \sqsubseteq C \sqcup \neg B$. This axiom can then be "absorbed" into another axiom $A \sqsubseteq D \in \mathcal{T}_a$ to give $A \sqsubseteq D \sqcap (C \sqcup \neg B)$, with $A \sqcap B \sqsubseteq C$ then being removed from $\mathcal{T}_g$ – provided that this preserves acyclicity of $\mathcal{T}_a$. Although a disjunction is still present in the axiom $A \sqsubseteq D \sqcap (C \sqcup \neg B)$, lazy unfolding ensures that this disjunction is only introduced for those individual names a such that $a : A$ is in the ABox.

Many refinements and extensions of absorption have been described in the literature. In some respects the more recently developed *hyper-tableau* algorithm used in the HermiT reasoner can be seen as the ultimate refinement of absorption: the algorithm uses a more complex form of expansion rule that allows for the lazy expansion of all (normalised) axioms.

Even if $\mathcal{T}_g$ is empty, disjunctive concepts in $\mathcal{T}_a$ can still lead to the exploration of large numbers of nondeterministic expansion choices, and pathological cases can arise when inherent unsatisfiability is concealed in subdescriptions. For example, expanding the assertion

$$a: \quad (\exists R.(A \sqcap B) \sqcup \exists R.(A \sqcap C)) \sqcap$$
$$(\forall R.D_1 \sqcup \forall R.E_1) \sqcap \ldots \sqcap (\forall R.D_n \sqcup \forall R.E_n) \sqcap$$
$$(\forall R.(\neg A \sqcap X) \sqcup \forall R.(\neg A \sqcap Y))$$

could lead to the fruitless exploration of 2^n possible expansions of $(\forall R.D_1 \sqcup \forall R.E_1) \sqcap \cdots \sqcap (\forall R.D_n \sqcup \forall R.E_n)$ before the inherent unsatisfiability of the first and last conjuncts is discovered. This problem is often addressed by adapting a form of dependency-directed backtracking called *backjumping*.

Backjumping works by labelling concepts with a dependency set indicating the nondeterministic expansion choices on which they depend. When a clash is discovered, the dependency sets of the clashing concepts can be used to identify the most recent nondeterministic expansion where an alternative choice might alleviate the cause of the clash. The algorithm can then "jump back" over intervening nondeterministic expansions *without* exploring any alternative choices.

4.4.2 And-branching

Although blocking ensures that the expansion process terminates, the ABox constructed by the algorithm can in some cases be large enough to cause serious performance problems. This problem is particularly prevalent in cases where the ontology describes structures that are not tree-like and/or where inverse roles are used. For example, in an ontology describing human anatomy, physical connections and part–whole relations between anatomical components are naturally cyclical:

$$\text{Head} \sqsubseteq \exists hasPart.\text{Skull},$$
$$\text{Skull} \sqsubseteq \exists hasPart^-.\text{Head}.$$

The tree-shaped ABox constructed by tableau algorithms can include numerous repetitions of large parts of the intended cyclical model.

One way to address this issue is to optimise blocking conditions so as to halt construction of the ABox at an earlier stage; examples include the use of more fine-grained blocking conditions [HS02] and of speculative blocking conditions that require subsequent checking in order to ensure correctness [GHM10].

Another way to address the same issue is to try to reuse parts of the ABox rather than reconstructing them. For example, if the ABox contains two individual names a and b such that $\text{con}_{\mathcal{A}}(a) = \text{con}_{\mathcal{A}}(b)$, then it might be possible to avoid further expansion of b by reusing the result of expanding a. This kind of technique can be particularly effective if many reasoning tasks are performed with respect to the same KB, for example during classification (see Section 4.4.3), as partial results may be reusable in multiple subsumption tests.

4.4.3 Classification

Classification is a basic reasoning task that is widely used to support ontology engineering, and as a precursor to other reasoning tasks (and optimisations) that exploit the concept hierarchy. Classification could, in the worst case, require $O(n^2)$ subsumption tests, where n is the number of concept names occurring in the TBox, with each subsumption test being transformed into a KB consistency test as described at the beginning of this chapter. However, implementations typically include a range of optimisations that can significantly reduce this number. The most commonly used technique is to construct the hierarchy iteratively, using top-down and bottom-up traversals of the partially constructed hierarchy to determine where to insert each concept name – a technique known as *enhanced traversal* [BFH$^+$94, GHM$^+$12]. Both traversals exploit the transitivity of the subsumption relation in order to avoid performing useless subsumption tests; e.g., if $\mathcal{T} \not\models D \sqsubseteq C$ and $\mathcal{T} \models B \sqsubseteq C$, then we can infer $\mathcal{T} \not\models D \sqsubseteq B$ without performing a test.

Refinements of this basic technique may exploit details of the subsumption reasoning procedure in order to further reduce the number of tests; e.g., when using tableau reasoning, determining $\mathcal{T} \not\models D \sqsubseteq C$ will typically involve the construction of a (partial) model of $D \sqcap \neg C$ that might also be used to prove other non-subsumptions.

Another widely used technique is to exploit more efficient but incomplete or unsound tests in order to avoid invoking a sound and complete tableau-based procedure. A common example is the use of sound but incomplete syntax-based reasoning to identify "obvious" subsumptions; e.g., if $A \sqsubseteq B \sqcap C \in \mathcal{T}$, then we can trivially infer $\mathcal{T} \models A \sqsubseteq B$ and $\mathcal{T} \models A \sqsubseteq C$, and if $\mathcal{T}$ additionally includes $C \sqsubseteq D$, then we can also infer $\mathcal{T} \models A \sqsubseteq D$. This technique is often used in conjunction with enhanced traversal in order to determine a good order in which to insert concept names in the subsumption hierarchy, the goal being to insert a concept name only after all subsuming concept names have already been inserted. Similarly, complete but unsound reasoning techniques can be used to cheaply identify non-subsumptions, an example being the so-called *model merging* technique [BCM$^+$07, Chapter 9].

4.5 Historical context and literature review

Early description logic reasoners such as KL-ONE [BS85], KRYPTON [BFL83], LOOM [Mac91b], CLASSIC [PSMB$^+$91] and BACK [Pel91] were mainly based on relatively ad-hoc structural subsumption algorithms; see [WS92] for a comprehensive historical account and overview. An alternative approach based on model construction was first introduced by Schmidt-Schauß and Smolka [SS91]; they apparently failed to notice the similarity to the tableau calculus for first-order logic [Smu68], but this was soon pointed out by Donini et al. [DHL$^+$92]. Schmidt-Schauß and Smolka considered only $\mathcal{ALC}$, but the "tableau" technique was soon extended to support a range of constructors including, for example, (qualified) number restrictions [HB91] and concrete domains [BH91]. Moreover, an implementation of one such algorithm in the KRIS system showed that, with suitable optimisations, performance on realistic problems could be comparable with or even superior to existing structural approaches [BFH$^+$92].

Initially, most such algorithms and systems, including KRIS, considered only concept subsumption or, equivalently, subsumption with respect to an acyclic TBox (see Section 4.2.2). Algorithms for DLs that support general TBoxes and other features that require some form of cycle detection (such as blocking) were soon developed [Baa91, BDS93], but were thought to be impractical due to their high worst-case complexity. However, the FaCT system subsequently demonstrated that a suitably optimised implementation of such a logic could work well in realistic applications [Hor97].

The success of the FaCT system prompted the development of tableau algorithms for increasingly expressive DLs with features such as inverse roles [HS99], qualified number restrictions [HSTT00], complex role inclusion axioms [HS04] and nominals [HS01]. These algorithms were implemented in systems such as FaCT, RACER [HM01], FaCT++ [TH06], Pellet [SPC$^+$07] and HermiT [GHM$^+$14]. The HermiT system is particularly interesting as it uses a so-called hypertableau algorithm in order to reduce the nondeterminism introduced by GCIs [MSH09].

This line of research culminated in the development of $\mathcal{SROIQ}$, a DL that combines all of the above mentioned features [HKS06]. This combination proved to be non-trivial due to complex interactions between inverse roles, number restrictions and nominals, and leads to an increase in complexity from NEXPTIME to N2EXPTIME [Kaz08]. Nevertheless, $\mathcal{SROIQ}$ has been successfully implemented in several of the above mentioned systems, as well as in hybrid systems such as MORe [ACH12] and Konclude [SLG14] that combine tableau with other reasoning techniques, including consequence-based approaches (see Chapter 6); it also forms the basis for the OWL ontology language (see Chapter 8).

5

Complexity

In Chapter 4, we looked at concrete algorithms for reasoning in $\mathcal{ALC}$ and some of its extensions. In this chapter, we are taking a more abstract viewpoint and discuss the computational complexity of reasoning, which essentially is the question of how efficient we can expect *any* reasoning algorithm for a given problem to be, even on very difficult ("worst-case") inputs. Although we will concentrate on the basic reasoning problems satisfiability and subsumption for the sake of simple exposition, all results established in this chapter also apply to the corresponding KB consistency problem. In fact, there are very few relevant cases in which the computational complexity of satisfiability and of KB consistency diverge. We start with $\mathcal{ALC}$ and show that the complexity of satisfiability and of subsumption depend on the TBox formalism that is used: without TBoxes and with acyclic TBoxes, it is PSPACE-complete while general TBoxes raise the complexity to EXPTIME-complete. Then we consider two extensions of $\mathcal{ALC}$, $\mathcal{ALCOI}$ and $\mathcal{ALCOIQ}$, and show that satisfiability and subsumption are more difficult in these DLs: in $\mathcal{ALCOI}$, satisfiability and subsumption are EXPTIME-complete already without TBoxes. We show only hardness to illustrate the increase in complexity. In $\mathcal{ALCOIQ}$, reasoning even becomes NEXPTIME-complete (without TBoxes). Again, we show only hardness. Finally, we consider two extensions of $\mathcal{ALC}$ that render reasoning undecidable: role value maps and a certain concrete domain based on the natural numbers and incrementation.

Before starting to analyse the computational complexity of DLs, let us recall some basics of complexity theory. A *complexity class* is a set of problems that share some relevant computational property such as being solvable within the same resource bounds. For example, PTIME is the class of all problems that can be solved by a deterministic Turing machine in time polynomial in the size of the input. In this chapter, we will mainly be concerned with the following standard complexity classes, which we order according to set inclusion:

$$\text{PTIME} \subseteq \text{NP} \subseteq \text{PSPACE} \subseteq \text{EXPTIME} \subseteq \text{NEXPTIME}.$$

The reader is referred to standard textbooks on complexity theory for the exact definition of these classes [AB09, Sip97, Pap94]. It is commonly believed that the inclusions shown above are all strict, but proofs have not yet been found. However, it is known that $\text{PTIME} \subsetneq \text{EXPTIME}$ and $\text{NP} \subsetneq \text{NEXPTIME}$.

For the purposes of this book, a problem is *hard* for a complexity class $\mathcal{C}$ if every problem in $\mathcal{C}$ can be reduced to it in polynomial time.[1] It is *complete* for $\mathcal{C}$ if it is hard for $\mathcal{C}$ and contained in $\mathcal{C}$. Intuitively, a problem that is $\mathcal{C}$-complete belongs to the hardest problems in $\mathcal{C}$. For example, an EXPTIME-complete problem is among the hardest problems in EXPTIME. In particular, it is not in PSPACE unless PSPACE = EXPTIME. Since the inclusion $\text{PTIME} \subseteq \text{EXPTIME}$ is strict, no EXPTIME-hard problem can be solved in polynomial time by a deterministic algorithm. When we prove that a problem P is hard for a complexity class $\mathcal{C}$, we will often call this a *lower bound* because it says that P is *at least* as hard as the other problems in $\mathcal{C}$ (but possibly much harder). Likewise, proving that P is contained in $\mathcal{C}$ will be called an *upper bound* because it means that solving P is *at least* as easy as $\mathcal{C}$-hard problems (but possibly much easier).

5.1 Concept satisfiability in $\mathcal{ALC}$

We begin our journey into the complexity of description logics by looking at concept satisfiability in the basic DL $\mathcal{ALC}$. As has been shown in Theorem 2.17, satisfiability and non-subsumption in $\mathcal{ALC}$ and its extensions can be mutually polynomially reduced. Therefore, we can concentrate on the complexity of satisfiability since it immediately yields the complexity of subsumption as well. Note, however, that the mutual polynomial reduction is between satisfiability and *non*-subsumption, and thus completeness of satisfiability for some complexity class $\mathcal{C}$ implies completeness of subsumption for the *complement* of $\mathcal{C}$. This is not an issue for

---

[1] This is not a useful definition for the class PTIME, but we will not consider PTIME-hardness anyway.

complexity classes that are closed under complement such as PTIME, PSPACE and EXPTIME, but it is important for NP and NEXPTIME, which are not known (or believed) to be closed under complement.

When looking at the complexity of concept satisfiability in $\mathcal{ALC}$, we have to be careful about the TBox formalism that we use. As we shall see, using no TBox at all and using acyclic TBoxes results in satisfiability being PSPACE-complete; in contrast, using general TBoxes results in EXPTIME-completeness. We start with the former.

5.1.1 Acyclic TBoxes and no TBoxes

We start with proving the upper bound, i.e., that concept satisfiability in $\mathcal{ALC}$ with respect to acyclic TBox is in PSPACE.

Upper Bound

Throughout Chapter 5, we develop several algorithms with the aim of proving upper complexity bounds. In this context, we are interested in algorithms that can be described as elegantly as possible, and will not pay attention to their practical feasibility. For example, when proving an EXPTIME upper bound, we shall not worry about an algorithm that requires exponential time in the best case (i.e., on *every* input), although this is clearly prohibitive for practically useful implementations.

We know from Theorem 3.24 that $\mathcal{ALC}$ has the tree model property; that is, if a concept C is satisfiable with respect to a TBox $\mathcal{T}$, then C has a tree model with respect to $\mathcal{T}$. We can even strenghten this statement by requiring that the outdegree of the tree model is bounded by the size of C and $\mathcal{T}$ because, intuitively, every element needs at most one successor for each existential restriction that occurs in C and $\mathcal{T}$. When we admit only acyclic TBoxes instead of general ones, we can further strengthen the statement by requiring also that the depth of the tree model is bounded by the size of the input. This suggests the following strategy for deciding satisfiability: when constructing a tree model, traverse it in a depth-first manner until the whole model has been explored; at any given time, keep only the single branch of the tree model in memory on which the algorithm is currently working. With this strategy, the tableau algorithm needs only polynomial space: although the size of the entire tree model is exponential, a single branch can be stored in polynomial space.

Although, in principle, the described strategy can be implemented with a tableau algorithm similar to those presented in Chapter 4, here we prefer to use an algorithm that can be described in a simpler way. This algorithm, which is very close to the so-called K-worlds algorithm from modal logic, reduces the described strategy to its essence: it non-deterministically "guesses" its way through a tree model in a depth-first manner, exploiting that the deterministic and nondeterministic versions of the complexity class PSPACE coincide by Savitch's theorem.

It is convenient to work with acyclic TBoxes in a particular normal form, which we introduce first. To start with, we assume without loss of generality that (i) the satisfiability of concept *names* with respect to acyclic TBoxes is to be decided and (ii) acyclic TBoxes contain only exact concept definitions, but no primitive ones. For (i), note that a compound concept C is satisfiable with respect to a TBox $\mathcal{T}$ if and only if A is satisfiable with respect to $\mathcal{T} \cup \{A \equiv C\}$, where A is a fresh concept name (that is, it does not appear in C and $\mathcal{T}$). For (ii), we can replace every primitive definition $A \sqsubseteq C$ with the exact one $A \equiv A' \sqcap C$, with A' a fresh concept name.

A precursor to the normal form is *negation normal form* (NNF). An acyclic TBox $\mathcal{T}$ is in NNF if negation is applied only to primitive concept names in $\mathcal{T}$, but neither to defined concept names nor to compound concepts. There is a close relation to the negation normal form of concepts defined in Chapter 4: if $\mathcal{T}'$ is the expansion of an acyclic TBox $\mathcal{T}$ in NNF, then all concepts on the right-hand side of concept definitions in $\mathcal{T}'$ are in NNF.

Proposition 5.1. *There is a polynomial time transformation of each acyclic TBox $\mathcal{T}$ into an acyclic TBox $\mathcal{T}'$ in NNF such that, for all concept names A occurring in $\mathcal{T}$, A is satisfiable with respect to $\mathcal{T}$ if and only if A is satisfiable with respect to $\mathcal{T}'$.*

Proof. Let $\mathcal{T}$ be an acyclic TBox. We proceed in three steps:

- For each defined concept name A in $\mathcal{T}$, introduce a fresh concept name $\overline{A}$. Extend $\mathcal{T}$ with the concept definition $\overline{A} \equiv \neg C$, for all $A \equiv C \in \mathcal{T}$.
- Convert the right-hand sides of all concept definitions into NNF in the sense of Chapter 4, not distinguishing between primitive and defined concept names.
- In all concept definitions, replace every subconcept $\neg A$, where A is a defined concept name, with $\overline{A}$.

The resulting TBox $\mathcal{T}'$ is as required. As an exercise, the reader might want to prove correctness of this procedure. □

An additional ingredient in our normal form is that concepts occurring on the right-hand side of concept definitions cannot be deeply nested. An acyclic TBox $\mathcal{T}$ is *simple* if all concept definitions are of the form

$$A \equiv P, \ A \equiv \neg P, \ A \equiv B_1 \sqcap B_2, \ A \equiv B_1 \sqcup B_2, \ A \equiv \exists r.B_1, \ \text{or} \ A \equiv \forall r.B_1,$$

where P is a primitive concept and B_1, B_2 are defined concept names. This is the normal form used by our algorithm. Observe that every simple TBox is in NNF.

Lemma 5.2. *Let A_0 be a concept name. There is a polynomial time transformation of each acyclic TBox $\mathcal{T}$ into a simple TBox $\mathcal{T}'$ such that A_0 is satisfiable with respect to $\mathcal{T}$ if and only if A_0 is satisfiable with respect to $\mathcal{T}'$.*

Proof. Let A_0 be a concept name and $\mathcal{T}$ an acyclic TBox. By Lemma 5.1, we can assume $\mathcal{T}$ to be in NNF. Apply the following additional modifications:

- To break down a concept definition $A \equiv C_1 \sqcap C_2$, with C or D not a defined concept name, introduce fresh concept names B_1 and B_2, and replace $A \equiv C \sqcap D$ with $A \equiv B_1 \sqcap B_2$, $B_1 \equiv C_1$ and $B_2 \equiv C_2$. Similarly for $A \equiv C \sqcup D$, $A \equiv \exists r.C$, and $A \equiv \forall r.C$.
- Delete each concept definition $A \equiv B$ with B a defined concept name and replace all occurrences of A with B if $A \neq A_0$, and all occurrences of B with A otherwise. $\square$

As justified by Lemmas 5.1 and 5.2, the algorithm for deciding the satisfiability of $\mathcal{ALC}$ concepts with respect to acyclic TBoxes takes as input a concept name A_0 and a simple TBox $\mathcal{T}$. The central notion underlying our algorithm is that of a *type*.

Definition 5.3. Let $\mathcal{T}$ be a simple TBox. Let $\mathsf{Def}(\mathcal{T})$ denote the set of defined concept names in $\mathcal{T}$. A *type* for $\mathcal{T}$ is a set $\tau \subseteq \mathsf{Def}(\mathcal{T})$ such that the following conditions are satisfied:

(i) $A \in \tau$ implies $B \notin \tau$, if $A \equiv P$ and $B \equiv \neg P$ in $\mathcal{T}$;
(ii) $A \in \tau$ implies $B \in \tau$ and $B' \in \tau$, if $A \equiv B \sqcap B' \in \mathcal{T}$;
(iii) $A \in \tau$ implies $B \in \tau$ or $B' \in \tau$, if $A \equiv B \sqcup B' \in \mathcal{T}$.

Intuitively, a type describes the concept memberships of an element d in an interpretation $\mathcal{I}$. This description is partial since we do not require a type to contain, for each defined concept name, either it or its negation (as enforced by the semantics). We could add this requirement,

---

define procedure $\mathcal{ALC}$-worlds$(A_0, \mathcal{T})$
    $i = \mathsf{rd}(A_0)$
    guess a set $\tau \subseteq \mathsf{Def}_i(\mathcal{T})$ with $A_0 \in \tau$
    recurse$(\tau, i, \mathcal{T})$

define procedure recurse$(\tau, i, \mathcal{T})$
    if τ is not a type for $\mathcal{T}$ **then return** false
    if $i = 0$ **then return** true
    for all $A \in \tau$ with $A \equiv \exists r.B \in \mathcal{T}$ **do**
       $S = \{B\} \cup \{B' \mid \exists A' : A' \in \tau \text{ and } A' \equiv \forall r.B' \in \mathcal{T}\}$
       guess a set $\tau' \subseteq \mathsf{Def}_{i-1}(\mathcal{T})$ with $S \subseteq \tau'$
       if recurse$(\tau', i - 1, \mathcal{T}) =$ false **then return** false
    return true

Fig. 5.1. Algorithm for concept satisfiability with respect to simple TBoxes.

but it is not necessary. Observe that Conditions (ii) and (iii) resemble the tableau rules for dealing with conjunction and disjunction, and that Condition (i) resembles clash-freeness.

The satisfiability algorithm constructs tree models whose depth is bounded by the *role depth* of the input concept name, which describes the nesting depth of existential and universal restrictions in the (unfolded!) definition of the concept name. Formally, we define the role depth of a defined concept name A by induction as follows:

- If $A \equiv (\neg)P \in \mathcal{T}$, then $\mathsf{rd}(A) = 0$.
- If $A \equiv B_1 * B_2 \in \mathcal{T}$ with $* \in \{\sqcap, \sqcup\}$, then
  $\mathsf{rd}(A) = \max(\mathsf{rd}(B_1), \mathsf{rd}(B_2))$.
- If $A \equiv Q\,r.B \in \mathcal{T}$ with $Q \in \{\exists, \forall\}$, then $\mathsf{rd}(A) = \mathsf{rd}(B) + 1$.

For $i \geq 0$, we define $\mathsf{Def}_i(\mathcal{T}) = \{A \in \mathsf{Def}(\mathcal{T}) \mid \mathsf{rd}(A) \leq i\}$.

The algorithm is given in Figure 5.1. It checks the existence of a tree model $\mathcal{I}$ of A_0 and $\mathcal{T}$, considering one element of $\Delta^{\mathcal{I}}$ in each recursion step. Intuitively, recusive calls correspond to a single application of the tableau rule for existential restrictions, together with multiple applications of the tableau rule for universal restrictions.

To show that the algorithm is correct and terminating and runs in polynomial space, it is convenient to work with recursion trees, which give a structured representation of the recursion calls made during a run of the algorithm. Such a recursion tree is a tuple $T = (V, E, \ell)$, with

(V, E) a tree and ℓ a node-labelling function that assigns with each node $v \in V$ the arguments $\ell(v) = (\tau, i, \mathcal{T})$ of the recursive call corresponding to v. Thus, $(v, v') \in E$ means that the call v' occurred during v.

The depth of the recursion tree is bounded by $\mathsf{rd}(A_0)$ since i is initialised to this value, decremented in each call, and never becomes negative. The outdegree is obviously bounded by the number of concept definitions in $\mathcal{T}$. This gives termination. Since $\mathsf{rd}(A_0)$ is bounded by the size of $\mathcal{T}$ (defined in Section 3.4) and the data stored in each call is polynomial in the size of the input, it also means that the algorithm only needs space polynomial in the size of $\mathcal{T}$. Thus, it remains to prove correctness.

Lemma 5.4. $\mathcal{ALC}$-worlds$(A_0, \mathcal{T}) = $ true *if and only if A_0 is satisfiable with respect to $\mathcal{T}$.*

Proof. (only if) Let $T = (V, E, \ell)$ be the recursion tree of a successful run of $\mathcal{ALC}$-worlds on A_0 and $\mathcal{T}$, with root $v_0 \in V$. For each node $v \in V \setminus \{v_0\}$, let $\sigma(v)$ be the role name that the **for all** loop was processing when making recursion call v. Set $\Delta^{\mathcal{I}} = V$ and define, for each primitive concept name P and role name r,

$$P^{\mathcal{I}} = \{v \in \Delta^{\mathcal{I}} \mid \exists A : A \in \ell(v) \text{ and } A \equiv P \in \mathcal{T}\}$$
$$r^{\mathcal{I}} = \{(v, v') \mid (v, v') \in E \text{ and } \sigma(v') = r\}.$$

For $A, B \in \mathsf{Def}(\mathcal{T})$, set $A \prec B$ if $A \equiv C \in \mathcal{T}$ and B is a subconcept of C. Let $\prec^+$ be the transitive closure of $\prec$. The interpretation of the defined concept names is defined by induction on $\prec^+$, setting

$$A^{\mathcal{I}} = C^{\mathcal{I}} \text{ if } A \equiv C \in \mathcal{T}.$$

Note that, since $\mathcal{T}$ is acyclic, $C^{\mathcal{I}}$ is well defined when we use it to define $A^{\mathcal{I}}$. Since $\mathcal{I}$ is a model of $\mathcal{T}$ by definition, it remains to show that it is also a model of A_0. To this end, one can prove the following by induction on $\prec^+$.

Claim. *For all $A \in \mathsf{Def}(\mathcal{T})$ and all $v \in V$, $A \in \ell(v)$ implies $v \in A^{\mathcal{I}}$.*

We leave the detailed proof to the reader and only consider the case $A \equiv \neg P$ as an example. Let $A \in \ell(v)$. By Property (i) of types, there is no $B \in \ell(v)$ with $B \equiv P \in \mathcal{T}$. By definition of $\mathcal{I}$, this yields $v \notin P^{\mathcal{I}}$ as required.

(if) Assume that A_0 is satisfiable with respect to $\mathcal{T}$. Let $\mathcal{I}$ be a model of A_0 and $\mathcal{T}$, and $d_0 \in A_0^{\mathcal{I}}$. For $d \in \Delta^{\mathcal{I}}$ and $i \leq \mathsf{rd}(A_0)$, set

$$\mathsf{tp}_i(d) = \{A \in \mathsf{Def}_i(\mathcal{T}) \mid d \in A^{\mathcal{I}}\}.$$

We use $\mathcal{I}$ to guide the nondeterministic decisions of the algorithm. To do this, it is convenient to pass an element $d \in \Delta^{\mathcal{I}}$ as a virtual fourth argument to the procedure recurse such that $d \in A^{\mathcal{I}}$ for all A in the first argument τ.

Initially, we guide the algorithm to guess $\mathsf{tp}_{\mathsf{rd}(A_0)}(d_0)$ as the set τ in $\mathcal{ALC}$-worlds. Now let recurse be called with arguments $(\tau, i, \mathcal{T}, d)$, and assume that the **for all** loop is processing $A \in \tau$ with $A \equiv \exists r.B \in \mathcal{T}$. Then $d \in A^{\mathcal{I}}$ and thus there is a $d' \in B^{\mathcal{I}}$ with $(d, d') \in r^{\mathcal{I}}$. We guide the algorithm to guess $\mathsf{tp}_{i-1}(d')$ as the set τ. It remains to show that, when guided in this way, the algorithm returns true. This boils down to showing that all the guessed sets τ are types, which is straightforward using the semantics. $\square$

We have thus proved the following result.

Theorem 5.5. *In $\mathcal{ALC}$, concept satisfiability and subsumption with respect to acyclic TBoxes are in* PSPACE.

Lower Bound

We now prove that the PSPACE upper bound from Theorem 5.5 is optimal by showing that concept satisfiability in $\mathcal{ALC}$ is PSPACE-hard, even without TBoxes. This implies that concept satisfiability is PSPACE-complete, both without TBoxes and with acyclic TBoxes.

The most common way to prove hardness for a complexity class $\mathcal{C}$ is to find an appropriate problem P that is already known to be hard for $\mathcal{C}$ and then to exhibit a polynomial time reduction from P to the problem at hand. In our case, the problem P is related to a game played on formulas of propositional logic and known to be PSPACE-complete [SC79].

A *finite Boolean game* (FBG) is a triple $(\varphi, \Gamma_1, \Gamma_2)$ with φ a formula of propositional logic and $\Gamma_1 \uplus \Gamma_2$ a partition of the variables used in φ into two sets of identical cardinality. The game is played by two players. Intuitively, Player 1 controls the variables in Γ_1 and Player 2 controls the variables in Γ_2. The game proceeds in $n = |\Gamma_1 \uplus \Gamma_2|$ rounds, with the players alternating. We assume that the variables in Γ_1 and Γ_2 are ordered. Player 1 moves first by choosing a truth value for the first variable from Γ_1. In the next round, Player 2 chooses a truth value for the first variable from Γ_2. Next, it is again Player 1's turn, who assigns a truth value to the second variable in Γ_1, and so on. After n rounds, Player 1 wins the game if the resulting truth assignment satisfies the formula φ; otherwise, Player 2 wins. The decision problem associated with this game is as follows: given a game $(\varphi, \Gamma_1, \Gamma_2)$, decide whether Player 1 has a *winning strategy*, i.e., whether he can force a win no matter what Player 2 does.

Before reducing FBGs to concept satisfiability in $\mathcal{ALC}$, we give a formal definition of winning strategies. Fix a game $G = (\varphi, \Gamma_1, \Gamma_2)$, and let $n = |\Gamma_1 \uplus \Gamma_2|$. We assume that $\Gamma_1 = \{p_1, p_3, \ldots, p_{n-1}\}$ and $\Gamma_2 = \{p_2, p_4, \ldots, p_n\}$. A *configuration* of G is a word $t \in \{0,1\}^i$, for some $i \leq n$. Intuitively, the kth symbol in this word assigns a truth value to the variable p_k. Thus, if the current configuration is t, then a truth value for $p_{|t|+1}$ is selected in the next round. This is done by Player 1 if $|t|$ is even and by Player 2 if $|t|$ is odd. The *initial configuration* is the empty word ε. A *winning strategy* for Player 1 in G is a finite node-labelled tree (V, E, ℓ) of depth n, where ℓ assigns to each node $v \in V$ a configuration $\ell(v)$. We say that a node $v \in V$ is of *depth i* if v is reachable from the root by travelling along i successor edges. Winning strategies are required to satisfy the following conditions:

- the root is labelled with the initial configuration;
- if v is a node of depth $i < n$ with i even and $\ell(v) = t$, then v has one successor v' with $\ell(v') \in \{t0, t1\}$;
- if v is a node of depth $i < n$ with i odd and $\ell(v) = t$, then v has two successors v' and v'' with $\ell(v') = t0$ and $\ell(v'') = t1$;
- if v is a node of depth n and $\ell(v) = t$, then t satisfies φ.

Consider the game $G = (\varphi, \{p_1, p_3\}, \{p_2, p_4\})$, with

$$\varphi = \left(\neg p_1 \to p_2 \right) \wedge \left((p_1 \wedge p_2) \to (p_3 \vee p_4) \right) \wedge \left(\neg p_2 \to (p_4 \to \neg p_3) \right).$$

Figure 5.2 shows a winning strategy for Player 1 in G. Intuitively, a winning strategy tells Player 1 how to play the game, no matter what Player 2 does. For example, if the current game configuration is 10, then Player 1 can look into the strategy tree for the (unique!) node $v \in V$ with $\ell(v) = 10$ and at its (unique!) successor v'. It is labelled 100, which advises Player 1 to set the truth value of p_3 to 0.

To reduce the existence of winning strategies in FBGs to the satisfiability of $\mathcal{ALC}$ concepts, we transform a game $G = (\varphi, \Gamma_1, \Gamma_2)$ into an $\mathcal{ALC}$ concept C_G such that Player 1 has a winning strategy in G if and only if C_G is satisfiable. The idea is to craft C_G such that every model

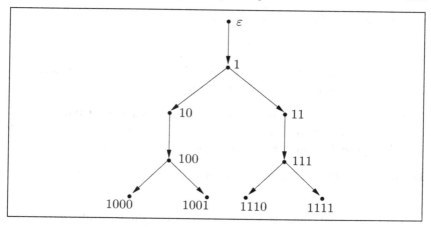

Fig. 5.2. A winning strategy for Player 1 in G.

of C_G describes a winning strategy for Player 1 in G and, vice versa, every such winning strategy gives rise to a model of C_G. The concept C_G uses a single role name r to represent the successor relation of the strategy tree. To describe the values of propositional variables, we use concept names $P_1, \ldots, P_n$. Throughout this chapter, we use $C \to D$ as an abbreviation for $\neg C \sqcup D$, for better readability. Now, C_G is a conjunction whose conjuncts we define step by step, along with intuitive explanations of their meaning:

- For each node of odd depth i (i.e., Player 2 is to move), there are two successors, one for each possible truth value of p_{i+1}:

$$C_1 = \prod_{i \in \{1,3,\ldots,n-1\}} \forall r^i.\big(\exists r.\neg P_{i+1} \sqcap \exists r.P_{i+1} \big),$$

where $\forall r^i.C$ denotes the i-fold nesting $\forall r.\cdots\forall r.C$.

- For each node of even depth i (i.e., Player 1 is to move), there is one successor:

$$C_2 = \prod_{i \in \{0,2,\ldots,n-2\}} \forall r^i.\exists r.\top.$$

Note that, since P_{i+1} must be either true or false at the generated successor, a truth value for p_{i+1} is chosen "automatically".

- Once a truth value is chosen, it remains fixed:

$$C_3 = \prod_{1 \leq i \leq j < n} \forall r^j.\big((P_i \to \forall r.P_i) \sqcap (\neg P_i \to \forall r.\neg P_i) \big).$$

- At the leaves, the formula φ is true:

$$C_4 = \forall r^n . \varphi^*,$$

where φ^* denotes the result of converting φ into an $\mathcal{ALC}$ concept by replacing each p_i with P_i, $\sqcap$ with $\wedge$, and $\sqcup$ with $\vee$.

Now, we define $C_G = C_1 \sqcap \cdots \sqcap C_4$. It is easily verified that the length of C_G is quadratic in n, and that C_G can be constructed in time polynomial in n. The next lemma states that the reduction is correct.

Lemma 5.6. *Player 1 has a winning strategy in G if and only if C_G is satisfiable.*

Proof. (only if) Assume that Player 1 has a winning strategy (V, E, ℓ) with root $v_0 \in V$. We define an interpretation $\mathcal{I}$ by setting

- $\Delta^{\mathcal{I}} = V$,
- $r^{\mathcal{I}} = E$,
- $P_i^{\mathcal{I}} = \{v \in V \mid \ell(v) \text{ sets } p_i \text{ to } 1\}$ for $1 \leq i \leq n$.

We leave it as an exercise to verify that $v_0 \in C_G^{\mathcal{I}}$.

(if) Let $\mathcal{I}$ be a model of C_G, and let $d_0 \in C_G^{\mathcal{I}}$. We define a winning strategy (V, E, ℓ) with $V \subseteq \mathbb{N} \times \Delta^{\mathcal{I}}$. The construction will be such that

(∗) if $(i, d) \in V$, then d is reachable from d_0 in $\mathcal{I}$ by travelling i steps along r.

Start by setting $V = \{(0, d_0)\}$, $E = \emptyset$ and $\ell(0, d_0)$ to the initial configuration. We proceed in rounds $1, \ldots, n$. In each odd round i, iterate over all nodes $(i - 1, d) \in V$ and do the following:

- select a $d' \in \Delta^{\mathcal{I}}$ such that $(d, d') \in r^{\mathcal{I}}$ (which exists since $d_0 \in C_2^{\mathcal{I}}$ and (∗) is satisfied by induction);
- add (i, d') to V, $((i - 1, d), (i, d'))$ to E, and set $\ell(i, d') = tj$, where $t = \ell(i - 1, d)$ and j is 1 if $d' \in P_i^{\mathcal{I}}$ and 0 otherwise.

In each even round i, iterate over all nodes $(i - 1, d) \in V$ and do the following:

- select $d', d'' \in \Delta^{\mathcal{I}}$ such that $d' \in P_i^{\mathcal{I}}$, $d'' \notin P_i^{\mathcal{I}}$ and $\{(d, d'), (d, d'')\} \subseteq r^{\mathcal{I}}$ (which exist since $d_0 \in C_1^{\mathcal{I}}$ and (∗) is satisfied by induction);
- add (i, d') and (i, d'') to V, $((i - 1, d), (i, d'))$ and $((i - 1, d), (i, d''))$ to E, and set $\ell(i, d') = t1$ and $\ell(i, d'') = t0$, where $t = \ell(i - 1, d)$.

Since $d_0 \in C_3^{\mathcal{I}}$ and $d_0 \in C_4^{\mathcal{I}}$, it is easy to prove that the resulting tree is a winning strategy for Player 1. $\qquad\square$

We have thus established PSPACE-hardness of concept satisfiability in $\mathcal{ALC}$. Together with Theorem 5.5, we obtain the following result.

Theorem 5.7. *In $\mathcal{ALC}$, concept satisfiability and subsumption without TBoxes and with acyclic TBoxes are PSPACE-hard, thus PSPACE-complete.*

As in the case of $\mathcal{ALC}$, it is rather often the case that satisfiability without TBoxes and with acyclic TBoxes have the same complexity. However, there are also notable exceptions. One example is $\mathcal{ALC}$ extended with concrete domains. For some natural concrete domains, satisfiability without TBoxes is PSPACE-complete, and with respect to acyclic TBoxes it is NEXPTIME-complete.

5.1.2 General TBoxes

The aim of this section is to show that, in $\mathcal{ALC}$, the transition from acyclic TBoxes to general TBoxes increases the computational complexity from PSPACE to EXPTIME.

Upper Bound

We prove an EXPTIME upper bound for satisfiability with respect to general $\mathcal{ALC}$ concepts using a so-called *type elimination* algorithm. The central notion of such an algorithm is that of a type, which is defined similarly to the types introduced in Section 5.1.1.

Let $\mathcal{T}$ be a general TBox. It can be seen that $\mathcal{T}$ is equivalent to the TBox

$$\top \sqsubseteq \underset{C \sqsubseteq D \in \mathcal{T}}{\bigsqcap} \neg C \sqcup D :$$

see Point (v) of Lemma 2.16 for a similar observation. We can thus assume without loss of generality that general TBoxes $\mathcal{T}$ have the form $\{\top \sqsubseteq C_{\mathcal{T}}\}$. Moreover, we can assume that $C_{\mathcal{T}}$ is in negation normal form (NNF); compare Chapter 4. As in Section 3.4, we use $\mathsf{sub}(C)$ to denote the set of subconcepts of the concept C. If $\mathcal{T}$ is a TBox, we set $\mathsf{sub}(\mathcal{T}) = \mathsf{sub}(C_{\mathcal{T}})$.

Definition 5.8. Let $\mathcal{T}$ be a general TBox. A *type* for $\mathcal{T}$ is a set $\tau \subseteq \mathsf{sub}(\mathcal{T})$ such that the following conditions are satisfied:

(i) $A \in \tau$ implies $\neg A \notin \tau$, for all $\neg A \in \mathsf{sub}(\mathcal{T})$;

(ii) $C \sqcap D \in \tau$ implies $C \in \tau$ and $D \in \tau$, for all $C \sqcap D \in \mathsf{sub}(\mathcal{T})$;

(iii) $C \sqcup D \in \tau$ implies $C \in \tau$ or $D \in \tau$, for all $C \sqcup D \in \mathsf{sub}(\mathcal{T})$;

(iv) $C_{\mathcal{T}} \in \tau$.

As in Section 5.1.1, a type (partially) describes the concept memberships of a single domain element.

The algorithm takes as input a concept name A_0 and general TBox $\mathcal{T}$ such that A_0 occurs in $\mathcal{T}$. If we want to decide satisfiability of a compound concept C with respect to $\mathcal{T}$, we can simply introduce a fresh concept name A_0, and add $A_0 \sqsubseteq C$ to $\mathcal{T}$. Obviously, the assumption that A_0 occurs in $\mathcal{T}$ can be made without loss of generality. The general idea is that the algorithm generates all types for $\mathcal{T}$, then repeatedly eliminates types that cannot occur in any model of $\mathcal{T}$, and finally checks whether A_0 is contained in one of the surviving types. The following definition serves to make the elimination step more precise.

Definition 5.9. Let Γ be a set of types and $\tau \in \Gamma$. Then τ is *bad* in Γ if there exists an $\exists r.C \in \tau$ such that the set

$$S = \{C\} \cup \{D \mid \forall r.D \in \tau\}$$

is no subset of any type in Γ.

Intuitively, a type τ is bad in Γ if there is an existential restriction $\exists r.C$ that cannot be satisfied in any interpretation in which the type of all domain elements is from Γ. Note the similarity of the set S in the above definition and the set S generated by the algorithm in Section 5.1.1. In both cases, the purpose is a combined treatment of existential and universal restrictions.

The algorithm is given in Figure 5.3. The algorithm terminates and runs in exponential time since (i) the number of types for $\mathcal{T}$ is exponential in the size of $\mathcal{T}$, (ii) in each execution of the **repeat** loop, at least one type is eliminated, and (iii) computing the set Γ_i inside the **repeat** loop can be done in time polynomial in the cardinality of Γ_{i-1} (thus in time exponential in the size of $\mathcal{T}$). Next, we prove correctness.

Lemma 5.10. $\mathcal{ALC}$-$\mathsf{Elim}(A_0, \mathcal{T}) = \mathsf{true}$ *if and only if* A_0 *is satisfiable with respect to* $\mathcal{T}$.

Proof. (only if) Assume that $\mathcal{ALC}$-$\mathsf{Elim}(A_0, \mathcal{T})$ returns true, and let Γ_i be the set of remaining types. Then there is a $\tau_0 \in \Gamma_i$ such that $A_0 \in \tau_0$. Define an interpretation $\mathcal{I}$ as follows:

---

define procedure $\mathcal{ALC}$-Elim$(A_0, \mathcal{T})$
    set Γ_0 to the set of all types for $\mathcal{T}$
    $i = 0$
    repeat
        $i = i + 1$
        $\Gamma_i = \{\tau \in \Gamma_{i-1} \mid \tau \text{ is not bad in } \Gamma_{i-1}\}$
    until $\Gamma_i = \Gamma_{i-1}$
    if there is $\tau \in \Gamma_i$ with $A_0 \in \tau$ **then return** true
    else return false

Fig. 5.3. Algorithm for concept satisfiability with respect to general TBoxes.

- $\Delta^{\mathcal{I}} = \Gamma_i$,
- $A^{\mathcal{I}} = \{\tau \in \Gamma_i \mid A \in \tau\}$,
- $r^{\mathcal{I}} = \{(\tau, \tau') \in \Gamma_i \times \Gamma_i \mid \forall r.C \in \tau \text{ implies } C \in \tau'\}$.

By induction on the structure of C, we can prove, for all $C \in \mathsf{sub}(\mathcal{T})$ and all $\tau \in \Gamma_i$, that $C \in \tau$ implies $\tau \in C^{\mathcal{I}}$. Most cases are straightforward, using the definition of $\mathcal{I}$ and the induction hypothesis. We only do the case $C = \exists r.D$ explicitly:

- Let $\exists r.D \in \tau$. Since τ has not been eliminated from Γ_i, it is not bad. Thus, there is a $\tau' \in \Gamma_i$ such that

$$\{C\} \cup \{D \mid \forall r.D \in \tau\} \subseteq \tau'.$$

By definition of $\mathcal{I}$, we have $(\tau, \tau') \in r^{\mathcal{I}}$. Since $\tau' \in C^{\mathcal{I}}$ by induction hypothesis, we obtain $\tau \in (\exists r.C)^{\mathcal{I}}$ by the semantics.

By Condition (iv) from Definition 5.8, we thus have $C^{\mathcal{I}} \subseteq D^{\mathcal{I}}$ for all $C \sqsubseteq D \in \mathcal{T}$. Hence, $\mathcal{I}$ is a model of $\mathcal{T}$. Since $A_0 \in \tau_0$, it is also a model of A_0.

(if) If A_0 is satisfiable with respect to $\mathcal{T}$, then there is a model $\mathcal{I}$ of A_0 and $\mathcal{T}$. Let $d_0 \in A_0^{\mathcal{I}}$. For all $d \in \Delta^{\mathcal{I}}$, set

$$\mathsf{tp}(d) = \{C \in \mathsf{sub}(\mathcal{T}) \mid d \in C^{\mathcal{I}}\}.$$

Define $\Psi = \{\mathsf{tp}(d) \mid d \in \Delta^{\mathcal{I}}\}$ and let $\Gamma_0, \Gamma_1, \ldots, \Gamma_k$ be the sequence of type sets computed by $\mathcal{ALC}$-Elim$(A_0, \mathcal{T})$. It is possible to prove by induction on i that no type from Ψ is ever eliminated from any set Γ_i, for $i \leq k$. Since $A_0 \in \mathsf{tp}(d_0) \in \Psi$, the algorithm returns "true". $\qquad\square$

This finishes the proof of the upper bound.

Theorem 5.11. *In $\mathcal{ALC}$, concept satisfiability and subsumption with respect to general TBoxes are in* EXPTIME.

Lower Bound

Our objective is to establish an EXPTIME lower bound for concept satisfiability in $\mathcal{ALC}$ with respect to general TBoxes. In Section 5.1.1, a PSPACE lower bound for concept satisfiability in $\mathcal{ALC}$ without TBoxes was proved by reducing the existence of winning strategies for finite Boolean games (FBGs). To show EXPTIME-hardness with general TBoxes, we use a similar kind of game, which proceeds over an infinite number of rounds.

An *infinite Boolean game* (IBG) is a tuple $(\varphi, \Gamma_1, \Gamma_2, t_0)$ with φ a formula of propositional logic, $\Gamma_1 \uplus \Gamma_2$ a partition of the variables used in φ, and t_0 an initial truth assignment for the variables in $\Gamma_1 \uplus \Gamma_2$. The game is played by two players, with Player 1 controlling the variables in Γ_1 and Player 2 controlling the variables in Γ_2. The game starts in configuration t_0 and Player 1 moves first. The players alternate, in each move choosing a variable they control and flipping its truth value. A skip move, in which all variables retain their truth values, is also allowed. Player 1 wins the game if the formula φ ever becomes true (no matter which player moved to make this happen). Player 2 wins if he manages to keep the game running forever, without φ ever becoming true.

Thus, the main difference between this game and the one in Section 5.1.1 is that players are not forced to choose variables in a fixed ordering. In particular, the same variable can be chosen more than once during the same game, and thus the game may continue indefinitely. Deciding the existence of a winning strategy is EXPTIME-complete, for both Player 1 and Player 2. In the reduction to $\mathcal{ALC}$ concept satisfiability, it is much easier to describe winning strategies for Player 2. Thus, the decision problem associated with IBGs is to decide, given a game $(\varphi, \Gamma_1, \Gamma_2, t_0)$, whether Player 2 has a winning strategy. We formally define such strategies in what follows.

Fix a game $G = (\varphi, \Gamma_1, \Gamma_2, t_0)$. A *configuration* of G has the form (i, t) with $i \in \{1, 2\}$ the player to move next and t a truth assignment for all variables in $\Gamma_1 \uplus \Gamma_2$. The *initial* configuration is $(1, t_0)$. A truth assignment t' is a *p-variation* of a truth assignment t, for $p \in \Gamma_1 \cup \Gamma_2$, if $t' = t$ or t' is obtained from t by flipping the truth value of p. It is a Γ_i-variation of t if it is a p-variation of t for some $p \in \Gamma_i$, $i \in \{1, 2\}$. A *winning strategy* for Player 2 in G is an infinite node-labelled tree

(V, E, ℓ), where ℓ assigns to each node $v \in V$ a configuration $\ell(v)$ such that

- the root is labelled with the initial configuration;
- if $\ell(v) = (2, t)$, then v has one successor v' with $\ell(v') = (1, t')$, t' a Γ_2-variation of t;
- if $\ell(v) = (1, t)$, then v has successors $v_0, \ldots, v_{|\Gamma_1|}$, $\ell(v_i) = (2, t_i)$ for $i < |\Gamma_1|$, such that $t_0, \ldots, t_{|\Gamma_1|}$ are all Γ_1-variations of t;
- if $\ell(v) = (i, t)$, then t does not satisfy φ.

Note that every configuration in which Player 1 is to move has $|\Gamma_1| + 1$ successors: one for each variable in Γ_1 that he can choose to flip and one for the skip move. In contrast to the finite strategies used in Section 5.1.1, the strategies above are trees in which every branch is infinite.

To reduce the existence of winning strategies for Player 2 in IBGs to satisfiability with respect to general $\mathcal{ALC}$ TBoxes, we transform a game instance $G = (\varphi, \Gamma_1, \Gamma_2, t_0)$ into a TBox $\mathcal{T}_G$ and select a concept name I such that Player 2 has a winning strategy in G if and only if I is satisfiable with respect to $\mathcal{T}_G$. Similarly to what was done in Section 5.1.1, the idea is that every joint model of I and $\mathcal{T}_G$ describes a winning strategy for Player 2 in G and, vice versa, every such winning strategy gives rise to a model of I and $\mathcal{T}_G$. Let $\Gamma_1 = \{p_1, \ldots, p_m\}$ and $\Gamma_2 = \{p_{m+1}, \ldots, p_n\}$. The TBox $\mathcal{T}_G$ uses a single role name r to represent the edges of the strategy tree, concept names $P_1, \ldots, P_n$ to describe truth values of the variables, T_1, T_2 to describe whether it is the turn of Player 1 or Player 2, and $F_1, \ldots, F_n$ to indicate which variable has been flipped in order to reach the current configuration. We now assemble $\mathcal{T}_G$:

- The initial configuration is as required:

$$I \sqsubseteq T_1 \sqcap \underset{1 \leq i \leq n, \, t_0(p_i)=0}{\bigsqcap} \neg P_i \sqcap \underset{1 \leq i \leq n, \, t_0(p_i)=1}{\bigsqcap} P_i.$$

- If it is the turn of Player 1, then there are $|\Gamma_1|+1$ successors:

$$T_1 \sqsubseteq \exists r.(\neg F_0 \sqcap \cdots \sqcap \neg F_{n-1}) \sqcap \underset{1 \leq i \leq m}{\bigsqcap} \exists r.F_i.$$

- If it is the turn of Player 2, then there is one successor:

$$T_2 \sqsubseteq \exists r.(\neg F_0 \sqcap \cdots \sqcap \neg F_{n-1}) \sqcup \underset{m < i \leq n}{\bigsqcup} \exists r.F_i.$$

- At most one variable is flipped in each move:

$$\top \sqsubseteq \prod_{1 \le i < j \le n} \neg(F_i \sqcap F_j).$$

- Variables that are flipped change their truth value:

$$\top \sqsubseteq \prod_{1 \le i \le n} \left(\, (\, P_i \to \forall r.(F_i \to \neg P_i) \,) \sqcap (\, \neg P_i \to \forall r.(F_i \to P_i) \,) \, \right).$$

- Variables that are not flipped keep their truth value:

$$\top \sqsubseteq \prod_{1 \le i \le n} \left(\, (\, P_i \to \forall r.(\neg F_i \to P_i) \,) \sqcap (\, \neg P_i \to \forall r.(\neg F_i \to \neg P_i) \,) \, \right).$$

- The players alternate:

$$T_1 \sqsubseteq \forall r.T_2 \qquad \text{and} \qquad T_2 \sqsubseteq \forall r.T_1.$$

- The formula φ is never satisfied:

$$\top \sqsubseteq \neg\varphi^*,$$

where φ^* denotes the result of converting φ into an $\mathcal{ALC}$ concept by replacing each p_i with P_i, $\sqcap$ with $\wedge$, and $\sqcup$ with $\vee$.

The TBox $\mathcal{T}_G$ is simply the set of all the TBox statements listed above. It is easily verified that the size of $\mathcal{T}_G$ is polynomial in that of G, and that $\mathcal{T}_G$ can be computed from G in polynomial time. The next lemma states that the reduction is correct.

Lemma 5.12. *Player 2 has a winning strategy in G if and only if I is satisfiable with respect to $\mathcal{T}_G$.*

The proof is similar to that of Lemma 5.6. Details are left as an exercise. Thus, we have established the desired EXPTIME lower bound. Together with Theorem 5.11, we obtain the following.

Theorem 5.13. *In $\mathcal{ALC}$, concept satisfiability and subsumption with respect to general TBoxes are EXPTIME-hard, thus EXPTIME-complete.*

Comparing Theorem 5.13 with the PSPACE results obtained in Section 5.1.1, one may wonder whether it is the particular shape of acyclic TBoxes or their acyclicity that makes reasoning with them easier than with general TBoxes. We show here that the latter is the case. Let a *classical TBox* $\mathcal{T}$ be an acyclic TBox with the acyclicity condition dropped; that is, all statements in $\mathcal{T}$ are of the form $A \equiv C$ or $A \sqsubseteq C$ with A a concept name, and left-hand sides have to be unique. For example, $\mathcal{T} = \{A \equiv \exists r.A\}$ is a classical TBox, but not an acyclic one. We show that concept satisfiability and subsumption with respect to classical TBoxes is not simpler than with respect to general TBoxes, namely ExpTime-complete. To do this, it suffices to observe that satisfiability of concepts with respect to general TBoxes can be polynomially reduced to satisfiability of concepts with respect to classical TBoxes.

Lemma 5.14. *Let $\mathcal{T}$ be a general $\mathcal{ALC}$ TBox, C an $\mathcal{ALC}$ concept and A a concept name not appearing in $\mathcal{T}$ and C. Then C is satisfiable with respect to $\mathcal{T}$ if and only if it is satisfiable with respect to the classical TBox*

$$\mathcal{T}' = \{\, A \equiv \neg A \sqcup (\underset{C \sqsubseteq D \in \mathcal{T}}{\sqcap} C \to D)\,\}.$$

Proof. (only if) Let $\mathcal{I}$ be a model of C and $\mathcal{T}$, and let $\mathcal{J}$ be obtained from $\mathcal{I}$ by setting $A^{\mathcal{I}} = \Delta^{\mathcal{I}}$. It is easily seen that $\mathcal{J}$ is a model of C and $\mathcal{T}'$.

(if) Let $\mathcal{I}$ be a model if C and $\mathcal{T}'$. We show that $\mathcal{I}$ is also a model of $\mathcal{T}$. Take a $C \sqsubseteq D \in \mathcal{T}$ and a $d \in \Delta^{\mathcal{I}}$. Assume $d \notin A^{\mathcal{I}}$. Then reading the concept definition in $\mathcal{T}'$ from right to left, we get $d \in A^{\mathcal{I}}$, which is a contradiction. Thus $d \in A^{\mathcal{I}}$. Now read the same concept definition from left to right to deduce that $d \in (C \to D)^{\mathcal{I}}$. Since this holds independently of the choice of $C \sqsubseteq D$ and d, we conclude that $\mathcal{I}$ is a model of $\mathcal{T}$. $\qquad\square$

5.2 Concept satisfiability beyond $\mathcal{ALC}$

Adding more expressive power to $\mathcal{ALC}$ sometimes leads to an increase in computational complexity, and sometimes not. For example, the DLs $\mathcal{ALCI}$, $\mathcal{ALCQ}$ and $\mathcal{ALCIQ}$ introduced in Chapter 3 behave like $\mathcal{ALC}$: reasoning is PSpace-complete without TBoxes and with acyclic TBoxes, and it is ExpTime-complete with general TBoxes. In this section, we review two extensions of $\mathcal{ALC}$ that are less well behaved. We prove only lower bounds to illustrate the complications introduced by the additional constructors. For corresponding upper bounds, we refer to the literature.

5.2.1 $\mathcal{ALC}$ with inverse roles and nominals

Recall that $\mathcal{ALCOI}$ is the extension of $\mathcal{ALC}$ with inverse roles and nominals. In this DL, satisfiability with respect to general TBoxes has the same complexity as in $\mathcal{ALC}$, namely ExpTime-complete. Interestingly,

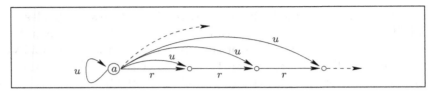

Fig. 5.4. A model of the concept C.

the complexity of concept satisfiability in $\mathcal{ALCOI}$ remains ExpTime-complete if we disallow TBoxes or allow only acyclic TBoxes, and thus $\mathcal{ALCOI}$ is more difficult than $\mathcal{ALC}$ in these cases. The increase in complexity is due to an interaction between inverse roles and nominals that leads to a more complex model theory. For example, in $\mathcal{ALC}$ (and $\mathcal{ALCI}$ and $\mathcal{ALCO}$), it is not possible to enforce that a model contains an infinite (possibly cyclic) r-chain for a role r without using a general TBox. In $\mathcal{ALCOI}$, this is easy:

$$C = \{a\} \sqcap \exists u.\{a\} \sqcap \forall u.\exists r.\exists u^-.\{a\}.$$

This concept enforces an infinite r-chain, as shown in Figure 5.4. PSpace algorithms such as $\mathcal{ALC}$-World cannot deal with such models since they rely on polynomially depth-bounded models. A variation of the above concept can be used for proving ExpTime-hardness.

Theorem 5.15. *In $\mathcal{ALCOI}$, concept satisfiability and subsumption (without TBoxes) are* ExpTime*-hard.*

Proof. We reduce satisfiability of $\mathcal{ALC}$ concepts with respect to general TBoxes. Let C be an $\mathcal{ALC}$ concept and $\mathcal{T}$ a general $\mathcal{ALC}$ TBox. Let $r_0, \ldots, r_{k-1}$ be all role names that occur in C and $\mathcal{T}$ and their inverses. Construct an $\mathcal{ALCOI}$ concept

$$D = C \sqcap \{a\} \sqcap \exists u.\{a\} \sqcap \forall u.\Big(\bigsqcap_{C \sqsubseteq D \in \mathcal{T}} C \to D\Big) \sqcap \forall u.\Big(\bigsqcap_{i<k} \forall r_i.\exists u^-.\{a\}\Big),$$

where u is a fresh role name. Then C is satisfiable with respect to $\mathcal{T}$ if and only if D is satisfiable.

(only if) Let $\mathcal{I}$ be a model of C and $\mathcal{T}$, and let $d_0 \in C^{\mathcal{I}}$. Modify $\mathcal{I}$ by setting $a^{\mathcal{I}} = d_0$ and $u^{\mathcal{I}} = \Delta^{\mathcal{I}} \times \Delta^{\mathcal{I}}$. It is easily seen that the modified interpretation is a model of D.

(if) Let $\mathcal{I}$ be a model of D, and $d_0 \in D^{\mathcal{I}}$. Let $\Delta^{\mathcal{J}}$ be the restriction of $\Delta^{\mathcal{I}}$ to those elements d such that d is reachable from d_0 by travelling an arbitrary number of steps along roles $r_0, \ldots, r_{k-1}$, and let $\mathcal{J}$ be the restriction of $\mathcal{I}$ to $\Delta^{\mathcal{J}}$. To make sure that all nominals are mapped to the restricted domain, put $b^{\mathcal{J}} = d_0$ for all individual names b (note that, consequently, $a^{\mathcal{J}} = a^{\mathcal{I}} = d_0$). By induction on the structure of E, it is possible to prove the following.

Claim. *For all ALCOI concepts E that contain no nominals except $\{a\}$ and all $d \in \Delta^{\mathcal{J}}$, we have $d \in E^{\mathcal{I}}$ if and only if $d \in E^{\mathcal{J}}$.*

By this claim, $d_0 \in D^{\mathcal{J}}$, and thus $d_0 \in C^{\mathcal{J}}$. It thus remains to prove that $\mathcal{J}$ is a model of $\mathcal{T}$. Let $E \sqsubseteq F \in \mathcal{T}$ and $d \in E^{\mathcal{J}}$. By the claim, $d \in E^{\mathcal{I}}$. Since d is reachable from d_0 along the roles $r_0, \ldots, r_{k-1}$ and by definition of D, $d \in (E \to F)^{\mathcal{I}}$, and thus $d \in F^{\mathcal{I}}$. By applying the claim once more, we get $d \in F^{\mathcal{J}}$ as required. $\qquad\square$

It is interesting that a single nominal suffices to prove this lower bound.

5.2.2 Further adding number restrictions

If we extend the description logic $\mathcal{ALCOI}$ from the previous section with qualifying number restrictions, the computational complexity further increases. In the resulting DL $\mathcal{ALCOIQ}$, concept satisfiability is NExpTime-complete whether or not TBoxes are present. Indeed, satisfiability of $\mathcal{ALCOIQ}$ concepts with respect to general TBoxes can be polynomially reduced to satisfiability of $\mathcal{ALCOIQ}$ concepts without TBoxes using the construction from the proof of Theorem 5.15, and thus satisfiability with and without TBoxes is of identical complexity. In this section, we prove NExpTime-hardness of satisfiability in $\mathcal{ALCOIQ}$ with respect to general TBoxes, and thus also without TBoxes.

Being closely related to the two-variable fragment of first-order logic extended with counting quantifiers, $\mathcal{ALCOIQ}$ has a more subtle model theory than the description logics that we have been concerned with so far. In particular, $\mathcal{ALCOIQ}$ concepts can enforce interpretations that are not tree-shaped. This is exploited in the subsequent proof, which is by a reduction of a NExpTime-complete version of the tiling problem and involves enforcing interpretations that have the shape of a torus. On an intuitive level, this tiling problem can be framed as follows. A *tile* is of square shape and has coloured edges. A *tile type* is a way to colour the edges of a tile. We are given a finite number of tile types, and have an unlimited supply of tiles of each type available. Additionally, we are given an initial sequence of tiles $t_0, \ldots, t_{n-1}$. The problem is whether

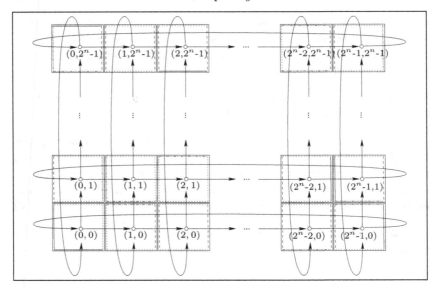

Fig. 5.5. An illustration of a tiling, where we use line styles instead of colours.

we can produce a tiling of the torus of size $2^{n+1} \times 2^{n+1}$ such that (i) all horizontally or vertically adjacent tiles are coloured identically at their touching edges and (ii) the position $(i, 0)$ is covered with t_i, for all $i < n$. See Figure 5.5 for an illustration.

Definition 5.16. A *torus tiling problem* P is a triple (T, H, V), where T is a finite set of *tile types* and $H, V \subseteq T \times T$ represent the horizontal and vertical matching conditions. Let P be a torus tiling problem and $c = t_0 \cdots t_{n-1} \in T^n$ an *initial condition*. A mapping

$$\tau : \{0, \ldots, 2^n - 1\} \times \{0, \ldots, 2^n - 1\} \to T$$

is a *solution* for P and c if and only if, for all $i, j < 2^{n}$, the following hold:

- if $\tau(i, j) = t$ and $\tau(i \oplus_{2^n} 1, j) = t'$, then $(t, t') \in H$;
- if $\tau(i, j) = t$ and $\tau(i, j \oplus_{2^n} 1) = t'$, then $(t, t') \in V$;
- $\tau(i, 0) = c_i$ for $i < n$,

where $\oplus_i$ denotes addition modulo i.

We want to reduce the torus tiling problem to satisfiability of $\mathcal{ALCOIQ}$ concepts with respect to general TBoxes. To this end, we show how to convert a torus tiling problem P and initial condition c

into a TBox $\mathcal{T}_{P,c}$ such that P and c have a solution if and only if $\top$ is satisfiable with respect to $\mathcal{T}_{P,c}$ (that is, if $\mathcal{T}_{P,c}$ has any model at all). The construction is such that models of $\mathcal{T}_{P,c}$ take the form of a torus that encodes solutions for P and c, and conversely, each such solution gives rise to a torus-shaped model of $\mathcal{T}_{P,c}$.

Let $P = (T, H, V)$ and $c = t_0 \cdots t_{n-1}$. We now show how to assemble the TBox $\mathcal{T}_{P,c}$. With every domain element d from a model $\mathcal{I}$ of $\mathcal{T}_{P,c}$, we associate a position $(x_d, y_d) \in \{0, \ldots, 2^n - 1\} \times \{0, \ldots, 2^n - 1\}$ in the torus. To this end, we introduce concept names $X_0, \ldots, X_{n-1}$ and $Y_0, \ldots, Y_{n-1}$. For any domain element d, we identify x_d with the number whose binary representation has a one in the ith position if $d \in X_i^{\mathcal{I}}$ and a zero otherwise (for all $i < n$); y_d is defined in the same way using the concept names $Y_0, \ldots, Y_{n-1}$, where in both cases we assume that the least significant bit is at position 0. To represent neighbourhood in the torus, we use role names r_x (horizontal neighbours to the right) and r_y (vertical neighbours to the top).

We now describe the desired behaviour of the concept and role names just introduced, starting by saying that every node in the torus has a (right) horizontal neighbour and an (upper) vertical neighbour:

$$\top \sqsubseteq \exists r_x.\top \sqcap \exists r_y.\top.$$

Next, we synchronise the positions represented by the concept names $X_0, \ldots, X_{n-1}, Y_0, \ldots, Y_{n-1}$ with the neighbourhoods represented by the role names r_x, r_y. When travelling along r_x the vertical position should not change, and likewise for r_y and the horizontal position:

$$
\begin{aligned}
Y_i \sqsubseteq \forall r_x.Y_i \quad &\text{and} \quad \neg Y_i \sqsubseteq \forall r_x.\neg Y_i \quad &\text{for all } i \leq n, \\
X_i \sqsubseteq \forall r_y.X_i \quad &\text{and} \quad \neg X_i \sqsubseteq \forall r_y.\neg X_i \quad &\text{for all } i \leq n.
\end{aligned}
$$

It is slightly more complicated to ensure that the horizontal position is incremented when travelling along r_x and likewise for the vertical position and r_y. We start with r_x:

$$\bigsqcap_{j<i} X_j \sqsubseteq (X_i \to \forall r_x.\neg X_i) \sqcap (\neg X_i \to \forall r_x.X_i) \quad \text{for all } i < n,$$

$$\bigsqcup_{j<i} \neg X_j \sqsubseteq (X_i \to \forall r_x.X_i) \sqcap (\neg X_i \to \forall r_x.\neg X_i) \quad \text{for all } i < n.$$

These GCIs capture binary incrementation in a straightforward way: if bits 0 to $i-1$ are all one, then bit i is flipped; if bits 0 to $i-1$ include at least one 0-bit, then bit i retains its value. Note that in the case that $i = 0$, the conjunction on the left-hand side of the top-most GCI is empty (thus equivalent to $\top$) and so is the disjunction on the left-hand side of the second GCI (which is thus equivalent to $\bot$). We also add the corresponding statements for incrementation of the vertical position along r_y, which are analogous:

$$\underset{j<i}{\bigsqcap} Y_j \sqsubseteq (Y_i \to \forall r_y.\neg Y_i) \sqcap (\neg Y_i \to \forall r_y.Y_i) \quad \text{for all } i < n,$$

$$\underset{j<i}{\bigsqcup} \neg Y_j \sqsubseteq (Y_i \to \forall r_y.Y_i) \sqcap (\neg Y_i \to \forall r_y.\neg Y_i) \quad \text{for all } i < n.$$

To represent tile types, we introduce a concept name A_t for each $t \in T$. Every node in the torus carries exactly one tile type and the initial condition $c = t_0 \cdots t_{n-1}$ is satisfied by this tiling:

$$\top \quad \sqsubseteq \quad \underset{t \in T}{\bigsqcup} A_t \sqcap \underset{t,t' \in T, t \neq t'}{\bigsqcup} \neg(A_t \sqcap A_{t'}),$$

$$A_{t_i} \quad \sqsupseteq \quad \underset{j<n, \text{bit}_j(i)=0}{\bigsqcap} \neg X_j \sqcap \underset{j<n, \text{bit}_j(i)=1}{\bigsqcap} X_j \sqcap \underset{j<n}{\bigsqcap} \neg Y_j \quad \text{for all } i < n,$$

where $\text{bit}_j(i)$ denotes the jth bit of the binary representation of i. We must also ensure that the horizontal matching conditions H and vertical matching conditions V of our torus tiling problem P are satisfied:

$$\top \sqsubseteq \underset{(t,t') \in H}{\bigsqcup} (A_t \sqcap \forall r_x.A_{t'}) \sqcap \underset{(t,t') \in V}{\bigsqcup} (A_t \sqcap \forall r_y.A_{t'}).$$

With what we have added to the TBox $\mathcal{T}_{P,c}$ so far, have we captured the torus tiling problem sufficiently well to make the reduction work? It is easy to see that this is not the case; that is, there are models of $\mathcal{T}_{P,c}$ which do not take the shape of a torus: there may be multiple nodes that represent the same torus position, there can be nodes with an $r_x r_y$-successor (first follow an r_x-edge, then an r_y-edge) that is not an $r_y r_x$-successor and so on. In fact, this is not surprising since so far we have only used the description logic $\mathcal{ALC}$, but no inverse roles, no qualified number restrictions and no nominals. It might thus seem that we have quite a bit of coding effort still ahead of us. Interestingly, this is not the case and it is very easy to finish the reduction at this point. We simply have to say that the inverses of the roles r_x and r_y are functional and that the grid position $(2^n - 1, 2^n - 1)$ occurs at most once, for which we use a single nominal a:

$$\top \quad \sqsubseteq \quad (\leqslant 1\, r_x^-.\top) \sqcap (\leqslant 1\, r_y^-.\top),$$

$$\{a\} \quad \sqsupseteq \quad X_0 \sqcap \cdots \sqcap X_{n-1} \sqcap Y_0 \sqcap \cdots \sqcap Y_{n-1}.$$

Why is this sufficient? Let $\mathcal{I}$ be a model of $\mathcal{T}_{P,c}$. The crucial point to observe is that

(∗) for each torus position (i, j), there is a unique element $d \in \Delta^{\mathcal{I}}$ with $(x_d, y_d) = (i, j)$.

In fact, because of the GCI $\top \sqsubseteq \exists r_x.\top \sqcap \exists r_y.\top$ and the synchronisation of the roles r_x, r_y with the concept names $X_0, \ldots, X_{n-1}, Y_0, \ldots, Y_{n-1}$, our TBox $\mathcal{T}_{P,c}$ ensures that there is *at least* one such d; the reader might like to attempt a formal proof. Additionally, we can prove by induction on $2^n - (i + j)$ that, for every torus position (i, j), there is also *at most* one $d \in \Delta^{\mathcal{I}}$ with $(x_d, y_d) = (i, j)$. The induction start is easy because $d = a^{\mathcal{I}}$ is the only element with $(x_d, y_d) = (2^n - 1, 2^n - 1)$. For the induction step, assume that $(x_d, y_d) = (x_e, y_e) = (i, j)$. We have to show that $d = e$. First assume that $i < 2^n - 1$. Then there is a d' with $(d, d') \in r_x^{\mathcal{I}}$ and $(x_{d'}, y_{d'}) = (i + 1, j)$ and an e' with $(e, e') \in r_x^{\mathcal{I}}$ and $(x_{e'}, y_{e'}) = (i + 1, j)$. By induction hypothesis, $d' = e'$. Because r_x^- is functional, we have $d = e$ as required. If $i = 2^n - 1$, then we must have $j < 2^n - 1$ and can argue analogously using the functionality of r_y^-.

We have thus established (∗). It is now possible to show that $\mathcal{I}$ is isomorphic to the $(2^n - 1, 2^n - 1)$-torus in the expected sense, but in fact this is not necessary since (∗) is essentially all that is needed to establish correctness of the reduction.

Lemma 5.17. *$\mathcal{T}_{P,c}$ has a model if and only if there exists a solution for P and c.*

Proof. (only if) Let $\mathcal{I}$ be a model of $\mathcal{T}_{P,c}$. For all $(i, j) \in \{0, \ldots, 2^n - 1\} \times \{0, \ldots, 2^n - 1\}$, set $\tau(i, j) = t$ if and only if there is a $d \in \Delta^{\mathcal{I}}$ with $(x_d, y_d) = (i, j)$ and $d \in A_t^{\mathcal{I}}$. By (∗) and since $\mathcal{T}_{P,c}$ ensures that every $d \in \Delta^{\mathcal{I}}$ is in the extension of exactly one concept A_t, τ is a well-defined and total function. It remains to argue that τ is a solution for P and c. Let us first show satisfaction of the horizontal matching condition H of P and consider a torus position (i, j) with $i < 2^n - 1$. By (∗), there are unique $d, e \in \Delta^{\mathcal{I}}$ with $(x_d, y_d) = (i, j)$ and $(x_e, y_e) = (i+1, j)$. Moreover, we must have $(d, e) \in r_x^{\mathcal{I}}$ because $d \in (\exists r_x.\top)^{\mathcal{I}}$, by (∗), and since $\mathcal{T}_{P,c}$ enforces that any r_x-successor e' of d must satisfy $(d', e') = (i + 1, j)$. Since H is satisfied in $\mathcal{I}$ along the role r_x, it is thus also satisfied by τ. The vertical matching condition V can be treated similarly. Moreover, by definition of τ and because of the GCI in $\mathcal{T}_{P,c}$ that deals with the initial condition c, it is clear that τ satisfies c.

(if) Let τ be a solution for P and c. Define an interpretation $\mathcal{I}$ as follows:

$$\Delta^{\mathcal{I}} = \{0,\ldots,2^n-1\} \times \{0,\ldots,2^n-1\},$$
$$r_x^{\mathcal{I}} = \{((i,j),(i+1,j)) \mid i < 2^n - 1, j < 2^n\},$$
$$r_y^{\mathcal{I}} = \{((i,j),(i,j+1)) \mid i < 2^n, j < 2^n - 1\},$$
$$A_t^{\mathcal{I}} = \{(i,j) \in \Delta^{\mathcal{I}} \mid \tau(i,j) = t\} \text{ for all } t \in T.$$

By going through the GCIs contained in it, it can be verified that $\mathcal{I}$ is a model of $\mathcal{T}_{P,c}$. $\qquad\Box$

The size of $\mathcal{T}_{P,c}$ is polynomial in n and satisfiability of $\mathcal{ALCOIQ}$ concepts with respect to TBoxes can be reduced to satisfiability without TBoxes, so we obtain the following theorem.

Theorem 5.18. *In* $\mathcal{ALCOIQ}$, *concept satisfiability and subsumption (without TBoxes) are* NExpTime-*hard.*

It is interesting to note that, to obtain this result, we do not need the full expressive power of qualified number restrictions. Indeed, all we need to say is that two roles are functional.

5.3 Undecidable extensions of $\mathcal{ALC}$

We consider two extensions of $\mathcal{ALC}$ in which satisfiability and subsumption are undecidable. Since Description Logic research aims at sound, complete and terminating algorithms, it is a commonly held opinion that constructors which lead to undecidability should not be included in a description logic, or only in a weakened form that is computationally better behaved.

5.3.1 Role value maps

Suppose that we are constructing a TBox about universities, which includes the statements

$$\text{Course} \sqsubseteq \exists\text{held-at.University},$$
$$\text{Lecturer} \sqsubseteq \exists\text{teaches.Course} \sqcap \exists\text{employed-by.University}.$$

To improve our knowledge base, we may want to express that if someone teaches a course held at a university, then he is employed by that specific university. This is not possible in $\mathcal{ALC}$ (which can be proved using the tree model property; see Section 3.5), but it can easily be done in the extension of $\mathcal{ALC}$ with so-called *role value maps* (RVMs), which come in two flavours: local and global. A *local* role value map is a new concept constructor with the syntax $(r_1 \circ \cdots \circ r_k \sqsubseteq s_1 \circ \cdots \circ s_\ell)$, where $r_1, \ldots, r_k$ and $s_1, \ldots, s_\ell$ are role names. To define the semantics, let

$$(r_1 \cdots r_k)^\mathcal{I}(d_0) = \{d_k \in \Delta^\mathcal{I} \mid \exists d_1, \ldots, d_k : (d_i, d_{i+1}) \in r_i^\mathcal{I} \text{ for } 0 \le i < k\}.$$

Then we define

$$(r_1 \circ \cdots \circ r_k \sqsubseteq s_1 \circ \cdots \circ s_\ell)^\mathcal{I} = \{d \in \Delta^\mathcal{I} \mid (r_1 \cdots r_k)^\mathcal{I}(d) \subseteq (s_1 \cdots s_\ell)^\mathcal{I}(d)\}.$$

In the *global* version of role value maps, $(r_1 \circ \cdots \circ r_k \sqsubseteq s_1 \circ \cdots \circ s_\ell)$ is not a concept constructor, but an expression that may occur in the TBox. The semantics of such an expression can be defined in terms of local RVMs: an interpretation $\mathcal{I}$ *satisfies* a global RVM $(r_1 \circ \cdots \circ r_k \sqsubseteq s_1 \circ \cdots \circ s_\ell)$ if it satisfies the TBox statement $\top \sqsubseteq (r_1 \circ \cdots \circ r_k \sqsubseteq s_1 \circ \cdots \circ s_\ell)$. In the initial example, we could now express the desired property using the global RVM

$$(\mathsf{teaches} \circ \mathsf{held\text{-}at} \sqsubseteq \mathsf{employed\text{-}by}).$$

Local role value maps were already present in the very first description logic system, KL-ONE. Several years after the invention of KL-ONE, it was proved that satisfiability in the underlying DL is undecidable, and that the reason for this is the presence of role value maps. In the following, we prove that satisfiability in $\mathcal{ALC}$ extended with RVMs is undecidable, whether or not the local or global version is used, and whether or not TBoxes are admitted.

We first show undecidability of satisfiability in $\mathcal{ALC}$ extended with global RVMs, and in the presence of general TBoxes. The proof is by a reduction of an undecidable version of the tiling problem: compare Section 5.2.2. The main differences are that (i) we tile $\mathbb{N} \times \mathbb{N}$, the first quadrant of the plane, instead of an exponentially sized torus; and (ii) there is no initial condition.

Definition 5.19. A *tiling problem* P is a triple (T, H, V), where T is a finite set of *tile types* and $H, V \subseteq T \times T$ represent the *horizontal and vertical matching conditions*. A mapping $\tau : \mathbb{N} \times \mathbb{N} \to T$ is a *solution* for P if and only if for all $i, j \ge 0$, the following hold:

- if $\tau(i, j) = t$ and $\tau(i + 1, j) = t'$, then $(t, t') \in H$;
- if $\tau(i, j) = t$ and $\tau(i, j + 1) = t'$, then $(t, t') \in V$.

Let $P = (T, H, V)$ be a tiling problem. We construct a general TBox $\mathcal{T}_P$ with global RVMs such that models of $\mathcal{T}_P$ represent solutions to P. In $\mathcal{T}_P$, we use concept names A_t, $t \in T$, to represent the tiling, and role names r_x and r_y to represent the horizontal and vertical successor relations between positions in the plane. The TBox $\mathcal{T}_P$ consists of the following parts:

(i) Every position has a horizontal and a vertical successor:

$$\top \sqsubseteq \exists r_x.\top \sqcap \exists r_y.\top.$$

(ii) Every position is labelled with exactly one tile type:

$$\top \sqsubseteq \bigsqcup_{t \in T} A_t \sqcap \bigsqcap_{t,t' \in T, t \neq t'} \neg(A_t \sqcap A_{t'}).$$

(iii) Adjacent tiles satisfy the matching conditions:

$$\top \sqsubseteq \bigsqcup_{(t,t') \in H} (A_t \sqcap \forall r_x.A_{t'}) \sqcap \bigsqcup_{(t,t') \in V} (A_t \sqcap \forall r_y.A_{t'}).$$

(iv) Every $r_x r_y$-successor is also a $r_y r_x$-successor and vice versa:

$$(r_x \circ r_y \sqsubseteq r_y \circ r_x),$$
$$(r_y \circ r_x \sqsubseteq r_x \circ r_y).$$

This finishes the construction of $\mathcal{T}_P$. Note that we have not enforced that the horizontal and vertical successors are unique (which they are in the first quadrant of the plane). Interestingly, this is not necessary for the reduction to be correct.

Lemma 5.20. $\top$ *is satisfiable with respect to $\mathcal{T}_P$ if and only if P has a solution.*

Proof. (only if) Let $\mathcal{I}$ be a model of $\mathcal{T}_P$. We construct a mapping $f : \mathbb{N} \times \mathbb{N} \to \Delta^{\mathcal{I}}$ such that, for all $i, j \geq 0$, $(f(i,j), f(i+1,j)) \in r_x^{\mathcal{I}}$ and $(f(i,j), f(i,j+1)) \in r_y^{\mathcal{I}}$, proceeding in two steps. First, we cut out a "staircase", i.e., define $f(i,j)$ for all $i, j \in \mathbb{N}$ such that $j \in \{i, i-1\}$:

- set $f(0,0)$ to an arbitrary element of $\Delta^{\mathcal{I}}$;
- if $f(i,i)$ was defined last, select a $d \in \Delta^{\mathcal{I}}$ with $(f(i,i), d) \in r_x^{\mathcal{I}}$, and set $f(i+1,i) = d$;
- if $f(i,i-1)$ was defined last, select a $d \in \Delta^{\mathcal{I}}$ with $(f(i,i-1), d) \in r_y^{\mathcal{I}}$, and set $f(i,i) = d$.

The required elements d exist since $\mathcal{I}$ is a model of $\mathcal{T}_P$. In the second step, we complete the construction of f as follows:

- if $f(i,j)$, $f(i+1,j)$ and $f(i+1,j+1)$ are defined and $f(i,j+1)$ is undefined, select a $d \in \Delta^{\mathcal{I}}$ with $(f(i,j),d) \in r_y^{\mathcal{I}}$ and $(d, f(i+1,j+1)) \in r_x^{\mathcal{I}}$, and set $f(i,j+1) = d$;
- if $f(i,j)$, $f(i,j+1)$ and $f(i+1,j+1)$ are defined and $f(i+1,j)$ is undefined, select a $d \in \Delta^{\mathcal{I}}$ with $(f(i,j),d) \in r_x^{\mathcal{I}}$ and $(d, f(i+1,j+1)) \in r_y^{\mathcal{I}}$, and set $f(i+1,j) = d$.

The required elements d exist due to the role value maps in $\mathcal{T}$. Intuitively, the mapping f "cuts out of $\mathcal{I}$" a representation of the first quadrant in which horizontal and vertical successors are unique. Now define a mapping $\tau : \mathbb{N} \times \mathbb{N} \to T$ by setting $\tau(i,j) = t$ if $f(i,j) \in A_t$. It is easily verified that this mapping is well defined and a solution for P.

(if) Let τ be a solution for P. Define an interpretation $\mathcal{I}$ as follows:

$$
\begin{aligned}
\Delta^{\mathcal{I}} &= \mathbb{N} \times \mathbb{N}, \\
r_x^{\mathcal{I}} &= \{((i,j),(i+1,j)) \mid i,j \geq 0\}, \\
r_y^{\mathcal{I}} &= \{((i,j),(i,j+1)) \mid i,j \geq 0\}, \\
A_t^{\mathcal{I}} &= \{(i,j) \mid \tau(i,j) = t\} \text{ for all } t \in T.
\end{aligned}
$$

Clearly, $\mathcal{I}$ is a model of $\mathcal{T}_P$ and we are done. $\qquad\square$

We have thus shown the following.

Theorem 5.21. *In $\mathcal{ALC}$ with global role value maps, concept satisfiability and subsumption with respect to general TBoxes are undecidable.*

Next, we strengthen this result by showing that satisfiability in $\mathcal{ALC}$ is undecidable even if general TBoxes are not admitted and global RVMs are replaced with local ones.

Theorem 5.22. *In $\mathcal{ALC}$ with local role value maps, concept satisfiability and subsumption (without TBoxes) are undecidable.*

Proof. The proof is by reduction from the satisfiability of $\mathcal{ALC}$ concepts with respect to general TBoxes and global role value maps. Let C be an $\mathcal{ALC}$ concept and $\mathcal{T}$ a general TBox with global role value maps. Let Γ be the set of all role names used in C and $\mathcal{T}$. Introduce a fresh role name u and define the concept D as the conjunction of the following:

- the concept $\exists u.C$ to generate an instance of C;
- the concept $\sqcap_{r \in \Gamma}(u \circ r \sqsubseteq u)$ to ensure that the element that satisfies D reaches all other "relevant" elements of the model by travelling a single step along u;

- the concept

$$\forall u.\big(\underset{C\sqsubseteq D\in\mathcal{T}}{\bigsqcap}C\to D\ \sqcap$$

$$\underset{(r_1\circ\cdots\circ r_k\sqsubseteq s_1\circ\cdots\circ s_\ell)\in\mathcal{T}}{\bigsqcap}(r_1\circ\cdots\circ r_k\sqsubseteq s_1\circ\cdots\circ s_\ell)\big),$$

which guarantees that all concept inclusions and global RVMs from $\mathcal{T}$ are satisfied.

The proof that D is satisfiable if and only if C is satisfiable with respect to $\mathcal{T}$, which we leave as an exercise, bears some similarity to the proof of Theorem 5.15. $\qquad\qquad\square$

There are not many ways to regain decidability in the presence of role value maps. Note, though, that role hierarchies are a special case of role value maps where sequences of roles are restricted to length one.

5.3.2 Concrete domains

In many applications of DLs, it is also necessary to describe concrete qualities of objects, such as the age of people, which is most appropriately represented by a non-negative integer value. Enabling such representations is the purpose of an extension of Description Logic known as concrete domains. In fact, concrete domains give rise to a class of extensions of a given DL rather than only to a single extension, depending on which concrete qualities we allow to be represented and how we can compare them using predicates. In this section, we show that satisfiability in $\mathcal{ALC}$ with general TBoxes becomes undecidable when we add a seemingly simple concrete domain based on the non-negative numbers, with a unary predicate for equality to zero and a binary predicate for incrementation.

A *concrete domain* is a pair $\mathsf{D}=(\Delta^{\mathsf{D}},\Phi^{\mathsf{D}})$, where Δ^{D} is a non-empty set and Φ^{D} is a finite set of predicates. Each *predicate* in Φ^{D} has a name P, an arity k_P and an extension $P^{\mathsf{D}}\subseteq(\Delta^{\mathsf{D}})^{k_P}$. The concrete domain used in this section is called D_{+1}. It is defined as $\mathsf{D}_{+1}=(\mathbb{N},\Phi^{\mathsf{D}_{+1}})$, where $\Phi^{\mathsf{D}_{+1}}$ consists of the unary predicate $=_0$ associated with the extension $(=_0)^{\mathsf{D}_{+1}}=\{0\}$ and the binary predicate $+1$ associated with the extension $(+1)^{\mathsf{D}_{+1}}=\{(i,j)\in\mathbb{N}\times\mathbb{N}\mid j=i+1\}$.

To integrate a concrete domain D into a description logic (in this case $\mathcal{ALC}$), we introduce *abstract features* and *concrete features*, as additional sorts. Every interpretation $\mathcal{I}$ assigns to each abstract feature g a partial function $g^{\mathcal{I}}:\Delta^{\mathcal{I}}\to\Delta^{\mathcal{I}}$ and to each concrete feature h a partial function

$h^{\mathcal{I}} : \Delta^{\mathcal{I}} \to \Delta^{\mathsf{D}}$. Note that an abstract feature is nothing but a role name whose interpretation is restricted to be a partial function. We then add a new concept constructor called a *predicate restriction*, taking the form $\exists c_1, \ldots, c_k.P$, where P is the name of a predicate from Φ^{D} of arity k and each c_i is a *feature chain*, that is, a sequence $g_1 \cdots g_n h$ of $n \geq 0$ abstract features g_i and one concrete feature h. For example, the following GCI expresses that every human has an age and a father who has a larger age:

$$\mathsf{Human} \sqsubseteq \exists \mathsf{age}, \mathsf{father\,age}. >,$$

where age is a concrete feature, father is an abstract feature and we assume a concrete domain based on the non-negative integers that includes the predicate $>$. We use $\mathcal{ALC}(\mathsf{D})$ to express the extension of $\mathcal{ALC}$ with the concrete domain D.

To prove undecidability of satisfiability in $\mathcal{ALC}(\mathsf{D}_{+1})$ with respect to general TBoxes, we use a reduction from the halting problem of two-register machines. A two-register machine M is similar to a Turing machine. It also has states, but instead of a tape, it has two registers which contain non-negative integers. In one step, the machine can increment the content of one of the registers or test whether the content of the given register is zero and, if not, then decrement it. In the second case, the successor state depends on whether the tested register was zero or not. There is a designated halting state, and M halts if it encounters that state.

Definition 5.23. A (deterministic) *two-register machine* (2RM) is a pair $M = (Q, P)$ with $Q = \{q_0, \ldots, q_\ell\}$ a set of *states* and $P = I_0, \ldots, I_{\ell-1}$ a sequence of *instructions*. By definition, q_0 is the *initial state* and q_ℓ the *halting state*. For all $i < \ell$,

- either $I_i = +(p, q_j)$ is an *incrementation instruction* with $p \in \{1, 2\}$ a register and q_j the subsequent state; or
- $I_i = -(p, q_j, q_k)$ is a *decrementation instruction* with $p \in \{1, 2\}$ a register, q_j the subsequent state if register p contains 0, and q_k the subsequent state otherwise.

A *configuration* of M is a triple (q, m, n), with q the current state and $m, n \in \mathbb{N}$ the register contents. We write $(q_i, n_1, n_2) \Rightarrow_M (q_j, m_1, m_2)$ if one of the following holds:

- $I_i = +(p, q_j)$, $m_p = n_p + 1$ and $m_{\overline{p}} = n_{\overline{p}}$, where $\overline{1} = 2$ and $\overline{2} = 1$;
- $I_i = -(p, q_j, q_k)$, $n_p = m_p = 0$ and $m_{\overline{p}} = n_{\overline{p}}$;

- $I_i = -(p, q_k, q_j)$, $n_p > 0$, $m_p = n_p - 1$ and $m_{\overline{p}} = n_{\overline{p}}$.

The *computation* of M on input $(n, m) \in \mathbb{N}^2$ is the unique longest configuration sequence $(p_0, n_0, m_0) \Rightarrow_M (p_1, n_1, m_1) \Rightarrow_M \cdots$ such that $p_0 = q_0$, $n_0 = n$ and $m_0 = m$.

The halting problem for 2RMs is to decide, given a 2RM M, whether its computation on input $(0, 0)$ is finite (which implies that its last state is q_ℓ). We reduce this problem to the *unsatisfiability* of $\mathcal{ALC}(\mathsf{D}_{+1})$ concepts with respect to general TBoxes by transforming a 2RM $M = (Q, P)$ into a TBox $\mathcal{T}_M$ and selecting a concept name I such that I is unsatisfiable with respect to $\mathcal{T}_M$ if and only if M halts. More precisely, every model of I and $\mathcal{T}_M$ describes an infinite computation of M on $(0, 0)$ and, conversely, every such computation gives rise to a model of I and $\mathcal{T}_M$. We use a single abstract feature g to describe the relation $\Rightarrow_M$, concrete features h_1 and h_2 to describe the register content, and concept names $Q_0, \ldots, Q_\ell$ for the states. For convenience, we first use an additional binary equality predicate $=$ (with the obvious extension), which is not actually contained in $\Phi^{\mathsf{D}+1}$, and later show how to replace it. We define the TBox $\mathcal{T}_M$ step by step, along with explanations:

- We start in state q_0 and with the registers containing zero:

$$I \sqsubseteq Q_0 \sqcap \exists h_1 =_0 \sqcap \exists h_2 =_0.$$

- Incrementation is executed correctly; that is, for all $I_i = +(p, q_j)$,

$$Q_i \sqsubseteq \exists g. Q_j \sqcap \exists h_p, gh_p. +_1 \sqcap \exists h_{\overline{p}}, gh_{\overline{p}} =.$$

Observe that all the existential restrictions talk about the same g-filler since g is functional.

- Decrementation is executed correctly; that is, for all $I_i = -(p, q_j, q_k)$

$$\begin{aligned} Q_i \sqcap \exists h_p =_0 &\sqsubseteq \exists g. Q_j \sqcap \exists h_p, gh_p. = \sqcap \exists h_{\overline{p}}, gh_{\overline{p}} =, \\ Q_i \sqcap \neg \exists h_p =_0 &\sqsubseteq \exists g. Q_j \sqcap \exists gh_p, h_p. +_1 \sqcap \exists h_{\overline{p}}, gh_{\overline{p}} =. \end{aligned}$$

Observe that we have swapped the arguments to $+_1$ to simulate a predicate $-_1$.

- The halting state q_ℓ is never reached, and thus the computation is infinite:

$$\top \sqsubseteq \neg Q_\ell.$$

It is not difficult to prove the following result.

Lemma 5.24. *The computation of M on $(0,0)$ is finite if and only if I is unsatisfiable with respect to $\mathcal{T}_M$.*

To establish undecidability of $\mathcal{ALC}(\mathsf{D}_{+1})$, it thus remains to show how to eliminate the binary equality predicate. The idea is to replace an equality test with repeated decrementations and tests for zero. We only treat the example concept $\exists h_1, h_2.=$. To eliminate it, we can replace it with a new concept name M, and then add the following, where g' is a new abstract feature:

$$ M \ \sqsubseteq \ (\exists h_1.=_0 \sqcap \exists h_2.=_0) \sqcup (\exists g'.M \sqcap \exists g'h_1, h_1.+_1 \sqcap \exists g'h_2, h_2.+_1). $$

Note that we again use $+_1$ to describe *decrementation*. It is now easy to remove binary equality from the above reduction, and we obtain the following result.

Theorem 5.25. *In $\mathcal{ALC}(\mathsf{D}_{+1})$, concept satisfiability and subsumption with respect to general TBoxes are undecidable.*

There are a number of ways to overcome undecidability of $\mathcal{ALC}$ extended with concrete domains. First, we can move to acyclic TBoxes, which results in decidability for a large number of concrete domains, including D_{+1}. Second, we may select concrete domains more carefully to achieve decidability even in the presence of general TBoxes. An example of such a more well-behaved concrete domain is based on the real numbers, with binary predicates for the comparisons $<, \leq, =, \neq, \geq$, and $>$, and unary predicates for the same comparisons with any fixed rational number. Third, we can stipulate that the concrete domain operator may contain only concrete features, but no sequences composed of abstract and concrete features. Then we obtain decidability even with general TBoxes and expressive concrete domains. The drawback is that it is no longer possible to relate the data values of *different* domain elements.

5.4 Historical context and literature review

PSPACE-completeness of satisfiability in $\mathcal{ALC}$ was first observed in the seminal paper by Schmidt-Schauß and Smolka, [SS91], which studied concept satisfiability and subsumption without TBoxes. Independently and previously, Ladner and others had proved that satisfiability in the modal logic K is PSPACE-complete [Lad77, HM92]. Later, Schild observed that $\mathcal{ALC}$ is a notational variant of K [Sch91], and thus the two mentioned results are identical. It has long been common knowledge in the DL community that the PSPACE upper bound can be extended to acyclic TBoxes; a published proof can be found in [Lut99]. Schmidt-Schauß and Smolka proved the PSPACE upper bound using a tableau-style algorithm. Our $\mathcal{ALC}$-worlds algorithm is an adaptation of the K-worlds algorithm for deciding satisfiability in the modal logic K, which goes back to Ladner [Lad77]. In both [SS91] and [Lad77], the PSPACE lower bound is proved using a reduction of the validity problem for quantified Boolean formulas (QBFs). This problem is very closely related to our finite Boolean games, taken from [SM73, Sch78] (the game is called $G_\omega(\text{CNF})$ in the latter). We have preferred to use finite Boolean games because they allow us to use a very similar problem, namely infinite Boolean games, for proving EXPTIME-hardness for the case with general TBoxes.

The EXPTIME upper bound for $\mathcal{ALC}$ with general TBoxes is a consequence of Schild's observation, mentioned above, and containment of propositional dynamic logic in EXPTIME, which was established by Fischer and Ladner [FL79]. The lower bound also follows from the corresponding bound for PDL, although in this case it is necessary to carefully analyze the proof, as has been done by Schild [Sch91]. The type elimination algorithm that we use for the upper bound was first used in the context of PDL, namely by Pratt [Pra79]. The original and most common way to establish the lower bound is by a reduction of the word problem for exponentially space-bounded alternating Turing machines [FL79]. Our infinite Boolean games are from [SC79] (where they are called G_5).

EXPTIME-completeness of $\mathcal{ALCOI}$ was first observed in modal logic. More precisely, description logics with nominals correspond to (a simple version of) so-called hybrid logics, and $\mathcal{ALCOI}$ is a fragment of hybrid logic with backwards modalities. It was shown by Areces *et al.* [ABM99] that this fragment is EXPTIME-complete, using for the hardness part the same approach that is followed in this chapter. The NEXPTIME-hardness of $\mathcal{ALCOIQ}$ was first established by Tobies [Tob99], who also gives a matching upper bound. As has been mentioned, $\mathcal{ALCOIQ}$ is closely related to the two-variable fragment of first-order logic extended with counting quantifiers in which satisfiability is also NEXPTIME-complete; see [GOR97, PST97, Pra09].

The undecidability of $\mathcal{ALC}$ with role value maps was first shown by Schmidt-Schauß [Sch89] using a reduction of the word problem for groups. This actually yields a stronger result than the one presented in this chapter because only the following constructors are needed: conjunction, value restriction and role value maps based on equality (instead of inclusion). The undecidability of $\mathcal{ALC}(D_{+1})$ with general TBoxes was proved in [Lut02] using a reduction of the post correspondence problem (PCP), building on a result by Baader and Hanschke [BH91].

All of the upper complexity bounds established in this section extend to KB consistency. Technically, this is typically not a big challenge. An interesting exception is presented in [DLNS94], where it is shown that, on the fragment $\mathcal{ALE}$ of $\mathcal{ALC}$, KB consistency is PSPACE-complete while satisfiability is only CONP-complete.

6

Reasoning in the $\mathcal{EL}$ Family of Description Logics

We saw in Chapter 5 that satisfiability and subsumption with respect to general $\mathcal{ALC}$ TBoxes is ExpTime-complete. Interestingly and quite surprisingly, subsumption with respect to general TBoxes is already ExpTime-complete in the small fragment $\mathcal{FL}_0$ of $\mathcal{ALC}$ that has conjunction, *value restriction*, and the top concept as its only concept constructors. In contrast to this negative complexity result for $\mathcal{FL}_0$, subsumption in the description logic $\mathcal{EL}$, which has conjunction, *existential restriction*, and the top concept as its only concept constructors, remains polynomial even in the presence of general TBoxes. Note that, due to the absence of constructors that could cause unsatisfiability, satisfiability is not an interesting inference problem in $\mathcal{FL}_0$ and $\mathcal{EL}$. Also, due to the absence of the complement constructor, subsumption cannot be reduced to unsatisfiability in $\mathcal{FL}_0$ and $\mathcal{EL}$.

The polynomial-time subsumption algorithm for $\mathcal{EL}$ that will be described below differs significantly from the algorithmic techniques for reasoning in DLs introduced in the two previous chapters. For subsumption, the tableau algorithms introduced in Chapter 4 are refutation procedures. In fact, to show that a subsumption $C \sqsubseteq D$ holds, these algorithms refute that a counterexample to the subsumption, i.e., an element of $C \sqcap \neg D$, exists by checking satisfiability of the concept $C \sqcap \neg D$. If $C \sqcap \neg D$ is unsatisfiable, then the subsumption holds, and otherwise it does not hold. The tableau algorithm that tests satisfiability of this concept is nondeterministic due to the presence of disjunction in $\mathcal{ALC}$, and thus an implementation needs to apply backtracking. In contrast, the subsumption algorithm for $\mathcal{EL}$ tries to prove directly that the subsumption holds by iteratively generating GCIs that follow from the TBox. This generation of consequences is deterministic, i.e., any GCI that is generated indeed follows from the TBox, and thus none of the generated consequences needs to be retracted. In the case of $\mathcal{EL}$, there are only polynomially many GCIs that need to be considered as consequences, and the rules generating consequences can be executed in polynomial time. Thus, we obtain a deterministic polynomial time algorithm for subsumption.

This algorithmic approach, which is sometimes called *consequence-based reasoning* in the literature, also turns out to be advantageous for DLs for which subsumption cannot be computed in polynomial time. In fact, for quite a number of interesting DLs (in particular, ones without disjunction and full negation) it is the approach used by highly efficient implemented reasoners. As an example of such a DL, we will consider $\mathcal{ELI}$, the extension of $\mathcal{EL}$ by inverse roles, for which subsumption is known to be EXPTIME-complete. In contrast to the tableau algorithm for $\mathcal{ALC}$, the consequence-based algorithm introduced in this chapter is still deterministic, but in the worst case it may, of course, need an exponential amount of time. At first sight, this sounds similar to the type elimination algorithm for satisfiability in $\mathcal{ALC}$ with respect to general TBoxes described in Chapter 5. There is, however, an important difference. The type elimination algorithm starts with the exponentially large set of all types, and then iteratively eliminates types. Consequently, a direct implementation of this approach is also exponential in the best case. In contrast, the subsumption algorithm for $\mathcal{ELI}$ to be introduced below starts with a polynomial number of GCIs that obviously follow from the TBox, and then iteratively adds implied ones. This process may in the worst case generate exponentially many GCIs following from the TBox, but this need not always be the case. In fact, for many practical ontologies, the number of actually implied GCIs is much smaller than the number of possibly implied GCIs.

6.1 Subsumption in $\mathcal{EL}$

The polynomial-time subsumption algorithm for $\mathcal{EL}$ introduced in this section actually classifies a given general TBox $\mathcal{T}$, i.e., it simultaneously computes all subsumption relationships between the concept names occurring in $\mathcal{T}$. Restricting the computation to subsumptions between concept names occurring in $\mathcal{T}$ is without loss of generality since, given compound concepts C, D, we can first add definitions $A \equiv C, B \equiv D$ to the TBox, where A, B are new concept names, and then decide the subsumption $A \sqsubseteq B$ with respect to the extended TBox rather than

$C \sqsubseteq D$ with respect to the original one. The following lemma shows that it is actually sufficient to add only "one half" of each definition.

Lemma 6.1. *Let $\mathcal{T}$ be a general $\mathcal{EL}$ TBox, C, D $\mathcal{EL}$ concepts and A, B concept names not occurring in $\mathcal{T}$ or C, D. Then*

$$\mathcal{T} \models C \sqsubseteq D \quad \text{if and only if} \quad \mathcal{T} \cup \{A \sqsubseteq C, D \sqsubseteq B\} \models A \sqsubseteq B.$$

Proof. First, assume that $\mathcal{T} \cup \{A \sqsubseteq C, D \sqsubseteq B\} \models A \sqsubseteq B$, and let $\mathcal{I}$ be a model of $\mathcal{T}$. Consider the interpretation $\mathcal{I}'$ that coincides with $\mathcal{I}$ on all role names and all concept names other than A, B, and satisfies $A^{\mathcal{I}'} = C^{\mathcal{I}}$ and $B^{\mathcal{I}'} = D^{\mathcal{I}}$. Since $\mathcal{T}, C, D$ do not contain A, B, the interpretation $\mathcal{I}'$ is a model of $\mathcal{T}$, and it satisfies $C^{\mathcal{I}'} = C^{\mathcal{I}}$ and $D^{\mathcal{I}'} = D^{\mathcal{I}}$. In addition, by the definition of the extensions of A, B in $\mathcal{I}'$, this interpretation is also a model of $\{A \sqsubseteq C, D \sqsubseteq B\}$. Consequently, it satisfies the GCI $A \sqsubseteq B$. Thus, we have $C^{\mathcal{I}} = A^{\mathcal{I}'} \subseteq B^{\mathcal{I}'} = D^{\mathcal{I}}$, which shows that $\mathcal{I}$ satisfies the GCI $C \sqsubseteq D$.

Conversely, assume that $\mathcal{T} \models C \sqsubseteq D$, and let $\mathcal{I}$ be a model of $\mathcal{T} \cup \{A \sqsubseteq C, D \sqsubseteq B\}$. Then, $\mathcal{I}$ is also a model of $\mathcal{T}$, and thus satisfies the GCI $C \sqsubseteq D$. This yields $A^{\mathcal{I}} \subseteq C^{\mathcal{I}} \subseteq D^{\mathcal{I}} \subseteq B^{\mathcal{I}}$, which shows that $\mathcal{I}$ satisfies the GCI $A \sqsubseteq B$. $\square$

6.1.1 Normalisation

To simplify the description of the algorithm, we first transform the given TBox into an appropriate normal form. We say that a general $\mathcal{EL}$ TBox $\mathcal{T}$ is *in normal form* (or *normalised*) if it only contains GCIs of the following form:

$$A \sqsubseteq B, \quad A_1 \sqcap A_2 \sqsubseteq B, \quad A \sqsubseteq \exists r.B, \quad \text{or} \quad \exists r.A \sqsubseteq B,$$

where A, A_1, A_2, B are concept names or the top concept $\top$, and r is a role name. One can transform a given TBox into a normalised one by applying the *normalisation rules* of Figure 6.1. Before showing this for general $\mathcal{EL}$ TBoxes, we illustrate by an example how a given (non-normalised) GCI can be transformed into a set of normalised GCIs using the rules of Figure 6.1:

$$
\begin{array}{lll}
\exists r.A \sqcap \exists r.\exists s.A \sqsubseteq A \sqcap B & \rightsquigarrow_{\mathsf{NF0}} & \exists r.A \sqcap \exists r.\exists s.A \sqsubseteq B_0, \quad B_0 \sqsubseteq A \sqcap B, \\
\exists r.A \sqcap \exists r.\exists s.A \sqsubseteq B_0 & \rightsquigarrow_{\mathsf{NF1}_\ell} & \exists r.A \sqsubseteq B_1, \quad B_1 \sqcap \exists r.\exists s.A \sqsubseteq B_0, \\
B_1 \sqcap \exists r.\exists s.A \sqsubseteq B_0 & \rightsquigarrow_{\mathsf{NF1}_r} & \exists r.\exists s.A \sqsubseteq B_2, \quad B_1 \sqcap B_2 \sqsubseteq B_0, \\
\exists r.\exists s.A \sqsubseteq B_2 & \rightsquigarrow_{\mathsf{NF2}} & \exists s.A \sqsubseteq B_3, \quad \exists r.B_3 \sqsubseteq B_2, \\
B_0 \sqsubseteq A \sqcap B & \rightsquigarrow_{\mathsf{NF4}} & B_0 \sqsubseteq A, \quad B_0 \sqsubseteq B.
\end{array}
$$

NF0	$\widehat{D} \sqsubseteq \widehat{E}$	$\longrightarrow$	$\widehat{D} \sqsubseteq A$, $\underline{A \sqsubseteq \widehat{E}}$
NF1$_r$	$C \sqcap \widehat{D} \sqsubseteq B$	$\longrightarrow$	$\underline{\widehat{D} \sqsubseteq A}$, $C \sqcap A \sqsubseteq B$
NF1$_\ell$	$\widehat{D} \sqcap C \sqsubseteq B$	$\longrightarrow$	$\underline{\widehat{D} \sqsubseteq A}$, $A \sqcap C \sqsubseteq B$
NF2	$\exists r.\widehat{D} \sqsubseteq B$	$\longrightarrow$	$\underline{\widehat{D} \sqsubseteq A}$, $\exists r.A \sqsubseteq B$
NF3	$B \sqsubseteq \exists r.\widehat{D}$	$\longrightarrow$	$\underline{A \sqsubseteq \widehat{D}}$, $B \sqsubseteq \exists r.A$
NF4	$B \sqsubseteq D \sqcap E$	$\longrightarrow$	$B \sqsubseteq D$, $B \sqsubseteq E$

where C, D, E denote arbitrary $\mathcal{EL}$ concepts,
$\widehat{D}, \widehat{E}$ denote $\mathcal{EL}$ concepts that are neither concept names nor $\top$,
B is a concept name, and
A is a *new* concept name.

Fig. 6.1. The normalisation rules for $\mathcal{EL}$.

On the right-hand side of each rule application, the GCIs that are not in normal form, and thus need to be further processed, are underlined. The concept names B_0, B_1, B_2, B_3 are new concept names that are introduced as "abbreviations" for compound concepts in the applications of the rules NF0, NF1$_\ell$, NF1$_r$ and NF2. Overall, the rule applications above transform the TBox $\mathcal{T} := \{\exists r.A \sqcap \exists r.\exists s.A \sqsubseteq A \sqcap B\}$ into the normalised TBox $\mathcal{T}' := \{\exists r.A \sqsubseteq B_1, B_1 \sqcap B_2 \sqsubseteq B_0, \exists s.A \sqsubseteq B_3, \exists r.B_3 \sqsubseteq B_2, B_0 \sqsubseteq A, B_0 \sqsubseteq B\}$.

Lemma 6.2. *Let $\mathcal{T}$ be a general $\mathcal{EL}$ TBox. Then $\mathcal{T}$ can be transformed into a normalised $\mathcal{EL}$ TBox $\mathcal{T}'$ by a linear number of applications of the rules of Figure 6.1. In addition, the size of the resulting TBox $\mathcal{T}'$ is linear in the size of $\mathcal{T}$.[1]*

Proof. We say that an occurrence of a concept $\widehat{D}$ within a general $\mathcal{EL}$ TBox is *abnormal* if one of the following conditions holds:

(i) $\widehat{D}$ is neither a concept name nor $\top$, and $\widehat{D}$ is the left-hand side of a GCI $\widehat{D} \sqsubseteq \widehat{E}$ whose right-hand side $\widehat{E}$ is neither a concept name nor $\top$;

(ii) $\widehat{D}$ is neither a concept name nor $\top$, and this occurrence is under a conjunction or an existential restriction operator;

(iii) this occurrence is under a conjunction operator on the right-hand side of a GCI.

---

[1] We use the definition of the size of a TBox as introduced in Chapter 3.

The *abnormality degree* of a general $\mathcal{EL}$ TBox is the number of abnormal occurrences of a concept in this TBox. Obviously, the abnormality degree of a TBox is bounded by the size of the TBox, and a TBox with abnormality degree 0 is normalised.

In a first phase of rule applications, we apply NF0 exhaustively. Each application of this rule decrements the abnormality degree by 1. In fact, the occurrence of the concept $\widehat{D}$ on the left-hand side of this rule is abnormal, while the occurrence of $\widehat{D}$ on the right-hand side is no longer abnormal. In addition, any abnormal occurrence of a concept within $\widehat{D}$ or $\widehat{E}$ in the new GCIs was also an abnormal occurrence in the old GCI. Thus, this first phase of rule applications stops after a linear number of steps. The resulting TBox contains only GCIs for which one of its sides is a concept name. Obviously, this property is preserved by applications of the other rules, which is the reason why on the left-hand sides of these rules we consider only GCIs satisfying this property.

In the second phase of rule applications, we apply the remaining rules exhaustively. Each application of such a rule decrements the abnormality degree by at least 1. For the rules $NF1_r$, $NF1_\ell$, NF2 and NF3, the occurrence of the concept $\widehat{D}$ on the left-hand side of these rules is abnormal, while the occurrence of $\widehat{D}$ on the right-hand side is no longer abnormal. In addition, no new abnormal occurrences of concepts are introduced by the rule application. For NF4, the occurrences of D and E are abnormal, and cease to be so after the rule is applied. Note that, because the left-hand side B of the GCI is a concept name, this left-hand side does not contain any abnormal occurrences of concepts, and thus the fact that the left-hand side is copied is harmless. This shows that the second phase of rule applications also stops after a linear number of steps. To be more precise, the overall number of rule applications in the two phases is bounded by the size of $\mathcal{T}$ since each rule application decrements the abnormality degree by at least 1 and the abnormality degree of $\mathcal{T}$ is bounded by the size of $\mathcal{T}$. When both phases are finished, the resulting TBox $\mathcal{T}'$ is normalised since a non-normalised GCI that has a concept name as one of its sides would trigger the application of one of the rules $NF1_r$, $NF1_\ell$, NF2, NF3, NF4.

Regarding the size of $\mathcal{T}'$, we note that an application of a rule adds at most 2 to the size of the TBox. The rules NF0, ..., NF3 increment the size by exactly 2 since they add two occurrences of A. The rule NF4 removes one conjunction operator, but duplicates B. However, since B is a concept name, which has size 1, the overall size of the TBox actually stays the same. Since the number of rule applications is bounded by the size of $\mathcal{T}$ and each rule application increments the size of the TBox by at most 2, the size of $\mathcal{T}'$ is at most three times the size of the original TBox $\mathcal{T}$. □

It remains to show that the original TBox $\mathcal{T}$ and the normalised TBox $\mathcal{T}'$ obtained from $\mathcal{T}$ using the rules of Figure 6.1 are in an appropriate semantic relationship that ensures that classification of the normalised TBox $\mathcal{T}'$ also yields the subsumption hierarchy for the concept names occurring in $\mathcal{T}$. One might be tempted to claim that $\mathcal{T}$ and $\mathcal{T}'$ are equivalent in the sense that they have the same models. This is not the case, however, because the rules of Figure 6.1 introduce new concept names. Thus, we first need to define an appropriate extension of the notion of equivalence.

Definition 6.3. For a given general $\mathcal{EL}$ TBox $\mathcal{T}_0$, its *signature* $sig(\mathcal{T}_0)$ consists of the concept and role names occurring in the GCIs of $\mathcal{T}_0$. Given general $\mathcal{EL}$ TBoxes $\mathcal{T}_1$ and $\mathcal{T}_2$, we say that $\mathcal{T}_2$ is a *conservative extension* of $\mathcal{T}_1$ if

- $sig(\mathcal{T}_1) \subseteq sig(\mathcal{T}_2)$,
- every model of $\mathcal{T}_2$ is a model of $\mathcal{T}_1$, and
- for every model $\mathcal{I}_1$ of $\mathcal{T}_1$ there exists a model $\mathcal{I}_2$ of $\mathcal{T}_2$ such that the extensions of concept and role names from $sig(\mathcal{T}_1)$ coincide in $\mathcal{I}_1$ and $\mathcal{I}_2$, i.e.,
  $A^{\mathcal{I}_1} = A^{\mathcal{I}_2}$ for all concept names $A \in sig(\mathcal{T}_1)$, and
  $r^{\mathcal{I}_1} = r^{\mathcal{I}_2}$ for all role names $r \in sig(\mathcal{T}_1)$.

It is easy to see that the notion of a conservative extension is *transitive*, i.e., if $\mathcal{T}_2$ is a conservative extension of $\mathcal{T}_1$ and $\mathcal{T}_3$ is a conservative extension of $\mathcal{T}_2$, then $\mathcal{T}_3$ is a conservative extension of $\mathcal{T}_1$.

In addition, the notion *preserves subsumption* in the following sense. If $\mathcal{T}_2$ is a conservative extension of $\mathcal{T}_1$, then subsumption with respect to $\mathcal{T}_1$ coincides with subsumption with respect to $\mathcal{T}_2$ for all concepts built using only symbols from $sig(\mathcal{T}_1)$.

Lemma 6.4. *Let $\mathcal{T}_1$ and $\mathcal{T}_2$ be general $\mathcal{EL}$ TBoxes such that $\mathcal{T}_2$ is a conservative extension of $\mathcal{T}_1$, and C, D are $\mathcal{EL}$ concepts containing only concept and role names from $sig(\mathcal{T}_1)$. Then $\mathcal{T}_1 \models C \sqsubseteq D$ if and only if $\mathcal{T}_2 \models C \sqsubseteq D$.*

Proof. First, assume that $\mathcal{T}_2 \not\models C \sqsubseteq D$. Then there is a model $\mathcal{I}$ of $\mathcal{T}_2$ such that $C^{\mathcal{I}} \not\subseteq D^{\mathcal{I}}$. Since $\mathcal{I}$ is also a model of $\mathcal{T}_1$, this implies $\mathcal{T}_1 \not\models C \sqsubseteq D$.

Second, assume that $\mathcal{T}_1 \not\models C \sqsubseteq D$. Then there is a model $\mathcal{I}_1$ of $\mathcal{T}_1$ such that $C^{\mathcal{I}_1} \not\subseteq D^{\mathcal{I}_1}$. Let $\mathcal{I}_2$ be a model of $\mathcal{T}_2$ such that the extensions of concept and role names from $sig(\mathcal{T}_1)$ coincide in $\mathcal{I}_1$ and $\mathcal{I}_2$. Since C, D contain only concept and role names from $sig(\mathcal{T}_1)$, we have $C^{\mathcal{I}_2} = C^{\mathcal{I}_1} \not\subseteq D^{\mathcal{I}_1} = D^{\mathcal{I}_2}$, and thus $\mathcal{T}_2 \not\models C \sqsubseteq D$. $\qquad\square$

Because of this lemma, it is enough to show that the rules of Figure 6.1 transform a given TBox into a conservative extension of this TBox.

Proposition 6.5. *Assume that $\mathcal{T}_2$ is obtained from $\mathcal{T}_1$ by applying one of the rules of Figure 6.1. Then $\mathcal{T}_2$ is a conservative extension of $\mathcal{T}_1$.*

Proof. We treat the rule NF1$_r$ in detail. The rules NF0, NF1$_\ell$, NF2 and NF3 can be treated similarly. The proposition holds trivially for NF4 since in that case $\mathcal{T}_1$ and $\mathcal{T}_2$ have the same signature and are obviously equivalent.

Regarding NF1$_r$, assume that $\mathcal{T}_2$ is obtained from $\mathcal{T}_1$ by replacing the GCI $C \sqcap \widehat{D} \sqsubseteq B$ with the two GCI $\widehat{D} \sqsubseteq A$ and $C \sqcap A \sqsubseteq B$, where A is a new concept name, i.e., $A \notin sig(\mathcal{T}_1)$. Obviously, $sig(\mathcal{T}_2) = sig(\mathcal{T}_1) \cup \{A\}$, and thus $sig(\mathcal{T}_1) \subseteq sig(\mathcal{T}_2)$. Next, assume that $\mathcal{I}$ is a model of $\mathcal{T}_2$. Then we have $\widehat{D}^{\mathcal{I}} \subseteq A^{\mathcal{I}}$ and $C^{\mathcal{I}} \cap A^{\mathcal{I}} \subseteq B^{\mathcal{I}}$. Obviously, this implies $C^{\mathcal{I}} \cap \widehat{D}^{\mathcal{I}} \subseteq C^{\mathcal{I}} \cap A^{\mathcal{I}} \subseteq B^{\mathcal{I}}$, and thus $\mathcal{I}$ is also a model of $\mathcal{T}_1$. Finally, assume that $\mathcal{I}_1$ is a model of $\mathcal{T}_1$. Let $\mathcal{I}_2$ be the interpretation that coincides with $\mathcal{I}_1$ on all concept and role names with the exception of A. For A, we define the extension in $\mathcal{I}_2$ as $A^{\mathcal{I}_2} := \widehat{D}^{\mathcal{I}_1}$. Since $\mathcal{I}_1$ is a model of $\mathcal{T}_1$, we have $C^{\mathcal{I}_1} \cap \widehat{D}^{\mathcal{I}_1} \subseteq B^{\mathcal{I}_1}$. In addition, since A does not occur in $C, \widehat{D}$ and B, we have $C^{\mathcal{I}_1} = C^{\mathcal{I}_2}$, $\widehat{D}^{\mathcal{I}_1} = \widehat{D}^{\mathcal{I}_2}$ and $B^{\mathcal{I}_1} = B^{\mathcal{I}_2}$. This yields $\widehat{D}^{\mathcal{I}_2} = \widehat{D}^{\mathcal{I}_1} = A^{\mathcal{I}_2}$ and $C^{\mathcal{I}_2} \cap A^{\mathcal{I}_2} = C^{\mathcal{I}_1} \cap \widehat{D}^{\mathcal{I}_1} \subseteq B^{\mathcal{I}_1} = B^{\mathcal{I}_2}$, which shows that $\mathcal{I}_2$ is a model of $\mathcal{T}_2$. $\qquad\square$

Because of transitivity, the following corollary is an immediate consequence of this proposition and Lemma 6.4.

Corollary 6.6. *Let $\mathcal{T}$ be a general $\mathcal{EL}$ TBox and $\mathcal{T}'$ the normalised TBox obtained from $\mathcal{T}$ using the rules of Figure 6.1, as described in the proof of Lemma 6.2. Then we have*

$$\mathcal{T} \models A \sqsubseteq B \text{ if and only if } \mathcal{T}' \models A \sqsubseteq B$$

for all concept names $A, B \in sig(\mathcal{T})$.

$$\text{CR1} \ \overline{A \sqsubseteq A} \qquad\qquad \text{CR2} \ \overline{A \sqsubseteq \top}$$

$$\text{CR3} \ \frac{A_1 \sqsubseteq A_2 \quad A_2 \sqsubseteq A_3}{A_1 \sqsubseteq A_3} \qquad \text{CR4} \ \frac{A \sqsubseteq A_1 \quad A \sqsubseteq A_2 \quad A_1 \sqcap A_2 \sqsubseteq B}{A \sqsubseteq B}$$

$$\text{CR5} \ \frac{A \sqsubseteq \exists r.A_1 \quad A_1 \sqsubseteq B_1 \quad \exists r.B_1 \sqsubseteq B}{A \sqsubseteq B}$$

Fig. 6.2. The classification rules for $\mathcal{EL}$.

6.1.2 The classification procedure

Let $\mathcal{T}$ be a general $\mathcal{EL}$ TBox in normal form. We start with the GCIs in $\mathcal{T}$ and add implied GCIs using appropriate inference rules. All the GCIs generated in this way are of a specific form.

Definition 6.7. A $\mathcal{T}$-*sequent* is a GCI of the form

$$A \sqsubseteq B, \quad A_1 \sqcap A_2 \sqsubseteq B, \quad A \sqsubseteq \exists r.B \ \text{ or } \ \exists r.A \sqsubseteq B,$$

where A, A_1, A_2, B are concept names in $sig(\mathcal{T})$ or the top concept $\top$, and r is a role name in $sig(\mathcal{T})$.

Obviously, the overall number of $\mathcal{T}$-sequents is polynomial in the size of $\mathcal{T}$, and every GCI in $\mathcal{T}$ is a $\mathcal{T}$-sequent. A set of $\mathcal{T}$-sequents consists of GCIs, and thus is a TBox. Inspired by its use in sequent calculi, we employ the name *sequent* rather than GCI to emphasise the fact that new $\mathcal{T}$-sequents can be derived using inference rules. The prefix $\mathcal{T}$ specifies the original TBox and restricts $\mathcal{T}$-sequents to being normalised GCIs containing only concept and role names from $sig(\mathcal{T})$.

Given the normalised input TBox $\mathcal{T}$, we define the current TBox $\mathcal{T}'$ to be initially $\mathcal{T}$, and then add new $\mathcal{T}$-sequents to $\mathcal{T}'$ by applying the *classification rules* of Figure 6.2. The rules given in this figure are, of course, not concrete rules, but rule schemata. To build a concrete instance of such a rule schema, the meta-variables A, A_1, A_2, B, B_1 must be replaced by a concrete $\mathcal{EL}$ concept and the meta-variable r by a concrete role name. However, it is important to note that *only instantiations are allowed for which all the GCIs occurring in the rule are $\mathcal{T}$-sequents*. A rule instance obtained in this way is then to be read as follows: if all the $\mathcal{T}$-sequents above the line occur in the current TBox $\mathcal{T}'$, then add the $\mathcal{T}$-sequent below the line to $\mathcal{T}'$ unless it already belongs to $\mathcal{T}'$. To simplify notation, we will in the following dispense with drawing a strict distinction between rule schemata and rule instances, and talk about applying a rule of Figure 6.2 rather than saying that we apply an instance of a rule schema.

Example 6.8. As an example, consider the TBox

$$\mathcal{T}_1 = \{A \sqsubseteq \exists r.A, \exists r.B \sqsubseteq B_1, \top \sqsubseteq B, A \sqsubseteq B_2, B_1 \sqcap B_2 \sqsubseteq C\}.$$

The rule CR2 can generate the $\mathcal{T}_1$-sequent $A \sqsubseteq \top$. Together with $\top \sqsubseteq B \in \mathcal{T}_1$, this $\mathcal{T}_1$-sequent can be used by rule CR3 to derive $A \sqsubseteq B$. This $\mathcal{T}_1$-sequent, together with the first and the second GCI in $\mathcal{T}_1$, can now be used by rule CR4 to infer $A \sqsubseteq B_1$. Finally, this $\mathcal{T}_1$-sequent, together with the third and the fourth GCI in $\mathcal{T}_1$, yields $A \sqsubseteq C$ by an application of rule CR5.

As a second example, consider the TBox

$$\mathcal{T}_2 = \{A \sqsubseteq \exists r.A, \exists r.A \sqsubseteq B\}.$$

Then there are two ways of deriving $A \sqsubseteq B$. One is by a direct application of rule CR3. The other is by first applying CR1 to derive $A \sqsubseteq A$, and then applying rule CR5.

The TBox obtained by an exhaustive application of the rules of Figure 6.2 to an initial normalised TBox $\mathcal{T}$ is denoted by $\mathcal{T}^*$. We call this process *saturation* of $\mathcal{T}$ with respect to the inference rules of Figure 6.2, and the resulting TBox $\mathcal{T}^*$ the *saturated* TBox. We will show that, for all concept names A, B (where $A, B \in sig(\mathcal{T}) \cup \{\top\}$), we then have

$$\mathcal{T} \models A \sqsubseteq B \quad \text{if and only if} \quad A \sqsubseteq B \in \mathcal{T}^*. \tag{6.1}$$

But first note that the saturated TBox $\mathcal{T}^*$ is uniquely determined and can be computed in polynomial time.

Lemma 6.9. *The saturated TBox $\mathcal{T}^*$ is uniquely determined by $\mathcal{T}$, and it can be computed by a polynomial number of applications of the inference rules of Figure 6.2.*

Proof. Each rule application adds one new $\mathcal{T}$-sequent to $\mathcal{T}'$, and there are only polynomially many $\mathcal{T}$-sequents. Thus, after a polynomial number of rule applications, no new sequents can be added by the rules, and thus the application of rules terminates.

The choice of which applicable rule to apply during the saturation process does not influence the resulting TBox $\mathcal{T}^*$. Indeed, note that $\mathcal{T}$-sequents may be added to, but are never removed from, the TBox $\mathcal{T}'$. Thus, if the condition that the $\mathcal{T}$-sequents above the line of a rule occur in the current TBox $\mathcal{T}'$ is satisfied at some stage of the saturation process, then it remains satisfied also at later stages. Consequently, each applicable rule remains applicable until its consequent (i.e., the $\mathcal{T}$-sequent below the line) is added to $\mathcal{T}'$. $\qquad\square$

Let us now show the "if" direction of (6.1). Obviously, this direction is an immediate consequence of the next lemma and the fact that any GCI in $\mathcal{T}$ follows from $\mathcal{T}$.

Lemma 6.10 (Soundness). *If all the GCIs in $\mathcal{T}'$ follow from $\mathcal{T}$ and the $\mathcal{T}$-sequents above the line of one of the inference rules of Figure 6.2 belong to $\mathcal{T}'$, then the $\mathcal{T}$-sequent below the line also follows from $\mathcal{T}$.*

Proof. This is an immediate consequence of the following facts:

- the subsumption relation $\sqsubseteq_{\mathcal{T}}$ is reflexive and transitive;
- $\top$ subsumes every concept with respect to any TBox;
- $A \sqsubseteq_{\mathcal{T}} A_1$ and $A \sqsubseteq_{\mathcal{T}} A_2$ implies $A \sqsubseteq_{\mathcal{T}} A_1 \sqcap A_2$;
- $A_1 \sqsubseteq_{\mathcal{T}} A_2$ implies $\exists r.A_1 \sqsubseteq_{\mathcal{T}} \exists r.A_2$.

Some of these facts have already been shown in Chapter 2. All of them are easy consequences of the semantics of the concept constructors of $\mathcal{EL}$ and the definition of subsumption. $\qquad\square$

Instead of showing the "only if" direction of (6.1) directly, we prove its contrapositive, i.e., if $A \sqsubseteq B \notin \mathcal{T}^*$ then $\mathcal{T} \not\models A \sqsubseteq B$. For this purpose, we construct a model of $\mathcal{T}$ that does not satisfy the GCI $A \sqsubseteq B$.

Definition 6.11. Let $\mathcal{T}$ be a general $\mathcal{EL}$ TBox in normal form and $\mathcal{T}^*$ the saturated TBox obtained by exhaustive application of the inference rules of Figure 6.2. The *canonical interpretation* $\mathcal{I}_{\mathcal{T}^*}$ induced by $\mathcal{T}^*$ is defined as follows:

$$\Delta^{\mathcal{I}_{\mathcal{T}^*}} = \{A \mid A \text{ is a concept name in } sig(\mathcal{T})\} \cup \{\top\},$$
$$A^{\mathcal{I}_{\mathcal{T}^*}} = \{B \in \Delta^{\mathcal{I}_{\mathcal{T}^*}} \mid B \sqsubseteq A \in \mathcal{T}^*\} \text{ for all concept names } A \in sig(\mathcal{T}),$$
$$r^{\mathcal{I}_{\mathcal{T}^*}} = \{(A, B) \in \Delta^{\mathcal{I}_{\mathcal{T}^*}} \times \Delta^{\mathcal{I}_{\mathcal{T}^*}} \mid A \sqsubseteq \exists r.B \in \mathcal{T}^*\}$$
$$\text{for all role names } r \in sig(\mathcal{T}).$$

Note that, according to this definition, we have $B \in A^{\mathcal{I}_{\mathcal{T}^*}}$ if and only if $B \sqsubseteq A \in \mathcal{T}^*$ for all concept names $A \in sig(\mathcal{T})$. The same is actually true for $A = \top$. In fact, $\top^{\mathcal{I}_{\mathcal{T}^*}} = \Delta^{\mathcal{I}_{\mathcal{T}^*}}$ according to the semantics of the top concept. Due to the presence of the rule CR2, $B \sqsubseteq \top \in \mathcal{T}^*$ for all $B \in \Delta^{\mathcal{I}_{\mathcal{T}^*}}$.

Lemma 6.12. *The canonical interpretation induced by $\mathcal{T}^*$ is a model of the saturated TBox $\mathcal{T}^*$.*

Proof. All the GCIs in $\mathcal{T}^*$ are $\mathcal{T}$-sequents, i.e., they are of the form described in Definition 6.7.

- Consider a GCI of the form $A \sqsubseteq B \in \mathcal{T}^*$. If $A' \in A^{\mathcal{I}_{\mathcal{T}^*}}$, then we have $A' \sqsubseteq A \in \mathcal{T}^*$. Since $\mathcal{T}^*$ is saturated, the rule CR3 is no longer applicable, and thus we must have $A' \sqsubseteq B \in \mathcal{T}^*$. This yields $A' \in B^{\mathcal{I}_{\mathcal{T}^*}}$, and thus shows that $\mathcal{I}_{\mathcal{T}^*}$ satisfies the GCI $A \sqsubseteq B$.
- GCIs of the form $A_1 \sqcap A_2 \sqsubseteq B$ can be treated analogously, using the semantics of conjunction and the rule CR4 instead of CR3.
- Consider a GCI of the form $A \sqsubseteq \exists r.B \in \mathcal{T}^*$. If $A' \in A^{\mathcal{I}_{\mathcal{T}^*}}$, then we have $A' \sqsubseteq A \in \mathcal{T}^*$, and thus (due to CR3) $A' \sqsubseteq \exists r.B \in \mathcal{T}^*$. The definition of the interpretation of roles in $\mathcal{I}_{\mathcal{T}^*}$ thus yields $(A', B) \in r^{\mathcal{I}_{\mathcal{T}^*}}$. Finally, due to rule CR1, $B \sqsubseteq B \in \mathcal{T}^*$, and thus $B \in B^{\mathcal{I}_{\mathcal{T}^*}}$. This shows that $A' \in (\exists r.B)^{\mathcal{I}_{\mathcal{T}^*}}$.
- Consider a GCI of the form $\exists r.A \sqsubseteq B \in \mathcal{T}^*$. If $A' \in (\exists r.A)^{\mathcal{I}_{\mathcal{T}^*}}$, then there is $B' \in \Delta^{\mathcal{I}_{\mathcal{T}^*}}$ such that $(A', B') \in r^{\mathcal{I}_{\mathcal{T}^*}}$ and $B' \in A^{\mathcal{I}_{\mathcal{T}^*}}$. This yields $A' \sqsubseteq \exists r.B' \in \mathcal{T}^*$ and $B' \sqsubseteq A \in \mathcal{T}^*$. Thus, due to rule CR5, $A' \sqsubseteq B \in \mathcal{T}^*$, which yields $A' \in B^{\mathcal{I}_{\mathcal{T}^*}}$.

Since all the GCIs in $\mathcal{T}^*$ are of one of the forms considered above, we have thus shown that $\mathcal{I}_{\mathcal{T}^*}$ does indeed satisfy every GCI in $\mathcal{T}^*$. $\qquad \square$

The "only if" direction of (6.1) is an easy consequence of this lemma.

Lemma 6.13 (Completeness). *Let $\mathcal{T}$ be a general $\mathcal{EL}$ TBox in normal form and $\mathcal{T}^*$ the saturated TBox obtained by exhaustive application of the inference rules of Figure 6.2. Then $\mathcal{T} \models A \sqsubseteq B$ implies $A \sqsubseteq B \in \mathcal{T}^*$.*

Proof. As mentioned above, we show the contrapositive of the statement of the lemma. Thus, assume that $A \sqsubseteq B \notin \mathcal{T}^*$. Then $A \notin B^{\mathcal{I}_{\mathcal{T}^*}}$ by the definition of the interpretation of concept names in $\mathcal{I}_{\mathcal{T}^*}$. Due to CR1, we have $A \sqsubseteq A \in \mathcal{T}^*$, and thus $A \in A^{\mathcal{I}_{\mathcal{T}^*}}$. This shows that $\mathcal{I}_{\mathcal{T}^*}$ does not satisfy the GCI $A \sqsubseteq B$. Since $\mathcal{I}_{\mathcal{T}^*}$ is a model of the saturated TBox $\mathcal{T}^*$, it is also a model of its subset $\mathcal{T}$, which yields $\mathcal{T} \not\models A \sqsubseteq B$. $\qquad \square$

If we put all the results of this section together, we obtain the following theorem.

Theorem 6.14. *Subsumption in $\mathcal{EL}$ with respect to general TBoxes is decidable in polynomial time.*

Proof. Let $\mathcal{T}_0$ be a general $\mathcal{EL}$ TBox and C, D $\mathcal{EL}$ concepts. To decide whether $\mathcal{T}_0 \models C \sqsubseteq D$ holds or not, we first add the GCIs $A \sqsubseteq C, D \sqsubseteq B$ to $\mathcal{T}_0$. The resulting TBox $\mathcal{T}_1$ is then normalised using the normalisation rules of Figure 6.1, as described in the proof of Lemma 6.2. The size of the normalised TBox $\mathcal{T}$ obtained this way is linear in the size of $\mathcal{T}_0$, and we have $\mathcal{T}_0 \models C \sqsubseteq D$ if and only if $\mathcal{T} \models A \sqsubseteq B$.

Let $\mathcal{T}^*$ be the TBox obtained by an exhaustive application of the rules of Figure 6.2, starting with $\mathcal{T}$. We know that the saturation process requires only a polynomial number of rule applications. Since a single rule application can be done in polynomial time, this shows that $\mathcal{T}^*$ can be computed in time polynomial in the size of $\mathcal{T}$, and thus also in the size of $\mathcal{T}_0$. In addition, we have $\mathcal{T} \models A \sqsubseteq B$ if and only if $A \sqsubseteq B \in \mathcal{T}^*$. Thus, by checking whether $A \sqsubseteq B$ is an element of $\mathcal{T}^*$, we can decide whether $\mathcal{T}_0 \models C \sqsubseteq D$ holds or not. $\qquad\square$

6.2 Subsumption in $\mathcal{ELI}$

In this section, we show that the ideas underlying the subsumption algorithm of the previous section can also be used to obtain a subsumption algorithm for $\mathcal{ELI}$, the extension of $\mathcal{EL}$ by inverse roles. However, as mentioned in the introduction to this chapter, subsumption in $\mathcal{ELI}$ is no longer polynomial, but ExpTime-complete. One reason for the higher complexity of subsumption in $\mathcal{ELI}$ is that it can express a restricted form of value restrictions, and thus comes close to $\mathcal{FL}_0$. In fact, it is easy to see that the GCI $\exists r^-.C \sqsubseteq D$ is equivalent to the GCI $C \sqsubseteq \forall r.D$. Thus, $\mathcal{ELI}$ can express value restrictions on the right-hand side of GCIs (but not on the left).

As usual, we will use r^- to denote s if $r = s^-$ for a role name s.

6.2.1 Normalisation

In principle, $\mathcal{ELI}$ admits a normal form that is similar to the one for $\mathcal{EL}$ introduced above. The only differences are that inverse roles can occur in place of role names and that we rewrite each GCIs of the form $\exists r^-.A \sqsubseteq B$ into the equivalent GCI $A \sqsubseteq \forall r.B$, where r is a role name or the inverse of a role name. To be more precise, we say that the general $\mathcal{ELI}$ TBox $\mathcal{T}$ is *in i.normal form* (or is *i.normalised*) if all its GCI are of one of the following forms:

$$A \sqsubseteq B, \quad A_1 \sqcap A_2 \sqsubseteq B, \quad A \sqsubseteq \exists r.B \text{ or } A \sqsubseteq \forall r.B,$$

where A, A_1, A_2, B are concept names or the top concept $\top$, and r is a role name or the inverse of a role name. The normalisation rules for $\mathcal{EL}$, extended by a rule that rewrites GCIs with existential restrictions on the left-hand side into the equivalent ones with value restrictions on the right-hand side, can be used to generate this i.normal form.

Corollary 6.15. *Given a general $\mathcal{ELI}$ TBox $\mathcal{T}$, we can compute in polynomial time an i.normalised $\mathcal{ELI}$ TBox $\mathcal{T}'$ that is a conservative extension of $\mathcal{T}$. In particular, we have*

$$\mathcal{T} \models A \sqsubseteq B \ \ \text{if and only if} \ \ \mathcal{T}' \models A \sqsubseteq B$$

for all concept names $A, B \in sig(\mathcal{T})$.

6.2.2 The classification procedure

In the following, we assume that $\mathcal{T}$ is a general $\mathcal{ELI}$ TBox in i.normal form. The higher complexity of subsumption in $\mathcal{ELI}$ necessitates the use of an extended notion of sequents within our classification procedure.

Definition 6.16. A $\mathcal{T}$-*i.sequent* is an expression of the form

$$K \sqsubseteq \{A\}, \quad K \sqsubseteq \exists r.K' \ \text{ or } \ K \sqsubseteq \forall r.\{A\},$$

where K, K' are *sets* of concept names in $sig(\mathcal{T})$, A is a concept name in $sig(\mathcal{T})$ and r is a role name in $sig(\mathcal{T})$ or the inverse of a role name in $sig(\mathcal{T})$.

From a semantic point of view, a set in a $\mathcal{T}$-i.sequent stands for the conjunction of its elements, where the empty conjunction corresponds to $\top$. Consequently, $\mathcal{T}$-i.sequents are GCIs, and thus a set of $\mathcal{T}$-i.sequents is a general $\mathcal{ELI}$ TBox. Obviously, the overall number of $\mathcal{T}$-i.sequents is exponential in the size of $\mathcal{T}$. In addition, every GCI in the i.normalised TBox $\mathcal{T}$ is either equivalent to a $\mathcal{T}$-i.sequent or a tautology, i.e., satisfied in every interpretation. In the first case, we respresent it as a $\mathcal{T}$-i.sequent, and in the second case, we remove it. For example, the GCI $\top \sqsubseteq A$ corresponds to the $\mathcal{T}$-i.sequent $\emptyset \sqsubseteq \{A\}$, and the GCI $A_1 \sqcap A_2 \sqsubseteq B$ corresponds to the $\mathcal{T}$-i.sequent $\{A_1, A_2\} \sqsubseteq \{B\}$. GCIs with $\top$ or $\forall r.\top$ on the right-hand side are obviously tautologies.

Given the i.normalised input TBox $\mathcal{T}$, we define the current TBox $\mathcal{T}'$ to consist initially of the non-tautological GCIs in $\mathcal{T}$ represented as $\mathcal{T}$-i.sequents. Then, we add new $\mathcal{T}$-i.sequents to $\mathcal{T}'$ by applying the *classification rules* of Figure 6.3.

i.CR1 $\dfrac{}{K \sqsubseteq \{A\}}$ if $A \in K$ and K occurs in $\mathcal{T}'$

i.CR2 $\dfrac{M \sqsubseteq \{B\} \text{ for all } B \in K \quad K \sqsubseteq C}{M \sqsubseteq C}$ if M occurs in $\mathcal{T}'$

i.CR3 $\dfrac{M_2 \sqsubseteq \exists r.M_1 \quad M_1 \sqsubseteq \forall r^-.\{A\}}{M_2 \sqsubseteq \{A\}}$

i.CR4 $\dfrac{M_1 \sqsubseteq \exists r.M_2 \quad M_1 \sqsubseteq \forall r.\{A\}}{M_1 \sqsubseteq \exists r.(M_2 \cup \{A\})}$

Fig. 6.3. The classification rules for $\mathcal{ELI}$.

As in the previous section, the rules given in this figure are actually rule schemata. To build a concrete instance of such a rule schema, the meta-variables K, M, M_1, M_2 must be replaced by sets of concept names in $sig(\mathcal{T})$, the meta-variable A by a concept name in $sig(\mathcal{T})$ and the meta-variable r by a role name in $sig(\mathcal{T})$ or the inverse of a role name in $sig(\mathcal{T})$. The meta-variable C can be replaced by any expression that is an admissible right-hand side of a $\mathcal{T}$-i.sequent.

For the rule schema i.CR1, only instantiations are allowed for which the set of concept names K actually occurs explicitly in some $\mathcal{T}$-i.sequent in the current TBox $\mathcal{T}'$. The reason for this restriction is that without it the procedure would always generate an exponential number of $\mathcal{T}$-i.sequents, since there are exponentially many sets K of concept names in $sig(\mathcal{T})$. The analogous restriction on M in rule i.CR2 is needed in the case where $K = \emptyset$. In fact, in this case the condition "$M \sqsubseteq \{B\}$ for all $B \in K$" is trivially satisfied for all sets M of concept names in $sig(\mathcal{T})$. Thus, without the restriction, the presence of a $\mathcal{T}$-i.sequent of the form $\emptyset \sqsubseteq C$ would cause the generation of exponentially many $\mathcal{T}$-i.sequents of the form $M \sqsubseteq C$.

Though in general the generation of exponentially many $\mathcal{T}$-i.sequents cannot be avoided, the restriction on the applicability of rules i.CR1 and i.CR2 to sets K and M, respectively, already occurring in $\mathcal{T}'$, prevents such an explosion in cases where it is not needed.

Example 6.17. For example, if $\mathcal{T} = \{A \sqsubseteq B\} \cup \{A_i \sqsubseteq A_i \mid 1 \leq i \leq n\}$, then we have $\mathcal{T} \models M \cup \{A\} \sqsubseteq \{B\}$ for all (exponentially many) sets $\emptyset \neq M \subseteq \{A_1, \ldots, A_n\}$. However, due to the restriction on the applicability of rule i.CR1, none of these $\mathcal{T}$-i.sequents is actually generated by the calculus when applied to $\mathcal{T}' = \{\{A\} \sqsubseteq \{B\}\} \cup \{\{A_i\} \sqsubseteq \{A_i\} \mid 1 \leq i \leq n\}$. In fact, since none of the sets $M \cup \{A\}$ occurs in $\mathcal{T}'$, the rule i.CR1 is not applicable.

What may seem to be a completeness problem is in fact an important feature of the calculus, aiming to avoid a combinatorial explosion due to the derivation of exponentially many "uninteresting" consequences such as the ones in the above example. The next example shows in what situations the rules i.CR1 and i.CR2 are actually needed.

Example 6.18. If $\mathcal{T} = \{A \sqsubseteq \exists r.(A_1 \sqcap A_2 \sqcap A_3), \exists r.(A_1 \sqcap A_2) \sqsubseteq B\}$, then obviously $\mathcal{T} \models A \sqsubseteq B$. The set of $\mathcal{T}$-i.sequents corresponding to $\mathcal{T}$ is $\mathcal{T}' = \{\{A\} \sqsubseteq \exists r.\{A_1, A_2, A_3\}, \{A_1, A_2\} \sqsubseteq \forall r^-.\{B\}\}$. We show that the rules of Figure 6.3 can be used to derive the $\mathcal{T}$-i.sequent $\{A\} \sqsubseteq \{B\}$.

In fact, two applications of i.CR1 yield the $\mathcal{T}$-i.sequents $\{A_1, A_2, A_3\} \sqsubseteq \{A_1\}$ and $\{A_1, A_2, A_3\} \sqsubseteq \{A_2\}$. These applications are admissible since $\{A_1, A_2, A_3\}$ occurs in $\mathcal{T}'$. Given the two derived $\mathcal{T}$-i.sequents together with the second $\mathcal{T}$-i.sequent in $\mathcal{T}'$, an application of i.CR2 now yields $\{A_1, A_2, A_3\} \sqsubseteq \forall r^-.\{B\}$. Given this $\mathcal{T}$-i.sequent together with the first $\mathcal{T}$-i.sequent in $\mathcal{T}'$, an application of i.CR3 yields $\{A\} \sqsubseteq \{B\}$.

Due to the occurrence restrictions, the rules i.CR1 and i.CR2 cannot introduce new sets of concept names into $\mathcal{T}'$. The same is obviously true (without any restriction) for i.CR3. In contrast, rule i.CR4 can generate sets not yet occurring in $\mathcal{T}'$, and thus may cause an exponential blowup.

Example 6.19. Consider the $\mathcal{ELI}$ TBox $\mathcal{T} := \{A \sqsubseteq \exists r.\top\} \cup \{\exists r^-.A \sqsubseteq A_i \mid i = 1, \ldots, n\}$. By i.normalisation, we can transform this TBox into the following set of $\mathcal{T}$-i.sequents:

$$\mathcal{T}' := \{\{A\} \sqsubseteq \exists r.\emptyset\} \cup \{\{A\} \sqsubseteq \forall r.\{A_i\} \mid i = 1, \ldots, n\}.$$

It is easy to see that repeated applications of rule i.CR4 can now be used to generate all $\mathcal{T}$-i.sequents $\{A\} \sqsubseteq \exists r.M$ for $M \subseteq \{A_1, \ldots, A_n\}$.

Thus, if we add $M \sqsubseteq \forall r^-.\{B\}$ to $\mathcal{T}'$ for some set $M \subseteq \{A_1, \ldots, A_n\}$, then $\{A\} \sqsubseteq \{B\}$ can be derived by an application of i.CR3. Note, however, that for this it would have been sufficient to derive (by n applications of i.CR4) only the "maximal" $\mathcal{T}$-i.sequent $\{A\} \sqsubseteq \exists r.\{A_1, \ldots, A_n\}$, and then use a derivation of $\{A\} \sqsubseteq \{B\}$ analogous to the one shown in Example 6.18. It is thus imaginable that the exponential blowup demonstrated by this example could actually be avoided by a clever strategy. That this cannot always be the case follows from the fact that subsumption in $\mathcal{ELI}$ is EXPTIME-complete. Later, in Section 6.3.1, we will give an example in which exponentially many $\mathcal{T}$-i.sequents need to be derived before the final $\mathcal{T}$-i.sequent $\{A\} \sqsubseteq \{B\}$ is reached.

Before analysing the complexity of the algorithm in more detail, we will show that it is actually sound and complete in the sense made precise in Proposition 6.20 below. Using the same notation as in the previous section, we denote the TBox obtained by an exhaustive application of the rules of Figure 6.3 as $\mathcal{T}^*$. We call this process *i.saturation* of $\mathcal{T}$ with respect to the inference rules of Figure 6.3, and the resulting TBox $\mathcal{T}^*$ the *i.saturated* TBox. As in the case of saturation for $\mathcal{EL}$, it is easy to see that the i.saturated TBox $\mathcal{T}^*$ is uniquely determined by $\mathcal{T}$.

Proposition 6.20. *For all concept names A, B in $sig(\mathcal{T})$ such that $\{A\}$ occurs in $\mathcal{T}^*$, we have $\mathcal{T} \models A \sqsubseteq B$ if and only if $\{A\} \sqsubseteq \{B\} \in \mathcal{T}^*$.*

Note that the condition "$\{A\}$ occurs in $\mathcal{T}^*$" can easily be satisfied for a given concept name A in $sig(\mathcal{T})$. For example, we can add the dummy GCI $A \sqsubseteq A$ to the input TBox, which is translated into the $\mathcal{T}$-i.sequent $\{A\} \sqsubseteq \{A\}$.

The "if" direction of this proposition is an immediate consequence of the next lemma and the fact that any GCI in $\mathcal{T}$ follows from $\mathcal{T}$.

Lemma 6.21 (Soundness). *If all the GCIs in $\mathcal{T}'$ follow from $\mathcal{T}$ and the $\mathcal{T}$-i.sequents above the line of one of the inference rules of Figure 6.3 belong to $\mathcal{T}'$, then the $\mathcal{T}$-i.sequent below the line also follows from $\mathcal{T}$.*

Proof. Soundness of rule i.CR1 follows from the fact that a conjunction of concept names is subsumed by each of its conjuncts.

Soundness of rule i.CR2 is due to transitivity of subsumption and the fact that $\mathcal{T} \models M \sqsubseteq \{B\}$ for all $B \in K$ if and only if $\mathcal{T} \models M \sqsubseteq K$. Note that this fact is also true in the case where K is the empty set.

To see soundness of i.CR3, note that $\mathcal{T} \models M_1 \sqsubseteq \forall r^-.\{A\}$ if and only if $\mathcal{T} \models \exists r.M_1 \sqsubseteq \{A\}$. Thus transitivity of subsumption yields $\mathcal{T} \models M_2 \sqsubseteq \{A\}$.

Finally, to show soundness of rule i.CR4, assume that $\mathcal{I}$ is a model of $\mathcal{T}$. Thus, according to the assumptions in the formulation of the lemma, $\mathcal{I}$ satisfies the two GCIs above the line of rule i.CR4. We must show that it also satisfies the GCI below the line. To this end, consider an element $d \in M_1^{\mathcal{I}}$. By the first GCI above the line, there is an element $e \in \Delta^{\mathcal{I}}$ such that $(d, e) \in r^{\mathcal{I}}$ and $e \in M_2^{\mathcal{I}}$. Due to the second GCI above the line, we know that $d \in (\forall r.\{A\})^{\mathcal{I}}$, and thus $e \in A^{\mathcal{I}}$. Together with $e \in M_2^{\mathcal{I}}$, this yields $e \in (M_1 \cup \{A\})^\mathcal{I}$. Consequently, we have $d \in (\exists r.(M_2 \cup \{A\}))^\mathcal{I}$ as required. $\qquad\square$

In order to show the "only if" direction of the proposition, we construct an appropriate canonical interpretation.

Definition 6.22 (Canonical interpretation). Let $\mathcal{T}$ be a general $\mathcal{ELI}$ TBox in i.normal form and $\mathcal{T}^*$ the i.saturated TBox obtained by exhaustive application of the inference rules of Figure 6.3. The *canonical interpretation* $\mathcal{I}_{\mathcal{T}^*}$ induced by $\mathcal{T}^*$ is defined as follows:

$\Delta^{\mathcal{I}_{\mathcal{T}^*}} = \{M \mid M$ is a set of concept names in $sig(\mathcal{T})$ that occurs in $\mathcal{T}^*\}$,

$A^{\mathcal{I}_{\mathcal{T}^*}} = \{M \in \Delta^{\mathcal{I}_{\mathcal{T}^*}} \mid M \sqsubseteq \{A\} \in \mathcal{T}^*\}$,

$s^{\mathcal{I}_{\mathcal{T}^*}} = \{(M,N) \in \Delta^{\mathcal{I}_{\mathcal{T}^*}} \times \Delta^{\mathcal{I}_{\mathcal{T}^*}} \mid M \sqsubseteq \exists s.N \in \mathcal{T}^*$ and N is maximal,
   i.e., there is no $N' \supsetneq N$ such that $M \sqsubseteq \exists s.N' \in \mathcal{T}^*\} \cup$
   $\{(N,M) \in \Delta^{\mathcal{I}_{\mathcal{T}^*}} \times \Delta^{\mathcal{I}_{\mathcal{T}^*}} \mid M \sqsubseteq \exists s^-.N \in \mathcal{T}^*$ and N is maximal,
   i.e., there is no $N' \supsetneq N$ such that $M \sqsubseteq \exists s^-.N' \in \mathcal{T}^*\}$,

where A ranges over all concept names in $sig(\mathcal{T})$ and s over all role names in $sig(\mathcal{T})$.

Our definition of the extension of role names in the canonical interpretation is symmetric with respect to the inverse operator, and thus also inverse roles satisfy the identity given in this definition.

Lemma 6.23. *Let r be a role name or the inverse of a role name. Then*

$$r^{\mathcal{I}_{\mathcal{T}^*}} = \{(M,N) \in \Delta^{\mathcal{I}_{\mathcal{T}^*}} \times \Delta^{\mathcal{I}_{\mathcal{T}^*}} \mid M \sqsubseteq \exists r.N \in \mathcal{T}^*, \; N \text{ maximal}\} \cup$$
$$\{(N,M) \in \Delta^{\mathcal{I}_{\mathcal{T}^*}} \times \Delta^{\mathcal{I}_{\mathcal{T}^*}} \mid M \sqsubseteq \exists r^-.N \in \mathcal{T}^*, \; N \text{ maximal}\}.$$

Proof. If $r = s$ is a role name, then this identity is just the definition of $s^{\mathcal{I}_{\mathcal{T}^*}}$. Otherwise, if $r = s^-$ for a role name s, then this identity follows from the fact that $r^- = s$, the semantics of the inverse operator and the definition of $s^{\mathcal{I}_{\mathcal{T}^*}}$:

$$r^{\mathcal{I}_{\mathcal{T}^*}} = (s^-)^{\mathcal{I}_{\mathcal{T}^*}} = \{(L,K) \in \Delta^{\mathcal{I}_{\mathcal{T}^*}} \times \Delta^{\mathcal{I}_{\mathcal{T}^*}} \mid (K,L) \in s^{\mathcal{I}_{\mathcal{T}^*}}\}$$
$$= \{(N,M) \in \Delta^{\mathcal{I}_{\mathcal{T}^*}} \times \Delta^{\mathcal{I}_{\mathcal{T}^*}} \mid M \sqsubseteq \exists s.N \in \mathcal{T}^*, \; N \text{ maximal}\} \cup$$
$$\{(M,N) \in \Delta^{\mathcal{I}_{\mathcal{T}^*}} \times \Delta^{\mathcal{I}_{\mathcal{T}^*}} \mid M \sqsubseteq \exists s^-.N \in \mathcal{T}^*, \; N \text{ maximal}\}$$
$$= \{(N,M) \in \Delta^{\mathcal{I}_{\mathcal{T}^*}} \times \Delta^{\mathcal{I}_{\mathcal{T}^*}} \mid M \sqsubseteq \exists r^-.N \in \mathcal{T}^*, \; N \text{ maximal}\} \cup$$
$$\{(M,N) \in \Delta^{\mathcal{I}_{\mathcal{T}^*}} \times \Delta^{\mathcal{I}_{\mathcal{T}^*}} \mid M \sqsubseteq \exists r.N \in \mathcal{T}^*, \; N \text{ maximal}\}.$$

$\qquad\square$

As in the case of $\mathcal{EL}$, it is now easy to show that the canonical interpretation is a model of the i.saturated TBox it is induced by.

Lemma 6.24. *The canonical interpretation induced by $\mathcal{T}^*$ is a model of the i.saturated TBox $\mathcal{T}^*$.*

Proof. All the GCIs in $\mathcal{T}^*$ are $\mathcal{T}$-i.sequents, i.e., they are of the form described in Definition 6.16.

- Consider a GCI of the form $K \sqsubseteq \{A\} \in \mathcal{T}^*$, and let $M \in K^{\mathcal{I}_{\mathcal{T}^*}}$, i.e., $M \sqsubseteq \{B\} \in \mathcal{T}^*$ for all $B \in K$. Then rule i.CR2 yields $M \sqsubseteq \{A\} \in \mathcal{T}^*$, and thus $M \in A^{\mathcal{I}_{\mathcal{T}^*}}$.

- Consider a GCI of the form $K \sqsubseteq \exists r.K' \in \mathcal{T}^*$ for a role name or the inverse of a role name r. Now assume that $M \in K^{\mathcal{I}_{\mathcal{T}^*}}$, i.e., $M \sqsubseteq \{B\} \in \mathcal{T}^*$ for all $B \in K$. Then rule i.CR2 yields $M \sqsubseteq \exists r.K' \in \mathcal{T}^*$, and thus there is a maximal set $K'' \supseteq K'$ with $M \sqsubseteq \exists r.K'' \in \mathcal{T}^*$ and $(M, K'') \in r^{\mathcal{I}_{\mathcal{T}^*}}$. Since K'' occurs in $\mathcal{T}^*$, rule i.CR1 yields $K'' \sqsubseteq \{A\} \in \mathcal{T}^*$ for all $A \in K''$. Since $K' \subseteq K''$, this implies $K'' \in K'^{\mathcal{I}_{\mathcal{T}^*}}$. Consequently, we have $M \in (\exists r.K')^{\mathcal{I}_{\mathcal{T}^*}}$.

- Consider a GCI of the form $K \sqsubseteq \forall r.\{A\} \in \mathcal{T}^*$ for a role name or the inverse of a role name r. Assume $M_1 \in K^{\mathcal{I}_{\mathcal{T}^*}}$ and that there is an M_2 such that $(M_1, M_2) \in r^{\mathcal{I}_{\mathcal{T}^*}}$. We must show that $M_2 \in A^{\mathcal{I}_{\mathcal{T}^*}}$.

  By the definition of $\mathcal{I}_{\mathcal{T}^*}$, $M_1 \in K^{\mathcal{I}_{\mathcal{T}^*}}$ yields $M_1 \sqsubseteq \{B\} \in \mathcal{T}^*$ for all $B \in K$. Because of rule i.CR2 we thus have $M_1 \sqsubseteq \forall r.\{A\} \in \mathcal{T}^*$.
  There are two possible reasons for (M_1, M_2) to belong to $r^{\mathcal{I}_{\mathcal{T}^*}}$.

  - First, assume that $M_1 \sqsubseteq \exists r.M_2 \in \mathcal{T}^*$ where M_2 is maximal with this property. Then rule i.CR4 yields $M_1 \sqsubseteq \exists r.(M_2 \cup \{A\}) \in \mathcal{T}^*$, and thus $A \in M_2$ due to the maximality of M_2. Since M_2 occurs in $\mathcal{T}^*$, rule i.CR1 yields $M_2 \sqsubseteq \{A\} \in \mathcal{T}^*$, and thus $M_2 \in A^{\mathcal{I}_{\mathcal{T}^*}}$ as required.

  - Second, assume that $M_2 \sqsubseteq \exists r^-.M_1 \in \mathcal{T}^*$, where M_1 is maximal with this property. Then rule i.CR3 yields $M_2 \sqsubseteq \{A\} \in \mathcal{T}^*$, and thus again $M_2 \in A^{\mathcal{I}_{\mathcal{T}^*}}$ as required.

Since all the elements of $\mathcal{T}^*$ are of one of the forms considered above, this shows that $\mathcal{I}_{\mathcal{T}^*}$ is indeed a model of $\mathcal{T}^*$. $\qquad\square$

The first case (i.e., where $M_1 \sqsubseteq \exists r.M_2 \in \mathcal{T}^*$) in the treatment of value restrictions in the above proof makes clear why we need the maximality condition in the definition of the extensions of roles in the canonical model. Let us illustrate this issue using Example 6.19. There, we obtain all the $\mathcal{T}$-i.sequents $\{A\} \sqsubseteq \exists r.M$ for $M \subseteq \{A_1, \ldots, A_n\}$. Thus, the set $\{A\}$ and all the sets $M \subseteq \{A_1, \ldots, A_n\}$ are in the domain of the canonical model. However, only the pair $(\{A\}, \{A_1, \ldots, A_n\})$ belongs to the interpretation of r. In fact, adding any other pair $(\{A\}, M)$ with $M \subset \{A_1, \ldots, A_n\}$ would violate one of the GCIs $\{A\} \sqsubseteq \forall r.\{A_i\}$. To be more precise, assume that $A_i \notin M$. Then $M \sqsubseteq \{A_i\}$ cannot be derived, and thus M does not belong to the extension of A_i in the canonical model.

Given Lemma 6.24, completeness is now easy to show.

Lemma 6.25 (Completeness). *Let A, B in $sig(\mathcal{T})$ be such that $\{A\}$ occurs in $\mathcal{T}^*$. Then $\mathcal{T} \models A \sqsubseteq B$ implies $\{A\} \sqsubseteq \{B\} \in \mathcal{T}^*$.*

Proof. We show the contrapositive. Assume that $\{A\} \sqsubseteq \{B\} \notin \mathcal{T}^*$. Since $\{A\}$ occurs in $\mathcal{T}^*$, we have $\{A\} \in \Delta^{\mathcal{I}_{\mathcal{T}^*}}$. Rule i.CR1 yields $\{A\} \sqsubseteq \{A\} \in \mathcal{T}^*$, and thus $\{A\} \in A^{\mathcal{I}_{\mathcal{T}^*}}$. However, $\{A\} \sqsubseteq \{B\} \notin \mathcal{T}^*$ shows that $\{A\} \notin B^{\mathcal{I}_{\mathcal{T}^*}}$. Since $\mathcal{I}_{\mathcal{T}^*}$ is a model of $\mathcal{T}^*$, and thus also of $\mathcal{T}$, this yields $\mathcal{T} \not\models A \sqsubseteq B$. $\qquad\square$

If we put all the results of this section together, we obtain the following theorem.

Theorem 6.26. *Subsumption in $\mathcal{ELI}$ with respect to general TBoxes is decidable in exponential time.*

Proof. Let $\mathcal{T}_0$ be a general $\mathcal{ELI}$ TBox and C, D $\mathcal{ELI}$ concepts. To decide whether $\mathcal{T}_0 \models C \sqsubseteq D$ holds or not, we first add the GCIs $A \sqsubseteq C, D \sqsubseteq B$ to $\mathcal{T}_0$. The resulting TBox $\mathcal{T}_1$ is then i.normalised using the normalisation rules of Figure 6.1 together with the rule that transforms a GCI with an existential restriction on the left-hand side into the equivalent one with a value restriction on the right-hand side. The size of the i.normalised TBox $\mathcal{T}$ obtained this way is linear in the size of $\mathcal{T}_0$, and we have $\mathcal{T}_0 \models C \sqsubseteq D$ if and only if $\mathcal{T} \models A \sqsubseteq B$.

Let $\mathcal{T}^*$ be the TBox obtained by an exhaustive application of the rules of Figure 6.3, starting with $\mathcal{T}'$, in which the non-tautological GCIs in $\mathcal{T}$ are represented as $\mathcal{T}$-i.sequents. The i.saturated TBox $\mathcal{T}^*$ can be computed in time exponential in the size of $\mathcal{T}$ (and thus also in the size of $\mathcal{T}_0$), since there are only exponentially many $\mathcal{T}$-i.sequents and every application of a rule adds a $\mathcal{T}$-i.sequent. Since $\mathcal{T}_0$ contains a GCI whose left-hand side is A, the initial set of $\mathcal{T}$-i.sequents $\mathcal{T}'$ contains the set $\{A\}$. Thus, Lemma 6.25 yields $\mathcal{T} \models A \sqsubseteq B$ if and only if $\{A\} \sqsubseteq \{B\} \in \mathcal{T}^*$. Consequently, by checking whether $\{A\} \sqsubseteq \{B\}$ is an element of $\mathcal{T}^*$, we can decide whether $\mathcal{T}_0 \models C \sqsubseteq D$ holds or not. $\qquad\square$

6.3 Comparing the two subsumption algorithms

First, we compare the two algorithms on the technical level of the rule sets, and then we take a more abstract point of view.

6.3.1 Comparing the classification rules

In principle, the classification rules for $\mathcal{ELI}$ are a generalisation of the rules for $\mathcal{EL}$, though at first sight the rules given in each of the two previous sections may look quite different from each other. In the following, we explain the connection between the two rule sets.

Obviously, rule CR1 is the special case of rule i.CR1 where $K = \{A\}$. The generalisation of rule CR1 to i.CR1 is needed to deal with the generalised form of sequents containing sets of concept names.

Rule CR2 does not have a corresponding rule in the calculus for $\mathcal{ELI}$. Basically, the reason for this is that rule i.CR2 implicitly covers the treatment of the top concept through its instances for which $K = \emptyset$. This point can best be clarified by an example. For instance, consider the normalised TBox $\mathcal{T} = \{A \sqsubseteq A, \top \sqsubseteq B\}$. We have $\mathcal{T} \models A \sqsubseteq B$, and thus completeness of the calculus for $\mathcal{EL}$ implies that the saturated TBox $\mathcal{T}^*$ must contain $A \sqsubseteq B$. To derive this GCI, the rule CR2 is needed. In fact, CR2 yields $A \sqsubseteq \top$, and then rule CR3 can be used to obtain $A \sqsubseteq B$. In the calculus for $\mathcal{ELI}$, we start with the i.normalised TBox $\{\{A\} \sqsubseteq \{A\}, \emptyset \sqsubseteq \{B\}\}$. If we instantiate M with $\{A\}$, K with $\emptyset$, and C with $\{B\}$, then rule i.CR2 yields $\{A\} \sqsubseteq \{B\}$ as required.

The rules CR3 and CR4 are obviously special cases of rule i.CR2.

If one takes into account that $M_1 \sqsubseteq \forall r^-.\{A\}$ is equivalent to $\exists r.M_1 \sqsubseteq \{A\}$, the rule i.CR3 looks similar to rule CR5. Rule i.CR3 realises transitivity through an existential restriction occurring on the right-hand side of one GCI and on the left-hand side of another GCI. One may wonder why, in the calculus for $\mathcal{EL}$, we need the rule CR5 rather than the more restricted transitivity rule

$$\text{CR5}' \quad \frac{A \sqsubseteq \exists r.A_1 \quad \exists r.A_1 \sqsubseteq B}{A \sqsubseteq B};$$

or, put the other way round, why the more restricted transitivity rule i.CR3 is sufficient in the calculus for $\mathcal{ELI}$. Again, this is best explained by a simple example. For instance, consider the normalised TBox $\mathcal{T} = \{A \sqsubseteq \exists r.A_1, A_1 \sqsubseteq B_1, \exists r.B_1 \sqsubseteq B\}$. If we replace CR5 in the calculus for $\mathcal{EL}$ by CR5′, then $A \sqsubseteq B$ can no longer be derived. In the calculus for

$\mathcal{ELI}$, we start with the i.normalised TBox

$$\{\{A\} \sqsubseteq \exists r.\{A_1\}, \{A_1\} \sqsubseteq \{B_1\}, \{B_1\} \sqsubseteq \forall r^-.\{B\}\}.$$

Applying rule i.CR2 to the second and the third GCI yields $\{A_1\} \sqsubseteq \forall r^-.\{B\}$. Now the rule i.CR3 can be applied to the first GCI in the above TBox and this derived GCI to obtain the desired GCI $\{A\} \sqsubseteq \{B\}$.

The rule i.CR4 does not have a corresponding rule in the calculus for $\mathcal{EL}$. It is required to deal with the additional expressive power caused by inverse roles, i.e, the fact that value restrictions on the right-hand side of GCIs can be expressed. Note that this is the only rule that can generate new sets of concept names other than singleton sets within $\mathcal{T}$-i.sequents: in fact, the set $M_2 \cup \{A\}$ may not have occurred in $\mathcal{T}'$ before.

This also shows that the algorithm for $\mathcal{ELI}$ runs in polynomial time if it receives a general $\mathcal{EL}$ TBox as input. Indeed, if we start with an $\mathcal{EL}$ TBox $\mathcal{T}_0$, then the corresponding i.normalised TBox $\mathcal{T}$ (written as a set of $\mathcal{T}$-i.sequents) contains only $\mathcal{T}$-i.sequents satisfying the following restrictions:

   (i) the only sets occurring in these $\mathcal{T}$-i.sequents are the empty set and singleton sets;
   (ii) value restrictions in these $\mathcal{T}$-i.sequents are only with respect to inverses of role names;
   (iii) existential restrictions in these $\mathcal{T}$-i.sequents are only with respect to role names.

Let us call a $\mathcal{T}$-i.sequent satisfying these three restrictions an $\mathcal{EL}$-$\mathcal{T}$-*i.sequent*.

Lemma 6.27. *There are only polynomially many $\mathcal{EL}$-$\mathcal{T}$-i.sequents in the size of $\mathcal{T}$. In addition, applying an inference rule of Figure 6.3 to a set $\mathcal{T}'$ of $\mathcal{EL}$-$\mathcal{T}$-i.sequents yields a set of $\mathcal{EL}$-$\mathcal{T}$-i.sequents.*

Proof. The first statement of the lemma is obviously true since there are only polynomially many sets of concept names in $sig(\mathcal{T})$ of cardinality ≤ 1.

The only rule that could generate a $\mathcal{T}$-i.sequent violating the above three conditions is rule i.CR4. However, this rule is not applicable since it requires the same role name r or inverse of a role name $r = s^-$ to occur in both an existential restriction and a value restriction in $\mathcal{T}'$, which is prevented by the second and third conditions above. $\square$

As an obvious consequence of this lemma, i.saturation terminates after a polynomial number of rule applications if applied to an i.normalised TBox that contains only $\mathcal{EL}$-$\mathcal{T}$-i.sequents.

Proposition 6.28. *The subsumption algorithm for $\mathcal{ELI}$ yields a polynomial-time decision procedure for subsumption in $\mathcal{EL}$.*

If we start with an $\mathcal{ELI}$ TBox whose i.normalisation does not yield a set of $\mathcal{EL}$-$\mathcal{T}$-i.sequents, then rule i.CR4 may cause the generation of an exponential number of $\mathcal{T}$-i.sequents, as illustrated by Example 6.19 above. However, though in this example the i.saturated TBox $\mathcal{T}^*$ indeed contains exponentially many $\mathcal{T}$-i.sequents, only a linear number of these $\mathcal{T}$-i.sequents is needed to derive the desired consequence $\{A\} \sqsubseteq \{B\}$. In the following example, one needs to derive exponentially many $\mathcal{T}$-i.sequents before the consequence $\{A\} \sqsubseteq \{B\}$ can be derived.

Example 6.29. Let A, B and $X_i, \overline{X}_i$ for $i = 0, \ldots, n-1$ be concept names and r a role name. Assume that $\mathcal{T}'$ consists of the following set of $\mathcal{T}$-i.sequents:

$$\begin{aligned}
\{A\} &\sqsubseteq \{\overline{X}_i\} \text{ for } 0 \leq i \leq n-1, \\
\emptyset &\sqsubseteq \exists r.\emptyset, \\
\{\overline{X}_i, X_0, \ldots, X_{i-1}\} &\sqsubseteq \forall r.\{X_i\} \text{ for } 0 \leq i \leq n-1, \\
\{X_i, X_0, \ldots, X_{i-1}\} &\sqsubseteq \forall r.\{\overline{X}_i\} \text{ for } 0 \leq i \leq n-1, \\
\{\overline{X}_i, \overline{X}_j\} &\sqsubseteq \forall r.\{\overline{X}_i\} \text{ for } 0 \leq j < i \leq n-1, \\
\{X_i, \overline{X}_j\} &\sqsubseteq \forall r.\{X_i\} \text{ for } 0 \leq j < i \leq n-1, \\
\{X_0, \ldots, X_{n-1}\} &\sqsubseteq \{B\}, \\
\{B\} &\sqsubseteq \forall r^-.\{B\}.
\end{aligned}$$

Subsets of $\{X_i, \overline{X}_i \mid i = 0, \ldots, n-1\}$ containing exactly one of the concept names $X_i, \overline{X}_i$ for each $i, 0 \leq i < n$, can obviously be used to represent natural numbers k between 0 and $2^n - 1$. The set corresponding to the number k will be denoted as $X(k)$, i.e.,

$$\begin{aligned}
X(0) &= \{\overline{X}_0, \overline{X}_1, \ldots, \overline{X}_{n-1}\}, \\
X(1) &= \{X_0, \overline{X}_1 \ldots, \overline{X}_{n-1}\}, \\
&\vdots \\
X(2^n - 2) &= \{\overline{X}_0, X_1, \ldots, X_{n-1}\}, \\
X(2^n - 1) &= \{X_0, X_1, \ldots, X_{n-1}\}.
\end{aligned}$$

Using rule i.CR2 we can derive

$$\{A\} \sqsubseteq \exists r.\emptyset \quad \text{and} \quad \{A\} \sqsubseteq \forall r.\{X_0\}$$

as well as

$$\{A\} \sqsubseteq \forall r.\{\overline{X}_i\} \text{ for all } i, 0 < i < n.$$

Using n applications of i.CR4 we can thus derive

$$\{A\} \sqsubseteq \exists r.X(1).$$

Since $X(1)$ occurs in the TBox generated in this way, we can now use i.CR1 to derive

$$X(1) \sqsubseteq X_0 \text{ and } X(1) \sqsubseteq \overline{X}_i \text{ for } i = 1, \ldots, n-1.$$

Thus, by applying the approach used above for $\{A\}$ to this set, we can derive $X(1) \sqsubseteq \exists r.X(2)$. Continuing this way, we obtain all the $\mathcal{T}$-i.sequents

$$X(k) \sqsubseteq \exists r.X(k+1) \text{ for } 1 \le k \le 2^n - 2.$$

Using the rule i.CR2, we can now derive

$$X(2^n - 1) \sqsubseteq \forall r^-.\{B\},$$

which together with $X(2^n - 2) \sqsubseteq \exists r.X(2^n - 1)$ yields $X(2^n - 2) \sqsubseteq \{B\}$ by an application of rule i.CR3. Continuing in this way, we can thus derive $X(1) \sqsubseteq \{B\}$, which then yields $X(1) \sqsubseteq \forall r^-.\{B\}$. Together with $\{A\} \sqsubseteq \exists r.X(1)$, we thus obtain

$$\{A\} \sqsubseteq \{B\}$$

by an application of rule i.CR3.

The derivation of $\{A\} \sqsubseteq \{B\}$ constructed above obviously has a length that is exponential in n, whereas the size of $\mathcal{T}'$ is polynomial in n. It is easy to see that there cannot be a derivation of this sequent that has polynomial length. In fact, one first needs to generate the exponentially many sequents $X(k) \sqsubseteq \exists r.X(k+1)$ for $1 \le k \le 2^n - 2$ before reaching B, which then has to be propagated back by generating the exponentially many sequents $X(k) \sqsubseteq \{B\}$ for $1 \le k \le 2^n - 1$.

6.3.2 A more abstract point of view

Both algorithms use inference rules to generate new GCIs that are consequences of the ones already obtained. This generation process is deterministic in the sense that GCIs, once added, are never removed. The two algorithms also have in common that it is sufficient to compute only consequences belonging to a certain *finite* set of *relevant* potential consequences, which is determined by the input TBox. Once all relevant consequences are computed, the subsumption query can be answered by a simple inspection of this set. The difference in the complexity of the two procedures stems from the fact that, for $\mathcal{EL}$, the cardinality of the set of relevant potential consequences is polynomial in the size of the input TBox, whereas it is exponential for $\mathcal{ELI}$.

From a semantic point of view, both algorithms generate *canonical models*, i.e., models $\mathcal{I}_{\mathcal{T}^*}$ of the normalised input TBox $\mathcal{T}$ in which subsumptions between concept names hold if and only if they follow from $\mathcal{T}$ (modulo certain occurrence restrictions formulated in the completeness results). For $\mathcal{EL}$, the domain of the canonical model consists of all the concept names occurring in the saturated TBox $\mathcal{T}^*$, the interpretation of the concept names is determined by the $\mathcal{T}$-sequents of the form $B \sqsubseteq A$ in $\mathcal{T}^*$, and the interpretation of the role names is determined by the $\mathcal{T}$-sequents of the form $A \sqsubseteq \exists r.B$ in $\mathcal{T}^*$. Similarly, for $\mathcal{ELI}$, the domain of the canonical model consists of all the sets of concept names occurring in the i.saturated TBox $\mathcal{T}^*$, the interpretation of the concept names is determined by the GCIs of the form $M \sqsubseteq \{A\}$ in $\mathcal{T}^*$, and the interpretation of the role names is determined by the GCIs of the form $M \sqsubseteq \exists r.N$ in $\mathcal{T}^*$.

In contrast to the type elimination algorithm for satisfiability in $\mathcal{ALC}$ with respect to general TBoxes, introduced in Chapter 5, the generation of the canonical model is a bottom-up procedure, i.e., it adds elements to the domain and to the extension of concepts and roles, rather than starting with a maximal set and successively removing elements.[2]

The tableau algorithms introduced in Chapter 4 compute a model of the TBox that refutes the subsumption in case it does not hold. But if the subsumption holds, then no model is computed. Another difference to the algorithms introduced in the present chapter is that the tableau algorithms are nondeterministic, i.e., different choices need to be made and backtracking is required if a decision was wrong.

The canonical model of an $\mathcal{ELI}$ TBox introduced in Definition 6.22 is not only a tool to show completeness of the classification algorithm for $\mathcal{ELI}$. It can also be employed to show other useful properties. As an example, we use the canonical model to show that $\mathcal{ELI}$ is convex. Intuitively, convexity says that $\mathcal{ELI}$ does not have any "hidden disjunctions":

---

[2] More formally speaking, type elimination computes a greatest fixpoint, whereas the algorithms introduced in the present chapter compute a least fixpoint.

Proposition 6.30. *$\mathcal{ELI}$ is convex, i.e., it satisfies the following convexity property: if $\mathcal{T}$ is an $\mathcal{ELI}$ TBox and $C, D_1, \ldots, D_n$ are $\mathcal{ELI}$ concepts, then*

$$\mathcal{T} \models C \sqsubseteq D_1 \sqcup \cdots \sqcup D_n \text{ if and only if } \mathcal{T} \models C \sqsubseteq D_i \text{ for some } i \in \{1, \ldots, n\}.$$

Note that the above definition of convexity makes sense even though $\mathcal{ELI}$ does not include disjunction as a constructor; in fact, the left-hand side of the above equivalence can simply be understood as a statement formulated in $\mathcal{ALCI}$.

Obviously, the DL $\mathcal{ALC}$ is not convex in the above sense as, for example, the TBox $\mathcal{T} = \{A \sqsubseteq B_1 \sqcup B_2\}$ satisfies $\mathcal{T} \models A \sqsubseteq B_1 \sqcup B_2$, but not $\mathcal{T} \models A \sqsubseteq B_i$ for any $i \in \{1, 2\}$. This is of course no surprise since $\mathcal{ALC}$ explicitly allows for disjunction.

However, things are not always that obvious. To see this, consider the DL $\mathcal{FLE}$, the extension of $\mathcal{EL}$ with value restrictions. In contrast to $\mathcal{ELI}$, an $\mathcal{FLE}$ TBox may have value restrictions on both the left- and the right-hand sides of GCIs. Despite not including disjunction as a concept constructor, this DL is not convex. To see this, take the TBox

$$\mathcal{T} = \{\exists r.\top \sqsubseteq B_1, \forall r.A \sqsubseteq B_2\}.$$

Then we have $\mathcal{T} \models \top \sqsubseteq B_1 \sqcup B_2$, but not $\mathcal{T} \models \top \sqsubseteq B_i$ for any $i \in \{1, 2\}$. In fact, the latter is easy to verify by giving a countermodel against the two subsumptions in question. To see the former, let $\mathcal{I}$ be a model of $\mathcal{T}$ and $d \in \Delta^{\mathcal{I}}$. Then either there is some $e \in \Delta^{\mathcal{I}}$ with $(d, e) \in r^{\mathcal{I}}$ or this is not the case. In the first case, $d \in (\exists r.\top)^{\mathcal{I}}$, thus $d \in B_1^{\mathcal{I}}$; in the second case, $d \in (\forall r.A)^{\mathcal{I}}$, thus $d \in B_2^{\mathcal{I}}$.

Convexity is of interest because reasoning algorithms for non-convex DLs typically need to employ nondeterminism or backtracking (such as tableau algorithms), or are best-case exponential (such as type elimination algorithms). They cannot be treated using consequence-based algorithms that are as simple and elegant as the ones presented in this chapter.

To prove Proposition 6.30, we first show a lemma, which will also turn out to be helpful in the next chapter.

Lemma 6.31. *Let $\mathcal{T}$ be an $\mathcal{ELI}$ TBox, C an $\mathcal{ELI}$ concept and Γ a finite set of $\mathcal{ELI}$ concepts. Then there is a model $\mathcal{I}$ of $\mathcal{T}$ and an element $d \in \Delta^{\mathcal{I}}$ such that the following holds for all concepts $D \in \Gamma$:*

$$\mathcal{T} \models C \sqsubseteq D \text{ if and only if } d \in D^{\mathcal{I}}.$$

Proof. Let $\Gamma = \{D_1, \ldots, D_n\}$. We introduce new concept names $A, B_1, \ldots, B_n$ and extend $\mathcal{T}$ by GCIs that say that A is equivalent to C and B_i is equivalent to D_i $(i = 1, \ldots, n)$, i.e., we define

$$\mathcal{T}' := \mathcal{T} \cup \{A \sqsubseteq C, C \sqsubseteq A\} \cup \{B_i \sqsubseteq D, D \sqsubseteq B_i \mid i = 1, \ldots, n\}.$$

Let $\mathcal{S}$ be the i.normalised $\mathcal{ELI}$ TBox obtained from $\mathcal{T}'$ by applying the $\mathcal{ELI}$ normalisation rules, and let $\mathcal{S}^*$ be the i.saturated TBox obtained from $\mathcal{S}$ by an exhaustive application of the inference rules of Figure 6.3.

We define $\mathcal{I} := \mathcal{I}_{\mathcal{S}^*}$, i.e., $\mathcal{I}$ is the canonical interpretation induced by $\mathcal{S}^*$. By Lemma 6.24, $\mathcal{I}$ is a model of $\mathcal{S}^*$, and thus also of $\mathcal{S}$, $\mathcal{T}'$ and $\mathcal{T}$. Since A is a concept name occurring in $\mathcal{S}$, and $\mathcal{S}$ contains a GCI with left-hand side A, it is easy to see that $\{A\}$ occurs in $\mathcal{S}^*$. For this reason, $\{A\}$ belongs to $\Delta^{\mathcal{I}}$ and we can define $d := \{A\}$.

By Proposition 6.20, we have, for all $i = 1, \ldots, n$,

$$\mathcal{S} \models A \sqsubseteq B_i \text{ if and only if } \{A\} \sqsubseteq \{B_i\} \in \mathcal{S}^*,$$

and the definition of the canonical interpretation yields

$$\{A\} \sqsubseteq \{B_i\} \in \mathcal{S}^* \text{ if and only if } d = \{A\} \in B_i^{\mathcal{I}}.$$

Finally, the definition of $\mathcal{T}'$ and the fact that $\mathcal{S}$ is a conservative extension of $\mathcal{T}'$ yield

$$\mathcal{S} \models A \sqsubseteq B_i \text{ if and only if } \mathcal{T} \models C \sqsubseteq D_i.$$

To complete the proof, we observe that $B_i^{\mathcal{I}} = D_i^{\mathcal{I}}$ since $\mathcal{I}$ is known to be a model of $\mathcal{T}'$. □

Proof of Proposition 6.30. It is easy to see that Lemma 6.31 implies this proposition. In fact, the "if" direction of the definition of convexity is trivially satisfied. Thus consider the contrapositive of the "only if" direction, and assume that $\mathcal{T} \not\models C \sqsubseteq D_i$ for all $i \in \{1, \ldots, n\}$. Let $\Gamma = \{C, D_1, \ldots, D_n\}$. Then Lemma 6.31 yields a model $\mathcal{I}$ of $\mathcal{T}$ and a $d \in \Delta^{\mathcal{I}}$ such that $d \in C^{\mathcal{I}}$ and $d \notin D_i^{\mathcal{I}}$ for all $i \in \{1, \ldots, n\}$. Consequently, $\mathcal{T} \not\models C \sqsubseteq D_1 \sqcup \cdots \sqcup D_n$. □

6.4 Historical context and literature review

In the early times of DL research, people concentrated on identifying formalisms for which reasoning is tractable, i.e., can be performed in polynomial time. In addition, the presence of both conjunction and value restriction was seen as indispensable in a true DL. The DL with only these two concept constructors is called $\mathcal{FL}_0$ [Baa90]. It came as surprise to the community when Bernhard Nebel [Neb90b] was able to show that subsumption in $\mathcal{FL}_0$ is intractable (more precisely, CONP-complete) with respect to acyclic TBoxes. Actually, the complexity of the subsumption problem increases even further if the TBox formalism is extended: it is PSPACE-complete with respect to cyclic TBoxes [Baa90, Baa96, KdN03] and even EXPTIME-complete with respect to general TBoxes [BBL05]. These negative complexity results, together with the advent of practically efficient, though worst-case intractable, tableau-based algorithms, were the main reasons why the DL community for more than a decade basically abandoned the search for DLs with tractable inference problems, and concentrated on the design of practical tableau-based algorithms for expressive DLs.

The DL $\mathcal{EL}$ was first introduced in [BKM99] in the context of non-standard inferences in DLs. There, it was shown that subsumption between $\mathcal{EL}$ concepts (without a TBox) is polynomial. Several years later, this polynomiality result was first extended to subsumption with respect to acyclic and cyclic TBoxes [Baa03] and then to subsumption with respect to general TBoxes [Bra04]. The subsumption algorithm introduced in [Bra04] is quite similar to the one described in Section 6.1 above, though the basic data structures used to present it look different. The proof-theoretic subsumption algorithm in [Hof05] uses a presentation that is quite similar to the one employed in Section 6.1.

In addition to providing new theoretical insights into the complexity of reasoning in DLs, these algorithms also turned out to be relevant in practice. In fact, quite a number of biomedical ontologies are built using $\mathcal{EL}$. Perhaps the most prominent example is the well-known medical ontology SNOMED CT,[3] which comprises about 380,000 concepts and is used to generate a standardised healthcare terminology employed as a standard for medical data exchange in a variety of countries including the US, UK, Canada and Australia.

Interestingly, the polynomiality result for subsumption in $\mathcal{EL}$ with respect to general TBoxes is stable under the addition of several interesting means of expressivity, such as the bottom concept, nominals and role hierarchies [BBL05, BBL08]. The papers [BBL05, BBL08] show that adding certain other constructors to $\mathcal{EL}$ makes subsumption with respect to general TBoxes intractable or even undecidable. In particular, it is shown in [BBL08] that, in $\mathcal{ELI}$, subsumption with respect to

---

[3] http://www.ihtsdo.org/snomed-ct/

general TBoxes is ExpTime-complete. Nevertheless, the ideas underlying the polynomial-time subsumption algorithm for $\mathcal{EL}$ can be extended to $\mathcal{ELI}$. This was independently shown by Kazakov [Kaz09] and Vu [Vu08], actually for extensions of $\mathcal{ELI}$ that can express the medical ontology GALEN.[4] The subsumption algorithm presented in Section 6.2 is similar to the one introduced in [Kaz09].

Regarding implementation, the CEL reasoner [BLS06], which basically implements the classification procedure introduced in [BBL05], was the first DL reasoner able to classify SNOMED CT in less than 30 minutes. More recent implementations of algorithms based on these ideas have significantly improved on these runtimes [LB10, Kaz09, KKS14], bringing the classification time down to a few seconds. The CB reasoner [Kaz09] was the first DL reasoner able to classify the full version of GALEN.

As explained above, an important feature of $\mathcal{EL}$ and $\mathcal{ELI}$ is their convexity, because this is what enables practically efficient reasoning based on consequence-based algorithms. There are other interesting and relevant DLs that are convex, in particular Horn-$\mathcal{SHIQ}$ and its variations. Horn-$\mathcal{SHIQ}$ originates from a translation of the description logic $\mathcal{SHIQ}$ into disjunctive Datalog and can be understood as a maximal fragment of $\mathcal{SHIQ}$ that is convex [HMS07]. Essentially, Horn-$\mathcal{SHIQ}$ extends $\mathcal{ELI}$ with functional roles, the $\bot$ concept, role hierarchies and at-least restrictions $(\geqslant n\, r.C)$ on the right-hand side of GCIs. In fact, the consequence-based algorithm by Kazakov mentioned above [Kaz09] is able to handle Horn-$\mathcal{SHIQ}$. The "Horn" in the name Horn-$\mathcal{SHIQ}$ refers to the fact that this DL can be viewed as a fragment of first-order Horn logic and, indeed, any such fragment must be convex.

---

[4] http://www.opengalen.org/

7

Query Answering

An important application of ontologies is to provide semantics and domain knowledge for data. Traditionally, data has been stored and managed inside relational database systems (aka SQL databases) where it is organised according to a pre-specified schema that describes its structure and meaning. In recent years, though, less and less data comes from such controlled sources. In fact, a lot of data is now found on the web, in social networks and so on, where typically neither its structure nor its meaning is explicitly specified; moreover, data coming from such sources is typically highly incomplete. Ontologies can help to overcome these problems by providing semantics and background knowledge, leading to a paradigm that is often called *ontology-mediated querying*. As an example, consider data about used-car offers. The ontology can add knowledge about the domain of cars, stating for example that a grand tourer is a kind of sports car. In this way, it becomes possible to return a car that the data identifies as a grand tourer as an answer to a query which asks for finding all sports cars. In the presence of data, a fundamental description logic reasoning service is answering database queries in the presence of ontologies. Since answers to full SQL queries are uncomputable in the presence of ontologies, the prevailing query language is conjunctive queries (CQs) and slight extensions thereof such as unions of conjunctive queries (UCQs) and positive existential queries. Conjunctive queries are essentially the select-from-where fragment of SQL, written in logic.

In this chapter, we study conjunctive query answering in the presence of ontologies that take the form of a DL TBox. In particular, we show how to implement this reasoning service using standard database systems such as relational (SQL) systems and Datalog engines, taking advantage of those systems' efficiency and maturity. Since database systems are not prepared to deal with TBoxes, we need a way to "sneak them in". While there are several approaches to achieve this, here we will concentrate on *query rewriting*: given a CQ q to be answered and a TBox $\mathcal{T}$, produce a query $q_{\mathcal{T}}$ such that, for any ABox $\mathcal{A}$, the answers to q on $\mathcal{A}$ and $\mathcal{T}$ are identical to the answers to $q_{\mathcal{T}}$ given by a database system that stores $\mathcal{A}$ as data. Thus, query rewriting can be thought of as integrating the TBox into the query. Different query languages for $q_{\mathcal{T}}$ such as SQL and Datalog give rise to different query rewriting problems. In general, it turns out that rewritten queries are guaranteed to exist only when the TBox is formulated in a very inexpressive DL. When rewriting into SQL queries, rewritings are in fact not guaranteed to exist for any of the DLs discussed in the earlier chapters of this book. This observation leads to the introduction of the DL-Lite family of description logics that was designed specifically to guarantee the existence of SQL rewritings. Rewriting into Datalog instead of into SQL enables the use of more expressive DLs for formulating the TBox. In fact, rewritings are guaranteed to exist when the TBox is formulated in $\mathcal{EL}$, $\mathcal{ELI}$ and several extensions thereof.

7.1 Conjunctive queries and FO queries

We introduce and discuss the essentials of conjunctive queries, starting with their syntax.

Definition 7.1 (Conjunctive query). Let $\mathbf{V}$ be a set of *variables*. A *term t* is a variable from $\mathbf{V}$ or an individual name from $\mathbf{I}$.

A *conjunctive query* (CQ) q has the form $\exists x_1 \cdots \exists x_k (\alpha_1 \wedge \cdots \wedge \alpha_n)$, where $k \geq 0$, $n \geq 1$, $x_1, \ldots, x_k \in \mathbf{V}$, and each α_i is a *concept atom* $A(t)$ or a *role atom* $r(t, t')$ with $A \in \mathbf{C}$, $r \in \mathbf{R}$, and t, t' terms.

We call $x_1, \ldots, x_k$ *quantified variables* and all other variables in q, *answer variables*. The *arity* of q is the number of answer variables.

To express that the answer variables in a CQ q are $\vec{x}$, we often write $q(\vec{x})$ instead of just q. Here are a number of simple examples of conjunctive queries; for easy identification, answer variables are underlined.

(i) Return all pairs of individual names (a, b) such that a is a professor who supervises student b:

$$q_1(\underline{x_1}, \underline{x_2}) = \mathsf{Professor}(\underline{x_1}) \wedge \mathsf{supervises}(\underline{x_1}, \underline{x_2}) \wedge \mathsf{Student}(\underline{x_2}).$$

(ii) Return all individual names a such that a is a student supervised by some professor:

$$q_2(x) = \exists y \, (\mathsf{Professor}(y) \wedge \mathsf{supervises}(y, \underline{x}) \wedge \mathsf{Student}(\underline{x})).$$

(iii) Return all pairs of students supervised by the same professor:

$$q_3(x_1, x_2) = \exists y \, (\mathsf{Professor}(y) \wedge \mathsf{supervises}(y, \underline{x_1}) \wedge \mathsf{supervises}(y, \underline{x_2}) \wedge$$
$$\mathsf{Student}(\underline{x_1}) \wedge \mathsf{Student}(\underline{x_2})).$$

(iv) Return all students supervised by professor smith (an individual name):

$$q_4(x) = (\mathsf{supervises}(\mathsf{smith}, \underline{x}) \wedge \mathsf{Student}(\underline{x})).$$

Observe that every conjunctive query q returns tuples of individual names $(a_1, \ldots, a_k)$, where k is the arity of q. Each such tuple is called an *answer* to the query. To formally define the semantics of CQs, we need to make precise which tuples of individual names qualify as answers. This is done in two steps: first on the level of interpretations and then on the level of knowledge bases.

Definition 7.2. Let q be a conjunctive query and $\mathcal{I}$ an interpretation. We use $\mathsf{term}(q)$ to denote the terms in q. A *match of q in $\mathcal{I}$* is a mapping $\pi : \mathsf{term}(q) \to \Delta^{\mathcal{I}}$ such that

- $\pi(a) = a^{\mathcal{I}}$ for all $a \in \mathsf{term}(q) \cap \mathbf{I}$,
- $\pi(t) \in A^{\mathcal{I}}$ for all concept atoms $A(t)$ in q, and
- $(\pi(t_1), \pi(t_2)) \in r^{\mathcal{I}}$ for all role atoms $r(t_1, t_2)$ in q.

Let $\vec{x} = x_1, \ldots, x_k$ be the answer variables in q and $\vec{a} = a_1, \ldots, a_k$ be individual names from $\mathbf{I}$. We call the match π of q in $\mathcal{I}$ an *$\vec{a}$-match* if $\pi(x_i) = a_i^{\mathcal{I}}$ for $1 \leq i \leq k$. Then $\vec{a}$ is an *answer to q on $\mathcal{I}$* if there is an $\vec{a}$-match π of q in $\mathcal{I}$. We use $\mathsf{ans}(q, \mathcal{I})$ to denote the set of all answers to q on $\mathcal{I}$.

Consider, for example, the interpretation $\mathcal{I}$ in Figure 7.1, where we assume for simplicity that all individual names are interpreted as themselves, as for example in $\mathsf{mark}^{\mathcal{I}} = \mathsf{mark}$. Then there are three answers to the above query $q_2(x)$ on $\mathcal{I}$, which are mark, alex, and lily. There are seven answers to $q_3(x_1, x_2)$ on $\mathcal{I}$, including (mark, alex), (alex, lily), (lily, alex) and (mark, mark). As illustrated by the last answer, a match need not be injective. Also note that, mathematically, a match is nothing but a *homomorphism* from the query (viewed as a graph) to the interpretation (also viewed as a graph). We now lift the notion of an answer

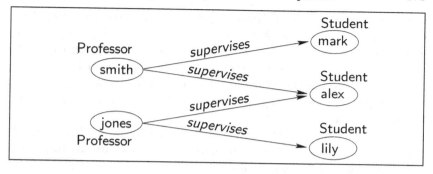

Fig. 7.1. An example interpretation $\mathcal{I}$.

from interpretations to knowledge bases, which have many possible interpretations as models. Thus, when querying a KB we are interested in querying a *set of interpretations* instead of only a single interpretation. In such a situation, so-called *certain answers* provide a natural semantics.

Definition 7.3. Let $\mathcal{K} = (\mathcal{A}, \mathcal{T})$ be a knowledge base. Then $\vec{a}$ is a *certain answer to q on $\mathcal{K}$* if all individual names from $\vec{a}$ occur in $\mathcal{A}$ and $\vec{a} \in \text{ans}(q, \mathcal{I})$ for every model $\mathcal{I}$ of $\mathcal{K}$. We use $\text{cert}(q, \mathcal{K})$ to denote the set of all certain answers to q on $\mathcal{K}$; that is, $\text{cert}(q, \mathcal{K}) = \bigcap_{\mathcal{I} \text{ model of } \mathcal{K}} \text{ans}(q, \mathcal{I})$.

As an example, consider the following knowledge base $\mathcal{K} = (\mathcal{T}, \mathcal{A})$ formulated in $\mathcal{ALCI}$:

$\mathcal{T} = \{\text{Student} \sqsubseteq \exists \text{supervises}^-.\text{Professor}\}$,

$\mathcal{A} = \{\text{smith} : \text{Professor}, \text{mark} : \text{Student}, \text{alex} : \text{Student}, \text{lily} : \text{Student},$
$\quad (\text{smith}, \text{mark}) : \text{supervises}, (\text{smith}, \text{alex}) : \text{supervises}\}$.

Note that the interpretation in Figure 7.1 is a model of this KB. Let us first consider the query $q_4(x)$ from above. As expected, we have $\text{cert}(q_4, \mathcal{K}) = \{\text{mark}, \text{alex}\}$. It is easy to find models of $\mathcal{K}$ in which smith supervises more students than mark and alex, but the latter are the only two students on whose supervision by smith *all* models are in agreement. It is illustrative to consider the role of domain elements whose existence is enforced by existential restrictions in the TBox. For the query $q_2(x)$, we find $\text{cert}(q_2, \mathcal{K}) = \{\text{mark}, \text{alex}, \text{lily}\}$. Note that lily is included because she is a student and thus the TBox enforces that she has a supervisor who is a professor in every model of $\mathcal{K}$. Now consider $q_1(x_1, x_2)$

and note that $\mathsf{cert}(q_1, \mathcal{K}) = \{(\mathsf{smith}, \mathsf{mark}), (\mathsf{smith}, \mathsf{alex})\}$, where lily does not occur. The reason is that different supervisors of lily are possible in different models, and thus there is no answer $(\mathsf{xyz}, \mathsf{lily})$ on which all models agree. In summary, elements that are required to satisfy existential restrictions in the TBox never occur in certain answers, but they can contribute to answers by enabling matches that use them as targets for quantified variables in the query.

We remark that, in Definition 7.3, the condition that all individual names from $\vec{a}$ occur in $\mathcal{A}$ prevents us from sometimes having to return infinitely many uninteresting answers, e.g., when the TBox contains $\top \sqsubseteq A$ and the query is $A(x)$ where otherwise *all* individual names would qualify as an answer.

The main reasoning problem for conjunctive queries is, given a knowledge base $\mathcal{K}$ and a CQ q, to compute the certain answers to q on $\mathcal{K}$. We refer to this reasoning problem as *conjunctive query answering*. To simplify algorithms and proofs, it is often convenient to consider conjunctive queries that do not include any individual names (that is, variables are the only terms that occur), which we call *pure*. As a warm-up exercise, we observe that individual names in queries can always be eliminated.

Lemma 7.4. *Conjunctive query answering can be reduced in polynomial time to answering pure conjunctive queries.*

Proof. Let $\mathcal{K} = (\mathcal{T}, \mathcal{A})$ be a knowledge base (formulated in any description logic) and q a conjunctive query that contains individual names. Let Γ be the set of individual names that occur in $\mathcal{A}$ or q, and introduce a fresh concept name A_a and a fresh variable x_a for each $a \in \Gamma$. Extend the ABox $\mathcal{A}$ to a new ABox $\mathcal{A}'$ by adding the assertions $A_a(a)$ for each $a \in \Gamma$. Furthermore, derive q' from q by replacing each $a \in \Gamma$ with x_a in q and adding the concept atom $A_a(x_a)$ for each $a \in \Gamma$. We show that $\mathsf{cert}(q, \mathcal{K}) = \mathsf{cert}(q', \mathcal{K}')$, where $\mathcal{K}' = (\mathcal{T}, \mathcal{A}')$.

For the "$\subseteq$" direction, assume that $\vec{a} \notin \mathsf{cert}(q', \mathcal{K}')$. Then there is a model $\mathcal{I}$ of $\mathcal{K}'$ such that $\vec{a}$ is not an answer to q' on $\mathcal{I}$; that is, there is no $\vec{a}$-match π of q' in $\mathcal{I}$. Since $\mathcal{A} \subseteq \mathcal{A}'$, $\mathcal{I}$ is also a model of $\mathcal{K}$. Moreover, any match π of q in $\mathcal{I}$ can be extended to a match of q' in $\mathcal{I}$ by setting $\pi(x_a) = a^{\mathcal{I}}$ for all $a \in \Gamma$. Consequently, there is no $\vec{a}$-match π of q in $\mathcal{I}$ (because there is no such match of q'). Thus, $\vec{a}$ is not an answer to q on $\mathcal{I}$, implying $\vec{a} \notin \mathsf{cert}(q, \mathcal{K})$.

For the "$\supseteq$" direction, assume that $\vec{a} \notin \mathsf{cert}(q, \mathcal{K})$. Then, for some model $\mathcal{I}$ of $\mathcal{K}$, there is no $\vec{a}$-match π of q in $\mathcal{I}$. Let $\mathcal{I}'$ be obtained from $\mathcal{I}$ by setting $A_a^{\mathcal{I}'} = \{a^{\mathcal{I}}\}$ for all $a \in \Gamma$. Clearly, $\mathcal{I}'$ is a model of $\mathcal{K}'$.

Moreover, any match π of q' in $\mathcal{I}'$ satisfies $\pi(x_a) = a^{\mathcal{I}}$ since $A_a^{\mathcal{I}'} = \{a^{\mathcal{I}}\}$ and is thus also a match of q in $\mathcal{I}'$ and, as the concept names A_a do not occur in q, a match of q in $\mathcal{I}$. Consequently, there is no $\vec{a}$-match π of q' in $\mathcal{I}'$ and thus $\vec{a} \notin \mathsf{cert}(q', \mathcal{K}')$. $\qquad\square$

From now on, we can thus assume, without loss of generality, that conjunctive queries are pure, which we do without further notice. As illustrated by the proof of Lemma 7.4, a tuple $\vec{a}$ *not* being an answer to a query q is always witnessed by a *counter model*, that is, by a model $\mathcal{I}$ of $\mathcal{K}$ such that there is no $\vec{a}$-match π of q in $\mathcal{I}$. In principle, one can thus view conjunctive query answering as a satisfiability problem: a tuple $\vec{a}$ is a certain answer to q on $\mathcal{K}$ if and only if the formula $\mathcal{K}^* \wedge \neg q[\vec{a}/\vec{x}]$ is unsatisfiable, where $\mathcal{K}^*$ is the first-order logic translation of $\mathcal{K}$ described in Section 2.6.1 and $q[\vec{a}/\vec{x}]$ is the first-order sentence obtained from q by consistently replacing the answer variables in $\vec{x}$ with the individual names in $\vec{a}$. Many algorithms for conjunctive query answering in Description Logic are based on this intuition.

We will be interested in query rewriting with SQL as a target language. Because dealing with SQL syntax is too unwieldy for our purposes and since, by Codd's theorem, SQL is equivalent to (a minor restriction of) first-order logic (FO) used as a query language, we instead use the standard syntax of FO.

Definition 7.5 (FO query). An *FO query* is a first-order formula that uses only unary predicates (concept names) and binary predicates (role names), and no function symbols or constants. The use of equality is allowed.

The free variables $\vec{x}$ of an FO query $q(\vec{x})$ are called *answer variables*. The *arity* of $q(\vec{x})$ is the number of answer variables.

Let $q(\vec{x})$ be an FO query of arity k, and $\mathcal{I}$ an interpretation. We say that $\vec{a} = a_1, \ldots, a_k$ is an *answer* to q on $\mathcal{I}$ if $\mathcal{I} \models q[\vec{a}]$; that is, $q(\vec{x})$ evaluates to true in $\mathcal{I}$ under the valuation that interprets the answer variables $\vec{x}$ as $\vec{a}$. We write $\mathsf{ans}(q, \mathcal{T})$ to denote the set of all answers to q in $\mathcal{I}$.

An example FO query of arity one is $A(x) \vee \forall y\, (r(x, y) \rightarrow s(y, x))$. Note that conjunctive queries are a special case of FO queries and that, for every conjunctive query q, the set $\mathsf{ans}(q, \mathcal{I})$ defined in Definition 7.2 agrees with the set set $\mathsf{ans}(q, \mathcal{I})$ defined in Definition 7.5. Computing the answers to an FO query q on an interpretation $\mathcal{I}$ as in Definition 7.5 is exactly the querying service offered by a relational database system, with $\mathcal{I}$ corresponding to the data stored in the database and q to an SQL query. We use FO queries only as a target language for rewriting, but not to query, knowledge bases because they are too expressive for the latter purpose: it is not hard to reduce satisfiability of FO formulas to answering FO queries on knowledge bases (with an empty TBox), and thus answers to FO queries on knowledge bases are uncomputable.

We will sometimes consider queries without answer variables. Such queries are a bit special in that they do not deliver proper answers but evaluate to true or false.

Definition 7.6 (Boolean queries). A conjunctive query or FO query is called *Boolean* if it has arity zero. For a Boolean FO query q and an interpretation $\mathcal{I}$, we write $\mathcal{I} \models q$ and say that $\mathcal{I}$ *entails* q if the empty tuple is an answer to q on $\mathcal{I}$. For a Boolean conjunctive query q and a knowledge base $\mathcal{K}$, we write $\mathcal{K} \models q$ and say that $\mathcal{K}$ *entails* q if the empty tuple is a certain answer to q on $\mathcal{K}$.

As a simple example, consider the Boolean CQ $\exists x\, \mathsf{Professor}(x)$. For the knowledge base $\mathcal{K} = (\mathcal{T}, \mathcal{A})$ introduced after Definition 7.3, we have $\mathcal{K} \models q$.

7.2 FO-rewritability and DL-Lite

Of course, it is possible to start from scratch when developing algorithms and systems for answering conjunctive queries in the presence of Description Logic knowledge bases, and this has in fact been done for many of the DLs treated in this book. However, conjunctive query answering is most useful in database-style applications where there is a huge amount of data, stored in the ABox. Even without a TBox, efficiently answering queries over large amounts of data is a challenging engineering enterprise, and the TBox makes it all the more difficult. It is thus a natural idea to make use of existing database systems for query answering. The obvious challenge is to accommodate the TBox, which the relational database system is not prepared to process. There are two fundamental ways in which a TBox can be sneaked into a relational database system, as well as various possible variations and combinations thereof. One approach is to replace the original ABox (which is now simply the data stored in the relational system) with a new ABox that includes all the consequences of the TBox, leaving untouched the query to be answered. This approach is often called *materialisation*. The second approach is to leave the data untouched and instead anticipate the consequences of the

TBox in the query. Here, we discuss only the second approach, known as *query rewriting*.

7.2.1 Introducing DL-Lite

In the query rewriting approach to conjunctive query answering, we aim to construct, given a TBox $\mathcal{T}$ and a conjunctive query q, a new query $q_{\mathcal{T}}$ such that, for any ABox $\mathcal{A}$, the certain answers to q on $\mathcal{K} = (\mathcal{T}, \mathcal{A})$ are exactly the answers that a relational database system returns when executing $q_{\mathcal{T}}$ on $\mathcal{A}$ stored as a relational dataset. With the exception of the preprocessing step of constructing $q_{\mathcal{T}}$, we can thus completely delegate query answering to the database system. We take a rather abstract view of relational database systems here, assuming that a relational dataset is simply a DL interpretation and that the queries that the system is able to process are exactly first-order (FO) queries as defined above. Consequently, we call the query $q_{\mathcal{T}}$ an *FO-rewriting* of q with respect to $\mathcal{T}$.

In the following, we restrict ourselves to *simple* ABoxes where, in all concept assertions $a : C$, the concept C must be a concept *name*. Note that it is always possible to make an ABox in a KB simple by replacing each concept assertion $a : C$ with $a : A_C$, where A_C is a fresh concept name, and adding $A_C \sqsubseteq C$ to the TBox. Simple ABoxes can be viewed as an interpretation $\mathcal{I}_{\mathcal{A}}$ and thus stored in a database system by taking $\Delta^{\mathcal{I}_{\mathcal{A}}}$ to be the set of individual names used in $\mathcal{A}$, setting $A^{\mathcal{I}_{\mathcal{A}}} = \{a \mid A(a) \in \mathcal{A}\}$ for all concept names A, $r^{\mathcal{I}_{\mathcal{A}}} = \{(a, b) \mid r(a, b) \in \mathcal{A}\}$ for all role names r, and $a^{\mathcal{I}} = a$ for all individual names a. In the remainder of Chapter 7, "*ABox*" always means *simple ABox*.

Definition 7.7. Let $\mathcal{T}$ be a TBox and q a conjunctive query. An FO query $q_{\mathcal{T}}$ is an *FO-rewriting* of q with respect to $\mathcal{T}$ if, for all ABoxes $\mathcal{A}$, we have $\mathsf{cert}(q, \mathcal{K}) = \mathsf{ans}(q_{\mathcal{T}}, \mathcal{I}_{\mathcal{A}})$ whenever $\mathcal{K} = (\mathcal{T}, \mathcal{A})$ is consistent.

As a first example of an FO-rewriting, consider the following TBox and conjunctive query:

$$\mathcal{T}_1 = \{B_1 \sqsubseteq A, B_2 \sqsubseteq A\}, \qquad q_1(x) = A(x).$$

It is not difficult to see that the FO query $A(x) \vee B_1(x) \vee B_2(x)$ is an FO-rewriting of q_1 with respect to $\mathcal{T}_1$. In fact, if the ABox contains the assertion $a : A$, then trivially $a \in \mathsf{cert}(q_1, \mathcal{K})$, which explains the first disjunct $A(x)$ in the rewriting. However, $a : B_1$ in the ABox also yields $a \in \mathsf{cert}(q_1, \mathcal{K})$ because of the inclusion $B_1 \sqsubseteq A$ in $\mathcal{T}_1$, which explains the second disjuct $B_1(x)$, and likewise for $B_2(x)$. As a second example, consider

$$\mathcal{T}_2 = \{A \sqsubseteq \exists r.A\}, \qquad q_2(x) = A(x).$$

In this case, q_2 itself is an FO-rewriting of q_2 with respect to $\mathcal{T}_2$, that is, we can simply ignore the TBox. The reason is that, although $\mathcal{T}_2$ might imply the existence of additional individuals that are instances of A, we have already seen that elements required to satisfy existential restrictions can never be returned as an answer. It is interesting to contrast this example with the rather similar TBox and query used in the following result which, slightly disturbingly, shows that even for very simple TBoxes and conjunctive queries, FO-rewritings are not guaranteed to exist.

Theorem 7.8. *There is no FO-rewriting of the conjunctive query* $q(x) = A(x)$ *with respect to the $\mathcal{EL}$ TBox* $\mathcal{T} = \{\exists r.A \sqsubseteq A\}$.

Proof. We only provide a sketch. It is not difficult to see that an FO-rewriting $\varphi(x)$ of q with respect to $\mathcal{T}$ has to satisfy $\mathcal{I} \models \varphi[d]$ exactly for those elements d of an interpretation $\mathcal{I}$ that reach an A-element along an r-chain, that is, there are elements $d_0, \ldots, d_n$ such that $d = d_0$, $(d_i, d_{i+1}) \in r^{\mathcal{I}}$ for all $i < n$, and $d_n \in A^{\mathcal{I}}$. It is well known that reachability properties of this sort are not expressible in first-order logic.

More specifically, we can use Gaifman locality to prove that there is no FO query $\varphi(x)$ with the above property. Let $\mathcal{I}$ be an interpretation and $d \in \Delta^{\mathcal{I}}$. For $k \geq 0$, the k-*neighbourhood* around d in $\mathcal{I}$, denoted $N_{\mathcal{I}}^k(d)$, is defined as the restriction of $\mathcal{I}$ to those elements that are reachable from d along a role chain of length at most k. It follows from a classical result of Gaifman that, for every FO query $\varphi(x)$, there is a number k such that the following holds: for all interpretations $\mathcal{I}$ and $d_1, d_2 \in \Delta^{\mathcal{I}}$ with $N_{\mathcal{I}}^k(d_1) = N_{\mathcal{I}}^k(d_2)$, we have $\mathcal{I} \models \varphi[d_1]$ if and only if $\mathcal{I} \models \varphi[d_2]$. Now assume that the desired FO-rewriting $\varphi(x)$ of q with respect to $\mathcal{T}$ exists and let k be the mentioned number. Take an interpretation $\mathcal{I}$ that is the disjoint union of two r-chains of length $k + 1$. The first one begins at element d_1 and ends at e_1 while the second one begins at d_2 and ends at e_2. Assume that $A^{\mathcal{I}} = \{e_1\}$ and thus in particular $e_2 \notin A^{\mathcal{I}}$. By the desired property of $\varphi(x)$, we should have $\mathcal{I} \models \varphi[d_1]$ and $\mathcal{I} \not\models \varphi[d_1]$. However, this contradicts Gaifman's observation and the fact that $N_{\mathcal{I}}^k(d_1) = N_{\mathcal{I}}^k(d_2)$. □

Theorem 7.8 casts serious doubt on the feasibility of the query rewriting approach to conjunctive query answering: FO-rewritings are not guaranteed to exist even when we confine ourselves to the tractable and moderately expressive description logic $\mathcal{EL}$. In fact, the proof of Theorem 7.8 illustrates that it is the recursive nature of the concept inclusion $\exists r.A \sqsubseteq A$ that conflicts with Gaifman locality and thus also with FO-rewritability. To make the query rewriting approach work, we therefore have to use a description logic that avoids such forms of recursion. The DL-Lite family of DLs has been introduced specifically for this purpose. In the following, we introduce one typical member of this family.

Definition 7.9. All of the following are *basic DL-Lite concepts*:

- every concept name,
- $\top$ (the top concept),
- $\exists r$ (unqualified existential restriction), and
- $\exists r^-$ (unqualified existential restriction on inverse role).

A *DL-Lite TBox* is a finite set of

- positive concept inclusions $B_1 \sqsubseteq B_2$,
- negative concept inclusions $B_1 \sqsubseteq \neg B_2$,
- role inclusion axioms $r \sqsubseteq s$,

where B_1 and B_2 range over basic DL-Lite concepts and r and s over role names and their inverses.

The above version of DL-Lite is a slight restriction of what in the literature is known as DL-Lite$_{\mathcal{R}}$.[1] We drop the subscript, which indicates the presence of role inclusions, for readability. The DL-Lite concept $\exists r$ is an abbreviation for $\exists r.\top$, which also clarifies its semantics (likewise for $\exists r^-$). Thus, DL-Lite replaces full existential restrictions with an *unqualified* version; that is, we can speak about the existence of an r-successor, but cannot further qualify its properties. Note that DL-Lite does not allow unbounded syntactic nesting of concept expressions.

The following is an example of a DL-Lite TBox; it consists of six concept inclusions and one role inclusion:

$$
\begin{array}{rclcrcl}
\mathsf{Professor} & \sqsubseteq & \mathsf{Teacher}, & & \mathsf{Teacher} & \sqsubseteq & \mathsf{Person}, \\
\mathsf{Teacher} & \sqsubseteq & \exists\mathsf{teaches}, & & \mathsf{Course} & \sqsubseteq & \neg\mathsf{Person}, \\
\exists\mathsf{teachesCourse}^- & \sqsubseteq & \mathsf{Course}, & & \mathsf{Course} & \sqsubseteq & \exists\mathsf{teachesCourse}^-, \\
& & \mathsf{teachesCourse} & \sqsubseteq & \mathsf{teaches}. & &
\end{array}
$$

---

[1] The restriction is that, for simplicity, we do not include negative role inclusions.

Suppose we want to answer the following CQ, which asks to return all persons that teach a course:

$$q(x) = \exists y\, \mathsf{Person}(x) \wedge \mathsf{teaches}(x, y) \wedge \mathsf{Course}(y).$$

The following is an FO-rewriting of $q(x)$ with respect to $\mathcal{T}$:

$$(\mathsf{Teacher}(x) \vee \mathsf{Professor}(x) \vee \mathsf{Person}(x))$$
$$\wedge\,((\mathsf{teaches}(x, y) \wedge \mathsf{Course}(y)) \vee \mathsf{teachesCourse}(x, y)).$$

Although DL-Lite is a seriously restricted language, a TBox such as the one above can still describe important aspects of the application domain. In fact, DL-Lite can capture the most important aspects of prominent conceptual modelling formalisms such as entity–relationship (ER) diagrams and UML class diagrams.

The most important property of DL-Lite is that FO-rewritings of conjunctive queries with respect to DL-Lite TBoxes are always guaranteed to exist and can often be constructed efficiently. Before we dig into this, we first take a brief look at the more basic reasoning problems of satisfiability and subsumption, which do not involve ABox data. In DL-Lite, satisfiability and subsumption (of basic concepts) turn out to be simple problems, both conceptually and computationally. As in more expressive DLs, subsumption and unsatisfiability are mutually reducible in polynomial time: deciding whether a subsumption $\mathcal{T} \models B_1 \sqsubseteq B_2$ holds is equivalent to deciding whether A is unsatisfiable with respect to $\mathcal{T} \cup \{A \sqsubseteq B_1, A \sqsubseteq \neg B_2\}$, where A is a fresh concept name. Conversely, a basic concept B is unsatisfiable with respect to $\mathcal{T}$ if and only if $\mathcal{T} \models B \sqsubseteq A$, where A is again a fresh concept name. We can thus concentrate on deciding satisfiability, for which the following closure operation is fundamental (NI stands for "negative inclusions"). As in Chapter 4, we use $\mathsf{Inv}(r)$ to denote r^- if r is a role name and s if $r = s^-$.

Definition 7.10. Let $\mathcal{T}$ be a DL-Lite TBox. The *NI-closure* of $\mathcal{T}$, denoted $\mathcal{T}^{\mathsf{NI}}$, is the TBox obtained by starting with $\mathcal{T}$ and then exhaustively applying the following rules:

- **C1** If $\mathcal{T}^{\mathsf{NI}}$ contains $\top \sqsubseteq \neg B$, then add $B \sqsubseteq \neg B$;
- **C2** If $\mathcal{T}^{\mathsf{NI}}$ contains $\top \sqsubseteq \neg\top$ and B is a basic concept that occurs in $\mathcal{T}$, then add $B \sqsubseteq \neg B$;
- **C3** If $\mathcal{T}^{\mathsf{NI}}$ contains $B_1 \sqsubseteq \neg B_2$, then add $B_2 \sqsubseteq \neg B_1$;
- **C4** if $\mathcal{T}^{\mathsf{NI}}$ contains $B_1 \sqsubseteq B_2$ and $B_2 \sqsubseteq \neg B_3$, then add $B_1 \sqsubseteq \neg B_3$;
- **C5** if $\mathcal{T}^{\mathsf{NI}}$ contains $B_1 \sqsubseteq B_2$ and $B_2 \sqsubseteq \neg B_2$, then add $B_1 \sqsubseteq \neg B_1$;

C6 if $\mathcal{T}^{\mathsf{NI}}$ contains $B \sqsubseteq \exists r$ and $\exists \, \mathsf{Inv}(r) \sqsubseteq \neg \exists \, \mathsf{Inv}(r)$, then add $B \sqsubseteq \neg B$;

C7 if $\mathcal{T}^{\mathsf{NI}}$ contains $r \sqsubseteq s$ and $\exists s \sqsubseteq \neg B$, then add $\exists r \sqsubseteq \neg B$;

C8 if $\mathcal{T}^{\mathsf{NI}}$ contains $r \sqsubseteq s$ and $\exists \, \mathsf{Inv}(s) \sqsubseteq \neg B$, then add $\exists \, \mathsf{Inv}(r) \sqsubseteq \neg B$;

C9 if $\mathcal{T}^{\mathsf{NI}}$ contains $r \sqsubseteq s$ and $\exists s \sqsubseteq \neg \exists s$ or $\exists \, \mathsf{Inv}(s) \sqsubseteq \neg \exists \, \mathsf{Inv}(s)$, then add $\exists r \sqsubseteq \neg \exists r$.

It is sufficient to decide the satisfiability of concept names instead of basic concepts because a basic concept B is satisfiable with respect to a TBox $\mathcal{T}$ if and only if A_B is satisfiable with respect to $\mathcal{T} \cup \{A_B \sqsubseteq B\}$, where A_B is a fresh concept name. The following result shows that deciding the satisfiability of concept names with respect to a DL-Lite TBox $\mathcal{T}$ merely requires a lookup in $\mathcal{T}^{\mathsf{NI}}$.

Theorem 7.11. *Let $\mathcal{T}$ be a DL-Lite TBox and A_0 a concept name. Then A_0 is satisfiable with respect to $\mathcal{T}$ if and only if $A_0 \sqsubseteq \neg A_0 \notin \mathcal{T}^{\mathsf{NI}}$.*

For proving the (contrapositive of the) "only if" direction, it is enough to prove that the rules applied in the construction of $\mathcal{T}^{\mathsf{NI}}$ are sound – that is, if such a rule is applied adding an inclusion $B_1 \sqsubseteq \neg B_2$ – then $\mathcal{T} \models B_1 \sqsubseteq \neg B_2$. This is straightforward using induction on the number of rule applications, a case distinction according to the rule applied, and the semantics of DL-Lite. The "if" direction is less straightforward and we defer its proof to Section 7.2.2. It is easy to see that, since the rules do not introduce any new basic concepts, the size of $\mathcal{T}^{\mathsf{NI}}$ is at most quadratic in the size of $\mathcal{T}$. The computation of $\mathcal{T}^{\mathsf{NI}}$ thus only takes polynomial time.

Theorem 7.12. *In DL-Lite, satisfiability and subsumption can be decided in polynomial time.*

It is interesting to note that, since in DL-Lite it is not possible to syntactically nest concepts, the set of all basic concepts that can be formed over a fixed finite signature (a set of concept and role names) is finite, and so is the set of concept and role inclusions. As a consequence, it is possible to effectively make explicit *all* inclusions implied by a DL-Lite TBox $\mathcal{T}$ which are formulated in the signature of $\mathcal{T}$ by finitely extending the TBox. This can be done, for example, by testing subsumption between all basic concepts using Theorem 7.12. The size of the completed TBox will be at most quadratic in the size of the signature, since every DL-Lite inclusion contains at most two concept or role names.

7.2.2 Universal models

We now introduce universal models of DL-Lite knowledge bases, which are a central tool for studying conjunctive query answering in DL-Lite. They will also be useful for proving the "if" direction of Theorem 7.11. Let $\mathcal{K} = (\mathcal{T}, \mathcal{A})$ be a DL-Lite knowledge base. To construct the universal model $\mathcal{I}_\mathcal{K}$ of $\mathcal{K}$, we start by defining an interpretation $\mathcal{I}_0$ as follows:

$$
\begin{aligned}
\Delta^{\mathcal{I}_0} &= \mathsf{Ind}(\mathcal{A}), \\
A^{\mathcal{I}_0} &= \{a \in \mathsf{Ind}(\mathcal{A}) \mid A(a) \in \mathcal{A}\}, \\
r^{\mathcal{I}_0} &= \{(a, b) \mid r(a, b) \in \mathcal{A}\}, \\
a^{\mathcal{I}_0} &= a,
\end{aligned}
$$

where $\mathsf{Ind}(\mathcal{A})$ denotes the set of individual names in $\mathcal{A}$. Next, we apply the concept and role inclusions in $\mathcal{T}$ as rules, obtaining the desired universal model in the limit of the resulting sequence of interpretations $\mathcal{I}_0, \mathcal{I}_1, \ldots$ This sequence is defined by starting with $\mathcal{I}_0$ and then exhaustively applying the following rules:

R1 if $d \in B^{\mathcal{I}_i}$, $B \sqsubseteq A \in \mathcal{T}$ and $d \notin B^{\mathcal{I}_i}$, then add d to $A^{\mathcal{I}_{i+1}}$;

R2 if $d \in B^{\mathcal{I}_i}$, $B \sqsubseteq \exists r \in \mathcal{T}$ and $d \notin (\exists r)^{\mathcal{I}_i}$, then add a fresh element f to $\Delta^{\mathcal{I}_{i+1}}$ and (d, f) to $r^{\mathcal{I}_{i+1}}$;

R3 if $(d, e) \in r^{\mathcal{I}_i}$, $r \sqsubseteq s \in \mathcal{T}$ and $(d, e) \notin s^{\mathcal{I}_i}$, then add (d, e) to $s^{\mathcal{I}_{i+1}}$.

In R2, r can be a role name or inverse thereof, and in the latter case "add (d, f) to $r^{\mathcal{I}_{i+1}}$" means adding (f, d) to $s^{\mathcal{I}_{i+1}}$ if $r = \mathsf{Inv}(s)$. The same is true for R3 and s. If no further rule application is possible after the construction of some interpretation $\mathcal{I}_i$, we simply set $\mathcal{I}_{i+\ell} = \mathcal{I}_i$ for all $\ell > 0$.

Note that applications of R3 might cause applications, previously possible, of R2 to become impossible. By applying the rules in a different order, we can thus obtain different universal models in the limit. To prevent this, we assume that applications of R3 are preferred to applications of R2. To make sure that all possible rule applications are eventually carried out, we assume fairness of application; that is, any rule that is applicable will eventually be applied. It can be proved that, with these assumptions, the interpretation obtained in the limit is unique. In the area of databases, the procedure we have just sketched is known as *the (restricted) chase*.

The *universal model* of $\mathcal{K}$ is the interpretation $\mathcal{I}_\mathcal{K}$ obtained as the limit of the sequence $\mathcal{I}_0, \mathcal{I}_1, \ldots$; that is, $\Delta^{\mathcal{I}_\mathcal{K}} = \bigcup_{i \geq 0} \Delta^{\mathcal{I}_i}$, $A^{\mathcal{I}_\mathcal{K}} = \bigcup_{i \geq 0} A^{\mathcal{I}_i}$ for all concept names A, $r^{\mathcal{I}_\mathcal{K}} = \bigcup_{i \geq 0} r^{\mathcal{I}_i}$ for all role names r, and $a^{\mathcal{I}_\mathcal{K}} = a$

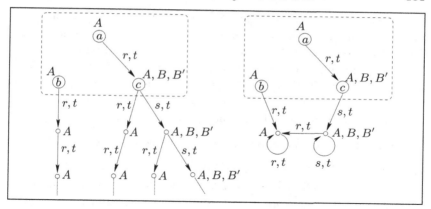

Fig. 7.2. The universal model (left) and another model (right).

for all individual names a. Note that $\mathcal{I}_\mathcal{K}$ might be finite or infinite. As an example, consider the following DL-Lite KB $\mathcal{K}$:

$$A \sqsubseteq \exists r, \qquad B \sqsubseteq \exists s, \qquad \exists t^- \sqsubseteq A, \qquad \exists s^- \sqsubseteq B, \qquad B \sqsubseteq B',$$

$$r \sqsubseteq t, \qquad s \sqsubseteq t,$$

$$a{:}A, \qquad b{:}A, \qquad c{:}B, \qquad (a,c){:}r.$$

The universal model $\mathcal{I}_\mathcal{K}$ is displayed on the left in Figure 7.2 with the dashed box enclosing the domain elements that consistute the ABox part of $\mathcal{K}$; all other domain elements are generated by rule R2 to satisfy existential restrictions. In this case, $\mathcal{I}_\mathcal{K}$ is infinite. On the right-hand side, we show another (finite) model of the same KB $\mathcal{K}$.

We will show shortly that $\mathcal{I}_\mathcal{K}$ is indeed a model of $\mathcal{K}$. However, it is not just *some* model but enjoys special properties which, together with its use for conjunctive query answering later on, earns it the name "universal". The most notable property of $\mathcal{I}_\mathcal{K}$ is that it can be found inside *any* model of $\mathcal{I}_\mathcal{K}$ in terms of a homomorphism; intuitively, this states a form of minimality in the sense that $\mathcal{I}_\mathcal{K}$ makes true only things that need to be true in any model of $\mathcal{K}$.

Definition 7.13. Let $\mathcal{I}_1$ and $\mathcal{I}_2$ be interpretations. A function $h : \Delta^{\mathcal{I}_1} \to \Delta^{\mathcal{I}_2}$ is a *homomorphism from $\mathcal{I}_1$ to $\mathcal{I}_2$* if the following conditions are satisfied:

(i) $d \in A^{\mathcal{I}_1}$ implies $h(d) \in A^{\mathcal{I}_2}$ for all concept names A;
(ii) $(d,e) \in r^{\mathcal{I}_1}$ implies $(h(d), h(e)) \in r^{\mathcal{I}_2}$ for all role names r; and
(iii) $h(a^{\mathcal{I}_1}) = a^{\mathcal{I}_2}$ for all individual names a.

If there is a homomorphism from $\mathcal{I}_1$ to $\mathcal{I}_2$, we write $\mathcal{I}_1 \to \mathcal{I}_2$.

As an example, consider again Figure 7.2, where it is not hard to find a homomorphism h from the universal model $\mathcal{I}_\mathcal{K}$ on the left-hand side to the model $\mathcal{I}$ on the right-hand side: map all ABox elements to themselves and, outside the ABox, map all elements in $\mathcal{I}_\mathcal{K}$ that satisfy A to the non-ABox element in $\mathcal{I}$ that satisfies A, and similarly for elements satisfying A, B, B'.

We now show that $\mathcal{I}_\mathcal{K}$ indeed behaves as described.

Lemma 7.14. *For every model $\mathcal{I}$ of $\mathcal{K}$, we have $\mathcal{I}_\mathcal{K} \to \mathcal{I}$.*

Proof. Let $\mathcal{I}_0, \mathcal{I}_1, \ldots$ be the interpretations used in the construction of $\mathcal{I}_\mathcal{K}$. We show by induction on i that there are $h_0, h_1, \ldots$ such that h_i is a homomorphism from $\mathcal{I}_i$ to $\mathcal{I}$ and h_i and h_{i+1} agree on $\Delta^{\mathcal{I}_i}$; that is, $h_{i+1}(d) = h_i(d)$ for all $d \in \Delta^{\mathcal{I}_i}$ (note that $\Delta^{\mathcal{I}_0} \subseteq \Delta^{\mathcal{I}_1} \subseteq \cdots$). The desired homomorphism h from $\mathcal{I}_\mathcal{K}$ to $\mathcal{I}$ is then obtained in the limit as $h = \bigcup_{i \geq 0} h_i$.

For the induction start, the homomorphism h_0 is defined by setting $h_0(a) = a^\mathcal{I}$ for all $a \in \mathsf{Ind}(\mathcal{A})$. Using the fact that $\mathcal{I}$ is a model of $\mathcal{A}$, it is easy to check that conditions (i)–(iii) in Definition 7.13 are satisfied.

For the induction step, assume that h_i has already been defined. To define h_{i+1}, we make a case distinction according to the rule that was applied to obtain $\mathcal{I}_{i+1}$ from $\mathcal{I}_i$:

R1. Then there is a $d \in B^{\mathcal{I}_i}$ and a GCI $B \sqsubseteq A \in \mathcal{T}$ such that $\mathcal{I}_{i+1}$ was obtained from $\mathcal{I}_i$ by adding d to the extension of A. We must have $h_i(d) \in B^\mathcal{I}$. Since $\mathcal{I}$ is a model of $\mathcal{T}$, this yields $h_{i+1}(d) \in A^\mathcal{I}$. Consequently, h_i is also a homomorphism from $\mathcal{I}_{i+1}$ to $\mathcal{I}$ and we can set $h_{i+1} = h_i$.

R2. Then there is a $d \in B^{\mathcal{I}_i}$ and a GCI $B \sqsubseteq \exists r \in \mathcal{T}$ such that $\mathcal{I}_{i+1}$ was obtained from $\mathcal{I}_i$ by adding a fresh element f to $\Delta^{\mathcal{I}_{i+1}}$ and (d, f) to the extension of r. We must have $h(d) \in B^\mathcal{I}$ and thus $h(d) \in (\exists r)^\mathcal{I}$. By the semantics, we thus find some $(d, e) \in r^\mathcal{I}$. Clearly, $h_{i+1} = h_i \cup \{f \mapsto e\}$ is a homomorphism from $\mathcal{I}_{i+1}$ to $\mathcal{I}$.

R3. Then there is a $(d, e) \in r^{\mathcal{I}_i}$ and a role inclusion $r \sqsubseteq s \in \mathcal{T}$ such that $\mathcal{I}_{i+1}$ was obtained from $\mathcal{I}_i$ by adding (d, e) to the extension of s. We must have $(h_i(d), h_i(e)) \in r^\mathcal{I}$ and, since $\mathcal{I}$ is a model of $\mathcal{T}$, also $(h_i(d), h_i(e)) \in s^\mathcal{I}$. Thus we can set $h_{i+1} = h_i$. □

Lemma 7.14 has many interesting applications. In Section 7.2.3, it will play a crucial role in our treatment of conjunctive query answering. It also helps in showing that, as intended, $\mathcal{I}_\mathcal{K}$ is a model of $\mathcal{K}$. Of course, we can only expect this if the knowledge base $\mathcal{K}$ is consistent, as otherwise it does not have any models.

Lemma 7.15. *If $\mathcal{K}$ is consistent, then $\mathcal{I}_\mathcal{K}$ is a model of $\mathcal{K}$.*

Proof. Since $\mathcal{A}$ is a simple ABox, the interpretation $\mathcal{I}_0$ from the construction of $\mathcal{I}_\mathcal{K}$ is clearly already a model of $\mathcal{A}$, and therefore so is $\mathcal{I}_\mathcal{K}$. Moreover, all positive concept inclusions and all role inclusions from $\mathcal{T}$ are satisfied in $\mathcal{I}_\mathcal{K}$ since none of the rules R1–R3 is applicable in $\mathcal{I}_\mathcal{K}$. It thus remains to show that, if $\mathcal{K}$ is consistent, then $\mathcal{I}_\mathcal{K}$ also satisfies the negative concept inclusions in $\mathcal{T}$. Assume to the contrary that there is some $B_1 \sqsubseteq \neg B_2 \in \mathcal{T}$ that is not satisfied in $\mathcal{I}_\mathcal{K}$. Then there is a $d \in B_1^{\mathcal{I}_\mathcal{K}} \cap B_2^{\mathcal{I}_\mathcal{K}}$. If $\mathcal{K}$ is consistent, then it has some model $\mathcal{I}$. By Lemma 7.14, there is a homomorphism h from $\mathcal{I}_\mathcal{K}$ to $\mathcal{I}$. But then $h(d) \in B_1^{\mathcal{I}} \cap B_2^{\mathcal{I}}$ contradicting that $\mathcal{I}$ is a model of $\mathcal{T}$. $\qquad\square$

We close this section by establishing the "only if" direction of Theorem 7.11, which was left open in Section 7.2.1. This completes the proof that satisfiability and subsumption in DL-Lite can be decided in polynomial time. While not using the central Lemma 7.14, the presented proof also relies on universal models.

Lemma 7.16. *Let $\mathcal{T}$ be a DL-Lite TBox and A_0 a concept name. If $A_0 \sqsubseteq \neg A_0 \notin \mathcal{T}^{\mathsf{NI}}$, then A_0 is satisfiable with respect to $\mathcal{T}$.*

Proof. Assume that $A_0 \sqsubseteq \neg A_0 \notin \mathcal{T}^{\mathsf{NI}}$ and consider the KB $\mathcal{K} = (\mathcal{T}, \mathcal{A})$ with $\mathcal{A} = \{a : A_0\}$ and the universal model $\mathcal{I}_\mathcal{K}$ of $\mathcal{K}$. By construction of the latter, we have $a \in A_0^{\mathcal{I}_\mathcal{K}}$. It thus suffices to show that $\mathcal{I}_\mathcal{K}$ is a model of $\mathcal{T}$. Note that we cannot invoke Lemma 7.15 because we do not know whether $\mathcal{K}$ is consistent – in fact this is equivalent to A_0 being satisfiable with respect to $\mathcal{T}$. However, we can argue exactly as in the proof of Lemma 7.15 that $\mathcal{I}_\mathcal{K}$ satisfies all positive concept inclusions and role inclusions in $\mathcal{T}$, since this was independent of $\mathcal{K}$ being consistent. To show that $\mathcal{I}_\mathcal{K}$ also satisfies all negative concept inclusions in $\mathcal{T}$, we prove by induction on i that $\mathcal{I}_i$ satisfies all negative concept inclusions in $\mathcal{T}^{\mathsf{NI}}$, where $\mathcal{I}_0, \mathcal{I}_1, \ldots$ are the interpretations used to construct $\mathcal{I}_\mathcal{K}$. Recall that $\mathcal{T} \subseteq \mathcal{T}^{\mathsf{NI}}$, so working with $\mathcal{T}^{\mathsf{NI}}$ instead of with $\mathcal{T}$ is sufficient.

For the induction start, consider $\mathcal{I}_0$. By definition and since $\mathcal{A} = \{a : A_0\}$, the only negative concept inclusions that $\mathcal{I}_0$ can potentially violate are $\top \sqsubseteq \neg A_0$, $A_0 \sqsubseteq \neg \top$, $\top \sqsubseteq \neg \top$, and $A_0 \sqsubseteq \neg A_0$. By rules C1–C3 for the construction of $\mathcal{T}^{\mathsf{NI}}$, the presence of any of these concept inclusions in $\mathcal{T}^{\mathsf{NI}}$ implies $A_0 \sqsubseteq \neg A_0 \in \mathcal{T}^{\mathsf{NI}}$, contradicting our initial assumption.

For the induction step, consider $\mathcal{I}_{i+1}$. Our aim is to show that if $\mathcal{I}_{i+1}$ violates a negative inclusion in $\mathcal{T}^{\mathsf{NI}}$, then so does $\mathcal{I}_i$, which yields a contradiction to the induction hypothesis. We make a case distinction according to the rule that was applied to obtain $\mathcal{I}_{i+1}$ from $\mathcal{I}_i$:

R1. Then there is a $d \in B^{\mathcal{I}_i}$ and a $B \sqsubseteq A \in \mathcal{T}$ such that $\mathcal{I}_{i+1}$ was obtained from $\mathcal{I}_i$ by adding d to the extension of A. This can result in the violation of negative GCIs from $\mathcal{T}^{\mathsf{NI}}$ that are of the form $A \sqsubseteq \neg B'$ or $B' \sqsubseteq \neg A$ for B' either A or any basic concept with $d \in B'^{\mathcal{I}_i}$. If $B' = A$, rule C5 of the construction of $\mathcal{T}^{\mathsf{NI}}$ yields $B \sqsubseteq \neg B \in \mathcal{T}^{\mathsf{NI}}$, and this inclusion is clearly violated by $\mathcal{I}_i$. Otherwise, $d \in B'^{\mathcal{I}_i}$. Thus the GCI $B \sqsubseteq \neg B' \in \mathcal{T}^{\mathsf{NI}}$ generated by rules C3 and C4 is violated by $\mathcal{I}_i$.

R2. Then there is a $d \in B^{\mathcal{I}_i}$ and a $B \sqsubseteq \exists r \in \mathcal{T}$ such that $\mathcal{I}_{i+1}$ was obtained from $\mathcal{I}_i$ by adding a fresh element f to $\Delta^{\mathcal{I}_{i+1}}$ and (d, f) to the extension of r. This can result in the violation of negative GCIs from $\mathcal{T}^{\mathsf{NI}}$ that are of the form $\exists \mathsf{Inv}(r) \sqsubseteq \neg \exists \mathsf{Inv}(r)$, $\exists r \sqsubseteq \neg B'$ or $B' \sqsubseteq \neg \exists r$ for B' either $\exists r$ or any basic concept with $d \in B'^{\mathcal{I}_i}$. The latter two cases can be dealt with exactly as for R1. Thus assume that $\exists \mathsf{Inv}(r) \sqsubseteq \neg \exists \mathsf{Inv}(r)$ is violated. Then rule C6 has added $B \sqsubseteq \neg B$ to $\mathcal{T}^{\mathsf{NI}}$, which is violated by $\mathcal{I}_i$.

R3. Then there is a $(d, e) \in r^{\mathcal{I}_i}$ and an $r \sqsubseteq s \in \mathcal{T}$ such that $\mathcal{I}_{i+1}$ was obtained from $\mathcal{I}_i$ by adding (d, e) to the extension of s. This can result in the violation of negative GCIs from $\mathcal{T}^{\mathsf{NI}}$ that are of the form $\exists s \sqsubseteq \neg \exists s$, $\exists \mathsf{Inv}(s) \sqsubseteq \neg \exists \mathsf{Inv}(s)$ or $\exists s \sqsubseteq \neg B'$ such that $d \in B'^{\mathcal{I}_i}$, or $\exists \mathsf{Inv}(s) \sqsubseteq \neg B'$ such that $e \in B'^{\mathcal{I}_i}$. In the first two cases, C9 ensures that $\mathcal{T}^{\mathsf{NI}}$ contains $\exists r \sqsubseteq \neg \exists r$, which is violated by $\mathcal{I}_i$. In the latter two cases, C7 and C8 make $\mathcal{T}^{\mathsf{NI}}$ contain $\exists r \sqsubseteq \neg B'$ and $\exists \mathsf{Inv}(r) \sqsubseteq \neg B'$, respectively, which are both violated by $\mathcal{I}_i$. $\qquad\square$

7.2.3 *FO-rewritability in DL-Lite*

We now study conjunctive query answering in DL-Lite and show that FO-rewritings of conjunctive queries with respect to DL-Lite TBoxes always exist. Thus, conjunctive query answering in DL-Lite can be delegated to a relational database system. We start by showing that the universal model plays a special role for conjunctive query answering: the certain answers to a CQ q on a DL-Lite KB $\mathcal{K}$ are identical to the answers to q on the interpretation $\mathcal{I}_\mathcal{K}$. Note that this is quite remarkable: while the definition of certain answers quantifies over all (infinitely many) models of $\mathcal{K}$, it turns out that it is still sufficient to consider only one single model, which is $\mathcal{I}_\mathcal{K}$. The proof relies crucially on the fundamental Lemma 7.14.

Lemma 7.17. *Let* $\mathcal{K} = (\mathcal{T}, \mathcal{A})$ *be a consistent DL-Lite KB and* q *a CQ. Then* $\mathsf{cert}(q, \mathcal{K}) = \mathsf{ans}(q, \mathcal{I}_\mathcal{K})$.

Proof. The "$\subseteq$" direction is clear: if $\vec{a} \notin \mathsf{ans}(q, \mathcal{I}_\mathcal{K})$, then $\vec{a} \notin \mathsf{cert}(q, \mathcal{K})$ since, by Lemma 7.15, $\mathcal{I}_\mathcal{K}$ is a model of $\mathcal{K}$.

For the "$\supseteq$" direction, assume that $\vec{a} \in \mathsf{ans}(q, \mathcal{I}_\mathcal{K})$. Then there is an $\vec{a}$-match π of q in $\mathcal{I}_\mathcal{K}$. Take any model $\mathcal{I}$ of $\mathcal{K}$. We have to show that there is an $\vec{a}$-match τ of q in $\mathcal{I}$. By Lemma 7.14, there is a homomorphism h from $\mathcal{I}_\mathcal{K}$ to $\mathcal{I}$. Define τ by setting $\tau(x) = h(\pi(x))$ for all variables x in q. Using the definitions of matches and homomorphisms, it is easy to verify that τ is an $\vec{a}$-match of q in $\mathcal{I}$, as required. $\square$

We have already remarked that a match is nothing but a homomorphism. In summary, the "$\supseteq$" direction of Lemma 7.17 is thus a consequence of Lemma 7.14 and the fact that the composition of two homomorphisms is again a homomorphism.

As a next step, it is interesting to observe that negative concept inclusions in the TBox can make the ABox inconsistent with respect to the TBox, but otherwise have no effect on query answering. This is stated more precisely by the following lemma. Note that, if $\mathcal{K}$ is an inconsistent KB and q a CQ of arity k, then $\mathsf{cert}(q, \mathcal{K})$ is the (uninteresting) set of all k-tuples over $\mathsf{Ind}(\mathcal{A})$.

Lemma 7.18. *Let* $\mathcal{K}$ *be a consistent DL-Lite KB and* q *a CQ. Then* $\mathsf{cert}(q, \mathcal{K}) = \mathsf{cert}(q, \mathcal{K}')$, *where* $\mathcal{K}'$ *is obtained from* $\mathcal{K}$ *by removing from* $\mathcal{T}$ *all negative concept inclusions.*

Proof. "$\subseteq$". Note that $\mathcal{I}_\mathcal{K} = \mathcal{I}_{\mathcal{K}'}$ since negative concept inclusions are not used in the construction of universal models. Thus by Lemma 7.17 we have $\mathsf{cert}(q, \mathcal{K}) = \mathsf{ans}(q, \mathcal{K}) = \mathsf{ans}(q, \mathcal{K}') = \mathsf{cert}(q, \mathcal{K}')$. $\square$

Recall from (the proof of) Theorem 7.8 that the non-existence of FO-rewritings is related to non-locality. For example, the query $A(x)$ turned out not to be FO-rewritable with respect to the $\mathcal{EL}$ TBox $\{\exists r.A \sqsubseteq A\}$ because there is no bound on how far the concept name A is propagated through the data, e.g., on the ABoxes $\mathcal{A}_i = \{A(a_0), r(a_1, a_0), \ldots, r(a_i, a_{i-1})\}$ for $i \geq 0$. DL-Lite is designed to avoid any such propagation and is thus "local in nature", which is responsible for the fact that FO-rewritings of CQs with respect to DL-Lite TBoxes always exist. The locality of DL-Lite is made precise by the following lemma. For a CQ q, we define $\mathsf{size}(q)$ by analogy with the size of concepts and TBoxes: $\mathsf{size}(q)$ is the number of symbols needed to write q, counting concept and role names as one and not counting brackets.

Lemma 7.19. *Let $\mathcal{K} = (\mathcal{T}, \mathcal{A})$ be a consistent DL-Lite KB, q a CQ and $\vec{a} \in \mathsf{cert}(q, \mathcal{K})$. Then there is an $\mathcal{A}' \subseteq \mathcal{A}$ such that $|\mathsf{Ind}(\mathcal{A}')| \leq \mathsf{size}(q) \cdot (\mathsf{size}(\mathcal{T}) + 1)$ and $\vec{a} \in \mathsf{cert}(q, \mathcal{K}')$ where $\mathcal{K}' = (\mathcal{T}, \mathcal{A}')$.*

Proof. Since $\vec{a} \in \mathsf{cert}(q, \mathcal{K})$, we have $\vec{a} \in \mathsf{ans}(q, \mathcal{I}_{\mathcal{K}})$ and thus there is an $\vec{a}$-match π of q in $\mathcal{I}_{\mathcal{K}}$. By construction, the universal model $\mathcal{I}_{\mathcal{K}}$ consists of an ABox part whose elements are exactly the individuals in $\mathcal{A}$ and (potentially infinite) tree-shaped parts, one rooted at each ABox individual (as an example, consider the universal model in Figure 7.2). Let I be the set of those individual names $a \in \mathsf{Ind}(\mathcal{A})$ such that π maps some variable in q to a or to a node in the tree in $\mathcal{I}_{\mathcal{K}}$ rooted at a. Clearly, $|I| \leq \mathsf{size}(q)$. Now extend I to J as follows: whenever $a \in I$ and r is a (potentially inverse) role in $\mathcal{T}$ such that there is an assertion $r(a, b) \in \mathcal{A}$, then choose such an $r(a, b)$ and include b in J. Clearly, $|J| \leq \mathsf{size}(q) \cdot (\mathsf{size}(\mathcal{T}) + 1)$. Let $\mathcal{A}'$ be the restriction of $\mathcal{A}$ to the individuals in J; that is, $\mathcal{A}'$ is obtained from $\mathcal{A}$ by dropping all assertions that involve an individual not in J. In the following, we show that $\vec{a} \in \mathsf{cert}(q, \mathcal{K}')$ as required.

It suffices to prove that there is an $\vec{a}$-match of q in $\mathcal{I}_{\mathcal{K}'}$. Let $\mathcal{I}_{\mathcal{K}}|_I^\downarrow$ be the restriction of $\mathcal{I}_{\mathcal{K}}$ to the elements that are either in I or located in a subtree rooted at some element of I. By choice of I, π is an $\vec{a}$-match of q in $\mathcal{I}_{\mathcal{K}}|_I^\downarrow$. Since the composition of two homomorphisms is a homomorphism, it thus remains to show that there is a homomorphism τ from $\mathcal{I}_{\mathcal{K}}|_I^\downarrow$ to $\mathcal{I}_{\mathcal{K}'}$ that is the identity on $\vec{a}$.

Let $\mathcal{I}_0, \mathcal{I}_1, \ldots$ be the interpretations from the construction of $\mathcal{I}_{\mathcal{K}}$; that is, $\mathcal{I}_{\mathcal{K}}$ is the limit of this sequence. Further, let $\mathcal{I}_i|_I^\downarrow$ be the restriction of $\mathcal{I}_i$ defined analogously to $\mathcal{I}_{\mathcal{K}}|_I^\downarrow$, for all $i \geq 0$. We show by induction on i that there is a homomorphism τ_i from $\mathcal{I}_i|_I^\downarrow$ to $\mathcal{I}_{\mathcal{K}'}$ such that τ_i is the identity on $\vec{a}$. In fact, we will construct these homomorphisms such that $\tau_0 \subseteq \tau_1 \subseteq \cdots$ and in the limit we obtain the desired homomorphism τ. Moreover, we construct τ_i such that the following condition is satisfied:

($*$) if $d \in C^{\mathcal{I}_i}$ with C a basic DL-Lite concept and $d \in \Delta^{\mathcal{I}_i|_I^\downarrow}$, then $\tau_i(d) \in C^{\mathcal{I}_{\mathcal{K}'}}$.

Note that ($*$) does not follow from the pure existence of the homomorphism τ_i because the precondition says $d \in C^{\mathcal{I}_i}$ and not $d \in C^{\mathcal{I}_i}|_I^{\downarrow}$. In fact, we have extended I to J before defining $\mathcal{K}'$ precisely in order to be able to attain Property $(*)$.

For the induction start, set $\tau_0(a) = a$ for all $a \in I$. Since $\mathcal{I}_0$ is read off from $\mathcal{A}$ and $\mathcal{I}_{\mathcal{K}'}$ satisfies the restriction of $\mathcal{A}$ to individuals from I, τ_0 is a homomorphism from $\mathcal{I}_i|_I^{\downarrow}$ to $\mathcal{I}_{\mathcal{K}'}$. Clearly, τ_0 is the identity on $\vec{a}$. Moreover, it is not hard to verify that τ_0 satisfies $(*)$. For example, assume that $d \in (\exists r)^{\mathcal{I}_0}$ and $d \in \Delta^{\mathcal{I}_0}|_I^{\downarrow}$. Then $d = a$ for some $a \in I$ and $d \in (\exists r)^{\mathcal{I}_0}$ means that there is an $r(a, b) \in \mathcal{A}$. Consequently, we have chosen such an $r(a, b)$ and included b in J, thus $(a, b) \in r^{\mathcal{I}_{\mathcal{K}'}}$, which implies $\tau_0(a) \in (\exists r)^{\mathcal{I}_{\mathcal{K}'}}$ as required by $(*)$.

For the induction step, we make a case distinction according to the rule that was applied to construct $\mathcal{I}_{i+1}$ from $\mathcal{I}_i$. Since all three cases are extremely similar, we consider only R2 explicitly. If this rule was applied to construct $\mathcal{I}_{i+1}$ from $\mathcal{I}_i$, then there is a $d \in B^{\mathcal{I}_i}$ and a $B \sqsubseteq \exists r \in \mathcal{T}$ such that $\Delta^{\mathcal{I}_{i+1}}$ contains a fresh element f with $(d, f) \in r^{\mathcal{I}_{i+1}}$. If $d \notin \Delta^{\mathcal{I}_i}|_I^{\downarrow}$, then neither is f and there is nothing to do. Otherwise, $(*)$ delivers $\tau_i(d) \in B^{\mathcal{I}_{\mathcal{K}'}}$. Since $\mathcal{I}_{\mathcal{K}'}$ is a model of $\mathcal{T}$, there is an $e \in \Delta^{\mathcal{I}_{\mathcal{K}'}}$ such that $(d, e) \in r^{\mathcal{I}_{\mathcal{K}'}}$. Set $\tau_{i+1} = \tau_i \cup \{f \mapsto e\}$. It is not hard to verify that τ_{i+1} is as required. In particular, $(*)$ is satisfied (also when d is the fresh element f) simply by induction hypothesis and construction of τ_{i+1}. $\qquad\square$

Lemma 7.19 suggests a way to produce an FO-rewriting $q_{\mathcal{T}}$ for a given CQ q of arity k and DL-Lite TBox $\mathcal{T}$, by making $q_{\mathcal{T}}$ check the existence of certain sub-ABoxes of bounded size. To make this precise, let $\mathcal{T}$ be a DL-Lite TBox and q a CQ of arity k. Further, let $m = \text{size}(q) \cdot (\text{size}(\mathcal{T}) + 1)$ be the bound from Lemma 7.19. Fix individual names $\text{Ind}_0 = \{a_1, \dots, a_m\}$. We will consider ABoxes that only use individual names from Ind_0, contain all of $\vec{a}_0 = a_1, \dots, a_k$ and use only concept and role names that occur in $\mathcal{T}$ or q. Such an ABox can be seen as a k-ary CQ $q_{\mathcal{A}}$ as follows:

- the variables are x_a, $a \in \text{Ind}(\mathcal{A})$, where $x_{a_1}, \dots, x_{a_k}$ are the answer variables and all other variables are quantified;

- every concept assertion $A(a)$ in $\mathcal{A}$ gives rise to a concept atom $A(x_a)$ in $q_{\mathcal{A}}$ and every role assertion $r(a, b) \in \mathcal{A}$ gives rise to a role atom $r(x_a, x_b)$ in $q_{\mathcal{A}}$; these are the only atoms.

Define $q_{\mathcal{T}}$ to be the disjunction of all CQs $q_{\mathcal{A}}$ such that $\mathcal{A}$ is an ABox as above and $\vec{a}_0 \in \text{cert}(q, \mathcal{K})$, where $\mathcal{K} = (\mathcal{T}, \mathcal{A})$.

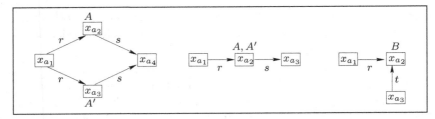

Fig. 7.3. Some disjuncts of $q_{\mathcal{T}}$.

As an example, consider the following TBox and CQ:

$$\mathcal{T} = \{\exists t^- \sqsubseteq A,\ B \sqsubseteq \exists s\},$$
$$q(x) = r(x, y_1) \wedge r(x, y_2) \wedge A(y_1) \wedge A'(y_2) \wedge s(y_1, z) \wedge s(y_2, z).$$

In Figure 7.3, we show three example disjuncts in $q_{\mathcal{T}}$. The left-most query is simply q itself, up to variable renaming. The middle query must always be a disjunct of $q_{\mathcal{T}}$, independently of what $\mathcal{T}$ actually is. In contrast, the presence of the right-most query as a disjunct in $q_{\mathcal{T}}$ does depend on $\mathcal{T}$. As a small exercise, the reader might want to convert this query into an ABox by replacing each variable x_{a_i} with an individual name a_i, construct the universal model $\mathcal{I}_{\mathcal{K}}$ of the resulting KB $\mathcal{K}$ and then verify that $a_1 \in \text{ans}(q, \mathcal{I}_{\mathcal{K}})$, thus $a_1 \in \text{cert}(q, \mathcal{K})$. Note that disjuncts of $q_{\mathcal{T}}$ might contain a larger number of variables than the original query, one example being obtained by replacing in $q(x)$ the atom $A(y_1)$ with $t(u, y_1)$.

It is easy to establish that $q_{\mathcal{T}}$ is *complete* as an FO-rewriting, meaning the following.

Lemma 7.20 (Completeness). *For any consistent KB* $\mathcal{K} = (\mathcal{T}, \mathcal{A})$, $\text{cert}(q, \mathcal{K}) \subseteq \text{ans}(q_{\mathcal{T}}, \mathcal{I}_{\mathcal{A}})$.

Proof. Let $\vec{a} \in \text{cert}(q, \mathcal{K})$. By Lemma 7.19, we find an $\mathcal{A}' \subseteq \mathcal{A}$ of size at most $\text{size}(q) \cdot (\text{size}(\mathcal{T}) + 1)$ and with $\vec{a} \in \text{cert}(q, \mathcal{K}')$ for $\mathcal{K}' = (\mathcal{T}, \mathcal{A}')$. By renaming the individual names, we obtain from $\mathcal{A}'$ an ABox $\mathcal{B}$ that uses only individual names from Ind_0 and such that $\vec{a}_0 \in \text{cert}(q, (\mathcal{T}, \mathcal{B}))$. Then $q_{\mathcal{B}}$ must be a disjunct of $q_{\mathcal{T}}$, and it can be verified that we find an $\vec{a}$-match π of $q_{\mathcal{B}}$ in $\mathcal{I}_{\mathcal{A}}$ by setting $\pi(x_a) = b$ if b is the individual name that was renamed to a when constructing $\mathcal{B}$. Consequently $\vec{a} \in \text{ans}(q_{\mathcal{T}}, \mathcal{I}_{\mathcal{A}})$ as required. $\qquad\square$

However, we also wish to show that $q_{\mathcal{T}}$ is sound, which means that the converse of Lemma 7.20 holds. As a technical preliminary, we first observe that query answers are preserved under taking the homomorphic pre-image of an ABox (and the answer). Homomorphisms between ABoxes are defined in the obvious way: $h : \mathsf{Ind}(\mathcal{A}_1) \to \mathsf{Ind}(\mathcal{A}_2)$ is a *homomorphism from ABox $\mathcal{A}_1$ to ABox $\mathcal{A}_2$* if the following conditions are satisfied:

(i) $A(a) \in \mathcal{A}_1$ implies $A(h(a)) \in \mathcal{A}_2$;
(ii) $r(a, b) \in \mathcal{A}_1$ implies $r(h(a), h(b)) \in \mathcal{A}_2$.

For later use, we state the lemma for KBs formulated in $\mathcal{ALCI}$, of which DL-Lite is a very moderate fragment. It actually holds true for all ontology languages that do not admit nominals.

Lemma 7.21. *Let $\mathcal{K}_i = (\mathcal{T}, \mathcal{A}_i)$ for $i \in \{1, 2\}$ be an $\mathcal{ALCI}$-KB, q a CQ and h a homomorphism from $\mathcal{A}_1$ to $\mathcal{A}_2$. Then $\vec{a} \in \mathsf{cert}(q, \mathcal{K}_1)$ implies $h(\vec{a}) \in \mathsf{cert}(q, \mathcal{K}_2)$.*

Proof. We show that $h(\vec{a}) \notin \mathsf{cert}(q, \mathcal{K}_2)$ implies $\vec{a} \notin \mathsf{cert}(q, \mathcal{K}_1)$. If $h(\vec{a}) \notin \mathsf{cert}(q, \mathcal{K}_2)$, then there is a model $\mathcal{I}$ of $\mathcal{K}_2$ such that q has no $h(\vec{a})$-match in $\mathcal{I}$. Define an interpretation $\mathcal{J}$ by starting with $\mathcal{I}$ and changing the interpretation of all $a \in \mathsf{Ind}(\mathcal{A}_1)$ by setting $a^{\mathcal{J}} = h(a)^{\mathcal{I}}$. Since the interpretation of TBoxes is independent of individual names, $\mathcal{J}$ is a model of $\mathcal{T}$. Using conditions (i) and (ii) in the definition of ABox homomorphisms, it is straightforward to verify that $\mathcal{J}$ is also a model of $\mathcal{A}_1$. For example, $A(a) \in \mathcal{A}_1$ implies $A(h(a)) \in \mathcal{A}_2$ and thus $h(a)^{\mathcal{I}} \in A^{\mathcal{I}}$ since $\mathcal{I}$ is a model of $\mathcal{A}_2$; consequently $a^{\mathcal{J}} \in A^{\mathcal{J}}$. It thus remains to observe that there is no $\vec{a}$-match of q in $\mathcal{J}$ as this implies $\vec{a} \notin \mathsf{cert}(q, \mathcal{K}_1)$ as desired. In fact, any $\vec{a}$-match of q in $\mathcal{J}$ is, by definition of $\mathcal{J}$, also an $h(\vec{a})$-match of q in $\mathcal{I}$, contradicting the fact that no such match exists. $\square$

Note that the (very simple) proof of Lemma 7.21 crucially relies on not making the unique name assumption. Lemma 7.21 also holds with the UNA, but is a bit more difficult to prove. We can now establish soundness of the FO-rewriting $q_{\mathcal{T}}$ of the CQ q relative to the TBox $\mathcal{T}$.

Lemma 7.22 (Soundness). *For any KB $\mathcal{K} = (\mathcal{T}, \mathcal{A})$, $\mathsf{ans}(q_{\mathcal{T}}, \mathcal{I}_{\mathcal{A}}) \subseteq \mathsf{cert}(q, \mathcal{K})$.*

Proof. Let $\vec{a} \in \mathsf{ans}(q_{\mathcal{T}}, \mathcal{I}_{\mathcal{A}})$. Then there is a disjunct $q_{\mathcal{B}}$ of $q_{\mathcal{T}}$ such that $\vec{a} \in \mathsf{ans}(q_{\mathcal{B}}, \mathcal{I}_{\mathcal{A}})$. Consequently, there is an $\vec{a}$-match π of $q_{\mathcal{B}}$ in $\mathcal{I}_{\mathcal{A}}$. Define a map $h : \mathsf{Ind}(\mathcal{B}) \to \mathsf{Ind}(\mathcal{A})$ by setting $h(b) = a$ if $\pi(x_b) = a$. It can be verified that h is a homomorphism from $\mathcal{B}$ to $\mathcal{A}$ with $h(\vec{a}_0) = \vec{a}$. Since $\vec{a}_0 \in \text{cert}(q, (\mathcal{T}, \mathcal{B}))$, Lemma 7.21 thus yields that $\vec{a} \in \text{cert}(q, \mathcal{K})$ as required. □

Summing up, we have established the following.

Theorem 7.23. *For every DL-Lite TBox $\mathcal{T}$ and CQ q, there exists an FO-rewriting $q_{\mathcal{T}}$.*

Note that, by definition of FO-rewritability, the FO-rewriting $q_{\mathcal{T}}$ is only guaranteed to deliver the desired answers when executed on an ABox $\mathcal{A}$ such that the KB $\mathcal{K} = (\mathcal{T}, \mathcal{A})$ is consistent. Before answering any queries, we would thus like to find out whether $\mathcal{K}$ is consistent and notify the user when this is not the case. Fortunately, the required check can be implemented by querying and thus also delegated to the relational database system that stores $\mathcal{A}$.

Theorem 7.24. *Let $\mathcal{T}$ be a DL-Lite TBox and $\mathcal{T}'$ be obtained from $\mathcal{T}$ by removing all negative concept inclusions. Then there is a finite set Q of Boolean CQs such that $\mathcal{K} = (\mathcal{T}, \mathcal{A})$ is consistent if and only if $\mathcal{K}' \not\models q$ for all $q \in Q$, where $\mathcal{K}' = (\mathcal{T}', \mathcal{A})$.*

Proof. We construct the desired set of Boolean CQs Q by including one query for every negative concept inclusion $B_1 \sqsubseteq \neg B_2$ in $\mathcal{T}$. For example, if $\mathcal{T}$ contains $A \sqsubseteq \neg B$, then we include $\exists x \, (A(x) \wedge B(x))$ in Q, and if $\mathcal{T}$ contains $\exists r \sqsubseteq \neg \exists s^-$ then we include $\exists x \exists y \exists z \, (r(x, y) \wedge s(z, x))$. It remains to show that Q is as required.

(if) Assume $\mathcal{K}' \not\models q$ for all $q \in Q$. Since $\mathcal{K}'$ contains no negative inclusions, it is consistent. Thus, $\mathcal{I}_{\mathcal{K}'}$ is a model of $\mathcal{K}'$. Moreover, $\mathcal{I}_{\mathcal{K}'} \not\models q$ for all $q \in Q$ by Lemma 7.17. By definition of the queries in Q, it follows that $\mathcal{I}_{\mathcal{K}'}$ satisfies all negative concept inclusions in $\mathcal{T}$. Thus $\mathcal{I}_{\mathcal{K}'}$ is a model of $\mathcal{K}$ and $\mathcal{K}$ is consistent.

(only if) If $\mathcal{K}$ is consistent, then $\mathcal{I}_{\mathcal{K}}$ is a model of $\mathcal{K}$ and thus all negative concept inclusions from $\mathcal{T}$ are satisfied in $\mathcal{I}_{\mathcal{K}}$. Consequently, $\mathcal{I}_{\mathcal{K}} \not\models q$ for all $q \in Q$. Since $\mathcal{I}_{\mathcal{K}}$ is a model $\mathcal{K}'$, we obtain $\mathcal{K}' \not\models q$ for all $q \in Q$. □

We remark that the construction of FO-rewritings $q_{\mathcal{T}}$ that underlies Theorem 7.23 is not yet effective since it requires us to decide, given a KB $\mathcal{K}$, CQ q and tuple $\vec{a}$, whether $\vec{a} \in \text{cert}(q, \mathcal{K})$. We briefly discuss how this can be done, but emphasise that, from a practical perspective, the described construction of $q_{\mathcal{T}}$ is suboptimal anyway since it often results in unnecessarily large rewritings. This is discussed further after the proof of Theorem 7.25.

Theorem 7.25. *Given a DL-Lite KB $\mathcal{K}$, CQ q and tuple of individual names $\vec{a}$, it is decidable whether $\vec{a} \in \mathsf{cert}(q, \mathcal{K})$.*

Sketch of Proof. Given $\mathcal{K}$, q and $\vec{a}$, we construct a finite initial part $\mathcal{I}_{\mathcal{K}}^{\mathsf{ini}}$ of $\mathcal{I}_{\mathcal{K}}$ and then check whether there is an $\vec{a}$-match of q in $\mathcal{I}_{\mathcal{K}}^{\mathsf{ini}}$ by considering all candidates, that is, all mappings from the variables in q to the elements of $\mathcal{I}_{\mathcal{K}}^{\mathsf{ini}}$. More precisely, $\mathcal{I}_{\mathcal{K}}^{\mathsf{ini}}$ is the restriction of $\mathcal{I}_{\mathcal{K}}$ to the domain elements d that are on level at most $\mathsf{size}(q) + \mathsf{size}(\mathcal{T})$, meaning that d can be reached from an ABox individual by travelling along a role path of length at most $\mathsf{size}(q) + \mathsf{size}(\mathcal{T})$. It thus remains to argue that, if there is an $\vec{a}$-match π of q in $\mathcal{I}_{\mathcal{K}}$, then there is such a match in $\mathcal{I}_{\mathcal{K}}^{\mathsf{ini}}$. It suffices to show this for all queries q that are connected (when viewed as a graph where the variables are the nodes and the role atoms the edges) since, for disconnected queries, we can treat all maximal connected components separately.

Thus assume that q is connected. The *depth* of a match is the minimum of the levels of all elements in the range of the match. Assume without loss of generality that π is of minimal depth. We aim to show that the depth of π is bounded by $\mathsf{size}(\mathcal{T})$ because then π maps all variables to elements of level $\leq \mathsf{size}(q) + \mathsf{size}(\mathcal{T})$ due to connectedness; thus π falls within $\mathcal{I}_{\mathcal{K}}^{\mathsf{ini}}$ as required.

Let d be an element of smallest level in the range of π. Since q is connected and d is of smallest level, π maps all variables in q to the subtree of $\mathcal{I}_{\mathcal{K}}$ rooted at d. Assume to the contrary of what we want to show that the level of d exceeds $\mathsf{size}(\mathcal{T})$. Then q must be a Boolean query. By construction of $\mathcal{I}_{\mathcal{K}}$, there is a unique path $a = d_0, \ldots, d_k = d$ from an ABox individual a to d. For $0 \leq i < k$, let C_i be the basic DL-Lite concept such that $d_i \in C_i^{\mathcal{I}_{\mathcal{K}}}$ and d_{i+1} was generated by an application of R1 or R2 to $d_i \in C_i^{\mathcal{I}_{\mathcal{K}}}$. Since the number of basic concepts is bounded by $\mathsf{size}(\mathcal{T})$, we must have $C_j = C_\ell$ for some j, ℓ with $0 \leq j < \ell < k$. The construction of $\mathcal{I}_{\mathcal{K}}$ ensures that the subtree rooted at d_j is identical to the subtree rooted at d_ℓ. Thus there must be an element e below d_j that, like d, was generated by an application of R1 or R2 to C_{k-1} but whose level is smaller than that of d (since the level of d_j is smaller than that of d_ℓ). The subtree rooted at e must be identical to that rooted at d and thus there is a match of q in $\mathcal{I}_{\mathcal{K}}$ that involves e, in contradiction to the minimal depth of π. $\qquad\square$

As mentioned above, the rewriting strategy presented here is not optimal from a practical perspective. In fact, it produces exponentially large rewritings in the *best case*, in the size of both the TBox and the query. We have chosen this form of rewriting only because it is conceptually simple and underlines the importance of locality (in the sense of Gaifman) for the existence of FO-rewritings and the design of DL-Lite.

Using results from the area of circuit complexity, it can be proved that exponentially-sized rewritings cannot be avoided in general. However, by constructing rewritings in a more goal-directed way and making use of various existing optimisation techniques, in practice it is often possible to find rewritings that are of reasonable size. While giving full details is beyond the scope of this chapter, we briefly mention that *backwards chaining* provides a more goal-directed approach to constructing rewritings. The idea is to (repeatedly and in all possible ways) replace atoms in the query by other atoms whenever $\mathcal{T}$ ensures that the latter imply the former. This approach is complicated by the fact that, additionally, it can sometimes be necessary to identify variables in the query. As an example, consider the query $q(x)$ and TBox $\mathcal{T}$ whose rewritings are displayed in Figure 7.3. The left-most rewriting is the original query and from it one reaches the middle rewriting by identifying the variables x_{a_2} and x_{a_3}. One backwards chaining step then replaces $A(x_{a_2})$ with $t(y, x_{a_2})$. Another backwards chaining step replaces $s(x_{a_2}, x_{a_3})$ with $B(x_{a_2})$, producing the right-most rewriting. Note that this last step is not possible without prior identification of x_{a_2} and x_{a_3}.

7.3 Datalog-rewritability in $\mathcal{EL}$ and $\mathcal{ELI}$

We now consider query answering in the description logics $\mathcal{EL}$ and $\mathcal{ELI}$ that, unlike DL-Lite, are able to express recursive queries. As a paradigmatic example, recall from Lemma 7.19 that $A(x)$ is not FO-rewritable with respect to the $\mathcal{EL}$ TBox $\mathcal{T} = \{\exists r.A \sqsubseteq A\}$ because the concept name A has to be propagated unboundedly far through the data. Since SQL provides only limited support of recursion, the query rewriting techniques for DL-Lite which we have developed in Section 7.2 cannot be adapted to $\mathcal{EL}$ and beyond.[2] One possible way around this problem is to admit only acyclic $\mathcal{EL}$ TBoxes (see Definition 2.9), which prevents unbounded recursion. In fact, it can be shown that conjunctive queries are always FO-rewritable with respect to acyclic $\mathcal{EL}$ TBoxes. If acyclic TBoxes are not sufficient, the only choice is to replace SQL as the target language of rewriting with a query language that admits recursion,

---

[2] SQL allows no recursion in Versions 1 and 2, and linear recursion from Version 3 on. The latter is not strong enough to guarantee the existence of rewritings in the context of $\mathcal{EL}$.

most notably Datalog. While Datalog engines are not as mainstream as SQL databases, there is still a substantial number of highly optimised such systems available, making Datalog a very suitable target for rewriting. In this section, we are concerned with rewriting into Datalog. For simplicity, we shall only consider conjunctive queries of the form $A(x)$, which from now on we call an *atomic query* (AQ). A few remarks on how to extend the presented results to full conjunctive queries are given at the end of the section.

7.3.1 Fundamentals of Datalog

Datalog is a simple and appealing query language with a rule-based syntax. A *Datalog rule* ρ has the form

$$R_0(\mathbf{x}_0) \leftarrow R_1(\mathbf{x}_1) \wedge \cdots \wedge R_n(\mathbf{x}_n),$$

with $n > 0$ and where each R_i is a relation symbol with an associated arity and each $\mathbf{x}_i$ is a tuple of variables whose length coincides with the arity of R_i. We refer to $R_0(\mathbf{x}_0)$ as the *head* of ρ and to $R_1(\mathbf{x}_1) \wedge \cdots \wedge R_n(\mathbf{x}_n)$ as the *body*. Every variable that occurs in the head of a rule is required to also occur in the body. A *Datalog program* Π is a finite set of Datalog rules, for example

$$\begin{aligned} X_A(x) &\leftarrow A(x), \\ X_A(x) &\leftarrow r(x, y) \wedge X_A(y), \\ \mathsf{goal}(x) &\leftarrow X_A(x). \end{aligned}$$

Relation symbols that occur in the head of at least one rule are *intensional* or *IDB* relations (X_A and goal in the above program) and all remaining relation symbols are *extensional* or *EDB* relations (A and r in the above program). Intuitively, the EDB relations are those relations that are allowed to occur in the data while the IDB relations are additional relations that only help in defining the query. We assume that there is a selected *goal relation* goal that does not occur in rule bodies. The *arity of* Π is the arity of the goal relation.

To fit within the framework of Description Logic, we assume that all relations (both EDB and IDB) are unary or binary, identifying unary relations with concept names and binary relations with role names. Given that we restrict ourselves to atomic query answering, we also assume that the goal relation is unary and, consequently, so are Datalog programs. Observe that the bodies of Datalog rules are actually conjunctive queries, and the heads are CQs that consist of a single atom. An interpretation $\mathcal{I}$ *satisfies* a Datalog rule ρ if every match of the (CQ that is the) body of ρ is also a match of the head. For example, the rule

$$r(x, y) \leftarrow r(x, z) \wedge r(z, y)$$

is satisfied in $\mathcal{I}$ if $r^{\mathcal{I}}$ is transitive.

Let Π be a Datalog program and $\mathcal{I}$ an interpretation that represents a database and in which the extension of all IDB relations is empty. Intuitively, an element $d \in \Delta^{\mathcal{I}}$ is an *answer* to Π on $\mathcal{I}$ if exhaustive application of the rules in Π to $\mathcal{I}$ results in d being in the extension of goal. Formally, we require that, for every interpretation $\mathcal{J}$ which can be obtained from $\mathcal{I}$ by extending the interpretation of IDB relations (concept and role names that occur in a rule head) and which satisfies all rules in Π, we have $d \in \text{goal}^{\mathcal{J}}$. We use $\text{ans}(\Pi, \mathcal{I})$ to denote the set of all answers to Π in $\mathcal{I}$.

Now that we have defined the syntax and semantics of Datalog, let us use this query language as a target for rewriting atomic queries with respect to TBoxes. Intuitively, it should be clear that the three-rule example Datalog program above is a rewriting of the atomic query $A(x)$ with respect to the TBox $\{\exists r.A \sqsubseteq A\}$. The formal definition is as follows.

Definition 7.26. Let $\mathcal{T}$ be a TBox and q a conjunctive query. A Datalog program Π is a *Datalog-rewriting* of q with respect to $\mathcal{T}$ if, for all ABoxes $\mathcal{A}$, we have $\text{cert}(q, \mathcal{K}) = \text{ans}(\Pi, \mathcal{I}_{\mathcal{A}})$, where $\mathcal{K} = (\mathcal{T}, \mathcal{A})$.

We have not required consistency of $\mathcal{K}$ in the above definition only because in this section we work with description logics that cannot produce inconsistencies. When inconsistency can occur, one would require $\mathcal{K}$ to be consistent, exactly as in Definition 7.7.

The following is an interesting first observation that relates Datalog-rewritings to FO-rewritings.

Lemma 7.27. *Let $A_0(x)$ be an AQ and $\mathcal{T}$ an $\mathcal{ALCI}$ TBox. If $A_0(x)$ is FO-rewritable with respect to $\mathcal{T}$, then $A_0(x)$ is Datalog-rewritable with respect to $\mathcal{T}$.*

Sketch of proof. An FO query q is *preserved under homomorphisms* if it satisfies the following property: if $\vec{d} \in \text{ans}(q, \mathcal{I})$ and h is a homomorphism from $\mathcal{I}$ to $\mathcal{J}$, then $h(\vec{d}) \in \text{ans}(q, \mathcal{J})$. A classical result in model theory states that an FO query is preserved under homomorphisms if and only if it is equivalent to a positive existential FO query, that is, a query composed only of conjunction, disjunction and existential quantifiers. This result was lifted to the class of finite interpretations by Rossman. As a consequence of Lemma 7.21, an FO-rewriting $q(x)$ of $A_0(x)$ with respect to $\mathcal{T}$ is preserved under homomorphisms on the class of finite interpretations: if h is a homomorphism from $\mathcal{I}$ to $\mathcal{J}$ with $\mathcal{I}$ and $\mathcal{J}$ finite, then $d \in \mathsf{ans}(q, \mathcal{I})$ implies $d \in \mathsf{cert}(A_0(x), \mathcal{K}_\mathcal{I})$ implies $h(d) \in \mathsf{cert}(A_0(x), \mathcal{K}_\mathcal{J})$ implies $h(d) \in \mathsf{ans}(q, \mathcal{J})$, where $\mathcal{K}_\mathcal{I} = (\mathcal{T}, \mathcal{A}_\mathcal{I})$ and $\mathcal{A}_\mathcal{I}$ is the ABox such that $\mathcal{I}_{\mathcal{A}_\mathcal{I}} = \mathcal{I}$, and likewise for $\mathcal{K}_\mathcal{J}$. Consequently, a rewriting $q(x)$ of $A_0(x)$ with respect to $\mathcal{T}$ is equivalent to a positive existential FO query, thus also to an FO query of the form $\bigvee_i q_i(x)$, where each $q_i(x)$ is a CQ; such a disjunction is commonly called a *union of conjunctive queries* (UCQ). Finally, a UCQ $\bigvee_i q_i(x)$ is equivalent to the Datalog program that consists of the rules $\mathsf{goal}(x) \leftarrow q_i(x)$. $\square$

7.3.2 Datalog-rewritings in $\mathcal{ELI}$

We show that Datalog-rewritings of atomic queries with respect to $\mathcal{ELI}$ TBoxes always exist, and how they can be constructed. The main challenge is to deal with existential restrictions on the right-hand sides of concept inclusions in the TBox. In fact, an $\mathcal{ELI}$ TBox in which no such restrictions occur is a notational variation of a Datalog program. Here, we show how to deal with the general case.

Let $\mathcal{T}$ be an $\mathcal{ELI}$ TBox and $A_0(x)$ an atomic query to be rewritten. We introduce a fresh concept name X_C for every $C \in \mathsf{sub}(\mathcal{T})$ to serve as an IDB relation in Π. The rules of Π are now as follows:

(i) for every concept name $A \in \mathsf{sub}(\mathcal{T})$, the rule $X_A(x) \leftarrow A(x)$;

(ii) for every $\exists r.C \in \mathsf{sub}(\mathcal{T})$, the rule $X_{\exists r.C}(x) \leftarrow r(x, y) \wedge X_C(y)$;

(iii) for every $C \in \mathsf{sub}(\mathcal{T})$ and every subset $\Gamma \subseteq \mathsf{sub}(\mathcal{T})$ such that $\mathcal{T} \models \bigsqcap \Gamma \sqsubseteq C$, the rule $X_C(x) \leftarrow \bigwedge_{D \in \Gamma} X_D(x)$;

(iv) the rule $\mathsf{goal}(x) \leftarrow X_{A_0}(x)$.

For readers who also expected rules of the form $X_{C \sqcap D} \leftarrow X_C \wedge X_D$, we note that these are just a special case of (iii). It is the rules of kind (iii) that deal with existential restrictions on the right-hand side. As a very simple example, consider the atomic query $A_0(x)$ and the TBox $\mathcal{T} = \{A \sqsubseteq \exists r.B, \exists r.B \sqsubseteq A_0\}$. For $\mathcal{K} = (\mathcal{T}, \mathcal{A})$ with $\mathcal{A} = \{A(a)\}$, we have $a \in \mathsf{cert}(A_0(x), \mathcal{K})$. The Datalog-rewriting Π of A_0 with respect to $\mathcal{T}$ contains, among others, the following rules:

$$X_A(x_0) \;\leftarrow\; A(x_0),$$
$$X_{A_0}(x) \;\leftarrow\; X_A(x),$$
$$\mathsf{goal}(x) \;\leftarrow\; X_{A_0}(x),$$

and thus $a \in \mathsf{ans}(\Pi, \mathcal{I}_{\mathcal{A}})$. The middle rule is of kind (iii), and intuitively it cuts short the existential restriction $\exists r.B$ in $\mathcal{T}$. Since such shortcuts are not always obvious (which is related to the fact that subsumption in $\mathcal{ELI}$ is ExpTime-complete), we use an exhaustive approach and consider all possible conjunctions of subconcepts in (iii).

Lemma 7.28. Π *is a Datalog-rewriting of* $A_0(x)$ *with respect to* $\mathcal{T}$.

Proof. We have to show that, for all ABoxes $\mathcal{A}$, $\mathsf{cert}(A_0(x), \mathcal{K}) = \mathsf{ans}(\Pi, \mathcal{I}_{\mathcal{A}})$, where $\mathcal{K} = (\mathcal{T}, \mathcal{A})$.

"$\subseteq$". Let $a_0 \notin \mathsf{ans}(\Pi, \mathcal{I}_{\mathcal{A}})$. Then there is an extension $\mathcal{J}$ of $\mathcal{I}_{\mathcal{A}}$ to the IDB relations in Π such that $\mathcal{J}$ satisfies all rules of Π and $a_0 \notin \mathsf{goal}^{\mathcal{J}}$. For every $a \in \mathsf{Ind}(\mathcal{A})$, let Γ_a be the set of all concepts $C \in \mathsf{sub}(\mathcal{T})$ such that $a \in X_C^{\mathcal{J}}$. Due to the rules of Π of kind (iii), Γ_a is closed under consequence; that is, if $\mathcal{T} \models \sqcap \Gamma_a \sqsubseteq C$ for some $C \in \mathsf{sub}(\mathcal{T})$, then $C \in \Gamma_a$. By Lemma 6.31, we find a model $\mathcal{I}_a$ of $\mathcal{T}$ with $a \in \Delta^{\mathcal{I}_a}$ and such that for all $C \in \mathsf{sub}(\mathcal{T})$, we have $\mathcal{T} \models \sqcap \Gamma_a \sqsubseteq C$ if and only if $a \in C^{\mathcal{I}_a}$; since Γ_a is closed under consequence, this means $C \in \Gamma_a$ if and only if $a \in C^{\mathcal{I}_a}$. Assume that each $\mathcal{I}_a$ shares only the element a with $\mathcal{I}_{\mathcal{A}}$ and that $\Delta^{\mathcal{I}_a} \cap \Delta^{\mathcal{I}_b} = \emptyset$ whenever $a \neq b$.

Define the interpretation $\mathcal{I}$ by first taking the disjoint union of all the interpretations $\mathcal{I}_a$ and then adding (a, b) to $r^{\mathcal{I}}$ whenever $r(a, b) \in \mathcal{A}$; for all individual names a, set $a^{\mathcal{I}} = a$. We show the following:

($*$) $d \in C^{\mathcal{I}_a}$ if and only if $d \in C^{\mathcal{I}}$ for all $C \in \mathsf{sub}(\mathcal{T})$, $a \in \mathsf{Ind}(\mathcal{A})$ and $d \in \Delta^{\mathcal{I}_a}$.

The proof is by induction on the structure of C. The case of concept names and conjunction is straightforward, so we consider only existential restrictions. Here, the "only if" direction is also easy, so we concentrate on "if". Assume that $d \in (\exists r.C)^{\mathcal{I}}$ with $d \in \Delta^{\mathcal{I}_a}$. Then there is a $(d, e) \in r^{\mathcal{I}}$ with $e \in C^{\mathcal{I}}$. By construction of $\mathcal{I}$, we have $(d, e) \in r^{\mathcal{I}_a}$ or there is a $b \in \mathsf{Ind}(\mathcal{A})$ such that $(d, e) = (a, b)$ and $r(a, b) \in \mathcal{A}$. In the former case, the induction hypothesis yields $e \in C^{\mathcal{I}_a}$ and thus $d \in (\exists r.C)^{\mathcal{I}_a}$ as required. Thus assume $(d, e) = (a, b)$ and $r(a, b) \in \mathcal{A}$. From $e \in C^{\mathcal{I}}$ and the induction hypothesis, we obtain $b \in C^{\mathcal{I}_b}$ and thus $C \in \Gamma_b$ by choice of $\mathcal{I}_b$ and $b \in X_C^{\mathcal{J}}$ by choice of Γ_b. Since $r(a, b) \in \mathcal{A}$ yields $(a, b) \in r^{\mathcal{J}}$ and the rules in Π of kind (ii) are satisfied in $\mathcal{J}$, we have $a \in X_{\exists r.C}^{\mathcal{J}}$, thus $\exists r.C \in \Gamma_a$ and $d \in (\exists r.C)^{\mathcal{I}_a}$, as required.

As a consequence of $(*)$ and since each $\mathcal{I}_a$ is a model of $\mathcal{T}$, $\mathcal{I}$ is also a model of $\mathcal{T}$. By construction, it satisfies all role assertions in $\mathcal{A}$. Concept assertions are also satisfied: $A(a) \in \mathcal{A}$ implies $a \in X_A^{\mathcal{J}}$ since the rules in Π of kind (i) are satisfied, thus $a \in A^{\mathcal{I}_a}$ and $(*)$ yields $a \in A^{\mathcal{I}}$. Finally, by the rules of kind (iv), $a_0 \notin \mathsf{goal}^{\mathcal{J}}$ implies $a_0 \notin X_{A_0}^{\mathcal{J}}$, and consequently $a_0 \notin A_0^{\mathcal{I}}$. We have thus shown that $a_0 \notin \mathsf{cert}(A_0(x), \mathcal{K})$.

"$\supseteq$". Let $a_0 \notin \mathsf{cert}(A_0(x), \mathcal{K})$. Then there is a model $\mathcal{I}$ of $\mathcal{A}$ and $\mathcal{K}$ such that $a_0^{\mathcal{I}} \notin A_0^{\mathcal{I}}$. Let $\mathcal{J}$ be the extension of $\mathcal{I}_{\mathcal{A}}$ to the IDB relations in Π by setting $X_C^{\mathcal{J}} = \{a \in \mathsf{Ind}(\mathcal{A}) \mid a^{\mathcal{I}} \in C^{\mathcal{I}}\}$ for every IDB relation of the form X_C and $\mathsf{goal}^{\mathcal{J}} = X_{A_0}^{\mathcal{J}}$. It can be verified that the extended $\mathcal{J}$ satisfies all rules in Π and that $a_0 \notin \mathsf{goal}^{\mathcal{J}}$, and thus $a_0 \notin \mathsf{ans}(\Pi, \mathcal{I}_{\mathcal{A}})$. $\square$

We have thus established the following result.

Theorem 7.29. *For every atomic query $A_0(x)$ and $\mathcal{ELI}$ TBox $\mathcal{T}$, there is a Datalog-rewriting Π.*

Theorem 7.29 is also true when the atomic queries A_0 are replaced with conjunctive queries q, but then the construction of Π becomes more complicated. The intuitive reason is that the existentially quantified part of a conjunctive query q can (fully or partially) be matched to elements that are generated by existential restrictions in $\mathcal{T}$, which we have "cut short" in the construction of Π as explained above. This means that it does not suffice to include in Π the rule $\mathsf{goal}(\vec{x}) \leftarrow q(\vec{x})$, but instead we have to "dissect" q according to which parts of it are matched in the ABox, and which parts are matched (implicitly!) inside the shortcuts, and then reflect this dissection in the rules. Of course, there is more than one possible such dissection of q, and all of them have to be considered.

Note that the Datalog-rewriting Π constructed above is of size exponential in the size of $\mathcal{T}$, due to the rules of kind (iii). In fact, it is known that Datalog-rewritings of polynomial size do not exist unless a standard complexity-theoretic assumption fails.[3] Of course, it is nevertheless possible to improve the presented construction of Π to make it shorter in many cases.

---

[3] The assumption is that $\textsc{ExpTime} \not\subseteq \textsc{coNP}/\textsc{Poly}$, where the latter is the non-uniform version of the complexity class $\textsc{coNP}$, commonly defined via Turing machines with *advice*; readers are referred to complexity theory textbooks for details.

7.3.3 Short Datalog-rewritings in $\mathcal{EL}$

We now consider the case of $\mathcal{EL}$ TBoxes and refine the construction of Datalog-rewritings given above so that the resulting program is of only polynomial size. Thus, let $\mathcal{T}$ be an $\mathcal{EL}$ TBox and $A_0(x)$ an atomic query. We again use a concept name X_C for every $C \in \mathsf{sub}(\mathcal{T})$ as an IDB relation. The rules of Π are:

(i) for every concept name $A \in \mathsf{sub}(\mathcal{T})$, the rule $X_A(x) \leftarrow A(x)$;

(ii) for every $C \sqcap D \in \mathsf{sub}(\mathcal{T})$, the rules $X_{C \sqcap D}(x) \leftarrow X_C(x) \wedge X_D(x)$, $X_C(x) \leftarrow X_{C \sqcap D}(x)$ and $X_D(x) \leftarrow X_{C \sqcap D}(x)$;

(iii) for every $\exists r.C \in \mathsf{sub}(\mathcal{T})$, the rule $X_{\exists r.C}(x) \leftarrow r(x,y) \wedge X_C(y)$;

(iv) for all $C, D \in \mathsf{sub}(\mathcal{T})$ with $\mathcal{T} \models C \sqsubseteq D$, the rule $X_D(x) \leftarrow X_C(x)$;

(v) the rule $\mathsf{goal}(x) \leftarrow X_{A_0}(x)$.

Note that the former rules of kind (iii) have been replaced by what are now rules of kinds (ii) and (iv).

Lemma 7.30. Π *is a Datalog-rewriting of $A_0(x)$ with respect to $\mathcal{T}$.*

Proof. An analysis of the proof of Lemma 7.28 shows that $\mathsf{cert}(A_0(x), \mathcal{K}) \supseteq \mathsf{ans}(\Pi, \mathcal{I}_\mathcal{A})$ is still straightforward to establish and that, in the converse direction, the only step that uses the former Datalog rules of kind (iii) which have been removed in the new translation is to show the following: if $\mathcal{J}$ is an extension of $\mathcal{I}_\mathcal{A}$ to the IDB relations in Π that satisfies all rules of Π, then for all $a \in \mathsf{Ind}(\mathcal{A})$ there is an interpretation $\mathcal{I}_a$ such that $a \in \Delta^{\mathcal{I}_a}$, and for all $C \in \mathsf{sub}(\mathcal{T})$ we have $a \in C^{\mathcal{I}_a}$ if and only if $C \in \Gamma_a$, where $\Gamma_a = \{C \mid a \in X_C^{\mathcal{J}}\}$. We show that, when $\mathcal{T}$ is formulated in $\mathcal{EL}$, this can be established using the new rules.

Let $\exists r_1.C_1, \ldots, \exists r_n.C_n$ be the existential restrictions in Γ_a. By Lemma 6.31, for $1 \leq i \leq n$ we find a model $\mathcal{I}_i$ of $\mathcal{T}$ and a $d_i \in \Delta^{\mathcal{I}_i}$ such that, for all $C \in \mathsf{sub}(\mathcal{T})$, we have $\mathcal{T} \models C_i \sqsubseteq C$ if and only if $d_i \in C^{\mathcal{I}_i}$. Assume without loss of generality that none of the $\Delta^{\mathcal{I}_i}$ contains a and that $\Delta^{\mathcal{I}_i} \cap \Delta^{\mathcal{I}_j} = \emptyset$ whenever $i \neq j$. Define the interpretation $\mathcal{I}_a$ by first taking the disjoint union of all interpretations $\mathcal{I}_i$ and then adding a as a fresh root; that is, a is added to $\Delta^{\mathcal{I}_a}$ and (a, d_i) is added to $r_i^{\mathcal{I}_a}$ for $1 \leq i \leq k$. Also, add a to $A^{\mathcal{I}_a}$ whenever $X_A \in \Gamma_a$.

It remains to show that $\mathcal{I}_a$ is the required model of $\mathcal{T}$. First note that, as a straightforward induction shows, we have $d \in C^{\mathcal{I}_a}$ if and only if $d \in C^{\mathcal{I}_i}$ for all $d \in \Delta^{\mathcal{I}_i}$ and all $\mathcal{EL}$ concepts C (this argument fails in the case of $\mathcal{ELI}$). Consequently, the elements $d \in \Delta^{\mathcal{I}_a} \setminus \{a\}$ satisfy the TBox $\mathcal{T}$ in the sense that $d \in C^{\mathcal{I}_a}$ implies $D^{\mathcal{I}_a}$ for all $C \sqsubseteq D \in \mathcal{T}$. We have to show that the same is true for a and that $a \in C^{\mathcal{I}_a}$ if and only if $X_C \in \Gamma_a$ for all $C \in \mathsf{sub}(\mathcal{T})$. We concentrate on the latter since, due to the rules of kind (iv), it implies the former.

The proof is by induction on the structure of C, where the induction start (C a concept name) is immediate by definition of $\mathcal{I}_a$. The case $C = D \sqcap E$ is straightforward based on the induction hypothesis, the semantics, and the rules of the form (ii). Thus consider the case $C = \exists r.D$.

(if) $X_{\exists r.D} \in \Gamma_a$ implies that $\exists r.D = \exists r_i.C_i$ for some i. By our choice of $\mathcal{I}_i$, $d_i \in C_i^{\mathcal{I}_i}$ and thus $d_i \in C_i^{\mathcal{I}_a}$. By construction of $\mathcal{I}_a$, we thus have $a \in (\exists r.C)^{\mathcal{I}_a}$.

(only if) By construction of $\mathcal{I}_a$, $a \in (\exists r.C)^{\mathcal{I}_a}$ implies $r = r_i$ and $d_i \in C^{\mathcal{I}_a}$ for some i. The latter yields $d_i \in C^{\mathcal{I}_i}$, which by our choice of $\mathcal{I}_i$ implies $\mathcal{T} \models C_i \sqsubseteq C$. From the latter, it easily follows that $\mathcal{T} \models \exists r.C_i \sqsubseteq \exists r.C$. Thus $X_{\exists r_i.C_i} \in \Gamma_a$ and the rules of kind (iv) give us $X_{\exists r.C} \in \Gamma_a$. $\qquad \square$

We summarise the obtained result as follows.

Theorem 7.31. *For every atomic query $A_0(x)$ and $\mathcal{EL}$ TBox $\mathcal{T}$, there is a Datalog-rewriting Π of size polynomial in the size of $\mathcal{T}$.*

The material presented in this section shows that query answering with respect to TBoxes formulated in description logics such as $\mathcal{EL}$ and $\mathcal{ELI}$ is closely related to query answering in Datalog. One main difference is that DLs allow existential quantification on the right-hand side of concept inclusions, whereas Datalog does not admit existential quantification in the rule head. Inspired by this difference, researchers have generalised Datalog with this kind of existential quantification, which leads to what is known as *existential rules* or *tuple-generating dependencies*. However, query answering with respect to sets of existential rules turns out to be undecidable and, therefore, various syntactic restrictions have been proposed that regain decidability, known under the name *Datalog$^\pm$*. In fact, there are many different versions of *Datalog$^\pm$*, several of which generalise the description logics DL-Lite, $\mathcal{EL}$ and $\mathcal{ELI}$.

7.4 Complexity aspects

In this chapter, we have focussed on rewriting-based approaches to query answering in the presence of Description Logic TBoxes. As alternatives, researchers have developed approaches that materialise the consequences of the TBox in the database instead of rewriting the query, as well as approaches that do not rely on existing database technology at all. One important motivation for the latter is to avoid the exponential blowups that are often inherent in rewriting-based approaches. Another is to enable TBox-aware querying for description logics that are too expressive to be rewritten into query languages such as SQL or Datalog. The latter is closely related to the subject of data complexity, which we briefly discuss in this section. When studying computational complexity, it is more convenient to work with decision problems than with computation problems. Therefore, from now on we will assume that queries are Boolean and speak of query entailment rather than query answering. In principle, though, everything said in the following also carries over to queries with answer variables.

Query answering in DLs is a problem with multiple inputs: the ABox (from now on called the data), the TBox and the query. The most obvious way to measure the complexity is to treat all inputs equally, which is called *combined complexity*. For example, conjunctive query entailment in the presence of TBoxes that are formulated in DL-Lite or in $\mathcal{EL}$ is NP-complete in combined complexity, and the same problem is EXPTIME-complete in combined complexity when the TBox is formulated in $\mathcal{ELI}$ or in $\mathcal{ALC}$, and even 2-EXPTIME-complete in $\mathcal{ALCI}$. In fact, conjunctive query entailment is NP-complete already without any TBoxes (it is then simply the homomorphism problem on directed graphs).

However, a moment of reflection reveals that combined complexity is probably *not* the most relevant form of complexity for query answering. In typical applications, the data is extremely large while the query and also the TBox are many orders of magnitude smaller. In database research, this observation has led to the notion of *data complexity*, which in the DL version reads as follows: when analyzing the complexity of query entailment, consider the ABox to be the only input while treating both the query and the TBox as parameters that are fixed and whose size therefore is a constant and does not contribute to the complexity. In effect, transitioning from combined complexity to data complexity thus means replacing a single decision problem (with three inputs) by infinitely many decision problems (with one input each): one problem for each query and each TBox.

The data complexity of a querying problem is typically much lower than its combined complexity and often reflects practical feasibility much better. For example, SQL query entailment (without TBoxes) is PSPACE-complete and thus intractable in combined complexity, but in the extremely small complexity class AC^0 (which is below LogSpace and PTime) in data complexity. Conjunctive query entailment is therefore also in AC^0 in data complexity while Datalog query entailment is known to be PTime-complete in data complexity.

The results on rewriting presented in this chapter allow us to infer results on data complexity. First consider conjunctive query entailment in the presence of DL-Lite TBoxes. Entailment of the (fixed) conjunctive query q with respect to the (fixed) TBox $\mathcal{T}$ is reduced to entailment of their FO-rewriting $q_{\mathcal{T}}$. As noted above, the latter problem is in AC^0 in data complexity (that is, with $q_{\mathcal{T}}$ regarded as fixed). In fact, if we neglect representational differences between an ABox $\mathcal{A}$ and the corresponding interpretation/relational instance $\mathcal{I}_{\mathcal{A}}$ (which can safely be done), entailment of q with respect to $\mathcal{T}$ and entailment of $q_{\mathcal{T}}$ are *exactly the same problem*: the inputs are identical and the "yes"-inputs also coincide. Consequently, conjunctive query entailment in DL-Lite is in AC^0 in data complexity. Note that the exponential size of $q_{\mathcal{T}}$ is irrelevant since $q_{\mathcal{T}}$ is fixed and not an input. Arguing in the same way and utilising the PTime data complexity of Datalog query entailment, we can derive from the rewritings presented in Section 7.3.2 that atomic query entailment in $\mathcal{EL}$ and in $\mathcal{ELI}$ is in PTime regarding data complexity. In fact, it is known to be PTime-complete, and the complexity does not change when we replace atomic queries with conjunctive queries.

Thus, query entailment in DL-Lite, $\mathcal{EL}$ and $\mathcal{ELI}$ is *tractable* in data complexity. In contrast, the use of description logics that include disjunction typically leads to intractability in data complexity. As an example, consider the following $\mathcal{ALC}$ TBox and Boolean CQ:

$$\mathcal{T} \ = \ \{ \qquad \top \sqsubseteq R \sqcup G \sqcup B$$
$$R \sqcap \exists r.R \sqsubseteq D$$
$$G \sqcap \exists r.G \sqsubseteq D$$
$$B \sqcap \exists r.B \sqsubseteq D \quad \},$$
$$q \ = \ \exists x\, D(x).$$

If we assume that the input ABox $\mathcal{A}$ contains only the role name r and no other symbols, thus representing a directed graph, then it is straightforward to prove that $(\mathcal{T}, \mathcal{A}) \models q$ if and only if $\mathcal{A}$ is not 3-colourable (counter models correspond to 3-colourings). Note that the concept name D represents a *defect* in the 3-colouring and the existence of defects is what q queries for. Consequently, CQ entailment is CONP-hard in data complexity in $\mathcal{ALC}$ and it is not hard to lift this result to the entailment of atomic queries (which do not admit the existential quantification used in the query above). A CONP upper bound can be established in various ways, such as through tableau algorithms, resolution or construction of a model-theoretic nature. Implicit forms of disjunction (see the discussion of convexity in Section 6.3.2) also easily lead to intractability in data complexity.

7.5 Historical context and literature review

Query answering over Description Logic knowledge bases has a long tradition and can be traced back to the very beginnings of the field. Originally, the most common choice for the query language was *concept queries*, that is, queries of the form $C(x)$ with C a DL concept, typically formulated in the description logic that is also used for the TBox. Over the years, query answering has become more and more important, and the setups and questions that have been considered have become more database-like in spirit. Conjunctive queries were first considered in a DL context in [LR98] and a little later in [CDGL98a]. Together with unions of conjunctive queries (UCQs), they are now the most common query language for DLs. A very large body of literature on the topic is available; in the following, we will give references relevant for this chapter, following roughly the order in which we have presented the material.

The DL-Lite family of description logics was introduced in [CDL+07], where the notions of query rewriting and FO-rewritability were also first considered in a DL context.[4] DL-Lite is the foundation for an approach to querying and integration of relational databases using ontologies and schema mappings that is called ontology-based data access (OBDA), discussed in detail in [CDL+09]. Gaifman locality, as used in the proof of Theorem 7.8 to analyse the limits of FO-rewritability, can be found in most textbooks on first-order logic and finite model theory such as [Lib04]. Universal models have been used under various names in the literature on query answering with DLs, for example in [CDL+07, LTW09, KZ14, BO15]. They can be viewed as a DL version of the chase procedure from database theory; see, e.g., [DNR08] and references therein. FO-rewritability of conjunctive queries in DL-Lite

---

[4] Query rewriting is also a popular tool in various subfields of database theory such as query answering under views [Hal01, Len02].

was first established in [CDL+07] by a procedure called PerfectRef. A more semantic approach based on so-called tree witnesses is presented in [KZ14]. Implemented systems for computing rewritings are available, such as OnTop [RKZ13]. Lower bounds on the size of rewritten queries are established in [GKK+14]. An alternative to query rewriting which materialises the consequences of the TBox in the ABox instead of anticipating them in the query was introduced in [LTW09] and applied to DL-Lite in [KLT+10]. This approach is also known as the combined approach.

Due to the limited expressive power of DL-Lite, query answering in more expressive DLs has also received significant interest. Datalog rewritings of concept queries in Horn DLs such as $\mathcal{ELI}$ were first studied in [HMS07]. Implemented systems are available, such as Rapid [TSCS15], Requiem [PUMH10] and Clipper [HS12]. A recent survey on query answering in Horn DLs is provided by [BO15]. One can also try to construct FO-rewritings of queries in Horn DLs beyond DL-Lite, although in general they are not guaranteed to exist. For concept queries, foundations are laid in [BLW13] and it is shown in [HLSW15] that FO-rewritings often exist in practice and can be computed efficiently.

For $\mathcal{ALC}$ and its extensions, even Datalog rewritings are not guaranteed to exist. One possibility is to rewrite into disjunctive Datalog instead [HMS07]; another is to give up on rewritings and implement query answering systems from scratch, based for example on tableau algorithms or resolution. Again, one can also try to construct FO-rewritings or Datalog-rewritings when they exist, as studied for example in [BtCLW14] and [GMSH13].

Both the combined complexity and the data complexity of query answering in DLs have received significant interest. Data complexity results for DLs first appeared in [DLNS98], where a CoNP lower bound is established for concept queries and (a fragment of) $\mathcal{ALC}$. Corresponding CoNP upper bounds can be established for conjunctive queries and a wide range of expressive DLs using various methods; see, e.g., [HMS07, OCE08, GLHS08]. Horn DLs typically have PTIME data complexity, but classes such as AC^0, LOGSPACE and NLOGSPACE also play a role; see [KL07, Ros07a, CDL+13] for a sample of results. A more fine-grained approach is taken in [LW12, BtCLW14], where data complexity is studied for single TBoxes and queries, instead of for entire description logics.

Regarding combined complexity, it is a classical result in database theory that conjunctive query entailment is NP-complete [CM77]. The combined complexity of answering both concept and conjunctive queries in $\mathcal{ALC}$ is ExpTime-complete [Lut08]. For the latter (but not for concept queries), the complexity rises to 2ExpTime-complete when inverse roles are added [Lut08]. Transitive roles and nominals are also known to increase combined complexity [ELOS09, NOS16]. In Horn DLs, the combined complexity of answering conjunctive queries is typically in ExpTime, even with inverse roles [EGOS08, ORS11]. For DLs for which subsumption is ExpTime-complete, such as $\mathcal{ELI}$, this problem (trivially) is also hard for ExpTime. Otherwise, it often turns out to be NP-complete, such as in DL-Lite (implicit in [CDL+07]) and in $\mathcal{EL}$ (simultaneously observed in [KL07, KRH07, Ros07b]).

When viewed from a database perspective, one obvious shortcoming of DLs is their restriction to unary and binary relations (concept and role names). To overcome this limitation, DLs with higher arity have been proposed, e.g., in [CDL08, CDL+13]. Another option is to give up DL syntax and instead use rule-based formalism as ontology languages, which naturally allow for relations of any arity. This approach has led to the development of the Datalog$^{\pm}$ family of ontology languages, also known as existential rules and tuple-generating dependencies. The literature on Datalog$^{\pm}$ has already become rather large, and we only mention [CGL12, CGK13, BLMS11, BMRT11, CGP11] to get the reader started.

8
Ontology Languages and Applications

As discussed in Section 1.2, DL systems have been used in a range of application domains, including configuration, software information and documentation systems and databases, where they have been used to support schema design, schema and data integration, and query answering. More recently, DLs have played a central role in the semantic web [Hor08], having been adopted as the basis for ontology languages such as OIL, DAML+OIL and OWL [HPSvH03]. This has rapidly become the most prominent application of DLs, and DL knowledge bases are now often referred to as ontologies.

In computer science, an ontology is a conceptual model specified using some ontology language; this idea was succinctly captured by Gruber in his definition of an ontology as "an explicit specification of a conceptualisation" [Gru93]. Early ontology languages were often based on frames, but as in the case of early DLs, a desire to provide them with precise semantics and well-defined reasoning procedures increasingly led to ontology languages becoming logic-based. The OIL ontology language was something of a compromise: it had a frame-based syntax, but complemented this with a formal semantics based on a mapping to $\mathcal{SHIQ}$. In DAML+OIL and OWL the DL-based semantics were retained, but the frame-based syntax of OIL was replaced with a structure much closer to DL-style axioms.

In Section 8.1 we will discuss OWL in more detail, examining its relationship to RDF and to $\mathcal{SROIQ}$, its syntax (or rather syntaxes), some features that go beyond what is typically found in a DL, and its various profiles or sub-languages. In Section 8.2 we will look at some interesting examples of OWL tools and applications.

8.1 The OWL ontology language

OWL is a semantic web ontology language developed by the World Wide Web Consortium (W3C), an international community that defines Web technologies. W3C follows a consensus-driven process for the publication of specification documents for Web technologies, in particular *Recommendations*, which are considered Web standards. OWL was first standardised in 2004, and then revised in 2012, with the revision being denoted OWL 2. Although using a variety of more "Web-friendly" syntaxes based, e.g., on XML and RDF, the basic structure of OWL corresponds closely with that of a DL, and includes such familiar constructs as existential and value restrictions, (qualified) number restrictions, inverse roles, nominals and role hierarchies (see Chapter 2). Moreover, the semantics of OWL can be defined via a mapping into an expressive DL.[1]

8.1.1 OWL and RDF

OWL was designed to extend RDF, a pre-existing W3C Recommendation. It is beyond the scope of this chapter to provide a detailed description of RDF, but a brief sketch will be useful in order to explain some of the features of OWL; interested readers are referred to `http://www.w3.org/RDF/` for complete information. RDF provides a very simple graph-like data model, with each statement, or *triple*, representing a labelled, directed edge in the graph. A triple consists of three elements called the subject, predicate and object, and they are often written

$$\langle s, p, o \rangle$$

where s is the subject, p the predicate and o the object. Such a triple represents a p-labelled edge from vertex s to vertex o; it can also be thought of as a first-order logic ground atomic formula $p(s, o)$, where p is a binary predicate and s and o are constants.

In RDF, all subject, predicate and object names are Internationalized Resource Identifiers (IRIs) [RFC05], a generalised version of the URLs that are used to identify resources on the Web. As they can be rather verbose, IRIs are often abbreviated by defining one or more common prefixes for the IRIs used in an ontology, e.g., by writing the IRI *http://dl.book/example#name* as *eg:name*, where *eg:* is defined to be the

---

[1] Roughly speaking, OWL can be mapped into $\mathcal{SHOIN}$, and OWL 2 into $\mathcal{SROIQ}$.

prefix *http://dl.book/example#*. Furthermore, a default prefix is often defined for all IRIs used in a given document, so we can simply write *:name* if *eg:* is the default prefix.

RDF assigns special meanings to certain predicates. In particular, *rdf:type* represents the "instance of" relationship, and is used to capture unary predicate formulae, where *rdf:* is the prefix *http://www.w3.org/1999/02/22-rdf-syntax-ns#*. For example, the triple $\langle s, rdf\!:\!type, o\rangle$ can be thought of as representing the first-order logic ground atomic formula $o(s)$, where o is a unary predicate and s is a constant. RDF thus provides a very natural way to capture ABox assertions, with a triple $\langle a, r, b\rangle$ corresponding to a role assertion $(a, b) : r$ and $\langle a, rdf\!:\!type, C\rangle$ corresponding to a concept assertion $a : C$. Note that in RDF and OWL, roles are referred to as properties and concepts are referred to as classes, so $\langle a, r, b\rangle$ would be called a property assertion and $\langle a, rdf\!:\!type, C\rangle$ a class assertion. In RDF C is always atomic (i.e., a class name), but in OWL C could be part of a graph that defines a compound class (see the OWL syntax example below).

RDF Schema (RDFS) extends the set of special predicates in order to capture a limited set of "schema" level statements, many of which correspond to TBox axioms;[2] for example, the triple $\langle C, rdfs\!:\!subClassOf, D\rangle$ corresponds to a TBox axiom $C \sqsubseteq D$.

OWL further extends this set of special predicates to capture more complex concept expressions and TBox axioms. Unlike a DL knowledge base, an OWL ontology makes no distinction between TBox and ABox – it consists of a single set of RDF triples (also known as an RDF graph) representing ABox assertions and/or TBox axioms. This style of syntax based on triples is flexible, but when extended to capture complex concepts it becomes quite cumbersome, and complicates even basic tasks; for example, it is difficult to constrain the syntax so as to allow only syntactically valid axioms and assertions, and to parse documents into an internal representation of a set of axioms. OWL is therefore defined using a functional-style syntax [OWL12c], along with a bidirectional mapping between this syntax and RDF triples [OWL12a]. In addition, other syntaxes for OWL have been specified, including the Manchester syntax, which presents an ontology in a succinct form easily readable by humans. The following example gives the DL axiom $C \sqsubseteq D \sqcap \exists r.E$ in these three syntaxes:

---

[2] The triple $\langle C, rdfs\!:\!comment, D\rangle$ is an example of an RDFS statement that has no correspondence with a TBox axiom; it states that D is a human-readable description of C.

Functional-style syntax

```
SubClassOf(
  :C
  ObjectIntersectionOf(
    :D
    ObjectSomeValuesFrom( :r :E))))
```

RDF/XML, an XML-based syntax for triples

```
<owl:Class rdf:about=":C">
  <rdfs:subClassOf>
    <owl:Class>
      <owl:intersectionOf rdf:parseType="Collection">
        <rdf:Description rdf:about=":D"/>
        <owl:Restriction>
          <owl:onProperty rdf:resource=":r"/>
          <owl:someValuesFrom rdf:resource=":E"/>
        </owl:Restriction>
      </owl:intersectionOf>
    </owl:Class>
  </rdfs:subClassOf>
</owl:Class>
```

Manchester syntax

```
Class: :C
  SubClassOf: :D and (:r some :E)
```

The OWL specification also includes two different methods of defining the semantics of OWL ontologies. The *direct* semantics is defined with respect to the functional-style syntax, and hence is only applicable to RDF graphs that can be mapped into an OWL functional-style syntax ontology; such ontologies are referred to as OWL (2) DL ontologies. The *RDF-based* semantics is defined directly on RDF graphs, and is applicable to any graph, even those that include apparently malformed OWL syntax, or nonsensical triples such as ⟨*rdf:type*, *rdf:type*, *rdf:type*⟩; in the 2004 version of OWL, such ontologies are referred to as OWL Full, but in OWL 2 they are referred to as OWL 2 ontologies interpreted under the RDF-based semantics.

It is easy to show that all standard reasoning problems are, in general, undecidable for OWL Full ontologies (which can only be interpreted using the RDF-based semantics) [Mot07]. Perhaps for this reason, most

Axiom	Syntax	Semantics
Complex role		
Inclusion (CRIA)	$R_1 \circ \ldots \circ R_n \sqsubseteq S$	$R_1^{\mathcal{I}} \circ \ldots \circ R_n^{\mathcal{I}} \subseteq S^{\mathcal{I}}$
Disjointness	$\mathsf{Disj}(R,S)$	$R^{\mathcal{I}} \cap S^{\mathcal{I}} = \emptyset$
Transitivity	$\mathsf{Trans}(R)$	$R^{\mathcal{I}} \circ R^{\mathcal{I}} \subseteq R^{\mathcal{I}}$
Reflexivity	$\mathsf{Ref}(R)$	$\{(x,x) \mid x \in \Delta^{\mathcal{I}}\} \subseteq R^{\mathcal{I}}$
Irreflexivity	$\mathsf{Irref}(R)$	$\{(x,x) \mid x \in \Delta^{\mathcal{I}}\} \cap R^{\mathcal{I}} = \emptyset$
Symmetry	$\mathsf{Sym}(R)$	$(x,y) \in R^{\mathcal{I}} \Rightarrow (y,x) \in R^{\mathcal{I}}$
Antisymmetry	$\mathsf{Asym}(R)$	$(x,y) \in R^{\mathcal{I}} \Rightarrow (y,x) \notin R^{\mathcal{I}}$

Table 8.1. $\mathcal{SROIQ}$ role axioms.

OWL tools support only OWL DL interpreted under the direct seman-
tics. In the remainder of this chapter we will only consider the OWL
DL setting, and we will treat OWL as being synonymous with OWL 2
DL.

8.1.2 OWL and $\mathcal{SROIQ}$

As mentioned above, OWL 2 corresponds closely to the $\mathcal{SROIQ}$ description logic. Before describing the features of OWL, it will therefore be
useful to briefly introduce $\mathcal{SROIQ}$. The $\mathcal{S}$ in $\mathcal{SROIQ}$ is a widely used
abbreviation for $\mathcal{ALC}$ extended with transitive roles (see the Appendix),
the letter $\mathcal{R}$ denotes an extended set of role axioms, sometimes called a
role box (RBox), and $\mathcal{O}$, $\mathcal{I}$ and $\mathcal{Q}$ denote, respectively, nominals, inverse
roles and qualified number restrictions as introduced in Chapter 2.

So far, we have considered DLs with a range of constructors for building concept descriptions, but with only two constructors for roles: inverse and transitive. Adding an RBox partly redresses the balance by
providing a generalisation of role inclusion axioms (RIAs) called complex
role inclusion axioms (CRIAs), as well as axioms asserting that roles are
disjoint, transitive, reflexive, irreflexive, symmetric or antisymmetric. In
addition, $\mathcal{SROIQ}$ provides concepts of the form $\exists R.\mathsf{Self}$, which can be
used to express "local reflexivity" of a role r, negated role assertions,
i.e., assertions of the form $(\mathsf{Mary}, \mathsf{Ph456}) : \neg teaches$, which states that
Mary does *not* teach Ph456, and the universal (or top) role, denoted U.[3]

Definition 8.1 ($\mathcal{SROIQ}$ RBox). Let **R** be a set of role names, with
$U \in \mathbf{R}$. A $\mathcal{SROIQ}$ role R is either a role name or the inverse S^- of a

---

[3] In any interpretation $\mathcal{I}$, U is interpreted as $\Delta^{\mathcal{I}} \times \Delta^{\mathcal{I}}$.

role name S. For R, R_i and S $\mathcal{SROIQ}$ roles, a $\mathcal{SROIQ}$ *role axiom* is an expression of one of the forms given in the second column of Table 8.1; a $\mathcal{SROIQ}$ *role box* is a set of such axioms. In any interpretation $\mathcal{I}$, the universal role U is interpreted as $\Delta^{\mathcal{I}} \times \Delta^{\mathcal{I}}$. An interpretation $\mathcal{I}$ *satisfies* a $\mathcal{SROIQ}$ role axiom if it satisfies the condition given in the third column of Table 8.1, where ∘ denotes the composition of two relations; i.e., for $R^{\mathcal{I}}, S^{\mathcal{I}}$ binary relations, we define

$$R^{\mathcal{I}} \circ S^{\mathcal{I}} = \{(e,g) \mid \text{there is some } f \text{ with } (e,f) \in R^{\mathcal{I}} \text{ and } (f,g) \in S^{\mathcal{I}}\}.$$

An interpretation $\mathcal{I}$ *satisfies* a $\mathcal{SROIQ}$ RBox $\mathcal{R}$ if it satisfies each axiom in $\mathcal{R}$; such an interpretation is called a *model* of $\mathcal{R}$.

Please note that a CRIA as defined in Table 8.1 and with $n = 1$ is a role inclusion axiom (RIA) as introduced in Section 2.5.4.

Before we discuss further syntactic restrictions, let us consider an example RBox which captures some axioms concerning family relationships and partonomic ones:

$$
\begin{aligned}
hasMother &\sqsubseteq hasParent, \\
hasSon &\sqsubseteq hasChild, \\
hasChild &\sqsubseteq childOf^-, \\
childOf &\sqsubseteq hasChild^-, \\
hasParent \circ hasBrother &\sqsubseteq hasUncle, \\
hasParent &\sqsubseteq hasAncestor, \\
\mathsf{Trans}&(hasAncestor), \\
\mathsf{Disj}&(hasSibling, childOf), \\
\mathsf{Irref}&(childOf), \\
\mathsf{Asym}&(childOf), \\
isLocatedIn \circ isPartOf &\sqsubseteq isLocatedIn, \\
\mathsf{Trans}&(isPartOf).
\end{aligned}
$$

While the axioms regarding family relations should be self-explanatory, it is worth pointing out the effect of the last two axioms, which motivated the support of complex inclusions in DLs and OWL [HS04]. For example, the last two axioms above together with the following concept inclusions:

$$
\begin{aligned}
FracOfFemur &\equiv Fracture \sqcap \exists isLocatedIn.Femur, \\
FracOfHeadOfFemur &\equiv Fracture \sqcap \exists isLocatedIn.HeadOfFemur, \\
HeadOfFemur &\sqsubseteq BodyPart \sqcap \exists isPartOf.Femur, \\
Femur &\sqsubseteq BodyPart \sqcap \exists isPartOf.Leg,
\end{aligned}
$$

entail

$$\text{HeadOfFemur} \sqsubseteq \exists isPartOf.\text{Leg},$$
$$\text{FracOfHeadOfFemur} \sqsubseteq \text{FracOfFemur}.$$

Further to Definition 8.1, to ensure that reasoning over $\mathcal{SROIQ}$ is decidable, $\mathcal{SROIQ}$ restricts RBoxes to *regular* ones and defines what it means for a role to be *simple* [HKS06]. Both conditions are rather tedious and technical, so we will only give an informal description here. For regularity, we know that the unrestricted use of CRIAs already leads to undecidability in $\mathcal{SHIQ}$ [HS04]. The regularity condition[4] ensures that the interactions between role names as enforced by an RBox can be captured by finite state automata which can then be used in a tableau algorithm. For simple roles, please note that role axioms such as $\text{Trans}(S)$ or $R_1 \circ \cdots \circ R_n \sqsubseteq S$ imply "shortcuts"; for example, in any model $\mathcal{I}$ of $\text{Trans}(S)$, an $S^\mathcal{I}$ path $\{(e_0, e_1), (e_1, e_2), \ldots, (e_{n-1}, e_n)\} \subseteq S^\mathcal{I}$ from e_0 to e_n implies a shortcut $(e_0, e_n) \in S^\mathcal{I}$. Using roles such as S for which shortcuts are implied in number restrictions is another source of undecidability [HST99]. To restore decidability, *simple* roles are defined as those for which no shortcuts are implied (e.g., that do not occur in transitivity axioms, and whose inverses also do not occur in transitivity axioms), and only simple roles can be used in role irreflexivity, antisymmetry and disjointness axioms, and in certain concept descriptions, as specified in the following definition.

Definition 8.2 ($\mathcal{SROIQ}$ Concepts). Let **C** and **I** be disjoint sets of, respectively, *concept names* and *individual names*, with both **C** and **I** disjoint from **R**. The set of $\mathcal{SROIQ}$ *concept descriptions* over **C** and **I** is inductively defined as follows:

- every concept name is a $\mathcal{SROIQ}$ concept description;
- $\top$ and $\bot$ are $\mathcal{SROIQ}$ concept descriptions;
- if C and D are $\mathcal{SROIQ}$ concept descriptions, R is a $\mathcal{SROIQ}$ role, S is a simple $\mathcal{SROIQ}$ role and n is a non-negative number, then the following are also $\mathcal{SROIQ}$ concept descriptions:
  - $C \sqcap D$ (conjunction),
  - $C \sqcup D$ (disjunction),
  - $\neg C$ (negation),
  - $\exists R.C$ (existential restriction),
  - $\forall R.C$ (value restriction),

---

[4] Interestingly, it has recently been shown that the version of these conditions given in the OWL 2 standard [OWL12c] is insufficient [Ste15].

- $\exists S.\mathsf{Self}$ (self restriction),
- $(\geqslant n\, S.C)$ (qualified number restriction), and
- $(\leqslant n\, S.C)$ (qualified number restriction).

Given an interpretation $\mathcal{I} = (\Delta^{\mathcal{I}}, \cdot^{\mathcal{I}})$, the mapping $\cdot^{\mathcal{I}}$ is extended to self restrictions as follows:

$$(\exists S.\mathsf{Self})^{\mathcal{I}} := \{d \in \Delta^{\mathcal{I}} \mid (d, d) \in S^{\mathcal{I}}\}.$$

Other concept descriptions are interpreted as per the definitions given in Chapter 2.

The only new concept constructor in Definition 8.2 is the self restriction: we can use it, for example, to describe people who love themselves by Person $\sqcap$ $\exists loves.\mathsf{Self}$.

Next, we define a $\mathcal{SROIQ}$ knowledge base: in addition to a TBox and an ABox, it also contains an RBox; the notion of "satisfaction" and "model" are extended to these in the usual way. It is a matter of taste whether we prefer to have three separate boxes or to allow role axioms in the TBox: here, we have opted for the former, but this choice is immaterial.

Definition 8.3 ($\mathcal{SROIQ}$ Knowledge Base). For C and D $\mathcal{SROIQ}$ concept descriptions, $C \sqsubseteq D$ is a $\mathcal{SROIQ}$ *general concept inclusion* (GCI); a $\mathcal{SROIQ}$ *TBox* is a finite set of $\mathcal{SROIQ}$ GCIs. An interpretation $\mathcal{I}$ *satisfies* a $\mathcal{SROIQ}$ GCI $C \sqsubseteq D$ if $C^{\mathcal{I}} \subseteq D^{\mathcal{I}}$, and it *satisfies* a $\mathcal{SROIQ}$ TBox $\mathcal{T}$ if it satisfies each GCI in $\mathcal{T}$; such an interpretation is called a *model* of $\mathcal{T}$.

For $a, b \in \mathbf{I}$ individual names, C a $\mathcal{SROIQ}$ concept description, and R a $\mathcal{SROIQ}$ role, $a : C$ is a $\mathcal{SROIQ}$ *concept assertion* and $(a, b) : R$ and $(a, b) : \neg R$ are $\mathcal{SROIQ}$ *role assertions*; a $\mathcal{SROIQ}$ *ABox* is a finite set of $\mathcal{SROIQ}$ concept and role assertions. An interpretation $\mathcal{I}$ *satisfies* $a : C$ if $a^{\mathcal{I}} \in C^{\mathcal{I}}$, it *satisfies* $(a, b) : R$ if $(a^{\mathcal{I}}, b^{\mathcal{I}}) \in R^{\mathcal{I}}$, and it *satisfies* $(a, b) : \neg R$ if $(a^{\mathcal{I}}, b^{\mathcal{I}}) \notin R^{\mathcal{I}}$. An interpretation $\mathcal{I}$ *satisfies* a $\mathcal{SROIQ}$ ABox $\mathcal{A}$ if it satisfies each concept and role assertion in $\mathcal{A}$; such an interpretation is called a *model* of $\mathcal{A}$.

A $\mathcal{SROIQ}$ *knowledge base* $\mathcal{K} = (\mathcal{R}, \mathcal{T}, \mathcal{A})$ consists of a regular $\mathcal{SROIQ}$ RBox $\mathcal{R}$, TBox $\mathcal{T}$ and ABox $\mathcal{A}$; an interpretation $\mathcal{I}$ is a *model* of $\mathcal{K}$ if it is a model of each of $\mathcal{R}$, $\mathcal{T}$ and $\mathcal{A}$.

Note that several of the axioms described in Table 8.1 are redundant in the sense that they could be expressed using other means, as captured by the following lemma.[5]

Lemma 8.4. *Let R, S be possibly inverse roles. Then we have the following:*

(i) $\mathsf{Trans}(R)$ *is equivalent to the CRIA $R \circ R \sqsubseteq R$;*

(ii) $\mathsf{Sym}(R)$ *is equivalent to $R \sqsubseteq R^-$;*

(iii) $\mathsf{Ref}(R)$ *is equivalent to $\top \sqsubseteq \exists R.\mathsf{Self}$;*

(iv) $\mathsf{Irref}(R)$ *is equivalent to $\top \sqsubseteq \neg\exists R.\mathsf{Self}$.*

8.1.3 OWL ontologies

An OWL ontology can be seen to correspond to a DL knowledge base $\mathcal{K} = (\mathcal{R}, \mathcal{T}, \mathcal{A})$ with its three boxes combined in a single set $\mathcal{R} \cup \mathcal{T} \cup \mathcal{A}$.[6] It is, however, trivial to sort this set into an RBox, TBox and ABox, and we will sometimes talk about an OWL TBox and ABox. In fact in the literature an OWL ontology is often assumed to be a TBox and an RBox, with the ABox assertions (if any) being stored separately as RDF triples.

As in a standard DL, an OWL TBox describes the domain in terms of *classes* (corresponding to concepts), *properties* (corresponding to roles) and *individuals* (corresponding to individual names), and consists of a set of *axioms* that assert, e.g., subsumption relationships between classes or properties.

As usual, OWL classes and properties may be names or expressions built up from simpler classes and properties using a variety of constructors. The main constructors supported by OWL, along with the equivalent DL syntax, are summarised in Table 8.2, where C (possibly subscripted) is a class, p is a property, x (possibly subscripted) is an individual and n is a non-negative integer. Note that:

- OWL provides an explicit bottom property (i.e., a property whose extension is empty in every interpretation), and an exact cardinality class constructor, but the semantics of these can be trivially simulated in $\mathcal{SROIQ}$. For example, if $\top \sqsubseteq \forall B.\bot \in \mathcal{T}$, then $B^{\mathcal{I}} = \emptyset$ in any model $\mathcal{I}$ of $\mathcal{T}$, and $(=n\,p.C)$ is equivalent to $(\geqslant n\,p.C) \sqcap (\leqslant n\,p.C)$.

---

[5] We remind the reader that two axioms α, β are equivalent if an interpretation satisfies α if and only if it satisfies β.

[6] The OWL specification uses "axiom" as a generic term for both TBox axioms and ABox assertions.

OWL functional syntax	DL syntax
`ObjectInverseOf( ` p ` )`	p^-
`ObjectPropertyChain( ` $p_1, \ldots, p_n$ ` )`	$p_1 \circ \ldots \circ p_n$
`owl:topObjectProperty`	U
`owl:bottomObjectProperty`	B
`owl:Thing`	$\top$
`owl:Nothing`	$\bot$
`ObjectIntersectionOf( ` $C_1 \ldots C_n$ ` )`	$C_1 \sqcap \ldots \sqcap C_n$
`ObjectUnionOf( ` $C_1 \ldots C_n$ ` )`	$C_1 \sqcup \ldots \sqcup C_n$
`ObjectComplementOf( ` C ` )`	$\neg C$
`ObjectOneOf( ` $x_1 \ldots x_n$ ` )`	$\{x_1\} \sqcup \ldots \sqcup \{x_n\}$
`ObjectAllValuesFrom( ` $p\ C$ ` )`	$\forall p.C$
`ObjectSomeValuesFrom( ` $p\ C$ ` )`	$\exists p.C$
`ObjectHasValue( ` $p\ x$ ` )`	$\exists p.\{x\}$
`ObjectHasSelf( ` p ` )`	$\exists p.Self$
`ObjectMinCardinality( ` $n\ p\ C$ ` )`	$(\geqslant n\, p.C)$
`ObjectMaxCardinality( ` $n\ p\ C$ ` )`	$(\leqslant n\, p.C)$
`ObjectExactCardinality( ` $n\ p\ C$ ` )`	$(= n\, p.C)$

Table 8.2. *OWL property and class constructors.*

- The use of the `ObjectPropertyChain` constructor is restricted to CRIAs of the form $p_1 \circ \ldots \circ p_n \sqsubseteq p$. In all other cases, OWL properties must be either property names (IRIs) or inverse properties.

An important feature of OWL is that, in addition to classes and individuals, the ontology can also use *datatypes* and *literals* (i.e., data values). The set of datatypes supported by OWL, including their syntax and semantics, is defined in the OWL 2 Datatype Map; most of these are taken from the set of XML Schema Datatypes (XSD) [XSD12], and include various number types (such as `xsd:float` and `xsd:integer`), string types (such as `xsd:string`), Booleans (`xsd:boolean`), IRIs (`xsd:anyURI`) and time instants (`xsd:dateTime` and `xsd:dateTimeStamp`). Literals may be either typed (e.g., `"42"^^xsd:integer`) or untyped (e.g., `"lifetheuniverseandeverything"`). OWL's datatypes and literals come with some useful "syntactic sugar", but semantically they can be seen as a restricted form of *concrete domains* which allows only unary predicates and feature paths of length one (see Section 5.3.2) [BH91, LAHS04, HS01].

Like classes, datatypes can be combined and constrained to form user-defined datatypes called *data ranges*. Each datatype is a data range, and many datatypes can additionally be constrained using *facets* such as *xsd:minInclusive*; for example,

$$xsd:integer\ \ xsd:minExclusive\ \ \texttt{"15"} \texttt{\textasciicircum\textasciicircum} xsd:integer$$

defines the data range based on integer whose values include all those integers greater than 15. Data ranges can also be combined using Boolean constructors similar to those used with classes, i.e., DataIntersectionOf, DataUnionOf, DataComplementOf and DataOneOf; for example,

$$\texttt{DataUnionOf(}\ xsd:string\ \ xsd:integer\ \texttt{)}$$

specifies a data range that contains all strings and all integers. Finally, OWL *datatype definitions* provide a simple mechanism for naming data ranges; for example,

$$\texttt{DatatypeDefinition(}\ :over15$$
$$xsd:integer\ \ xsd:minExclusive\ \ \texttt{"15"} \texttt{\textasciicircum\textasciicircum} xsd:integer\ \texttt{)}$$

introduces the name *:over15* as an abbreviation for the data range consisting of integers greater than 15. Datatype definitions are restricted (e.g., to be acyclic) such that the datatypes they define can be treated as macros; i.e., given an ontology $\mathcal{O}$ containing the above datatype definition, other occurrences of *:over15* can be replaced with *xsd:integer xsd:minExclusive* $\texttt{"15"} \texttt{\textasciicircum\textasciicircum} xsd:integer$ without affecting the semantics of $\mathcal{O}$.

As in DL Datatypes [HS01], OWL imposes a strict separation between classes and datatypes: the interpretation domain of classes is disjoint from that of datatypes, and the set of properties that relate pairs of individuals (called *object properties*) is disjoint from the set of properties that relate individuals to literals (called *data properties*). This ensures that reasoning algorithms can be relatively straightforwardly extended to support datatypes by employing a *datatype oracle* that decides basic reasoning problems about datatypes and literals [MH08]. Moreover, in order to avoid any syntactic ambiguity, OWL distinguishes class constructors used with classes and individuals ("object" constructors) from those used with datatypes and literals ("data" constructors); this allows object and data properties to be correctly typed without the need for typing declarations (OWL does allow for such declarations, but they are not mandatory); by dint of its occurrence in object constructors, the property p used in Table 8.2 is thus unambiguously an object property. Class constructors using data ranges and literals are otherwise similar to object constructors, and are shown in Table 8.3, where D (possibly

OWL functional syntax	DL syntax
`DataAllValuesFrom( d D )`	$\forall d.D$
`DataSomeValuesFrom( d D )`	$\exists d.D$
`DataHasValue( d v )`	$\exists d.\{v\}$
`DataMinCardinality( n d D )`	$(\geqslant n\, d.D)$
`DataMaxCardinality( n d D )`	$(\leqslant n\, d.D)$
`DataExactCardinality( n d C )`	$(= n\, d.D)$

Table 8.3. *OWL data property class constructors.*

subscripted) is a datatype, d is a data property, v is a data value and n is a non-negative integer.

The distinction between object and data properties is maintained in property axioms and assertions; e.g., there are distinct axioms for asserting subsumption between object properties and data properties. The axioms and assertions provided by OWL, along with the equivalent DL syntax, are summarised in Tables 8.4 and 8.5, where C (possibly subscripted) is a class, p (possibly subscripted) is an object property, d (possibly subscripted) is a data property, a (possibly subscripted) is an individual and v is a data value. Recall that in `SubObjectPropertyOf` axioms p_1 can be a property name (an IRI), an inverse property or a property chain; in all other cases properties are restricted to being property names or inverse properties.

Note that some OWL axioms are equivalent to sets of $\mathcal{SROIQ}$ axioms; for example, an OWL `EquivalentObjectProperties` axiom takes two or more object properties, and is semantically equivalent to two or more role inclusion axioms in $\mathcal{SROIQ}$. Similarly, we can say that two or more (object or data) properties are pairwise disjoint, e.g., in `DisjointObjectProperties`$(p_1 \dots p_n)$; the $\mathcal{SROIQ}$ equivalent is a set of axioms of the form $p_i \sqsubseteq \neg p_j$, each of which states that a pair of roles are disjoint. The semantics of such axioms is straightforward: an interpretation $\mathcal{I}$ satisfies $p_i \sqsubseteq \neg p_j$ if $p_i^{\mathcal{I}} \subseteq \Delta^{\mathcal{I}} \times \Delta^{\mathcal{I}} \setminus p_j^{\mathcal{I}}$ or, in other words, if $p_i^{\mathcal{I}} \cap p_j^{\mathcal{I}} = \emptyset$.

A final point to mention is that we can, explicitly, state that two or more individuals are the same via `SameIndividual`$(a_1 \dots a_n)$ or that they are pairwise different via `DifferentIndividuals`$(a_1 \dots a_n)$.

Axiom	DL Syntax
SubObjectPropertyOf(p_1 p_2)	$p_1 \sqsubseteq p_2$
EquivalentObjectProperties($p_1 \ldots p_n$)	$\cup_{i \neq j}\{p_i \sqsubseteq p_j\}$
DisjointObjectProperties($p_1 \ldots p_n$)	$\cup_{i \neq j}\{p_i \sqsubseteq \neg p_j\}$
InverseObjectProperties(p_1 p_2)	$p_1 \equiv p_2^-$
ObjectPropertyDomain(p C)	$\exists p.\top \sqsubseteq C$
ObjectPropertyRange(p C)	$\top \sqsubseteq \forall p.C$
FunctionalObjectProperty(p)	$\top \sqsubseteq (\leqslant 1\,p)$
InverseFunctionalObjectProperty(p)	$\top \sqsubseteq (\leqslant 1\,p^-)$
ReflexiveObjectProperty(p)	$\mathsf{Ref}(p)$
IrreflexiveObjectProperty(p)	$\mathsf{Irref}(p)$
SymmetricObjectProperty(p)	$\mathsf{Sym}(p)$
AsymmetricObjectProperty(p)	$\mathsf{Asym}(p)$
TransitiveObjectProperty(p)	$\mathsf{Trans}(p)$
SubDataPropertyOf(d_1 d_2)	$d_1 \sqsubseteq d_2$
EquivalentDataProperties($d_1 \ldots d_n$)	$\cup_{i \neq j}\{d_i \sqsubseteq d_j\}$
DisjointDataProperties($d_1 \ldots d_n$)	$\cup_{i \neq j}\{d_i \sqsubseteq \neg d_j\}$
DataPropertyDomain(d C)	$(\geqslant 1\,d) \sqsubseteq C$
DataPropertyRange(d D)	$\top \sqsubseteq \forall d.D$
FunctionalDataProperty(d)	$\top \sqsubseteq (\leqslant 1\,d)$

Table 8.4. *OWL property axioms, where unions range over i,j between 1 and n.*

Axiom	DL Syntax
SubClassOf(C_1 C_2)	$C_1 \sqsubseteq C_2$
EquivalentClasses($C_1 \ldots C_n$)	$\cup_{i \neq j}\{C_i \sqsubseteq C_j\}$
DisjointClasses($C_1 \ldots C_n$)	$\cup_{i \neq j}\{C_i \sqsubseteq \neg C_j\}$
DisjointUnion(C $C_1 \ldots C_n$)	$\cup_{i \neq j}\{C_i \sqsubseteq \neg C_j\} \cup$ $\{C \equiv C_1 \sqcup \ldots \sqcup C_n\}$
SameIndividual($a_1 \ldots a_n$)	$\cup_{i \neq j}\{a_i = a_j\}$
DifferentIndividuals($a_1 \ldots a_n$)	$\cup_{i \neq j}\{a_i \neq a_j\}$
ClassAssertion(C a)	$a : C$
ObjectPropertyAssertion(p a_1 a_2)	$(a_1, a_2) : p$
NegativeObjectPropertyAssertion(p a_1 a_2)	$(a_1, a_2) : \neg p$
DataPropertyAssertion(d a v)	$(a, v) : d$
NegativeDataPropertyAssertion(d a v)	$(a, v) : \neg d$

Table 8.5. *OWL class axioms and assertions, where unions range over i,j between 1 and n.*

8.1.4 Non-DL features

Although largely a syntactic variant of $\mathcal{SROIQ}$, OWL also includes a number of features that are not found in standard DLs.

Keys

OWL ontologies can additionally include `HasKey` axioms, the purpose of which is to provide funcionality similar to keys in relational databases. A `HasKey` axiom is of the form

$$\text{HasKey}(\ C\ (\ p_1 \ldots p_n\ )\ (\ d_1 \ldots d_m)\ ),$$

where C is a class, p_i is an object property and d_j is a data property. Such an axiom states that no two distinct *named* instances of class C can be related to the same set of individuals and literals via the given properties, i.e., that *named* instances of C are uniquely identified by these relationships, where an individual is *named* if it occurs syntactically in the ontology.

More precisely, given an ontology $\mathcal{O}$ with a `HasKey` axiom

$$\text{HasKey}(\ C\ (\ p_1 \ldots p_n\ )\ (\ d_1 \ldots d_m)\ ) \in \mathcal{O},$$

a model $\mathcal{I}$ of $\mathcal{O}$ has to satisfy the following condition: if a, b are individuals occurring in $\mathcal{O}$, $\{a^{\mathcal{I}}, b^{\mathcal{I}}\} \subseteq C^{\mathcal{I}}$, and for each $e \in \Delta^{\mathcal{I}}$, $v \in \Delta^{\mathsf{D}}$, $i \le n$, and $j \le m$, we have

- $(a^{\mathcal{I}}, e) \in p_i^{\mathcal{I}}$ if and only if $(b^{\mathcal{I}}, e) \in p_i^{\mathcal{I}}$, and
- $(a^{\mathcal{I}}, v) \in d_j^{\mathcal{I}}$ if and only if $(b^{\mathcal{I}}, v) \in d_j^{\mathcal{I}}$,

then $a^{\mathcal{I}} = b^{\mathcal{I}}$.

For example, if an ontology $\mathcal{O}$ includes the following axiom and assertions:

> HasKey(:*Person* (:*hasChild*) (:*hasGender*)),
> ClassAssertion(:*Person* :*Elizabeth*),
> ObjectPropertyAssertion(:*hasChild* :*Elizabeth* :*Mary*),
> DataPropertyAssertion(:*hasGender* :*Elizabeth* "F"),
> ClassAssertion(:*Person* :*Liz*),
> ObjectPropertyAssertion(:*hasChild* :*Liz* :*Mary*),
> DataPropertyAssertion(:*hasGender* :*Liz* "F"),

then $\mathcal{O}$ entails `SameIndividual`(:*Elizabeth* :*Liz*). If $\mathcal{O}$ additionally includes the following axioms and assertions:

> ClassAssertion(ObjectSomeValuesFrom(*hasFriend* :*P*) :*John*),
> SubClassOf(:*P* ObjectHasValue(*hasChild* :*Mary*)),
> SubClassOf(:*P* DataHasValue(*hasGender* "F")),
> SubClassOf(:*P* :*Person*), SubClassOf(:*P* :*Happy*),
> ClassAssertion(ObjectComplementOf(:*Happy*) :*Liz*),

then it might at first appear that Peter has at least one friend who is also entailed to be the same individual as :*Elizabeth* and :*Liz* (because they too have :*Mary* as their child and "F" as their gender), and that when combined with the fact that Peter's friend is :*Happy* while :*Liz* is ¬:*Happy*, this would make $\mathcal{O}$ inconsistent. However, the key axiom does not apply to Peter's friend, because this friend is not explicitly named in $\mathcal{O}$, and so does not lead to an inconsistency.

Anonymous individuals

As we saw in Section 8.1.1, ABox assertions in OWL directly correspond to RDF triples of the form $\langle a, rdf\!:\!type, C\rangle$ and $\langle a, p, b\rangle$, where C is a class, p is a property and a and b are IRIs. Unlike standard DLs, a and b do not have to be named individuals, but can also be RDF *blank nodes*. Blank nodes are denoted by the use of _: as an IRI prefix (e.g., _:*x*), and are treated as variables that are existentially quantified at the outer level of the ABox [MAHP11]. In OWL, blank nodes used in ABox assertions are called *anonymous individuals*. For example, the assertions

```
ObjectPropertyAssertion( :hasFriend :Liz _:x ),
ObjectPropertyAssertion( :livesIn _:x _:y ),
ObjectPropertyAssertion( :livesIn :Mary _:y )
```

assert that :*Liz* has a friend who lives in the same place as :*Mary* without explicitly naming the friend or the place where they live; they are semantically equivalent to a first-order logic sentence of the form

$$\exists x \exists y \, (hasFriend(Liz, x) \wedge livesIn(x, y) \wedge livesIn(Mary, y)).$$

These assertions can also be written as the semantically equivalent $\mathcal{SROIQ}$ concept assertion

$$Liz : \exists hasFriend.(\exists livesIn.(\exists livesIn^-.\{Mary\})),$$

and hence can be similarly written in OWL without recourse to blank nodes.

This rewriting procedure, where existential restrictions are used to transform property assertions into semantically equivalent class assertions, is often referred to in the literature as *rolling up* [HT00]. Rolling up can be used to eliminate anonymous individuals, as in the above example, only if the property assertions that connect them have a tree-like structure, i.e., provided that anonymous individuals are not cyclically connected. For example, if we extended the above ABox with the assertion

$$\texttt{ObjectPropertyAssertion(}\ :bornIn\ \_\!:x\ \_\!:y\ ),$$

then it would no longer be possible to use rolling up to eliminate $\_\!:x$ and $\_\!:y$.

OWL 2 DL ontologies must satisfy syntactic restrictions on the use of anonymous individuals which ensure that rolling up is always possible; hence any OWL 2 DL ontology $\mathcal{O}$ can be rewritten as a semantically equivalent OWL 2 DL ontology $\mathcal{O}'$ in which there are no anonymous individuals.

Metamodelling

In some applications it may be desirable to use the same name for both a class (or property) and an individual. For example, we might want to state that :*Harry* is an instance of :*Eagle*

$$\texttt{ClassAssertion(}\ :Eagle\ :Harry\ )$$

and that :*Eagle* is an instance of :*EndangeredSpecies*

$$\texttt{ClassAssertion(}\ :EndangeredSpecies\ :Eagle\ ).$$

We could then extend our modelling of the domain to describe classes of classes, e.g., by stating that it is illegal to hunt any class of animal that is an instance of :*EndangeredSpecies*; this is often called *metamodelling*. Metamodelling is not possible in a standard DL, where it is usually assumed that the sets **C**, **R** and **I** (of, respectively, concept, role and individual names) are pairwise disjoint, and where class assertions can only be used to describe individual names; i.e., in an assertion $a:C$, a must be an individual name.

OWL 2 uses a mechanism known as *punning* to provide a simple form of metamodelling while still retaining the correspondence between OWL ontologies and $\mathcal{SROIQ}$ KBs. Punning allows for the same IRI (name) to be used as an individual, a class and a property, but it applies the *contextual semantics* described by Motik in [Mot07]. In the contextual semantics, IRIs used in the individual, class and property contexts are semantically unrelated; this semantics is equivalent to rewriting the ontology by adding unique prefixes such as i:, c: and p: to IRIs according to the context in which they occur. For example, the above assertions would be treated as though they were written

$$\texttt{ClassAssertion(}\ c{:}Eagle\ i{:}Harry\ )$$

and

ClassAssertion(*c:EndangeredSpecies i:Eagle*),

with *c:Eagle* a class name and *i:Eagle* an individual name. This is easy to achieve as the context of each IRI occurrence is clear from the syntactic structure of the ontology. Punning thus has no effect on standard reasoning tasks (such as classification), but it does allow for queries that, e.g., return individuals that are instances of species that are themselves instances of *c:EndangeredSpecies*.

Annotations

OWL includes a flexible annotation mechanism that allows for comments and other "non-logical" information to be included in the ontology. An OWL annotation consists of an annotation property and a literal, and zero or more annotations can be attached to class, property and individual names, to axioms and assertions, to datatypes, to the ontology as a whole and even to annotations themselves; for example,

ClassAssertion(Annotation(*rdfs:comment* "Liz is a person")

:*Person* :*Liz*)

annotates the class assertion with the property *rdfs:comment* and the literal "Liz is a person".

Annotation properties can be used to distinguish different kinds of annotations, with OWL even providing for a basic type structure via annotation property specific range, domain and sub-property axioms. Note, however, that annotations and annotation property axioms have no formal semantics, and can simply be discarded when translating the ontology into a DL knowledge base. As with other OWL properties, annotation property names are IRIs, and the set of annotation property names is pairwise disjoint from the sets of object property and data property names.

Imports

Each OWL ontology is associated with an *ontology document* in which the various statements that make up the ontology are stored. OWL makes no assumptions about the structure of such documents, but it is assumed that each ontology document can be accessed via an IRI, and that its contents can be converted into an ontology. For the sake of brevity, we will from now on refer to ontology documents using the IRIs via which they are accessed; for example, we will refer to the ontology document that can be accessed via :*ont* simply as :*ont*.

The OWL `Import` statement provides a mechanism for "importing" the contents of one ontology document into another; for example, if :*ont1* includes the statement

`Import(` :*ont2* `),`

then :*ont1* is treated as though it also includes all of the contents of :*ont2* and, recursively, any ontology documents imported by :*ont2*. The OWL specification defines a parsing procedure that extracts ontological content from the current ontology document and all those that it (possibly recursively) imports, while ensuring termination even if ontology documents (directly or indirectly) import each other cyclically.

8.1.5 OWL profiles

An important change in OWL 2 was the introduction of *profiles*. A profile is "a trimmed down version of OWL 2 that trades some expressive power for efficiency of reasoning" [OWL12b], i.e., a syntactic subset (sometimes called a fragment) of the language that enjoys better computational properties. Three profiles are defined: OWL 2 EL, OWL 2 QL and OWL 2 RL, each of which provides different expressive power and targets different application scenarios. The OWL 2 profiles are defined by placing restrictions on the functional-style syntax of OWL 2; in OWL 2 EL, for example, one such restriction forbids the use of the `ObjectComplementOf` (class negation) constructor in class expressions.

Note that the original OWL language specification also defined a subset, called OWL Lite. The computational properties of this subset are, however, only marginally better than those of the unrestricted language (ontology satisfiability is EXPTIME-complete [HPSvH03]); as a result OWL Lite was little used, and was not included as one of the OWL 2 profiles.

OWL 2 EL is based on $\mathcal{EL}^{++}$, a family of description logics that extend $\mathcal{EL}$ (see Chapter 6) while ensuring that satisfiability and subsumption with respect to general TBoxes remains polynomial in the size of the TBox [BBL05]. Optimised implementations of PTIME algorithms for TBox classification have proved to be very effective in practice, and are widely used in the development of healthcare and life science ontologies, including the SNOMED healthcare ontology which is developed and maintained by the International Health Terminology Standards Development Organisation [BLS06, KKS11, SSBB09].

OWL 2 QL is based on the DL-Lite family of description logics [ACKZ09], for which conjunctive queries are FO-rewritable, and for which conjunctive query answering is thus in AC^0 with respect to the size of the data. More specifically, OWL 2 QL is based on DL-Lite$_{\mathcal{R}}$, a variant of DL-Lite that additionally allows for role inclusion and role disjointness axioms. FO-rewritability allows for query answering to be implemented on top of relational database systems, with query evaluation being delegated to the DB system.

OWL 2 RL is based on *description logic programs* [GHVD03], a logic that aims to capture the intersection between Description Logic and Datalog, i.e., a description logic whose TBox axioms can be translated into Datalog rules. As the resulting language can be seen as a subset of Datalog, query answering is in PTIME with respect to the size of the data [DEGV01]; moreover, implementations can exploit existing rule engines, several of which have been shown to be highly scalable in practice [BKO+11, MNP+14].

8.2 OWL tools and applications

The correspondence between OWL and Description Logic means that DL algorithms and systems can be used to provide reasoning services for OWL tools and applications. A wide range of DL-based OWL reasoners is available, including both general-purpose and profile-specific systems (see, e.g., `http://www.w3.org/2001/sw/wiki/OWL/Implementations` and `http://owl.cs.manchester.ac.uk/tools/list-of-reasoners/` for lists maintained by, respectively, the W3C and the University of Manchester). On the other hand, OWL tools and infrastructure provide convenient and practical mechanisms for both developing and deploying DL knowledge bases. In the following we will briefly mention a few prominent and interesting examples of OWL tools and applications.

8.2.1 The OWL API

The OWL API is a Java API and reference implementation for creating, manipulating and serialising OWL Ontologies (see `http://owlcs.github.io/owlapi/`). Although not a tool or application per se, the

OWL API is an important component of numerous tools and applications, and is widely used for parsing and writing OWL ontologies in various syntaxes (including RDF/XML), and for interfacing with reasoners.

8.2.2 OWL reasoners

As mentioned above, a wide range of DL-based OWL reasoners is available, including both general-purpose and profile-specific systems. Currently, all fully fledged OWL reasoners (i.e., those that support most or all of the OWL language), are based on tableau algorithms similar to those described in Chapter 4, although efforts are being made to extend the consequence-based techniques described in Chapter 6 to larger fragments of OWL [SKH11, BMG+15]. Prominent examples of tableau-based OWL reasoners include FaCT++ [TH06], HermiT [GHM+14], Konclude [SLG14] and Pellet [SPC+07].

Several profile-specific reasoners are also available. For the OWL 2 EL profile, most reasoners are based on consequence-based techniques as described in Chapter 6; prominent examples include CEL [BLS06], ELK [KKS14] and SnoRocket [MJL13]. However, there are also several systems for query answering over RDF data with respect to (subsets of) OWL 2 EL ontologies that use rewriting techniques similar to those described in Section 7.3; these include REQUIEM [PUMH10], KARMA [SMH13] and EOLO [SM15]. For the OWL 2 QL profile, most systems are based on the query rewriting techniques described in Chapter 7; prominent examples include Mastro [CCD+13], Grind [HLSW15] and Ontop [KRR+14]. Such systems typically answer (unions of) conjunctive queries with respect to an OWL 2 QL ontology and data stored in a relational database. For the OWL 2 RL profile, most systems exploit Datalog reasoning techniques, including both forward chaining (also known as materialisation) and backwards chaining; prominent examples include GraphDB [BKO+11] (formerly known as OWLIM), RD-Fox [MNP+14] and Oracle's RDF store [WED+08]. Such systems typically answer SPARQL queries [SPA13] with respect to an OWL 2 RL ontology, where the data may be stored separately as RDF triples.

8.2.3 Ontology engineering tools

Numerous tools are available for developing and maintaining OWL ontologies (see http://www.w3.org/wiki/Ontology_editors). Prominent examples include Protégé [KFNM04], a "free, open-source ontology editor and framework" developed by the Center for Biomedical Informatics Research at Stanford University School of Medicine, and TopBraid Composer, a commercial ontology "modelling environment" developed by TopQuadrant (see `http://www.topquadrant.com//`).

Protégé has played an important role in the popularisation of OWL by providing a sophisticated ontology development environment that is freely available for download (see `http://protege.stanford.edu/`). Protégé uses reasoning to support the development and maintenance process, e.g., checking for inconsistent classes, discovering implicit subsumption relationships and answering queries over the ABox. Protégé interfaces to reasoners via the OWL API, and so can exploit a wide range of reasoners, including many of those mentioned above.

Tools are also available for managing various aspects of ontology evolution, including ontology versioning [JRCHB11], merging [JRCZH12] and modularisation [JGS+08].

8.2.4 OWL applications

The availability of tools and systems, including those mentioned above, has contributed to the increasingly widespread use of OWL, and it is currently by far the most widely used ontology language, with applications in fields as diverse as agriculture [SLL+04], astronomy [DeRP06], biology [RB11, OSRM+12], defence [LAF+05], education [CBV+14], energy management [CGH+13], geography [Goo05], geoscience [RP05], medicine [CSG05, GZB06, HDG12, TNNM13], oceanography [KHJ+15b] and oil and gas [SLH13, KHJ+15a]. We discuss below a few representative applications, but this is very far from an exhaustive survey; interested readers should investigate the "industry" and/or "applications" tracks that are often organised by semantic web conferences (e.g., the International Semantic Web Conference[7] and European Semantic Web Conference[8]), and specialised conferences and journals in relevant areas (e.g., the *Journal of Biomedical Semantics*[9]).

Applications of OWL are particularly prevalent in the life sciences, where it has been used by the developers of several large biomedical ontologies, including the Biological Pathways Exchange (BioPAX) ontology [RRL05], the GALEN ontology [RR06], the Foundational Model of Anatomy (FMA) [GZB06] and the National Cancer Institute thesaurus [HdD+05]. The National Centre for Biomedical Ontol-

---

[7] `http://swsa.semanticweb.org/`
[8] `http://www.eswc-conferences.org`
[9] `https://jbiomedsem.biomedcentral.com/`

ogy (see `http://www.bioontology.org/`) supports the ongoing development and maintenance of Protégé, and provides numerous resources, including a repository of biomedical ontologies (called BioPortal) and ontology-based tools for accessing and analysing biomedical data. The BioPortal repository contains several hundred ontologies, almost all of which are available in OWL and/or OBO formats, the latter being a text-based ontology language developed in the Open Biomedical Ontologies project and corresponding to a subset of OWL [GHH+07].

The SNOMED CT ontology is particularly noteworthy as it is very large (more than 300,000 classes) and is used in the healthcare systems of many countries (see `http://www.ihtsdo.org/snomed-ct`). The ontology is developed and maintained by the International Health Terminology Standards Development Organisation (IHTSDO), which is funded by member organisations from (at the time of writing) 27 countries. SNOMED CT uses a bespoke syntax, but this can be directly translated into OWL 2 EL, and reasoners such as ELK and SnoRocket are used to support the development and adaptation of SNOMED CT.

The importance of reasoning support in biomedical applications was highlighted in [KFP+06], which describes a project in which the Medical Entities Dictionary (MED), a large ontology (100,210 classes and 261 properties) that is used at the Columbia Presbyterian Medical Center, was converted into OWL, and checked using an OWL reasoner. This check revealed "systematic modelling errors", and a significant number of missed subClass relationships which, if not corrected, "could have cost the hospital many missing results in various decision support and infection control systems that routinely use MED to screen patients".

Another important application of OWL is in tools that help non-expert users to access data stored in relational databases, a technique that is often called ontology-based data access (OBDA). In the EU Optique project (see `http://optique-project.eu/`), for example, OBDA was used to help geologists and geophysicists at the Norwegian oil and gas company Statoil to access data gathered from past and present operations and stored in large and complex relational databases; their Exploration and Production Data Store (EPDS), for example, stores around 700GB of data in more than 3,000 tables [KHJ+15a]. In the Optique system, an OWL 2 QL ontology provides a more user-friendly schema for query formulation, and the Ontop query rewriting system is then used to answer these queries over the EPDS database.

The Électricité de France (EDF) Energy Management Adviser (EMA) uses the HermiT OWL reasoner to produce personalised energy saving advice for EDF's customers. The EMA uses an OWL ontology to model both relevant features of the domain (housing, environment, and so on) and a range of energy-saving "tips". Customers are then described using RDF, and SPARQL queries are used to generate a personalised set of tips for each customer. The system has been used to provide tips to more than 300,000 EDF customers in France.

Appendix
Description Logic Terminology

The purpose of this appendix is to summarise the syntax and semantics of the DL constructors and axioms used in this book. More information and explanations can be found in the relevant chapters. We will also comment on the naming schemes for DLs that are employed in the literature and in this book.

A.1 Syntax and semantics of concept and role constructors

The *concept descriptions* of a DL are built from *concept names, role names* and *individual names* using the *concept* and *role constructors* available in the DL. Table A.1 lists the name, syntax and semantics of such constructors. In this table, C, D stand for concepts (concept names or compound concepts), r, s for roles (role names or compound roles) and a for an individual name. The symbol $\#$ in the semantics of number restrictions maps a set to its cardinality. With r^n we denote the n-fold composition of r with itself, i.e., $r^1 = r$ and $r^{n+1} = r^n \circ r$. Note that, for historical reasons, role value maps are written $(r \sqsubseteq s)$, where r and s are role names or compositions of role names. Role value maps are concept descriptions – they denote the set of individuals whose role values satisfy the relevant inclusion – and should not be confused with role inclusion axioms.

Predicate restrictions need a bit more explanation. They presuppose that a fixed so-called *concrete domain* $\mathsf{D} = (\Delta^{\mathsf{D}}, \Phi^{\mathsf{D}})$ is given, where Δ^{D} is a non-empty set and Φ^{D} is a finite set of predicates. Each *predicate* in Φ^{D} has a name P, an arity k_P and an extension $P^{\mathsf{D}} \subseteq (\Delta^{\mathsf{D}})^{k_P}$. In the predicate restriction $\exists c_1, \ldots, c_k.P$, the symbol P is the name of a predicate from Φ^{D}, which has arity k, and the symbols $c_1, \ldots, c_k$ stand for feature chains. A *feature chain* c is a sequence of the form $g_1 \cdots g_n h$

Name	Syntax	Semantics
Top	$\top$	$\Delta^{\mathcal{I}}$
Bottom	$\bot$	$\emptyset$
Conjunction	$C \sqcap D$	$C^{\mathcal{I}} \cap D^{\mathcal{I}}$
Disjunction	$C \sqcup D$	$C^{\mathcal{I}} \cup D^{\mathcal{I}}$
Negation	$\neg C$	$\Delta^{\mathcal{I}} \setminus C^{\mathcal{I}}$
Exist. restr.	$\exists r.C$	$\{d \in \Delta^{\mathcal{I}} \mid \exists e \in \Delta^{\mathcal{I}}.(d,e) \in r^{\mathcal{I}} \wedge e \in C^{\mathcal{I}}\}$
Value restr.	$\forall r.C$	$\{d \in \Delta^{\mathcal{I}} \mid \forall e \in \Delta^{\mathcal{I}}.(d,e) \in r^{\mathcal{I}} \rightarrow e \in C^{\mathcal{I}}\}$
Self restr.	$\exists r.\mathsf{Self}$	$\{d \in \Delta^{\mathcal{I}} \mid (d,d) \in r^{\mathcal{I}}\}$
Unqualified number restr.	$(\leqslant n\, r)$ $(\geqslant n\, r)$	$\{d \in \Delta^{\mathcal{I}} \mid \#\{e \mid (d,e) \in r^{\mathcal{I}}\} \leq n\}$ $\{d \in \Delta^{\mathcal{I}} \mid \#\{e \mid (d,e) \in r^{\mathcal{I}}\} \geq n\}$
Qualified number restr.	$(\leqslant n\, r.C)$ $(\geqslant n\, r.C)$	$\{d \in \Delta^{\mathcal{I}} \mid \#\{e \mid (d,e) \in r^{\mathcal{I}} \wedge e \in C^{\mathcal{I}}\} \leq n\}$ $\{d \in \Delta^{\mathcal{I}} \mid \#\{e \mid (d,e) \in r^{\mathcal{I}} \wedge e \in C^{\mathcal{I}}\} \geq n\}$
Nominal	$\{a\}$	$\{a^{\mathcal{I}}\}$
Role value map	$(r \sqsubseteq s)$	$\{d \in \Delta^{\mathcal{I}} \mid \{e \mid (d,e) \in r^{\mathcal{I}}\} = \{e' \mid (d,e') \in s^{\mathcal{I}}\}\}$
Predicate restr.	$\exists c_1, \dots, c_k.P$	$\{d \in \Delta^{\mathcal{I}} \mid (c_1^{\mathcal{I}}(d), \dots, c_k^{\mathcal{I}}(d)) \in P^{\mathsf{D}}\}$
Role composition	$r \circ s$	$\{(d,f) \in \Delta^{\mathcal{I}} \times \Delta^{\mathcal{I}} \mid \exists e \in \Delta^{\mathcal{I}}.(d,e) \in r^{\mathcal{I}} \wedge (e,f) \in s^{\mathcal{I}}\}$
Inverse role	r^-	$\{(e,d) \in \Delta^{\mathcal{I}} \times \Delta^{\mathcal{I}} \mid (d,e) \in r^{\mathcal{I}}\}$
Feature chain	$g_1 \cdots g_n h$	$(g_1 \cdots g_n h)^{\mathcal{I}}(d) = h^{\mathcal{I}}(g_n^{\mathcal{I}}(\cdots(g_1^{\mathcal{I}}(d))\cdots))$

Table A.1. *Some Description Logic concept and role constructors.*

of $n \geq 0$ *abstract features* g_i and one *concrete feature* h. Thus, from the syntactic point of view we need to assume that, in addition to concept, role and individual names, abstract and concrete feature names are also available.

The semantics of concept and role descriptions is defined using the notion of an *interpretation* $\mathcal{I} = (\Delta^{\mathcal{I}}, \cdot^{\mathcal{I}})$, where $\Delta^{\mathcal{I}}$ is a non-empty set and the interpretation function $\cdot^{\mathcal{I}}$ maps concept names A to sets $A^{\mathcal{I}} \subseteq \Delta^{\mathcal{I}}$, role names r to binary relation $r^{\mathcal{I}} \subseteq \Delta^{\mathcal{I}} \times \Delta^{\mathcal{I}}$ and individual names a to elements $a^{\mathcal{I}} \in \Delta^{\mathcal{I}}$. In the presence of a concrete domain $D = (\Delta^D, \Phi^D)$, abstract features g are interpreted as partial functions $g^{\mathcal{I}} : \Delta^{\mathcal{I}} \to \Delta^{\mathcal{I}}$ and concrete features h as partial functions $h^{\mathcal{I}} : \Delta^{\mathcal{I}} \to \Delta^D$. The interpretation function $\cdot^{\mathcal{I}}$ is inductively extended to compound concepts, roles and feature chains using the identities given in the semantics column of Table A.1. In the definition of the semantics of predicate restrictions, the condition that the tuple $(c_1^{\mathcal{I}}(d), \dots, c_k^{\mathcal{I}}(d))$ belongs to P^D includes the requirement that all the elements of this tuple are well-defined, i.e., d belongs to the domains of the partial functions $c_1^{\mathcal{I}}, \dots, c_k^{\mathcal{I}}$. For the feature chain $c = g_1 \cdots g_n h$, the elements $d \in \Delta^{\mathcal{I}}$ belong to the domain of $c^{\mathcal{I}}$ if d belongs to the domain of $g_1^{\mathcal{I}}$, $g_1^{\mathcal{I}}(d)$ belongs to the domain of $g_2^{\mathcal{I}}$ etc. and $g_n^{\mathcal{I}}(\cdots (g_1^{\mathcal{I}}(d))\cdots)$ belongs to the domain of $h^{\mathcal{I}}$.

A.2 Syntax and semantics of knowledge bases

Knowledge bases consist of terminological axioms and assertions. Terminological axioms restrict the interpretation of concepts (concept axioms) and roles (role axioms), whereas assertions restrict the interpretation of individuals. In Table A.2, C, D again stand for concepts (concept names or compound concepts) and r, s for roles (role names or compound roles); in addition, A stands for a concept name and a, b stand for individual names. A *TBox* is a finite set of concept and role axioms, and an *ABox* is a finite set of assertions. A *knowledge base* $\mathcal{K} = (\mathcal{T}, \mathcal{A})$ consists of a TBox $\mathcal{T}$ and an ABox $\mathcal{A}$.

The semantics of axioms is defined using the notion of a *model*. An interpretation $\mathcal{I}$ *satisfies* an axiom if it satisfies the condition formulated in the semantics column of Table A.2. Recall that a binary relation $r^{\mathcal{I}}$ is *transitive* if it satisfies

$$(d, e) \in r^{\mathcal{I}} \wedge (e, f) \in r^{\mathcal{I}} \Rightarrow (d, f) \in r^{\mathcal{I}};$$

it is *functional* if it satisfies

$$(d, e) \in r^{\mathcal{I}} \wedge (d, f) \in r^{\mathcal{I}} \Rightarrow e = f;$$

it is *reflexive* if it satisfies

$$d \in \Delta^{\mathcal{I}} \Rightarrow (d, d) \in r^{\mathcal{I}};$$

it is *irreflexive* if it satisfies

$$d \in \Delta^{\mathcal{I}} \Rightarrow (d, d) \notin r^{\mathcal{I}};$$

Name	Syntax	Semantics
General concept inclusion	$C \sqsubseteq D$	$C^{\mathcal{I}} \subseteq D^{\mathcal{I}}$
Concept definition	$A \equiv C$	$A^{\mathcal{I}} = C^{\mathcal{I}}$
Role inclusion	$r \sqsubseteq s$	$r^{\mathcal{I}} \subseteq s^{\mathcal{I}}$
Role disjointness	$\mathsf{Disj}(r, s)$	$r^{\mathcal{I}} \cap s^{\mathcal{I}} = \emptyset$
Role transitivity	$\mathsf{Trans}(r)$	$r^{\mathcal{I}}$ is transitive
Role functionality	$\mathsf{Func}(r)$	$r^{\mathcal{I}}$ is functional
Role reflexivity	$\mathsf{Ref}(r)$	$r^{\mathcal{I}}$ is reflexive
Role irreflexivity	$\mathsf{Irref}(r)$	$r^{\mathcal{I}}$ is irreflexive
Role symmetry	$\mathsf{Sym}(r)$	$r^{\mathcal{I}}$ is symmetrical
Role antisymmetry	$\mathsf{Asym}(r)$	$r^{\mathcal{I}}$ is antisymmetrical
Concept assertion	$a : C$	$a^{\mathcal{I}} \in C^{\mathcal{I}}$
Role assertion	$(a, b) : r$	$(a^{\mathcal{I}}, b^{\mathcal{I}}) \in r^{\mathcal{I}}$

Table A.2. *Terminological and assertional axioms.*

it is *symmetrical* if it satisfies

$$(d, e) \in r^{\mathcal{I}} \Rightarrow (e, d) \in r^{\mathcal{I}};$$

and it is antisymmetrical if it satisfies

$$(d, e) \in r^{\mathcal{I}} \Rightarrow (e, d) \notin r^{\mathcal{I}}.$$

An interpretation that satisfies each axiom in a TBox $\mathcal{T}$ (ABox $\mathcal{A}$) is called a *model* of $\mathcal{T}$ ($\mathcal{A}$). It is a model of a knowledge base $\mathcal{K} = (\mathcal{T}, \mathcal{A})$ if it is a model of both $\mathcal{T}$ and $\mathcal{A}$.

A.3 Naming schemes for description logics

A particular DL is determined by the constructors and axioms available in the DL. In order to distinguish between different DLs, certain naming schemes have been introduced in the DL community. These schemes start with (the name for) a basic DL, and then add letters or symbols to indicate additional concept constructors, role constructors and kinds of role axiom.

Name	Syntax	Sym	$\mathcal{AL}$	$\mathcal{EL}$	$\mathcal{S}$
Top	$\top$		✓	✓	✓
Bottom	$\bot$		✓		✓
Conjunction	$C \sqcap D$		✓	✓	✓
Atomic negation	$\neg A$		✓		✓
Value restr.	$\forall r.C$		✓		✓
Disjunction	$C \sqcup D$	$\mathcal{U}$			✓
Negation	$\neg C$	$\mathcal{C}$			✓
Exist. restr.	$\exists r.C$	$\mathcal{E}$		✓	✓
Unqualified number restr.	$(\leqslant n\, r)$ $(\geqslant n\, r)$	$\mathcal{N}$			
Qualified number restr.	$(\leqslant n\, r.C)$ $(\geqslant n\, r.C)$	$\mathcal{Q}$			
Nominal	$\{a\}$	$\mathcal{O}$			
Inverse role	r^-	$\mathcal{I}$			
Role inclusion	$r \sqsubseteq s$	$\mathcal{H}$			
Complex role inclusion	$r_1 \circ \ldots \circ r_n \sqsubseteq s$	$\mathcal{R}$			
Functionality	$\mathsf{Func}(r)$	$\mathcal{F}$			
Transitivity	$\mathsf{Trans}(r)$	$_{R^+}$			✓

Table A.3. *The $\mathcal{AL}$, $\mathcal{EL}$, and $\mathcal{S}$ naming schemes.*

Three common such schemes are illustrated in Table A.3, where the columns $\mathcal{AL}$, $\mathcal{EL}$ and $\mathcal{S}$ show the features of the corresponding basic DL, and the column Sym shows the symbols used to indicate additional features. As above, C, D stand for concepts (concept names or compound concepts), r, s stand for roles (role names or compound roles), A stands for a concept name and a, b stand for individual names.

The most common scheme starts with the basic DL $\mathcal{AL}$; for example, $\mathcal{ALC}$ is the DL obtained from $\mathcal{AL}$ by adding (full) negation. Note that we consider DLs modulo expressivity of constructors. Since negation can be used to define disjunction from conjunction and existential restriction from value restriction, $\mathcal{ALC}$ is the same DL as $\mathcal{ALCEU}$. Similarly, the fact that every $\mathcal{ALC}$ concept can be transformed into an equivalent one in negation normal form shows that $\mathcal{ALC}$ is actually the same DL as $\mathcal{ALEU}$.

The second naming scheme illustrated in Table A.3 starts with the basic DL $\mathcal{EL}$; for example, $\mathcal{ELI}$ stands for $\mathcal{EL}$ extended with inverse roles, and $\mathcal{ELIRO}$ for $\mathcal{ELI}$ extended with complex role inclusions and nominals.

The $\mathcal{S}$ naming scheme was introduced to avoid very long names for DLs. Its basic DL $\mathcal{S}$ is $\mathcal{ALC}$ extended with transitive roles. The DL $\mathcal{SHIQ}$, for example, extends this basic DL with role inclusion axioms,[1] inverse roles and qualified number restrictions, while $\mathcal{SROIQ}$ also includes a role box (RBox) and nominals. Note that in this context $\mathcal{R}$ signifies an RBox, which can include not only complex role inclusion axioms but also disjointness, transitivity, reflexivity, irreflexivity, symmetry and antisymmetry axioms (see Table A.2), as well as the self restriction concept constructor (see Table A.1).

Unfortunately, things are not quite so simple since the unrestricted combination of the constructors indicated by the name $\mathcal{SHIQ}$ would lead to a DL with undecidable inference problems. For this reason, the qualified number restrictions in $\mathcal{SHIQ}$ are restricted to *simple roles*, i.e., roles that do not have transitive subroles (see [HST00] for details). Similarly, the use of complex role inclusions in DLs like $\mathcal{SROIQ}$ must be restricted to so-called regular collections of role inclusion axioms [HKS06].

---

[1] Role inclusion axioms are named with an $\mathcal{H}$ as they can be used to define a role hierarchy.

References

[AB09] Sanjeev Arora and Boaz Barak. *Computational Complexity: A Modern Approach.* Cambridge University Press, 2009.

[ABM99] Carlos Areces, Patrick Blackburn, and Maarten Marx. A road-map on complexity for hybrid logics. In Jörg Flum and Mario Rodríguez-Artalejo, editors, *Proc. of the Annual Conf. of the Eur. Assoc. for Computer Science Logic (CSL-99)*, volume 1683 of *Lecture Notes in Computer Science*, pages 307–321. Springer, 1999.

[ACG⁺05] Andrea Acciarri, Diego Calvanese, Giuseppe De Giacomo, Domenico Lembo, Maurizio Lenzerini, Mattia Palmieri, and Riccardo Rosati. QuOnto: Querying ontologies. In Manuela M. Veloso and Subbarao Kambhampati, editors, *Proc. of the 20th Nat. Conf. on Artificial Intelligence (AAAI-05)*, pages 1670–1671. AAAI Press/The MIT Press, 2005.

[ACH12] Ana Armas Romero, Bernardo Cuenca Grau, and Ian Horrocks. MORe: Modular combination of OWL reasoners for ontology classification. In Philippe Cudré-Mauroux, Jeff Heflin, Evren Sirin, Tania Tudorache, Jérôme Euzenat, Manfred Hauswirth, Josiane Xavier Parreira, Jim Hendler, Guus Schreiber, Abraham Bernstein, and Eva Blomqvist, editors, *Proc. of the 11th International Semantic Web Conference (ISWC-12)*, volume 7649 of *Lecture Notes in Computer Science*, pages 1–16. Springer, 2012.

[ACKZ09] Alessandro Artale, Diego Calvanese, Roman Kontchakov, and Michael Zakharyaschev. The DL-Lite family and relations. *J. of Artificial Intelligence Research*, 36:1–69, 2009.

[ANvB98] Hajnal Andréka, István Németi, and Johan van Benthem. Modal languages and bounded fragments of predicate logic. *J. Philosophical Logic*, 27(3):217–274, 1998.

[Are00] Carlos Areces. *Logic Engineering: The Case of Description and Hybrid Logics.* PhD thesis, Institute for Logic, Language and Computation, University of Amsterdam, 2000. ILLC Dissertation Series 2000–5.

[Baa90] Franz Baader. Terminological cycles in KL-ONE-based knowledge representation languages. In Howard E. Shrobe, Thomas G. Dietterich, and William R. Swartout, editors, *Proc. of the 8th Nat. Conf. on Artificial Intelligence (AAAI-90)*, pages 621–626. AAAI Press, 1990.

[Baa91] Franz Baader. Augmenting concept languages by transitive closure of roles: An alternative to terminological cycles. In John Mylopoulos and

Raymond Reiter, editors, *Proc. of the 12th Int. Joint Conf. on Artificial Intelligence (IJCAI-91)*, pages 446–451. Morgan Kaufmann, Los Altos, 1991.

[Baa96] Franz Baader. Using automata theory for characterizing the semantics of terminological cycles. *Ann. of Mathematics and Artificial Intelligence*, 18:175–219, 1996.

[Baa03] Franz Baader. Terminological cycles in a description logic with existential restrictions. In Georg Gottlob and Toby Walsh, editors, *Proc. of the 18th Int. Joint Conf. on Artificial Intelligence (IJCAI-03)*, pages 325–330. Morgan Kaufmann, Los Altos, 2003.

[BBL05] Franz Baader, Sebastian Brandt, and Carsten Lutz. Pushing the $\mathcal{EL}$ envelope. In Leslie Pack Kaelbling and Alessandro Saffiotti, editors, *Proc. of the 19th Int. Joint Conf. on Artificial Intelligence (IJCAI-05)*, pages 364–369. Morgan Kaufmann, Los Altos, 2005.

[BBL08] Franz Baader, Sebastian Brandt, and Carsten Lutz. Pushing the $\mathcal{EL}$ envelope further. In Kendall Clark and Peter F. Patel-Schneider, editors, *Proc. of OWL: Experiences and Directions 2008 DC*, volume 496 of *CEUR Workshop Proceedings* (http://ceur-ws.org/), 2008.

[BCDG01] Daniela Berardi, Diego Calvanese, and Giuseppe De Giacomo. Reasoning on UML class diagrams using description logic based systems. In Günther Görz, Volker Haarslev, Carsten Lutz, and Ralf Möller, editors, *Proc. of the KI-01 Workshop on Applications of Description Logics*, volume 44 of *CEUR Workshop Proceedings* (http://ceur-ws.org/), 2001.

[BCM+07] Franz Baader, Diego Calvanese, Deborah McGuinness, Daniele Nardi, and Peter F. Patel-Schneider, editors. *The Description Logic Handbook: Theory, Implementation and Applications*. Cambridge University Press, 2nd edition, 2007.

[BDNS98] Martin Buchheit, Francesco M. Donini, Werner Nutt, and Andrea Schaerf. A refined architecture for terminological systems: Terminology = schema + views. *Artificial Intelligence*, 99(2):209–260, 1998.

[BdRV01] Patrick Blackburn, Maarten de Rijke, and Yde Venema. *Modal Logic*, volume 53 of *Cambridge Tracts in Theoretical Computer Science*. Cambridge University Press, 2001.

[BDS93] Martin Buchheit, Francesco M. Donini, and Andrea Schaerf. Decidable reasoning in terminological knowledge representation systems. *J. of Artificial Intelligence Research*, 1:109–138, 1993.

[BFH+92] Franz Baader, Enrico Franconi, Bernhard Hollunder, Bernhard Nebel, and Hans-Jürgen Profitlich. An empirical analysis of optimization techniques for terminological representation systems, or, making KRIS get a move on. In Bernhard Nebel, Charles Rich, and William R. Swartout, editors, *Proc. of the 3rd Int. Conf. on the Principles of Knowledge Representation and Reasoning (KR-92)*, pages 270–281. Morgan Kauffman, Los Altos, 1992.

[BFH+94] Franz Baader, Enrico Franconi, Bernhard Hollunder, Bernhard Nebel, and Hans-Jürgen Profitlich. An empirical analysis of optimization techniques for terminological representation systems or, making KRIS get a move on. *Applied Artificial Intelligence. Special Issue on Knowledge Base Management*, 4:109–132, 1994.

[BFL83] Ronald J. Brachman, Richard E. Fikes, and Hector J. Levesque. KRYPTON: A functional approach to knowledge representation. *IEEE Computer*, October:67–73, 1983.

[BH91] Franz Baader and Philipp Hanschke. A schema for integrating concrete domains into concept languages. In John Mylopoulos and Raymond Reiter, editors, *Proc. of the 12th Int. Joint Conf. on Artificial Intelligence (IJCAI-91)*, pages 452–457. Morgan Kaufmann, Los Altos, 1991.

[BK06] Franz Baader and Ralf Küsters. Nonstandard inferences in description logics: The story so far. In Dov Gabbay, Sergei Goncharov, and Michael Zakharyaschev, editors, *Mathematical Problems from Applied Logic I*, volume 4 of *International Mathematical Series*, pages 1–75. Springer, 2006.

[BKL+16] Elena Botoeva, Boris Konev, Carsten Lutz, Vladimir Ryzhikov, Frank Wolter, and Michael Zakharyaschev. Inseparability and conservative extensions of description logic ontologies: A survey. In *Proc. of the 12th Int. Reasoning Web Summer School, Lecture Notes in Computer Science*. Springer, 2016.

[BKM99] Franz Baader, Ralf Küsters, and Ralf Molitor. Computing least common subsumers in description logics with existential restrictions. In Thomas Dean, editor, *Proc. of the 16th Int. Joint Conf. on Artificial Intelligence (IJCAI-99)*, pages 96–101. Morgan Kaufmann, Los Altos, 1999.

[BKO+11] Barry Bishop, Atanas Kiryakov, Damyan Ognyanoff, Ivan Peikov, Zdravko Tashev, and Ruslan Velkov. OWLIM: A family of scalable semantic repositories. *J. of Web Semantics*, 2(1):33–42, 2011.

[BL84] Ronald J. Brachman and Hector J. Levesque. The tractability of subsumption in frame-based description languages. In Ronald J. Brachman, editor, *Proc. of the 4th Nat. Conf. on Artificial Intelligence (AAAI-84)*, pages 34–37. AAAI Press, 1984.

[BLMS11] Jean-François Baget, Michel Leclère, Marie-Laure Mugnier, and Eric Salvat. On rules with existential variables: Walking the decidability line. *Artificial Intelligence*, 175(9-10):1620–1654, 2011.

[BLS06] Franz Baader, Carsten Lutz, and Boontawee Suntisrivaraporn. CEL: a polynomial-time reasoner for life science ontologies. In Ulrich Furbach and Natarajan Shankar, editors, *Proc. of the Int. Joint Conf. on Automated Reasoning (IJCAR-06)*, volume 4130 of *Lecture Notes in Artificial Intelligence*, pages 287–291. Springer, 2006.

[BLW13] Meghyn Bienvenu, Carsten Lutz, and Frank Wolter. First-order rewritability of atomic queries in Horn description logics. In Francesca Rossi, editor, *Proc. of the 23nd Int. Joint Conf. on Artificial Intelligence (IJCAI-13)*, pages 754–760. AAAI Press, 2013.

[BMG+15] Andrew Bate, Boris Motik, Bernardo Cuenca Grau, František Simančík, and Ian Horrocks. Extending consequence-based reasoning to SHIQ. In Diego Calvanese and Boris Konev, editors, *Proc. of the 2015 Description Logic Workshop (DL-15)*, volume 1350 of *CEUR Workshop Proceedings* (http://ceur-ws.org/), 2015.

[BMRT11] Jean-François Baget, Marie-Laure Mugnier, Sebastian Rudolph, and Michaël Thomazo. Walking the complexity lines for generalized guarded existential rules. In Toby Walsh, editor, *Proc. of the 22nd Int. Joint Conf. on Artificial Intelligence (IJCAI-11)*, pages 712–717. AAAI Press/IJCAI, 2011.

[BO15] Meghyn Bienvenu and Magdalena Ortiz. Ontology-mediated query answering with data-tractable description logics. In Wolfgang Faber and Adrian Paschke, editors, *Proc. of the 11th Int. Reasoning Web Summer School*, volume 9203 of *Lecture Notes in Computer Science*, pages 218–307. Springer, 2015.

[Bor96] Alexander Borgida. On the relative expressiveness of description logics and predicate logics. *Artificial Intelligence*, 82(1–2):353–367, 1996.

[Bra92] Ronald J. Brachman. "Reducing" CLASSIC to practice: Knowledge representation meets reality. In Bernhard Nebel, Charles Rich, and William R. Swartout, editors, *Proc. of the 3rd Int. Conf. on the Principles of Knowledge Representation and Reasoning (KR-92)*, pages 247–258. Morgan Kaufmann, Los Altos, 1992.

[Bra04] Sebastian Brandt. Polynomial time reasoning in a description logic with existential restrictions, GCI axioms, and—what else? In Ramon López de Mántaras and Lorenza Saitta, editors, *Proc. of the 16th Eur. Conf. on Artificial Intelligence (ECAI-04)*, pages 298–302. IOS Press, 2004.

[BS85] Ronald J. Brachman and James G. Schmolze. An overview of the KL-ONE knowledge representation system. *Cognitive Science*, 9(2):171–216, 1985.

[BtCLW14] Meghyn Bienvenu, Balder ten Cate, Carsten Lutz, and Frank Wolter. Ontology-based data access: A study through disjunctive datalog, CSP, and MMSNP. *ACM Trans. on Database Systems*, 39(4):33:1–33:44, 2014.

[Bv07] Patrick Blackburn and Johan van Benthem. Modal logic: A semantic perspective. In Patrick Blackburn, Johan van Benthem, and Frank Wolter, editors, *The Handbook of Modal Logic*, pages 1–84. Elsevier, 2007.

[CBV⁺14] Sofia Cramerotti, Marco Buccio, Giampiero Vaschetto, Luciano Serafini, and Marco Rospocher. ePlanning: An ontology-based system for building individualized education plans for students with special educational needs. In Axel Polleres, Alexander Garcia, and Richard Benjamins, editors, *Proc. of the Industry Track at the 13th International Semantic Web Conference (ISWC-14)*, volume 1383 of *CEUR Workshop Proceedings* (http://ceur-ws.org/), 2014.

[CCD⁺13] Cristina Civili, Marco Console, Giuseppe De Giacomo, Domenico Lembo, Maurizio Lenzerini, Lorenzo Lepore, Riccardo Mancini, Antonella Poggi, Riccardo Rosati, Marco Ruzzi, Valerio Santarelli, and Domenico Fabio Savo. MASTRO STUDIO: Managing ontology-based data access applications. *Proceedings of the VLDB Endowment*, 6(12):1314–1317, 2013.

[CDGL98a] Diego Calvanese, Giuseppe De Giacomo, and Maurizio Lenzerini. On the decidability of query containment under constraints. In Alberto O. Mendelzon and Jan Paredaens, editors, *Proc. of the 17th ACM SIGACT SIGMOD SIGART Symp. on Principles of Database Systems (PODS-98)*, pages 149–158. ACM, 1998.

[CDGL⁺98b] Diego Calvanese, Giuseppe De Giacomo, Maurizio Lenzerini, Daniele Nardi, and Riccardo Rosati. Description logic framework for information integration. In Anthony G. Cohn, Lenhart K. Schubert, and Stuart C. Shapiro, editors, *Proc. of the 6th Int. Conf. on the Principles of Knowledge Representation and Reasoning (KR-98)*, pages 2–13. Morgan Kaufmann, Los Altos, 1998.

[CDGL99] Diego Calvanese, Giuseppe De Giacomo, and Maurizio Lenzerini. Modeling and querying semi-structured data. *Network and Information Systems*, 2(2), 1999.

[CDGR99] Diego Calvanese, Giuseppe De Giacomo, and Riccardo Rosati. Data integration and reconciliation in data warehousing: Conceptual modeling and reasoning support. *Network and Information Systems*, 2(4), 1999.

[CDL+07] Diego Calvanese, Giuseppe De Giacomo, Domenico Lembo, Maurizio Lenzerini, and Riccardo Rosati. Tractable reasoning and efficient query answering in description logics: The DL-Lite family. *J. of Automated Reasoning*, 39(3):385–429, 2007.

[CDL08] Diego Calvanese, Giuseppe De Giacomo, and Maurizio Lenzerini. Conjunctive query containment and answering under description logic constraints. *ACM Trans. on Computational Logic*, 9(3), 2008.

[CDL+09] Diego Calvanese, Giuseppe De Giacomo, Domenico Lembo, Maurizio Lenzerini, Antonella Poggi, Mariano Rodriguez-Muro, and Riccardo Rosati. Ontologies and databases: The DL-Lite approach. In Sergio Tessaris, Enrico Franconi, Thomas Eiter, Claudio Gutierrez, Siegfried Handschuh, Marie-Christine Rousset, and Renate A. Schmidt, editors, *Proc. of the 5th Int. Reasoning Web Summer School*, volume 5689 of *Lecture Notes in Computer Science*, pages 255–356. Springer, 2009.

[CDL+13] Diego Calvanese, Giuseppe De Giacomo, Domenico Lembo, Maurizio Lenzerini, and Riccardo Rosati. Data complexity of query answering in description logics. *Artificial Intelligence*, 195:335–360, 2013.

[CGH+13] Pierre Chaussecourte, Birte Glimm, Ian Horrocks, Boris Motik, and Laurent Pierre. The energy management adviser at EDF. In Harith Alani, Lalana Kagal, Achille Fokoue, Paul Groth, Chris Biemann, Josiane Xavier Parreira, Lora Aroyo, Natasha Noy, Chris Welty, and Krzysztof Janowicz, editors, *Proc. of the 12th International Semantic Web Conference (ISWC-13)*, volume 8219 of *Lecture Notes in Computer Science*, pages 49–64. Springer, 2013.

[CGK13] Andrea Calì, Georg Gottlob, and Michael Kifer. Taming the infinite chase: Query answering under expressive relational constraints. *J. of Artificial Intelligence Research*, 48:115–174, 2013.

[CGL+05] Diego Calvanese, Giuseppe De Giacomo, Domenico Lembo, Maurizio Lenzerini, and Riccardo Rosati. DL-Lite: Tractable description logics for ontologies. In Manuela M. Veloso and Subbarao Kambhampati, editors, *Proc. of the 20th Nat. Conf. on Artificial Intelligence (AAAI-05)*, pages 602–607. AAAI Press/The MIT Press, 2005.

[CGL12] Andrea Calì, Georg Gottlob, and Thomas Lukasiewicz. A general datalog-based framework for tractable query answering over ontologies. *J. of Web Semantics*, 14:57–83, 2012.

[CGP11] Andrea Calì, Georg Gottlob, and Andreas Pieris. New expressive languages for ontological query answering. In Wolfram Burgard and Dan Roth, editors, *Proc. of the 25th Nat. Conf. on Artificial Intelligence (AAAI-12)*. AAAI Press/The MIT Press, 2011.

[Che76] Peter Pin-Shan Chen. The entity-relationship model: Toward a unified view of data. *ACM Trans. on Database Systems*, 1(1):9–36, 1976.

[CLN94] Diego Calvanese, Maurizio Lenzerini, and Daniele Nardi. A unifying framework for class based representation formalisms. In Jon Doyle, Erik Sandewall, and Pietro Torasso, editors, *Proc. of the 4th Int. Conf. on the Principles of Knowledge Representation and Reasoning (KR-94)*, pages 109–120. Morgan Kaufmann, Los Altos, 1994.

[CLN98] Diego Calvanese, Maurizio Lenzerini, and Daniele Nardi. Description logics for conceptual data modeling. In Jan Chomicki and Günter Saake, editors, *Logics for Databases and Information Systems*, pages 229–264. Kluwer Academic Publisher, 1998.

[CM77] Ashok K. Chandra and Philip M. Merlin. Optimal implementation of conjunctive queries in relational data bases. In John E. Hopcroft, Emily P. Friedman, and Michael A. Harrison, editors, *Proc. of the 9th ACM Symp. on Theory of Computing (STOC-77)*, pages 77–90. ACM, 1977.

[CSG05] Werner Ceusters, Barry Smith, and Louis Goldberg. A terminological and ontological analysis of the NCI Thesaurus. *Methods of Information in Medicine*, 44(4):498–507, 2005.

[DBSB91] Premkumar Devambu, Ronald J. Brachman, Peter J. Selfridge, and Bruce W. Ballard. LASSIE: A knowledge-based software information system. *Communications of the ACM*, 34(5):36–49, 1991.

[DEGV01] Evgeny Dantsin, Thomas Eiter, Georg Gottlob, and Andrei Voronkov. Complexity and expressive power of logic programming. *ACM Computing Surveys*, 33(3):374–425, 2001.

[DeRP06] Sebastian Derriere, André Richard, and Andrea Preite-Martinez. An ontology of astronomical object types for the virtual observatory. *Proc. of Special Session 3 of the 26th meeting of the IAU: Virtual Observatory in Action: New Science, New Technology, and Next Generation Facilities*, 2006.

[DGL94a] Giuseppe De Giacomo and Maurizio Lenzerini. Boosting the correspondence between description logics and propositional dynamic logics. In *Proc. of the 12th Nat. Conf. on Artificial Intelligence (AAAI-94)*, pages 205–212. AAAI Press/The MIT Press, 1994.

[DGL94b] Giuseppe De Giacomo and Maurizio Lenzerini. Concept language with number restrictions and fixpoints, and its relationship with μ-calculus. In *Proc. of the 11th Eur. Conf. on Artificial Intelligence (ECAI-94)*, pages 411–415. John Wiley & Sons, 1994.

[DGM00] Giuseppe De Giacomo and Fabio Massacci. Combining deduction and model checking into tableaux and algorithms for converse-pdl. *Information and Computation*, 160(1–2), 2000.

[DHL+92] Francesco M. Donini, Bernhard Hollunder, Maurizio Lenzerini, Alberto Marchetti Spaccamela, Daniele Nardi, and Werner Nutt. The complexity of existential quantification in concept languages. *Artificial Intelligence*, 53(2–3):309–327, 1992.

[DLNN91a] Francesco M. Donini, Maurizio Lenzerini, Daniele Nardi, and Werner Nutt. The complexity of concept languages. In James Allen, Richard Fikes, and Erik Sandewall, editors, *Proc. of the 2nd Int. Conf. on the Principles of Knowledge Representation and Reasoning (KR-91)*, pages 151–162. Morgan Kaufmann, Los Altos, 1991.

[DLNN91b] Francesco M. Donini, Maurizio Lenzerini, Daniele Nardi, and Werner Nutt. Tractable concept languages. In John Mylopoulos and Ray Reiter, editors, *Proc. of the 12th Int. Joint Conf. on Artificial Intelligence (IJCAI-91)*, pages 458–463. Morgan Kaufmann, Los Altos, 1991.

[DLNS94] Francesco M. Donini, Maurizio Lenzerini, Daniele Nardi, and Andrea Schaerf. Deduction in concept languages: From subsumption to instance checking. *J. of Logic and Computation*, 4(4):423–452, 1994.

[DLNS98] Francesco M. Donini, Maurizio Lenzerini, Daniele Nardi, and Andrea Schaerf. $\mathcal{AL}$-log: Integrating Datalog and description logics. *J. of Intelligent Information Systems*, 10(3):227–252, 1998.

[DNR08] Alin Deutsch, Alan Nash, and Jeffrey B. Remmel. The chase revisited. In Maurizio Lenzerini and Domenico Lembo, editors, *Proc. of the 27th ACM SIGACT SIGMOD SIGART Symp. on Principles of Database*

Systems (PODS-08), pages 149–158. AAAI Press, 2008.

[dR00] Maarten de Rijke. A note on graded modal logic. *Studia Logica*, 64(2):271–283, 2000.

[EGOS08] Thomas Eiter, Georg Gottlob, Magdalena Ortiz, and Mantas Simkus. Query answering in the description logic Horn-$\mathcal{SHIQ}$. In Steffen Hölldobler, Carsten Lutz, and Heinrich Wansing, editors, *Proc. of the 11th Eur. Workshop on Logics in Artificial Intelligence (JELIA-08)*, volume 5293 of *Lecture Notes in Computer Science*, pages 166–179. Springer, 2008.

[ELOS09] Thomas Eiter, Carsten Lutz, Magdalena Ortiz, and Mantas Simkus. Query answering in description logics with transitive roles. In Craig Boutilier, editor, *Proc. of the 21st Int. Joint Conf. on Artificial Intelligence (IJCAI-09)*, pages 759–764. AAAI Press/IJCAI, 2009.

[FL79] Michael J. Fischer and Richard E. Ladner. Propositional dynamic logic of regular programs. *J. of Computer and System Sciences*, 18:194–211, 1979.

[GG00] M. Elisabeth Gonçalvès and Erich Grädel. Decidability issues for action guarded logics. In *Proc. of the 2000 Description Logic Workshop (DL-00)*, volume 33 of *CEUR Workshop Proceedings* (http://ceur-ws.org/), pages 123–132, 2000.

[GHH⁺07] Christine Golbreich, Matthew Horridge, Ian Horrocks, Boris Motik, and Rob Shearer. OBO and OWL: Leveraging semantic web technologies for the life sciences. In *Proc. of the 6th International Semantic Web Conference (ISWC-07)*, volume 4825 of *Lecture Notes in Computer Science*, pages 169–182. Springer, 2007.

[GHKS08] Bernardo Cuenca Grau, Ian Horrocks, Yevgeny Kazakov, and Ulrike Sattler. Modular reuse of ontologies: Theory and practice. *J. of Artificial Intelligence Research*, 31:273–318, 2008.

[GHM10] Birte Glimm, Ian Horrocks, and Boris Motik. Optimized description logic reasoning via core blocking. In Jürgen Giesl and Reiner Hähnle, editors, *Proc. of the Int. Joint Conf. on Automated Reasoning (IJCAR-10)*, volume 6173 of *Lecture Notes in Artificial Intelligence*, pages 457–471. Springer, 2010.

[GHM⁺12] Birte Glimm, Ian Horrocks, Boris Motik, Rob Shearer, and Giorgos Stoilos. A novel approach to ontology classification. *J. of Web Semantics*, 14:84–101, 2012.

[GHM⁺14] Birte Glimm, Ian Horrocks, Boris Motik, Giorgos Stoilos, and Zhe Wang. Hermit: An OWL 2 reasoner. *J. of Automated Reasoning*, 53(3):245–269, 2014.

[GHVD03] Benjamin N. Grosof, Ian Horrocks, Raphael Volz, and Stefan Decker. Description logic programs: Combining logic programs with description logic. In *Proc. of the Twelfth International World Wide Web Conference (WWW-03)*, pages 48–57. ACM, 2003.

[GKK⁺14] Georg Gottlob, Stanislav Kikot, Roman Kontchakov, Vladimir V. Podolskii, Thomas Schwentick, and Michael Zakharyaschev. The price of query rewriting in ontology-based data access. *Artificial Intelligence*, 213:42–59, 2014.

[GKV97] Erich Grädel, Phokion G. Kolaitis, and Moshe Y. Vardi. On the decision problem for two-variable first-order logic. *Bulletin of Symbolic Logic*, 3(1):53–69, 1997.

[GLHS08] Birte Glimm, Carsten Lutz, Ian Horrocks, and Ulrike Sattler. Conjunctive query answering for the description logic $\mathcal{SHIQ}$. *J. of Artificial Intelligence Research*, 31:157–204, 2008.

[GLW06] Silvio Ghilardi, Carsten Lutz, and Frank Wolter. Did I damage my ontology? A case for conservative extensions in description logics. In Patrick Doherty, John Mylopoulos, and Christopher A. Welty, editors, *Proc. of the 10th Int. Conf. on Principles of Knowledge Representation and Reasoning (KR-06)*, pages 187–197. AAAI Press, 2006.

[GMSH13] Bernardo Cuenca Grau, Boris Motik, Giorgos Stoilos, and Ian Horrocks. Computing datalog rewritings beyond Horn ontologies. In Francesca Rossi, editor, *Proc. of the 23nd Int. Joint Conf. on Artificial Intelligence (IJCAI-13)*, pages 832–838. AAAI Press/IJCAI, 2013.

[GN13] Rajeev Goré and Linh Anh Nguyen. ExpTime tableaux for $\mathcal{ALC}$ using sound global caching. *J. of Automated Reasoning*, 50(4):355–381, 2013.

[GO07] Valentin Goranko and Martin Otto. Model theory of modal logic. In Patrick Blackburn, Johan van Benthem, and Frank Wolter, editors, *The Handbook of Modal Logic*, pages 249–329. Elsevier Science Publishers (North-Holland), 2007.

[Goo05] John Goodwin. Experiences of using OWL at the ordnance survey. In *Proc. of the First OWL Experiences and Directions Workshop (OWLED-05)*, volume 188 of *CEUR Workshop Proceedings* (http://ceur-ws.org/), 2005.

[GOR97] Erich Grädel, Martin Otto, and Eric Rosen. Two-variable logic with counting is decidable. In *Proc. of the 12th IEEE Symp. on Logic in Computer Science (LICS-97)*, pages 306–317. IEEE Computer Society Press, 1997.

[Grä98] Erich Grädel. Guarded fragments of first-order logic: A perspective for new description logics? In *Proc. of the 1998 Description Logic Workshop (DL-98)*, volume 11 of *CEUR Workshop Proceedings* (http://ceur-ws.org/), 1998.

[Grä99] Erich Grädel. On the restraining power of guards. *J. of Symbolic Logic*, 64:1719–1742, 1999.

[Gru93] Thomas R. Gruber. A translation approach to portable ontology specifications. *Knowledge Acquisition*, 5(2):199–220, 1993.

[GZB06] Christine Golbreich, Songman Zhang, and Olivier Bodenreider. The foundational model of anatomy in OWL: Experience and perspectives. *J. of Web Semantics*, 4(3), 2006.

[Hal01] Alon Y. Halevy. Answering queries using views: A survey. *VLDB J.*, 10(4), 270–294, 2001.

[HB91] Bernhard Hollunder and Franz Baader. Qualifying number restrictions in concept languages. In *Proc. of the 2nd Int. Conf. on the Principles of Knowledge Representation and Reasoning (KR-91)*, pages 335–346. Morgan Kauffman, Los Altos, 1991.

[HdD⁺05] Frank W. Hartel, Sherri de Coronado, Robert Dionne, Gilberto Fragoso, and Jennifer Golbeck. Modeling a description logic vocabulary for cancer research. *J. of Biomedical Informatics*, 38(2):114–129, 2005.

[HDG12] Robert Hoehndorf, Michel Dumontier, and Georgios V. Gkoutos. Evaluation of research in biomedical ontologies. *Briefings in Bioinformatics*, 14(6):696–712, 2012.

[HKS06] Ian Horrocks, Oliver Kutz, and Ulrike Sattler. The even more irresistible $\mathcal{SROIQ}$. In Patrick Doherty, John Mylopoulos, and Christopher A. Welty, editors, *Proc. of the 10th Int. Conf. on Principles of*

Knowledge Representation and Reasoning (KR-06), pages 57–67. AAAI Press, 2006.

[HLSW15] Peter Hansen, Carsten Lutz, Inanc Seylan, and Frank Wolter. Efficient query rewriting in the description logic $\mathcal{EL}$ and beyond. In Qiang Yang and Michael Wooldridge, editors, *Proc. of the 24th Int. Joint Conf. on Artificial Intelligence (IJCAI-15)*, pages 3034–3040. AAAI Press, 2015.

[HM92] Joseph Y. Halpern and Yoram Moses. A guide to completeness and complexity for modal logics of knowledge and belief. *Artificial Intelligence*, 54:319–379, 1992.

[HM01] Volker Haarslev and Ralf Möller. RACER system description. In *Proc. of the Int. Joint Conf. on Automated Reasoning (IJCAR-01)*, volume 2083 of *Lecture Notes in Artificial Intelligence*, pages 701–706. Springer, 2001.

[HMS07] Ullrich Hustadt, Boris Motik, and Ulrike Sattler. Reasoning in description logics by a reduction to disjunctive datalog. *J. of Automated Reasoning*, 39(3):351–384, 2007.

[Hod93] Wilfried Hodges. *Model Theory*. Cambridge University Press, 1993.

[Hof05] Martin Hofmann. Proof-theoretic approach to description-logic. In Prakash Panangaden, editor, *Proc. of the 20th IEEE Symp. on Logic in Computer Science (LICS-05)*, pages 229–237. IEEE Computer Society Press, 2005.

[Hor97] Ian Horrocks. Optimisation techniques for expressive description logics. Technical Report UMCS-97-2-1, University of Manchester, Department of Computer Science, 1997.

[Hor08] Ian Horrocks. Ontologies and the semantic web. *Communications of the ACM*, 51(12):58–67, 2008.

[HPS98] Ian Horrocks and Peter F. Patel-Schneider. Optimising propositional modal satisfiability for description logic subsumption. In Jacques Calmet and Jan A. Plaza, editors, *Proc. of the 4th Int. Conf. on Artificial Intelligence and Symbolic Computation (AISC'98)*, volume 1476 of *Lecture Notes in Computer Science*, pages 234–246. Springer, 1998.

[HPS09] Matthew Horridge, Bijan Parsia, and Ulrike Sattler. Explaining inconsistencies in OWL ontologies. In Lluis Godo and Andrea Pugliese, editors, *Proc. of the 3rd Int. Conf. on Scalable Uncertainty Management (SUM-09)*, volume 5785 of *Lecture Notes in Computer Science*, pages 124–137. Springer, 2009.

[HPSvH03] Ian Horrocks, Peter F. Patel-Schneider, and Frank van Harmelen. From $\mathcal{SHIQ}$ and RDF to OWL: The making of a web ontology language. *J. of Web Semantics*, 1(1):7–26, 2003.

[HS99] Ian Horrocks and Ulrike Sattler. A description logic with transitive and inverse roles and role hierarchies. *J. of Logic and Computation*, 9(3):385–410, 1999.

[HS01] Ian Horrocks and Ulrike Sattler. Ontology reasoning in the $\mathcal{SHOQ}(D)$ description logic. In Bernhard Nebel, editor, *Proc. of the 17th Int. Joint Conf. on Artificial Intelligence (IJCAI-01)*, pages 199–204. Morgan Kaufmann, Los Altos, 2001.

[HS02] Ian Horrocks and Ulrike Sattler. Optimised reasoning for $\mathcal{SHIQ}$. In Frank van Harmelen, editor, *Proc. of the 15th Eur. Conf. on Artificial Intelligence (ECAI-02)*, pages 277–281. IOS Press, 2002.

[HS04] Ian Horrocks and Ulrike Sattler. Decidability of $\mathcal{SHIQ}$ with complex role inclusion axioms. *Artificial Intelligence*, 160(1–2):79–104, 2004.

[HS12] Jörg Hoffmann and Bart Selman, editors. *Proc. of the 26th Nat. Conf.*

on *Artificial Intelligence (AAAI-12)*. AAAI Press/The MIT Press, 2012.

[HST99] Ian Horrocks, Ulrike Sattler, and Stephan Tobies. Practical reasoning for expressive description logics. In Harald Ganzinger, David McAllester, and Andrei Voronkov, editors, *Proc. of the 6th Int. Conf. on Logic for Programming and Automated Reasoning (LPAR-99)*, number 1705 in Lecture Notes in Artificial Intelligence, pages 161–180. Springer, 1999.

[HST00] Ian Horrocks, Ulrike Sattler, and Stefan Tobies. Practical reasoning for very expressive description logics. *J. of the Interest Group in Pure and Applied Logic*, 8(3):239–264, 2000.

[HSTT00] Ian Horrocks, Ulrike Sattler, Sergio Tessaris, and Stephan Tobies. How to decide query containment under constraints using a description logic. In Michel Parigot and Andrei Voronkov, editors, *Proc. of the 7th Int. Conf. on Logic for Programming and Automated Reasoning (LPAR-00)*, volume 1955 of *Lecture Notes in Artificial Intelligence*, pages 326–343. Springer, 2000.

[HT00] Ian Horrocks and Sergio Tessaris. A conjunctive query language for description logic ABoxes. In Henry A. Kautz and Bruce W. Porter, editors, *Proc. of the 17th Nat. Conf. on Artificial Intelligence (AAAI-00)*, pages 399–404. AAAI Press/The MIT Press, 2000.

[JGS+08] Ernesto Jiménez-Ruiz, Bernardo Cuenca Grau, Ulrike Sattler, Thomas Schneider, and Rafael Berlanga Llavori. Safe and economic reuse of ontologies: A logic-based methodology and tool support. In Sean Bechhofer, Manfred Hauswirth, Jörg Hoffmann, and Manolis Koubarakis, editors, *Proc. of the 5th European Semantic Web Conf. (ESWC-08)*, volume 5021 of *Lecture Notes in Computer Science*, pages 185–199. Springer, 2008.

[JRCHB11] Ernesto Jiménez-Ruiz, Bernardo Cuenca Grau, Ian Horrocks, and Rafael Berlanga Llavori. Supporting concurrent ontology development: Framework, algorithms and tool. *Data and Knowledge Engineering*, 70(1):146–164, 2011.

[JRCZH12] Ernesto Jiménez-Ruiz, Bernardo Cuenca Grau, Yujiao Zhou, and Ian Horrocks. Large-scale interactive ontology matching: Algorithms and implementation. In Luc De Raedt, Christian Bessière, Didier Dubois, Patrick Doherty, Paolo Frasconi, Fredrik Heintz, and Peter J. F. Lucas, editors, *Proc. of the 20th Eur. Conf. on Artificial Intelligence (ECAI-12)*, pages 444–449. IOS Press, 2012.

[Kaz08] Yevgeny Kazakov. $\mathcal{RIQ}$ and $\mathcal{SROIQ}$ are harder than $\mathcal{SHOIQ}$. In *Proc. of the 11th Int. Conf. on Principles of Knowledge Representation and Reasoning (KR-08)*, pages 274–284. AAAI Press, 2008.

[Kaz09] Yevgeny Kazakov. Consequence-driven reasoning for Horn $\mathcal{SHIQ}$ ontologies. In Craig Boutilier, editor, *Proc. of the 21st Int. Joint Conf. on Artificial Intelligence (IJCAI-09)*, pages 2040–2045. AAAI Press, 2009.

[Kd99] Natasha Kurtonina and Maarten de Rijke. Expressiveness of concept expressions in first-order description. *Artificial Intelligence*, 107(2):303–333, 1999.

[KdN03] Yevgeny Kazakov and Hans de Nivelle. Subsumption of concepts in $\mathcal{FL}_0$ for (cyclic) terminologies with respect to descriptive semantics is PSPACE-complete. In *Proc. of the 2003 Description Logic Workshop (DL-03)*, volume 81 of *CEUR Workshop Proceedings* (http://ceur-ws.org/), 2003.

[KdR97] Natasha Kurtonina and Maarten de Rijke. Simulating without negation. *J. of Logic and Computation*, 7(4):501–522, 1997.

[KFNM04] Holger Knublauch, Ray Fergerson, Natalya Noy, and Mark Musen. The Protégé OWL plugin: An open development environment for semantic web applications. In Sheila A. McIlraith, Dimitris Plexousakis, and Frank van Harmelen, editors, *Proc. of the 3rd International Semantic Web Conference (ISWC-04)*, number 3298 in Lecture Notes in Computer Science, pages 229–243. Springer, 2004.

[KFP⁺06] Aaron Kershenbaum, Achille Fokoue, Chintan Patel, Christopher Welty, Edith Schonberg, James Cimino, Li Ma, Kavitha Srinivas, Robert Schloss, and J William Murdock. A view of OWL from the field: Use cases and experiences. In *Proc. of the Second OWL Experiences and Directions Workshop (OWLED-06)*, volume 216 of *CEUR Workshop Proceedings* (http://ceur-ws.org/), 2006.

[KHJ⁺15a] Evgeny Kharlamov, Dag Hovland, Ernesto Jiménez-Ruiz, Davide Lanti, Christoph Pinkel, Martin Rezk, Martin G. Skjæveland, Evgenij Thorstensen, Guohui Xiao, Dmitriy Zheleznyakov, Eldar Bjørge, and Ian Horrocks. Ontology based access to exploration data at Statoil. In *Proc. of the 14th International Semantic Web Conference (ISWC-15)*, volume 9367 of *Lecture Notes in Computer Science*, pages 93–112. Springer, 2015.

[KHJ⁺15b] Adila Krisnadhi, Yingjie Hu, Krzysztof Janowicz, Pascal Hitzler, Robert A. Arko, Suzanne Carbotte, Cynthia Chandler, Michelle Cheatham, Douglas Fils, Timothy W. Finin, Peng Ji, Matthew B. Jones, Nazifa Karima, Kerstin A. Lehnert, Audrey Mickle, Thomas W. Narock, Margaret O'Brien, Lisa Raymond, Adam Shepherd, Mark Schildhauer, and Peter Wiebe. The GeoLink modular oceanography ontology. In Marcelo Arenas, Oscar Corcho, Elena Simperl, Markus Strohmaier, Mathieu d'Aquin, Kavitha Srinivas, Paul Groth, Michel Dumontier, Jeff Heflin, Krishnaprasad Thirunarayan, Krishnaprasad Thirunarayan, and Steffen Staab, editors, *Proc. of the 14th International Semantic Web Conference (ISWC-15)*, volume 9367 of *Lecture Notes in Computer Science*, pages 301–309. Springer, 2015.

[KKS11] Yevgeny Kazakov, Markus Krötzsch, and František Simančík. Concurrent classification of $\mathcal{EL}$ ontologies. In Lora Aroyo, Chris Welty, Harith Alani, Jamie Taylor, Abraham Bernstein, Lalana Kagal, Natasha Fridman Noy, and Eva Blomqvist, editors, *Proc. of the 10th International Semantic Web Conference (ISWC-11)*, volume 7031 of *Lecture Notes in Computer Science*, pages 305–320. Springer, 2011.

[KKS14] Yevgeny Kazakov, Markus Krötzsch, and František Simančík. The incredible ELK – from polynomial procedures to efficient reasoning with $\mathcal{EL}$ ontologies. *J. of Automated Reasoning*, 53(1):1–61, 2014.

[KL07] Adila Krisnadhi and Carsten Lutz. Data complexity in the $\mathcal{EL}$ family of description logics. In Nachum Dershowitz and Andrei Voronkov, editors, *Proc. of the 14th Int. Conf. on Logic for Programming, Artificial Intelligence and Reasoning (LPAR-07)*, volume 4790 of *Lecture Notes in Artificial Intelligence*, pages 333–347. Springer, 2007.

[KLT⁺10] Roman Kontchakov, Carsten Lutz, David Toman, Frank Wolter, and Michael Zakharyaschev. The combined approach to query answering in DL-Lite. In Fangzhen Lin, Ulrike Sattler, and Miroslaw Truszczynski, editors, *Proc. of the 12th Int. Conf. on the Principles of Knowledge Representation and Reasoning (KR-10)*, pages 247–257. AAAI Press, 2010.

[KRH07] Markus Krötzsch, Sebastian Rudolph, and Pascal Hitzler. Conjunctive queries for a tractable fragment of OWL 1.1. In Karl Aberer, Key-Sun Choi, Natasha Fridman Noy, Dean Allemang, Kyung-Il Lee, Lyndon J. B. Nixon, Jennifer Golbeck, Peter Mika, Diana Maynard, Riichiro Mizoguchi, Guus Schreiber, and Philippe Cudré-Mauroux, editors, *Proc. of the 6th International Semantic Web Conference (ISWC-07)*, volume 4825 of *Lecture Notes in Computer Science*, pages 310–323. Springer, 2007.

[KRR+14] Roman Kontchakov, Martin Rezk, Mariano Rodriguez-Muro, Guohui Xiao, and Michael Zakharyaschev. Answering SPARQL queries over databases under OWL 2 QL entailment regime. In Peter Mika, Tania Tudorache, Abraham Bernstein, Chris Welty, Craig A. Knoblock, Denny Vrandecic, Paul T. Groth, Natasha F. Noy, Krzysztof Janowicz, and Carole A. Goble, editors, *Proc. of the 13th International Semantic Web Conference (ISWC-14)*, volume 8796 of *Lecture Notes in Computer Science*, pages 552–567. Springer, 2014.

[KWW08] Boris Konev, Dirk Walther, and Frank Wolter. The logical difference problem for description logic terminologies. In Alessandro Armando, Peter Baumgartner, and Gilles Dowek, editors, *Proc. of the Int. Joint Conf. on Automated Reasoning (IJCAR-08)*, volume 5195 of *Lecture Notes in Computer Science*, pages 259–274. Springer, 2008.

[KZ14] Roman Kontchakov and Michael Zakharyaschev. An introduction to description logics and query rewriting. In Manolis Koubarakis, Giorgos B. Stamou, Giorgos Stoilos, Ian Horrocks, Phokion G. Kolaitis, Georg Lausen, and Gerhard Weikum, editors, *Proc. of the 10th Int. Reasoning Web Summer School*, volume 8714 of *Lecture Notes in Computer Science*, pages 195–244. Springer, 2014.

[Lad77] Richard E. Ladner. The computational complexity of provability in systems of modal propositional logic. *SIAM J. on Computing*, 6(3):467–480, 1977.

[LAF+05] Lee Lacy, Gabriel Aviles, Karen Fraser, William Gerber, Alice Mulvehill, and Robert Gaskill. Experiences using OWL in military applications. In *Proc. of the First OWL Experiences and Directions Workshop (OWLED-05)*, volume 188 of *CEUR Workshop Proceedings* (http://ceur-ws.org/), 2005.

[LAHS04] Carsten Lutz, Carlos Areces, Ian Horrocks, and Ulrike Sattler. Keys, nominals, and concrete domains. *J. of Artificial Intelligence Research*, 23:667–726, 2004.

[LB10] Michael Lawley and Cyril Bousquet. Fast classification in Protégé: Snorocket as an OWL 2 EL reasoner. In T. Meyer, M.A. Orgun, and K. Taylor, editors, *Australasian Ontology Workshop 2010 (AOW 2010): Advances in Ontologies*, volume 122 of *CRPIT*, pages 45–50. ACS, 2010.

[Len02] Maurizio Lenzerini. Data Integration: A Theoretical Perspective. In Lucian Popa, Serge Abiteboul and Phokion G. Kolaitis, editors, *Proc. of the 21st ACM SIGACT-SIGMOD-SIGART Symp. on Principles of Database Systems (PODS-02)*, pages 233–246. ACM, 2002.

[Lib04] Leonid Libkin. *Elements of Finite Model Theory*. Texts in Theoretical Computer Science. An EATCS series. Springer, 2004.

[LPW11] Carsten Lutz, Robert Piro, and Frank Wolter. Description logic TBoxes: Model-theoretic characterizations and rewritability. In Toby Walsh, editor, *Proc. of the 22nd Int. Joint Conf. on Artificial Intelligence (IJCAI-11)*, pages 983–988. IJCAI/AAAI, 2011.

[LR96] Alon Y. Levy and Marie-Christine Rousset. CARIN: A representation language combining Horn rules and description logics. In Wolfgang Wahlster, editor, *Proc. of the 12th Eur. Conf. on Artificial Intelligence (ECAI-96)*, pages 323–327. John Wiley & Sons, 1996.

[LR98] Alon Y. Levy and Marie-Christine Rousset. Verification of knowledge bases based on containment checking. *Artificial Intelligence*, 101(1-2):227–250, 1998.

[LS08] Thomas Lukasiewicz and Umberto Straccia. Managing uncertainty and vagueness in description logics for the semantic web. *J. of Web Semantics*, 6(4):291–308, 2008.

[LSW01] Carsten Lutz, Ulrike Sattler, and Frank Wolter. Description logics and the two-variable fragment. In Carole A. Goble, Deborah L. McGuinness, Ralf Möller, and Peter F. Patel-Schneider, editors, *Proc. of the 2001 Description Logic Workshop (DL-01)*, volume 49 of *CEUR Workshop Proceedings* (http://ceur-ws.org/), 2001.

[LTW09] Carsten Lutz, David Toman, and Frank Wolter. Conjunctive query answering in the description logic $\mathcal{EL}$ using a relational database system. In Craig Boutilier, editor, *Proc. of the 21st Int. Joint Conf. on Artificial Intelligence (IJCAI-09)*, pages 2070–2075. AAAI Press/IJCAI, 2009.

[Lut99] Carsten Lutz. Complexity of terminological reasoning revisited. In Harald Ganzinger, David A. McAllester, and Andrei Voronkov, editors, *Proc. of the 6th Int. Conf. on Logic for Programming and Automated Reasoning (LPAR-99)*, volume 1705 of *Lecture Notes in Artificial Intelligence*, pages 181–200. Springer, 1999.

[Lut02] Carsten Lutz. *The Complexity of Description Logics with Concrete Domains.* PhD thesis, RWTH Aachen, Germany, 2002.

[Lut08] Carsten Lutz. The complexity of conjunctive query answering in expressive description logics. In Alessandro Armando, Peter Baumgartner, and Gilles Dowek, editors, *Proc. of the Int. Joint Conf. on Automated Reasoning (IJCAR-08)*, volume 5195 of *Lecture Notes in Computer Science*, pages 179–193. Springer, 2008.

[LW12] Carsten Lutz and Frank Wolter. Non-uniform data complexity of query answering in description logics. In Gerhard Brewka, Thomas Eiter, and Sheila A. McIlraith, editors, *Proc. of the 13th Int. Conf. on the Principles of Knowledge Representation and Reasoning (KR-12)*, pages 247–257. AAAI Press, 2012.

[LWZ08] Carsten Lutz, Frank Wolter, and Michael Zakharyaschev. Temporal description logics: A survey. In Stéphane Demri and Christian S. Jensen, editors, *Proc. of the 15th Int. Symp. on Temporal Representation and Reasoning (TIME-08)*, pages 3–14. IEEE Computer Society Press, 2008.

[Mac91a] Robert MacGregor. The evolving technology of classification-based knowledge representation systems. In John F. Sowa, editor, *Principles of Semantic Networks*, pages 385–400. Morgan Kaufmann, Los Altos, 1991.

[Mac91b] Robert MacGregor. Inside the LOOM description classifier. *SIGART Bull.*, 2(3):88–92, 1991.

[MAHP11] Alejandro Mallea, Marcelo Arenas, Aidan Hogan, and Axel Polleres. On blank nodes. In *Proc. of the 10th International Semantic Web Conference (ISWC-11)*, volume 7031 of *Lecture Notes in Computer Science*, pages 421–437. Springer, 2011.

[MDW91] Eric Mays, Robert Dionne, and Robert Weida. K-REP system overview. *SIGART Bull.*, 2(3), 1991.

[MH08] Boris Motik and Ian Horrocks. OWL datatypes: Design and implementation. In *Proc. of the 7th International Semantic Web Conference (ISWC-08)*, volume 5318 of *Lecture Notes in Computer Science*, pages 307–322. Springer, 2008.

[MJL13] Alejandro Metke-Jimenez and Michael Lawley. Snorocket 2.0: Concrete domains and concurrent classification. In *Informal Proceedings of the 2nd International Workshop on OWL Reasoner Evaluation (ORE-2013)*, volume 1015 of *CEUR Workshop Proceedings* (http://ceur-ws.org/), pages 32–38, 2013.

[MNP⁺14] Boris Motik, Yavor Nenov, Robert Piro, Ian Horrocks, and Dan Olteanu. Parallel materialisation of Datalog programs in centralised, main-memory RDF systems. In Carla E. Brodley and Peter Stone, editors, *Proc. of the 28th Nat. Conf. on Artificial Intelligence (AAAI-14)*, pages 129–137. AAAI Press, 2014.

[Mot07] Boris Motik. On the Properties of Metamodeling in OWL. *J. of Logic and Computation*, 17(4):617–637, 2007.

[MSH09] Boris Motik, Rob Shearer, and Ian Horrocks. Hypertableau reasoning for description logics. *J. of Artificial Intelligence Research*, 36:165–228, 2009.

[MW98] Deborah McGuinness and Jon R. Wright. Conceptual modelling for configuration: A description logic-based approach. *Artificial Intelligence for Engineering Design, Analysis, and Manufacturing J. – Special Issue on Configuration*, 12:333–344, 1998.

[Neb90a] Bernhard Nebel. *Reasoning and Revision in Hybrid Representation Systems*, volume 422 of *Lecture Notes in Artificial Intelligence*. Springer, 1990.

[Neb90b] Bernhard Nebel. Terminological reasoning is inherently intractable. *Artificial Intelligence*, 43:235–249, 1990.

[NOS16] Nhung Ngo, Magdalena Ortiz, and Mantas Simkus. Closed predicates in description logics: Results on combined complexity. In Chitta Baral, James Delgrande, and Frank Wolter, editors, *Proc. of the 15th Int. Conf. on the Principles of Knowledge Representation and Reasoning (KR-16)*, pages 237–246. AAAI Press, 2016.

[OCE08] Magdalena Ortiz, Diego Calvanese, and Thomas Eiter. Data complexity of query answering in expressive description logics via tableaux. *J. of Automated Reasoning*, 41(1):61–98, 2008.

[ORS11] Magdalena Ortiz, Sebastian Rudolph, and Mantas Simkus. Query answering in the Horn fragments of the description logics $\mathcal{SHOIQ}$ and $\mathcal{SROIQ}$. In Toby Walsh, editor, *Proc. of the 22nd Int. Joint Conf. on Artificial Intelligence (IJCAI-11)*, pages 1039–1044. AAAI Press/IJCAI, 2011.

[OSRM⁺12] David Osumi-Sutherland, Simon Reeve, Christopher J. Mungall, Fabian Neuhaus, Alan Ruttenberg, Gregory S.X.E. Jefferis, and J. Douglas Armstrong. A strategy for building neuroanatomy ontologies. *Bioinformatics*, 28(9):1262–1269, 2012.

[OWL12a] OWL 2 Web Ontology Language Mapping to RDF Graphs (Second Edition). W3C Recommendation, 2012. Available at http://www.w3.org/TR/owl2-mapping-to-rdf/.

[OWL12b] OWL 2 Web Ontology Language Profiles (Second Edition). W3C Recommendation, 2012. Available at http://www.w3.org/TR/owl2-profiles/.

[OWL12c] OWL 2 Web Ontology Language Structural Specification and

Functional-style Syntax (Second Edition). W3C Recommendation, 2012. Available at http://www.w3.org/TR/owl2-syntax/.

[Pap94] Christos H. Papadimitriou. *Computational Complexity*. Addison Wesley, 1994.

[Pel91] Christof Peltason. The BACK system: An overview. *SIGART Bull.*, 2(3):114–119, 1991.

[Pra79] Vaugham R. Pratt. Models of program logic. In *Proc. of the 20th Annual Symp. on the Foundations of Computer Science (FOCS-79)*, pages 115–122. IEEE Computer Society, 1979.

[Pra09] Ian Pratt-Hartmann. Data-complexity of the two-variable fragment with counting quantifiers. *Information and Computation*, 207(8):867–888, 2009.

[PS89] Peter F. Patel-Schneider. Undecidability of subsumption in NIKL. *Artificial Intelligence*, 39:263–272, 1989.

[PSMB+91] Peter F. Patel-Schneider, Deborah L. McGuiness, Ronald J. Brachman, Lori A. Resnick, and Alexander Borgida. The CLASSIC knowledge representation system: Guiding principles and implementation rational. *SIGART Bull.*, 2(3):108–113, 1991.

[PST97] Leszek Pacholski, Wieslaw Szwast, and Lidia Tendera. Complexity of two-variable logic with counting. In *Proc. of the 12th IEEE Symp. on Logic in Computer Science (LICS-97)*, pages 318–327. IEEE Computer Society Press, 1997.

[PST00] Leszek Pacholski, Wiesław Szwast, and Lidia Tendera. Complexity results for first-order two-variable logic with counting. *SIAM J. on Computing*, 29(4):1083–1117, 2000.

[PUMH10] Héctor Pérez-Urbina, Boris Motik, and Ian Horrocks. Tractable query answering and rewriting under description logic constraints. *J. of Applied Logic*, 8(2):186–209, 2010.

[RB11] Peter N. Robinson and Sebastian Bauer. *Introduction to Bio-Ontologies*. CRC Press, 2011.

[RFC05] RFC 3987: Internationalized Resource Identifiers (IRIs). Internet Engineering Task Force (IETF) Request For Comments (RFC), 2005. Available at http://www.ietf.org/rfc/rfc3987.txt.

[RKZ13] Mariano Rodriguez-Muro, Roman Kontchakov, and Michael Zakharyaschev. Ontology-based data access: *Ontop* of databases. In Harith Alani, Lalana Kagal, Achille Fokoue, Paul T. Groth, Chris Biemann, Josiane Xavier Parreira, Lora Aroyo, Natasha F. Noy, Chris Welty, and Krzysztof Janowicz, editors, *Proc. of the 12th International Semantic Web Conference (ISWC-13)*, volume 8218 of *Lecture Notes in Computer Science*, pages 558–573. Springer, 2013.

[Ros07a] Riccardo Rosati. The limits of querying ontologies. In Thomas Schwentick and Dan Suciu, editors, *Proc. of the 11th Int. Conf. on Database Theory (ICDT-07)*, volume 4353 of *Lecture Notes in Computer Science*, pages 164–178. Springer, 2007.

[Ros07b] Riccardo Rosati. On conjunctive query answering in $\mathcal{EL}$. In Diego Calvanese, Enrico Franconi, Volker Haarslev, Domenico Lembo, Boris Motik, Anni-Yasmin Turhan, and Sergio Tessaris, editors, *Proc. of the 2007 Description Logic Workshop (DL-07)*, volume 250 of *CEUR Workshop Proceedings* (http://ceur-ws.org/), 2007.

[RP05] Robert G. Raskin and Michael J. Pan. Knowledge representation in the semantic web for earth and environmental terminology (SWEET).

Computers & Geosciences, 31(9):1119–1125, 2005.

[RR06] Alan Rector and Jeremy Rogers. Ontological and practical issues in using a description logic to represent medical concept systems: Experience from GALEN. In Pedro Barahona, François Bry, Enrico Franconi, Nicola Henze, and Ulrike Sattler, editors, *Proc. of the 2nd Int. Reasoning Web Summer School*, volume 4126 of *Lecture Notes in Computer Science*, pages 197–231. Springer, 2006.

[RRL05] Alan Ruttenberg, Jonathan Rees, and Joanne Luciano. Experience using OWL DL for the exchange of biological pathway information. In Bernardo Cuenca Grau, Ian Horrocks, Bijan Parsia, and Peter Patel-Schneider, editors, *Proc. of the First OWL Experiences and Directions Workshop (OWLED-05)*, volume 188 of *CEUR Workshop Proceedings* (http://ceur-ws.org/), 2005.

[SC79] Larry J. Stockmeyer and Ashok K. Chandra. Provably difficult combinatorial games. *SIAM J. on Computing*, 8(2):151–174, 1979.

[Sch78] Thomas J. Schaefer. On the complexity of some two-person perfect-information games. *J. of Computer and System Sciences*, 16(2):185–225, 1978.

[Sch89] Manfred Schmidt-Schauß. Subsumption in KL-ONE is undecidable. In Ron J. Brachman, Hector J. Levesque, and Ray Reiter, editors, *Proc. of the 1st Int. Conf. on the Principles of Knowledge Representation and Reasoning (KR-89)*, pages 421–431. Morgan Kaufmann, Los Altos, 1989.

[Sch91] Klaus Schild. A correspondence theory for terminological logics: Preliminary report. In John Mylopoulos and Ray Reiter, editors, *Proc. of the 12th Int. Joint Conf. on Artificial Intelligence (IJCAI-91)*, pages 466–471. Morgan Kaufmann, Los Altos, 1991.

[Sch94] Klaus Schild. Terminological cycles and the propositional μ-calculus. In Jon Doyle, Erik Sandewall, and Pietro Torasso, editors, *Proc. of the 4th Int. Conf. on the Principles of Knowledge Representation and Reasoning (KR-94)*, pages 509–520. Morgan Kaufmann, Los Altos, 1994.

[Sch95] Klaus Schild. *Querying Knowledge and Data Bases by a Universal Description Logic with Recursion*. PhD thesis, Universität des Saarlandes, Germany, 1995.

[Sip97] Michael Sipser. *Introduction to the Theory of Computation*. PWS Publishing Company, 1997.

[SKH11] František Simančík, Yevgeny Kazakov, and Ian Horrocks. Consequence-based reasoning beyond Horn ontologies. In Toby Walsh, editor, *Proc. of the 22nd Int. Joint Conf. on Artificial Intelligence (IJCAI-11)*, pages 1093–1098. AAAI Press/IJCAI, 2011.

[SLG14] Andreas Steigmiller, Thorsten Liebig, and Birte Glimm. Konclude: System description. *J. of Web Semantics*, 27(1):78–85, 2014.

[SLH13] Martin G. Skjæveland, Espen H. Lian, and Ian Horrocks. Publishing the Norwegian Petroleum Directorate's FactPages as semantic web data. In Harith Alani, Lalana Kagal, Achille Fokoue, Paul Groth, Chris Biemann, Josiane Xavier Parreira, Lora Aroyo, Natasha Noy, Chris Welty, and Krzysztof Janowicz, editors, *Proc. of the 12th International Semantic Web Conference (ISWC-13)*, volume 8219 of *Lecture Notes in Computer Science*, pages 162–177. Springer, 2013.

[SLL+04] Dagobert Soergel, Boris Lauser, Anita Liang, Frehiwot Fisseha, Johannes Keizer, and Stephen Katz. Reengineering thesauri for new applications: The AGROVOC example. *J. of Digital Information*, 4(4),

2004.

[SM73] Larry J. Stockmeyer and Albert R. Meyer. Word problems requiring exponential time: Preliminary report. In *Proc. of the 5th ACM Symp. on Theory of Computing (STOC-73)*, pages 1–9. ACM, 1973.

[SM15] Giorgio Stefanoni and Boris Motik. Answering conjunctive queries over $\mathcal{EL}$ knowledge bases with transitive and reflexive roles. In Blai Bonet and Sven Koenig, editors, *Proc. of the 29th Nat. Conf. on Artificial Intelligence (AAAI-15)*, pages 1611–1617. AAAI Press/The MIT Press, 2015.

[SMH13] Giorgio Stefanoni, Boris Motik, and Ian Horrocks. Introducing nominals to the combined query answering approaches for $\mathcal{EL}$. In *Proc. of the 27th Nat. Conf. on Artificial Intelligence (AAAI-13)*, pages 1177–1183. AAAI Press, 2013.

[Smu68] Raymond M. Smullyan. *First-Order Logic*. Springer, 1968.

[SPA13] SPARQL 1.1 Entailment Regimes. W3C Recommendation, 2013. Available at http://www.w3.org/TR/sparql11-entailment/.

[SPC+07] Evren Sirin, Bijan Parsia, Bernardo Cuenca Grau, Aditya Kalyanpur, and Yarden Katz. Pellet: A practical OWL-DL reasoner. *J. of Web Semantics*, 5(2):51–53, 2007.

[SS91] Manfred Schmidt-Schauß and Gert Smolka. Attributive concept descriptions with complements. *Artificial Intelligence*, 48(1):1–26, 1991.

[SSBB09] Stefan Schulz, Boontawee Suntisrivaraporn, Franz Baader, and Martin Boeker. SNOMED reaching its adolescence: Ontologists' and logicians' health check. *Int. J. of Medical Informatics*, 78(Supplement 1):S86–S94, 2009.

[Ste15] Giorgio Stefanoni. *Evaluating Conjunctive and Graph Queries over the EL Profile of OWL 2*. PhD thesis, University of Oxford, 2015.

[TH06] Dmitry Tsarkov and Ian Horrocks. FaCT++ description logic reasoner: System description. In Ulrich Furbach and Natarajan Shankar, editors, *Proc. of the Int. Joint Conf. on Automated Reasoning (IJCAR-06)*, volume 4130 of *Lecture Notes in Artificial Intelligence*, pages 292–297. Springer, 2006.

[THPS07] Dmitry Tsarkov, Ian Horrocks, and Peter F. Patel-Schneider. Optimizing terminological reasoning for expressive description logics. *J. of Automated Reasoning*, 39(3):277–316, 2007.

[TNNM13] Tania Tudorache, Csongor Nyulas, Natalya Fridman Noy, and Mark A. Musen. Using semantic web in ICD-11: Three years down the road. In Harith Alani, Lalana Kagal, Achille Fokoue, Paul Groth, Chris Biemann, Josiane Xavier Parreira, Lora Aroyo, Natasha Noy, Chris Welty, and Krzysztof Janowicz, editors, *Proc. of the 12th International Semantic Web Conference (ISWC-13)*, volume 8219 of *Lecture Notes in Computer Science*, pages 195–211. Springer, 2013.

[Tob99] Stephan Tobies. A NEXPTIME-complete description logic strictly contained in C^2. In Jörg Flum and Mario Rodríguez-Artalejo, editors, *Proc. of the Annual Conf. of the Eur. Assoc. for Computer Science Logic (CSL-99)*, volume 1683 of *Lecture Notes in Computer Science*, pages 292–306. Springer, 1999.

[TSCS15] Despoina Trivela, Giorgos Stoilos, Alexandros Chortaras, and Giorgos B. Stamou. Optimising resolution-based rewriting algorithms for OWL ontologies. *J. of Web Semantics*, 33:30–49, 2015.

[Vu08] Quoc Huy Vu. Subsumption in the description logic $\mathcal{ELHIf}_{\mathcal{R}+}$ with respect to general TBoxes. Master's thesis, Chair for Automata Theory,

TU Dresden, Germany, 2008.

[WED⁺08] Zhe Wu, George Eadon, Souripriya Das, Eugene Inseok Chong, Vladimir Kolovski, Melliyal Annamalai, and Jagannathan Srinivasan. Implementing an inference engine for RDFS/OWL constructs and user-defined rules in oracle. In *Proc. of the 24th IEEE Int. Conf. on Data Engineering (ICDE-08)*, pages 1239–1248. IEEE Computer Society, 2008.

[WS92] William A. Woods and James G. Schmolze. The KL-ONE family. In Fritz W. Lehmann, editor, *Semantic Networks in Artificial Intelligence*, pages 133–178. Pergamon Press, 1992. Published as a special issue of *Computers & Mathematics with Applications*, Volume 23, Number 2–9.

[XSD12] W3C XML Schema Definition Language (XSD) 1.1 Part 2: Datatypes. W3C Recommendation, 2012. Available at http://www.w3.org/TR/xmlschema11-2/.

Index